Exploring

Oregon's
Wild Areas

A GUIDE FOR

HIKERS • BACKPACKERS • CLIMBERS
CROSS-COUNTRY SKIERS • PADDLERS

Exploring

Oregon's
Wild Areas

To Rachel,

with deep gratitude and

appreciation !

Regina and

William Sullivan

THIRD EDITION
William L. Sullivan

THE MOUNTAINEERS BOOKS

Published by
The Mountaineers Books
1001 SW Klickitat Way, Suite 201
Seattle, WA 98134

Published simultaneously in Great Britain by Cordee, 3a DeMontfort Street, Leicester, England, LE1 7HD

Manufactured in the United States of America

Project Editor: Laura Slavik
Editor: Paula Thurman
Cover and Book Design: The Mountaineers Books
Layout Artist: Marge Mueller, Gray Mouse Graphics
Mapmaker: William L. Sullivan
Photographer: William L. Sullivan

Cover photograph: *Mount Jefferson from Jefferson Park* © William L. Sullivan
Frontispiece: *Mount Hood from Lost Lake* © William L. Sullivan

Library of Congress Cataloging-in-Publication Data

Sullivan, William L
     Exploring Oregon's wild areas : a guide for hikers, backpackers, climbers, X-C skiers & paddlers / by William L. Sullivan.-- 3rd ed.
          p. cm.
Includes bibliographical references (p.351) and index.
     ISBN 0-89886-793-2 (pbk.)
     1. Outdoor recreation--Guidebooks. 2. Wilderness areas--Oregon--Guidebooks. 3. Oregon--Guidebooks.
I. Title.
     GV191.42.07 S85 2002
     917.9504'44--dc21

                                                                                                      2001007163

   Printed on recycled paper

CONTENTS

Chapter Three. **Northeast Oregon**

Chapter Four. **Southeast Oregon**

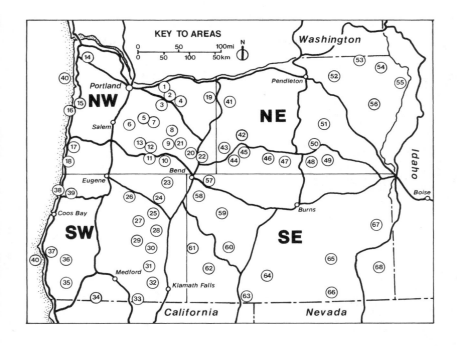

KEY TO AREAS

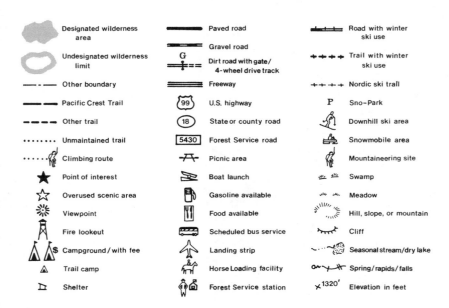

KEY TO MAP SYMBOLS

Designated wilderness area	Paved road	Road with winter ski use
Undesignated wilderness limit	Gravel road	Trail with winter ski use
Other boundary	G Dirt road with gate/ 4-wheel drive track	Nordic ski trail
Pacific Crest Trail	Freeway	P Sno–Park
Other trail	99 U.S. highway	Downhill ski area
Unmaintained trail	18 State or county road	Snowmobile area
Climbing route	5430 Forest Service road	Mountaineering site
Point of interest	Picnic area	Swamp
Overused scenic area	Boat launch	Meadow
Viewpoint	Gasoline available	Hill, slope, or mountain
Fire lookout	Food available	Cliff
Campground/with fee	Scheduled bus service	Seasonal stream/dry lake
Trail camp	Landing strip	Spring/rapids/falls
Shelter	Horse Loading facility	X 1320' Elevation in feet
	Forest Service station	

PREFACE

Wilderness is part of the Oregon experience. To stand on a mountain top and look across an unbroken expanse of forest, to feel the wind on your face, to smell the scent of pine and cedar, to drink from a forest stream—these are the things that define us as Oregonians.

Oregonians have had the foresight to protect more than 2 million acres as wilderness. However, several million more acres of pristine wild lands remain unprotected. This book serves as a guide to all of the designated wilderness areas in Oregon (shown in gray on the maps) and to many of the undesignated areas (shown by gray borders on the maps).

Unfortunately, only 11 percent of our federal public forest lands are officially protected as wilderness, and according to the U.S. Forest Service, one-quarter of that unprotected wilderness will be logged and roaded in little more than a decade. Two-thirds of Oregonians want to see that change—66 percent say they want to see more federal forest lands designated as wilderness. Additionally, 77 percent of Northwest residents agree that protecting pristine forest as wilderness is an effective means to protect clean drinking water, salmon habitat, and ancient forests.

At the Oregon Natural Resources Council (ONRC), we agree with what Oregonians have to say about wilderness. This is why we have launched the Oregon Wild Campaign to designate and protect more wilderness areas in the state. Here's how you can help:

- Explore the areas in this book to see what is at stake.
- Adopt a wilderness. The ONRC's volunteers help document the values of special places and work to protect them permanently.
- Join the ONRC and support our Oregon Wild Campaign. For information, call (503) 283-6343, visit our website at *www.onrc.org*, or write to one of the ONRC's addresses at the back of this book.
- Contact your local and federal elected officials to let them know you think we ought to protect our wilderness heritage and legacy.

Future generations will judge us by the Oregon we pass along to them, whether it be clearcut hillsides or the magical light and rich life of an ancient forest. Which legacy do we prefer to leave? Exploring the wild areas in this book will help you decide.

Regna Merritt, Executive Director
Oregon Natural Resources Council

Opposite: *South Falls in Silver Falls State Park (Area 6)*

INTRODUCTION

How can we love Oregon's fragile wilderness without loving it to death? If we intend to walk lightly on the land, we cannot all continue to beat dusty paths to Mount Jefferson's sorely trammeled Jeff Park, Mount Hood's Paradise Park, and the Three Sisters' Green Lakes Basin.

Oregon is chock full of alternative trips with both beauty and isolation. This guide describes more than 600 hikes and 130 cross-country ski tours, as well as prime spots for white-water rafting, mountaineering, and even hang gliding.

The popular High Cascades wildernesses are all included, of course, but so are less crowded areas in four other major mountain ranges. And there is more: the deepest white-water river canyons in the country. Fog-bound oceanshore rain forests. Winter hideaways at snowy lakes. Turquoise hot-spring pools in stark deserts. Two areas of sand dunes. And thousands of miles of quiet trails.

HOW TO USE THIS BOOK
The Maps

A *locator map* following the Contents identifies the book's sixty-eight areas by number and shows which quarter of the state each area is in. Turn to the appropriate *quadrant overview map* (pages 24–25, 116–117, 208–209, or 288–289) to find the best highway approach to an area.

Individual *area maps* use symbols identified in a key on page 7. Note that solid gray areas denote wilderness designated by an act of Congress. Undesignated wilderness—managed under quite different rules—is shown only by thin gray borders. Beyond the gray borders lies land unsuitable as wilderness because of clearcuts, roads, private ownership, development, or insufficient size.

Stars denote points of interest, but *hollow* stars indicate scenic spots already badly worn by overuse. Visitors heading for such fragile spots should tread lightly and plan to camp elsewhere.

The maps' north arrows always point to true north; magnetic north lies approximately 20° east of true north in Oregon. In the few instances where north is not at the top of the map, a square of gray shading helps draw attention to the north arrow.

Dirt roads shown with dashed lines are 'ways'—unimproved four-wheel-drive tracks that are probably not drivable by passenger cars. The maps do not show all the ways and roads. Particularly in southeast Oregon's desert country, backroad drivers may find the proliferation of unmarked ways confusing. Bureau of Land Management district maps are good insurance here (see Appendix C).

Opposite: *The Crooked River at Smith Rock State Park (Area 22)*

Long-distance recreation trails connecting many of the areas in this book are featured in the *State Trail Plan* map in Appendix A.

The Information Blocks

Each entry begins with a synopsis of the area's facts. The *location* tells the highway mileage and direction from major cities to the closest portion of a roadless area. The *size* reflects the approximate extent (in square miles) of all the roadless lands in each featured area. For state parks, the size is the total extent of parkland. An area's *status* tells how many square miles have been Congressionally designated as wilderness so far and the dates of those additions to the National Wilderness System. Other, less protective designations are also noted.

Next, each entry notes the roadless area's dominant types of *terrain*, as well as the highest and lowest *elevation* in feet. The *management* listing advises whether a National Forest (NF), a district of the Bureau of Land Management (BLM), or some other agency administers the area. These agencies can answer specific questions about road conditions, regulations, and permits. Their addresses and phone numbers appear in Appendix B.

An essential back-up for the maps in this book are *topographic maps,* which show landforms by means of contour lines. The best topographic maps are listed first. Appendix C includes detailed information for ordering topographic maps.

The Text Descriptions

An area's *climate* information generally includes average snow levels, temperature ranges, and likeliest seasons to find mosquitoes, wildflowers, or huckleberries. Average annual precipitation reflects the total of rain and melted snow. All of these figures vary substantially from year to year. In addition, some of the data for remote areas are approximate, extrapolated from weather station records. Wilderness visitors should always prepare for inclement weather.

All areas include descriptions of *plants and wildlife* and *geology.* However, only areas with a substantial history of human contact have *history* entries.

A FEW WILDERNESS RULES

The 1964 Wilderness Act defines wilderness as "an area where the earth and its community of life are untrammeled by man, where man himself is a visitor who does not remain." That law established strict rules that govern the thirty-nine Oregon areas Congress has thus far designated as wilderness. These include the following:

- No mechanical transport. This bans off-road vehicles (ORVs), motorcycles, bicycles, airplane drops, hang gliders, and helicopter landings—except rarely for rescue or fire fighting.
- No new mining claims. Mining on a few pre-1984 claims, however, continues.
- No commercial enterprises. An exception currently allows some cattle grazing. Guides and outfitters may operate only under permit.
- No motorized equipment (such as generators or chainsaws).

- Fishing and hunting are permitted with a state license. Check with the Oregon Department of Fish and Wildlife for regulations.

Many designated wilderness areas have other restrictions as well. The most common "No's" are the following:

- Cutting, chopping, or clipping live trees or dead snags.
- Grazing, picketing, or tying saddle stock within 200 feet of a lake or stream.
- Discharging firearms within 150 yards of a campsite, or across any trail or body of water.
- Smoking while traveling.
- Traveling in groups larger than twelve.

In addition, some rules extend to all federal lands, wilderness or not:

- Collecting arrowheads or other cultural artifacts is a federal crime.
- Disturbing archaeological sites or pictographs is likewise a criminal offense (even making tracings or rubbings of pictographs can damage them).
- National Forests limit campers to fourteen days' stay at the same campsite in any calendar year.
- Permits are required to dig up plants on federal land.
- Rare plants and animals are sometimes protected by both federal and state law. Picking wildflowers may in fact be illegal.

Rockpile Lake in the Mount Jefferson Wilderness (Area 9)

HAZARDS IN THE WILDS

The Wilderness Act of 1964 insists that a wilderness should offer outstanding opportunities for solitude. One backwoods hiker paraphrased this, suggesting a wilderness should offer outstanding opportunities for death.

I think the dangers of the wilderness have been overrated. Consider the Portland businessman who decided to commit suicide, so he drove to Bend and walked into the Three Sisters Wilderness with nothing but the Armani suit he was wearing. Three days later he was hungry and sore, and his suit was very wrinkled, but he was still not dead, so he walked back out. Grizzly bears are extinct in Oregon, so there is no need to decorate backpacks with bear-warning bells. Oregon's black bears huff and scramble out of a hiker's way as fast as their little legs will take them—generally even when the hiker has accidentally passed a mother bear's cubs. In a very few areas (notably the Wild Rogue Wilderness), bears have been trained over the years by careless campers to rip open packs and coolers at night for bacon, tuna, and sweets. Here a standard wilderness precaution will suffice: hang all food from a tree limb, at least 10 feet high and 5 feet away from the trunk. This will also keep food safe from the real scoundrels—chipmunks.

Mountain lion (cougar) populations are recovering from years of being hunted with dogs, but because the lions are nocturnal, they have almost no interaction with humans. Wolves were hunted to extinction in Oregon long ago, and although a few individual wolves have explored northeastern Oregon from reintroduced packs in Idaho, there is still no established population on this side of the Snake River. No one in the history of Oregon has been killed by either a bear, a mountain lion, or a wolf.

Likewise, rattlesnakes will disappoint the danger seeker. These reptiles are rare enough that most people will not see one in 1000 miles of wilderness hiking. What's more, the aggressive diamondback species is not found in the state at all. Oregon's subspecies, *Crotalis viridis oreganius,* is a retiring sort, absolutely incapable of such spuriously attributed feats of daring as crawling into a sleeping bag for warmth.

These days, the most threatening beast in the woods is a microscopic paramecium by the name of *Giardia.* This water-borne pest has forever changed the tradition of casually dipping a drink from cold, clear mountain streams. Those who ingest *Giardia* can expect debilitating diarrhea and nausea to appear in six to fifteen days, symptoms that abate only after medical treatment. Many hikers and nearly all backpackers now carry a commercial filter, attached to a bottle lid or hand pump, that has been approved to remove *Giardia.* Some water purification tablets are also effective, but they tend to make the water unpalatable. Boiling water for ten minutes is a reliably safe treatment, but it requires both fuel and time. A few daring souls prefer to second-guess the little paramecium. *Giardia* is spread only by mammals (often beaver, deer, cattle, or mice), enters the water by defecation, and only moves downstream. Thus, water from a spring or a high mountain watershed unfrequented by mammals has a lower risk of contamination.

Hikers in dry, grassy areas should check occasionally for ticks under their collars and cuffs, especially in May or June. If you find that a tick has attached itself to your skin, do not attempt to pull it off. Instead, twist its body like a screw for several complete rotations and it will let go. In Oregon, only a handful of cases have been reported of Lyme disease, an ailment carried by tiny deer ticks. Lyme disease progressively affects the joints and nerves. Keep an eye on the site of any tick bite to make sure it doesn't develop the disease's characteristic bull's-eye-shaped sore (red with a white ring), followed within a month by a rash.

Of course, those who enter the wilderness without basic survival gear and skills are bringing hazard with them. Hypothermia is the number one killer in the wilds. It results from being wet and cold too long, and can be prevented by bringing proper clothing and shelter. Useful books and classes abound on preparation for hiking, backpacking, and climbing—with far more detail than this Introduction can possibly include. Be prepared for the worst, and you will be able to enjoy the wilderness confidently at its best.

Finally, errors in mileage, trail location, and the like are inevitable in any guidebook—especially when new roads and logging are constantly adding confusion. Despite all our effort to the contrary, the author, publisher, and research consultant cannot guarantee the accuracy of the information included here, nor that the trips described are safe for everyone.

Without danger, wilderness would not be wild. Of course, it seems obvious, but visitors in the wild are on their own. Pack some common sense and caution for safety's sake.

A WORD TO HIKERS
Choosing a Trip

The easiest trips in each area are generally described first. Those who rarely hike should look for the nature trails, lakeshore paths, and short riverside hikes listed near the beginning of an area's *hiking* section. Remember that most mileages reflect the one-way length of a trail. Thus, a "1.4-mile trail to Twin Lakes" means a 2.8-mile round-trip hike. Also, the term "easy" is used only in relation to other hikes. Someone who puffs climbing a few flights of stairs will not find a 2.8-mile walk easy at all.

Speaking of climbing, pay attention to the *elevation gains*—they warn of steep uphill trails. Many of the hike descriptions mention the elevation gain in feet, but even when they do not, the elevations shown on the maps make gains for most hikes calculable. A 1000-foot gain is an arduous uphill trudge for out-of-shape walkers, particularly if the climb is packed into less than 2 miles. A 2000-foot gain requires frequent rest stops even when hikers are in good condition. Hikers must be in very good shape—strong hearts and strong knees—to handle a 3000-foot elevation gain in a day. Only those in prime condition should tackle the 5000-foot climbs required by trails up Hat Point or South Sister.

Trail mileages given in this book are approximate and may not agree with trail sign mileages (which are often incorrect). Likewise, official signs and maps often offer a confusion of names and numbers for the same trail. This guide generally avoids the debate by identifying trails according to their destination and starting point.

Road directions to trailheads are provided only when the map does not clearly show the route. When several obscure trailheads cluster together, complete car directions may be given to only one of them, with the understanding that drivers can then use the map to find the others.

A *car shuttle* allows a group with two cars to end their hike at a different trailhead. Drive both cars to the trip's end point, leave one there, and then drive the other to the hike's starting point. A *key-swap hike* requires less driving, but more careful planning. For this arrangement, two carloads of hikers walk the same trail, starting at opposite trailheads. When the two groups meet at a specified time at the trail's midpoint, they swap car keys for the drive home. Better yet, swap duplicate keys before leaving for the hike.

Advanced hikers may be interested in the *cross-country hiking routes* suggested for many areas. Bushwhacking, not to be confused with machete-style trail chopping, can be surprisingly easy and immensely rewarding. It is the only way to hike in Oregon's trailless desert country. Although off-trail travel is more difficult in the dense forests of western Oregon's wildernesses, you do not need to bushwhack very far in such terrain before finding true isolation—even in an area billed as crowded. Perhaps the best way to walk lightly on the land is to walk where no one else has. Cross-country hikers in particular should keep a topographic map and compass at hand and have experience using them. All hikers should inform someone of their route before leaving so that the county sheriff's office can be called to organize a search and rescue, if necessary.

Emergency Gear

Even on the tamest hike a surprise storm or a wrong turn can suddenly make the gear you carry very important. If you are lost, stay put and keep warm. The biggest killer in the woods is hypothermia—being cold and wet too long.

For safety's sake, your backpack should always contain the following Ten Essentials:

1. Warm, water-repellent coat (or parka and extra shirt)
2. Sunglasses
3. Extra food and drinking water
4. Knife
5. Matches in waterproof container
6. Firestarter (butane lighter or candle)
7. First-aid kit
8. Flashlight
9. Map (topographic, if possible)
10. Compass

Global Positioning System Devices

A global positioning system (GPS) device can be helpful in certain situations. By tracking signals from satellites, these handheld, battery-operated instruments are able to display the latitude and longitude of their location with a precision that varies by only a few feet. If you mark your location with a GPS device, it will be easy to return later to the exact same place. However, a GPS device is no substitute for a map and compass.

If you are lost, a GPS device will not point out north, nor will it show you your location on most maps. The devices are useless if their batteries fail. And they rarely work in forested areas where trees block satellite signals.

On the other hand, a GPS device can be the simplest way to locate a poorly marked desert trailhead or to find a high-country ski shelter in a blizzard whiteout. This book occasionally gives a destination's coordinates using standard latitude-longitude notation (for example, *GPS location N43°37.931' W122°00.202'*). To locate the destination, use your GPS device's on-screen menu to mark a new "waypoint," edit the waypoint's latitude and longitude to match those of the given destination, and then select the device's *Go To* feature to show the direction and distance you will need to travel to reach that destination.

Trailhead and Wilderness Permits

Northwest Forest Pass permits are required to park within a quarter mile of many trailheads in National Forests. These permits cost $5 per car per day or $30 per year and can be purchased at ranger stations or outdoor stores. Note, however, that some areas are not included in this program. Northwest Forest Passes are not needed in the Umpqua, Winema, Ochoco, Malheur, Fremont, and Umatilla National Forests. Even in participating National Forests, some trailheads are free—for example, at Timberline Lodge and Multnomah Falls.

A wilderness permit is sometimes required to enter a wilderness area, but these are free and can generally be filled out at the trailhead. *For Mount Jefferson's Pamelia Lake Trailhead, the Three Sisters' Obsidian Trailhead, and Mount Hood's Burnt Lake Trailhead, however, entry permits are strictly limited and must be picked up in advance at a ranger station.*

Trail Courtesies

Finally, remember a few "rules of the trail":

- Step off the trail on the downhill side to let horses pass. Talking quietly to the horses can help prevent them from spooking.
- Pick no flowers.
- Leave no litter. Trailside orange peels and eggshells last for decades.
- Do not shortcut switchbacks.
- Divide large groups into independent hiking parties of twelve or fewer.
- Do not bring pets into the wilderness. A dog can dangerously anger bears, porcupines, and other wilderness users.
- Respect private land. This guide makes an effort to steer hikers clear of private property, but even designated wildernesses include some private inholdings.

A WORD TO BACKPACKERS

Wilderness campers face a serious challenge: leaving no trace of their camp. Choosing the right campsite is critical. Savvy campers will not pitch a tent over the wildflower meadow they came to see, but instead will choose a spot in the forest—and never in a

Dry River's gorge (Area 57)

hollow where rainwater will gather, making trenching a temptation. Likewise, never camp in a fragile alpine area, on a streambank, or within 100 feet of a lake. Choose a less delicate site on sand, snow, or bare pine-needle duff. Best of all, bring a gallon's worth of water bottles per camper and pitch a dry camp, away from the water sources that attract camping overuse.

Campfires are banned in many of the wilderness areas' popular and fragile alpine areas. The truth is, open fires are a luxury the wilderness can no longer afford to provide. Instead, cook on a lightweight campstove using gas, alcohol, or butane. For warmth, wear more clothing. Even when an emergency requires a campfire, do not build a rock campfire ring; this needlessly blackens stones. Clear a circle of ground to mineral soil. Gather only small pieces of wood that can be broken off by hand; never hack limbs with a hatchet. After use, drown the fire, scatter the cold ashes, and restore the site.

Do not bury or burn garbage. Limit the trash that must be packed out by bringing no canned or bottled foods, and by repackaging bulky foods into compact, lightweight plastic bags or containers.

Never wash dishes or bathe with soap directly in a lake or stream. Carry water at least 100 feet away from the shore and wash there.

Bury human waste in a small hole dug at least 100 feet from water. Choose a site where no one would ever camp. Fill the hole with dirt and cover the spot with a natural-looking arrangement of rocks or sticks. Do not bury toilet paper, because animals will dig it up. If you must use toilet paper (instead of leaves), seal the used paper in a plastic bag and pack it out.

When camping at an established site in the wilderness, try to restore it a little. Remove nails and clotheslines from trees. Dismantle racks, benches, or lean-to frames. Pick aluminum foil and trash from campfire rings and scatter the ashes. Remember, campers in the wilderness are visitors who should leave no trace of their stay. "Developed" campsites belong only at automobile campgrounds.

A WORD TO MOUNTAINEERS

This guide identifies mountaineering sites in seventeen areas across the state—including Mount Hood, the world's second most-climbed snowpeak, and Smith Rock, a mecca for technical climbers with hundreds of named routes. In addition, *hiking* entries describe popular nontechnical climbs such as South Sister, Eagle Cap, and Mount McLoughlin.

Because available guidebooks discuss climbing techniques and safety and describe Oregon's technical climbs in detail, this book restricts itself to noting the chief attractions of each climbing area and the range of difficulty of the most important routes. The rating system used here, known as the Yosemite Decimal System, expresses the climb's overall difficulty first by a Roman numeral, then the climb's athletic difficulty by a number from 1 to 5.15, and finally (when appropriate) the difficulty of available artificial aid by symbols from A1 to A5, as follows:

Overall Difficulty

(length of climb, degree of commitment)

I—up to 2 hours

II—up to a half day

III—a full day

IV—possibly requires a bivouac

Oregon has no grade V or VI climbs

Athletic Difficulty

(class of technical skill needed)

1—hiking

2—scrambling over talus or through brush

3—steep slopes or exposed ridges

4—rope required

5—rope and protection required

Class 5 climbs are broken down from 5.1 to 5.15 to indicate increasingly difficult pitches requiring rope and protection. Climbs above 5.7 are demanding even for experienced climbers.

Artificial Aid Difficulty

A1—solid placements

A2—strenuous placements

A3—several marginal placements

A4—many marginal placements

A5—marginal protection throughout

Thus, the east face of Smith Rock's Monkey Face, rated II-5.7-A3, requires most of a day with advanced free-climbing skills and has several marginally secure aids.

Climbers should not add new bolts to established routes, both to decrease clutter and to preserve a route's challenge.

A WORD TO CROSS-COUNTRY SKIERS

This guide covers most of Oregon's popular cross-country ski touring areas and many little-known spots as well. In the area maps, hatch marks along trails and unplowed roads indicate feasible winter routes for nordic skiers. Snowmobile-shaped symbols designate winter ORV staging areas. These have been included on the maps because other winter users may wish to avoid such areas.

"P" symbols along highways represent plowed sno-park lots. From November 15 to April 30, cars parked in or near sno-park lots must display a valid permit or face a fine. Because the permit costs only $3 per day or $15 per season, it pays to stop by a sporting goods store, ski shop, or Department of Motor Vehicles office to pick one up.

The Forest Service generally identifies the route of winter trails near sno-parks with plastic markers nailed to trees. Snowmobile routes are signed with orange diamonds while ski and snowshoe trails are posted with blue diamonds. Because plastic markers are considered inappropriate inside designated wilderness areas, however, travelers on wilderness routes will need advanced routefinding skills. In some areas, tree blazes or wooden markers help identify wilderness trails in winter.

Oregon's extremely variable snow conditions can produce delightful powder, heavy mush, and clattery ice all within a day's time. Waxless skis are usually the boards of choice.

Nordic skiers and snowshoers in Oregon need raingear, plenty of warm clothing (wool is best), a rucksack with the *Ten Essentials* (page 16), a repair kit, and an insulated seating pad for rests. Never set out without a topographic map and compass. Wilderness exploration can be great fun in winter, but the need for caution and survival training is likewise great.

Avalanches, though infrequent in Oregon, may occur during or immediately after a snowstorm or high wind. Avoid slopes of more than 25 percent steepness—especially treeless slopes, because these may have a history as "avalanche chutes." Also beware of frozen lakes. Particularly in the Cascades, heavy snows can insulate the water, preventing it from forming solid ice. Even when skiers succeed in crossing the snow-covered slush, those on foot may fall through.

Finally, a few winter manners:

■ Yield the right of way to downhill skiers.

■ Do not stop to rest in a ski track; step aside.

■ Do not walk or snowshoe in a ski track; this ruins the smooth grooves.
■ Leave pets at home.

A WORD TO BOATERS

This guide describes eight of Oregon's wildest white-water river runs and numerous quiet spots for canoeing, sailing, or sailboarding.

The descriptions use a six-point scale to rate a rapids' difficulty for rafters, kayakers, and drift boaters:

    class 1—easy
    class 2—moderate
    class 3—dangerous. Novices should consider lining or portaging boats.
    class 4—very dangerous. Novices should line or portage.
    class 5—extremely dangerous. Even experts should consider portaging.
    class 6—unrunnable. Portage boats.

Those in decked canoes should add one point to the difficulty of each rapids. For open canoes, add two points.

Note that most of the featured rivers can be run only when water is high—but not too high. Suitable months for running rivers vary dramatically from year to year. Check with the Water Resources Data Center at (503) 249-0666 for daily updates of river gauge levels.

Because floatboating concentrates visitor impact on the fragile camping beaches of wilderness rivers, it is important to follow the strictest no-trace camping guidelines:

■ Cook on campstoves. Those who insist on using campfires must bring all of their own firewood, build the fire in a firepan they have brought, and then pack up both pan and ashes without a trace.

■ Use toilets when provided. When they are not, do not bury toilet paper. Buried human waste decomposes within a few weeks, but paper remains for a year or more in riverbank soils and can be exposed by wind or water. Pack out the used paper in a sealed plastic bag.

Proper boating skills and safety are essential on wilderness runs because escape or rescue after an accident can be extremely difficult. Check the references listed at the back of this book for information on these important subjects.

A WORD TO EQUESTRIANS

The role of horses in the wilderness is in transition. A few new routes have been added for horses, but more and more trails bear the sign "Hikers Only." The National Park Service at Crater Lake bans horses everywhere except on the Pacific Crest Trail and allows no grazing.

As the no-trace ethic spreads, so have restrictions on saddle stock. Here's a list of guidelines that have grown into iron-clad rules in most wilderness areas:

■ Keep saddle stock at least 200 feet from streams or lakes except for loading, unloading, watering, or traveling on a trail.
■ Carry all the feed an animal will need. This cuts down on grazing.

- Bring no hay. It spreads weed seeds.
- Feed oats or hay pellets morning and evening from a nose bag, and not from piles on the ground.
- Never tie stock to a tree, even temporarily. Tethers can girdle trees, and hooves can dig circular pits.
- Hobble, do not picket stock. This disperses grazing damage.
- Do not build corrals or hitching racks.
- When breaking camp, fill in paw holes and scatter manure.

Gone are the days of campfires, big coffee pots, beans and bacon, and canvas tents. As equestrians limit their loads and their pack strings, their gear increasingly resembles that of the no-trace backpacker: lightweight nylon tents, lightweight campstoves, and freeze-dried food.

Many wilderness visitors who might once have used a pack horse now hire a llama. Llamas must be led on foot, because they can only carry a 60-pound pack. But llamas weigh a fifth as much as a horse, leave only deerlike pellets for droppings, and do a tenth of the damage to trails and meadows.

A FINAL WORD

Once Oregon was entirely wilderness, from the Pacific Ocean to the Snake River. Now, only scattered islands of that great wilderness survive, and most of these still lack protection. Use this guide to discover the beautiful but fragile heritage that remains to show Oregon as it once was.

For the areas in this book, there is still time.

A NOTE ABOUT SAFETY

Safety is an important concern in all outdoor activities. No guidebook can alert you to every hazard or anticipate the limitations of every reader. Therefore, the descriptions of roads, trails, routes, and natural features in this book are not representations that a particular place or excursion will be safe for your party. When you follow any of the routes described in this book, you assume responsibility for your own safety. Under normal conditions, such excursions require the usual attention to traffic, road and trail conditions, weather, terrain, the capabilities of your party, and other factors. Keeping informed on current conditions and exercising common sense are the keys to a safe, enjoyable outing.

The Mountaineers Books

Opposite: *Mount Jefferson and snowy Jefferson Park in April*

chapter 1 **Northwest Oregon**

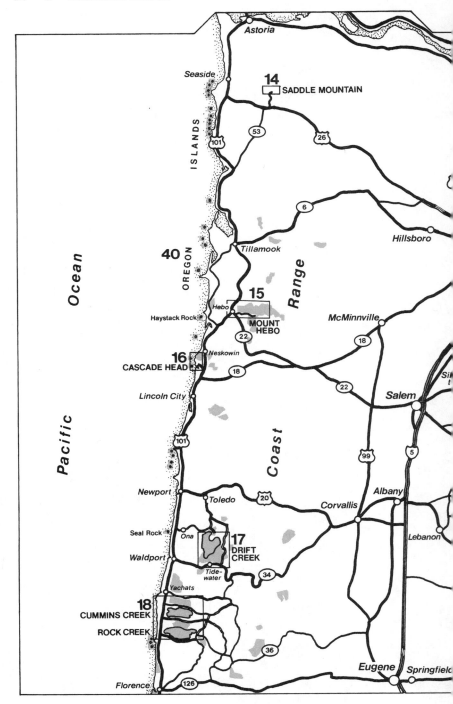

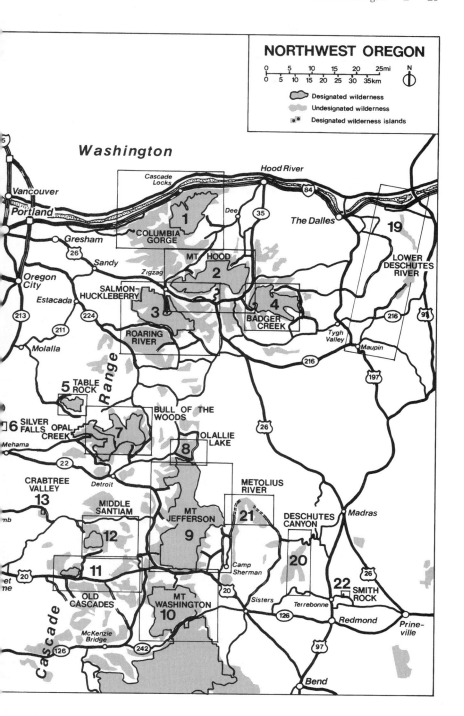

1 Columbia Gorge

Location: 24 miles east of Portland
Size: 107 square miles
Status: 62 square miles designated wilderness (1984)
Terrain: Cliffs, densely forested canyons
Elevation: 100 feet–4960 feet
Management: Columbia Gorge National Scenic Area
Topographic maps: Forest Trails of the Columbia Gorge (Geo-Graphics); Columbia Wilderness, PCT Northern Oregon Portion (USFS); Bridal Veil, Bonneville Dam, Hood River (Green Trails); Multnomah Falls, Bonneville Dam, Tanner Butte, Carson, Wahtum Lake, Mt. Defiance (USGS)

Several worlds collide in the Columbia Gorge. In the west, moss-covered rain forests cling to misty green cliffs. A few miles east, only scrub oaks dot a semiarid scabland. And in between, a colonnade of more than twenty major waterfalls separates the alpine meadows of the Cascade Range from the mudflats of the Columbia River, nearly at sea level.

In the midst of these colliding ecosystems is the remarkable Hatfield Wilderness. Although it lies a mere half-hour freeway drive from Portland and overlooks a busy transportation corridor along the Columbia, it remains delightfully wild, protected by a ribbon of breathtaking 3000-foot cliffs. Originally called the Columbia Wilderness, the Hatfield area was renamed by Congress in the 1990s—ironically, for a politician dubbed "Senator Stumpfield" by conservationists.

Climate

The annual rainfall varies from a soggy 150 inches in the Bull Run Watershed to 75 inches at Cascade Locks, and just 29 inches at Hood River on the eastern end of the Gorge. Summers, however, are dry throughout. Snow covers trails above 3600 feet from December to May, but lower trails may be clear for hiking even in midwinter. Occasionally, winter ice storms drape the cliffs with icicles and coat trees and highways with silvery freezing rain—a result of warm Pacific clouds dropping rain through a layer of freezing air blown in from east of the mountains.

Plants and Wildlife

Between the dense Douglas fir and sword fern rain forests of the west and the open oak grasslands of the east, the Columbia Gorge hosts twelve plant species found nowhere else in the world—including six strictly confined to the wilderness lands. Look for rare plants and flowers on the rock walls of the Gorge's cool, north-facing canyons, where even alpine wildflowers are often tricked into growing nearly at sea level.

The California condors that Lewis and Clark reported here in 1805, attracted by the Columbia's salmon runs, are now gone, although bald eagles may yet be sighted.

Ponytail Falls, on the trail from Horsetail Falls to Oneonta Creek

The darling of the Gorge's many waterfalls is the water ouzel, a chubby little slate-gray bird that builds its mossy nests behind waterfalls. Ouzels spend their days walking along the bottom of rushing mountain streams, poking about for insect larvae with their deft little bills. When this robin-sized bird is not marching around underwater it can be seen doing bobbing knee-bend exercises on creek rocks or whirring along just above the water with rapid, constant little wingbeats. Though common throughout western North America, this dipper can live only where water runs wild and white.

Geology

The many layers of columnar basalt exposed in the cliffs of the Gorge are all part of the massive lava outpourings that inundated 50,000 square miles of eastern Washington, eastern Oregon, and Idaho to a depth of up to a mile 10 to 17 million years ago. These rock floods—a result of the North American continent overriding the Pacific Ocean floor—surged down the ancient Columbia as far as the sea, pushing the river north to its present location. When the crest of the Cascade Range then gradually warped upward, making those mountains ever higher, the Columbia kept pace by cutting its gorge deeper and deeper. The original surface of the lava flows is now a tilted and well-eroded upland, evident in the 2000-foot plateau above Multnomah Falls and the 4000-foot Benson Plateau. More recent volcanoes—Larch Mountain, Tanner Butte, and Mount Defiance—protrude above this general silhouette.

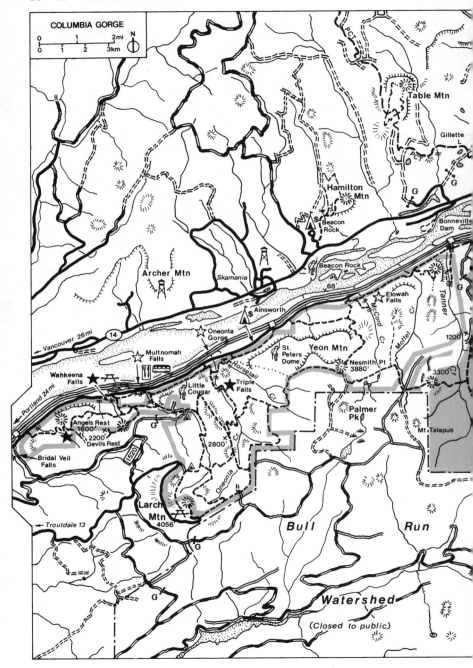

COLUMBIA GORGE

0 1 2mi
0 1 2 3km

N

Table Mtn

Gillette

PCT

PCT

G

G

Hamilton Mtn

Beacon Rock

Bonneville Dam

Beacon Rock

Archer Mtn

Skamania

68'

Elowah Falls

McCord Cr

Moffet

Tanner

G

Ainsworth

Oneonta Gorge

St. Peters Dome

Yeon Mtn

Nesmith Pt 3880'

1200'

Vancouver 26mi

14

Multnomah Falls

Horsetail

3300'

Wahkeena Falls

Little Cougar

Triple Falls

Palmer Pk

Portland 24mi

Angels Rest 1600'

2200' Devils Rest

Cr

2800'

Mt Talapus

1520

Bridal Veil Falls

G

Oneonta

Bull

Run

Troutdale 13

Larch Mtn 4056'

G

Watershed

(Closed to public)

During the Ice Age twenty small glaciers formed on the Gorge's southern rim, carving the hanging amphitheaters that lie above many of the waterfalls. Much of the scenery of the Gorge, however, can be attributed to a series of monumental Ice Age floods of the Columbia River. These "Missoula Floods" occurred when the continental ice sheet then covering Canada temporarily dammed the Clark Fork River in western Montana. The most recent such flood, 13,000 years ago, unleashed a body of water half the volume of Lake Michigan across eastern Washington and through the narrow Columbia Gorge. The flood denuded the Gorge to an elevation of 800 feet and undercut the cliffs, leaving the graceful waterfalls visible today.

THINGS TO DO
Hiking
The thorough trail network is very heavily used on weekends, particularly in the vicinity of Multnomah Falls and along Eagle Creek. The dramatic elevation gains on many trails (as much as 4000 feet) should be taken into consideration when planning trips.

Oregon's tallest waterfall, Multnomah Falls, has inspired a cluster of trails well-suited to day hikes. Paths within roughly 0.5 mile of this 542-foot double cascade are paved due to frequent foot traffic. A good way to beat the crowds is to park at nearby Wahkeena Falls and make a 5-mile loop up the Wahkeena Trail to Multnomah Falls' top, passing half a dozen falls on the way.

Long, slotlike Oneonta Gorge, though less well-known than neighboring Multnomah Falls, has perhaps equal charm. A 2.7-mile loop trail peers down into this mossy chasm from its rim, but it can be more directly experienced by wading knee-deep up the narrow creekbed 0.5 mile from the old Columbia River Highway bridge to an otherwise hidden 100-foot falls.

The historic Columbia River Highway was built 1913–15 as a winding pleasure drive through the scenic Columbia Gorge. Several long-abandoned sections have been reopened as trails for hikers, equestrians, and bicyclists, including a 4-mile stretch paralleling Interstate 5 from Bonneville Dam exit 40 to Cascade Locks exit 44. This section includes the bridgelike, cliff-edge Tooth Rock Viaduct just west of Eagle Creek.

Half a dozen exhilarating day hikes switchback up to viewpoints of the Gorge. The spectacular rock bluff at Angels Rest is a 1500-foot climb in 2.2 miles from the old Columbia River Highway at the Bridal Veil exit of Interstate 5. Nesmith Point, just west of elegant Elowah Falls, is an ambitious 3800-foot climb in 4.9 miles to a stunning view. Two viewpoint hikes climb through natural wildflower rock gardens: the rugged 4.8-mile Ruckel Creek Trail from the Eagle Creek Campground, and the steep 3.3-mile path up Nick Eaton Ridge from the Herman Creek Campground. Both have loop options.

The spectacular Eagle Creek Trail features seven waterfalls, a high bridge, and one tunnel (which actually goes behind Tunnel Falls). Blasted out of the sheer cliffs in the 1910s, this trail is now very popular. A day trip can hardly do the trail justice; it is better seen on a two-day backpack trip, perhaps returning via the beautiful Benson Plateau or the quiet Tanner Creek or Herman Creek Trails. Camping along the Eagle

Creek Trail is restricted to designated sites. On summer weekends space can be tight. Cars at the Eagle Creek Trailhead are unusually susceptible to break-ins.

The area's largest lake, Wahtum Lake, shimmers in a forested bowl at the headwaters of Eagle Creek. It is a popular campsite for backpackers on the Eagle Creek-to-Benson Plateau Loop. Tenters at the lake are restricted to designated sites. Because the lake can also be accessed by a mere 0.2-mile walk from paved Road 1310, use has been so heavy that the Forest Service plans to require permits for day hikers and backpackers alike, starting in about 2004. Once this system is in place, you will be able to apply for the free but limited permits online at *www.fs.fed.us/r6/mthood* or from the Mount Hood Information Center on Highway 26 (1-888-622-4822).

Three long-distance trail routes traverse the Oregon side of the Columbia Gorge. The 35.5-mile low-elevation Gorge Trail, between Bridal Veil and Wyeth, avoids the steep climbs found on many other trails and is snow-free year round. It is used primarily to connect other trails, but it makes good hiking from end to end. Because of the Gorge Trail's many trailheads along the Columbia River Highway, sections of the path make for accessible and undemanding day hikes.

A higher elevation trail route winds 38 miles from 4056-foot Larch Mountain to 4960-foot Mount Defiance. Together with the low-elevation Gorge Trail, this route makes it possible to convert any of the area's fifteen north–south trails into scenic loop hikes. Hiking the length of this high-elevation Gorge route is a challenging four-day backpack trip, zigzagging across several steep canyons in the most remote part of the wilderness.

The third long-distance trail in the Gorge is the Pacific Crest Trail (PCT), which passes Wahtum Lake and crosses the 2-square-mile forested Benson Plateau. Those who just can not wait to see the summer display of alpine wildflowers will find them blooming as early as June along the Benson Plateau's northeast rim. Huckleberry aficionados can profitably prowl about Wahtum Lake in late August.

For those able to arrange a car shuttle between trailheads, Larch Mountain and Mount Defiance can be the starting points of dramatic, downhill day hikes. The Larch Mountain Trail drops 4000 feet in 6.7 miles to Multnomah Falls Lodge. The Mount Defiance Trail loses fully 4800 feet elevation to Starvation Creek Falls in just 5.8 miles. Both mountains offer dramatic views of Mount Hood, Mount Adams, and Mount St. Helens.

Throughout the Columbia Gorge, hikers should remember that poison oak is common below 800 feet, that trailside cliffs make some paths inappropriate for unsupervised children, and that underbrush and steep slopes virtually prohibit cross-country travel. Only the wider, well-graded Herman Creek and Pacific Crest Trails are recommended for horses or pack stock. The Bull Run Watershed to the south, the source of Portland's water supply, is closed to the public except specifically for travel on the PCT.

Climbing

The Columbia Gorge is a center for testing technical climbing skills. For starters, good conditioning hikes include the nearly 5000-foot climb from Starvation Creek Falls to Mount Defiance and the numerous trails up to the 4000-foot Benson Plateau. Then,

3 miles west of Bridal Veil Falls are Rooster Rock (a 200-foot pinnacle with routes varying in difficulty from level I-4 to II-5.6-A3) and Crown Point (a 700-foot bluff with routes of difficulty II-5.4 and III-5.6). The Pillars of Hercules, a group of 100-foot basalt towers immediately west of Bridal Veil, rate difficulty levels from I-5.2 to II-5.8.

Little Cougar, a small thumb of rotten rock at 1300-foot elevation 1 mile east of Multnomah Falls, is a level I-4 or I-5.4 climb, depending on the route taken. St. Peters Dome, 1 mile east of Ainsworth State Park, consists of similarly poor rock but requires level II-5.6 or III-5.6-A3 skills. It is a 200-foot thumb at 1525 feet and was unclimbed until 1940.

By far the most popular and most extensive climbing challenges in the area, however, are on Beacon Rock, just across the Columbia River in Washington. This impressive 848-foot andesite monolith requires about five rope lengths of skilled climbing. Difficulty levels of II-5.6 to IV-5.11 are encountered on a total of forty-five named routes and variations.

Mount Hood

Location: 34 miles east of Portland
Size: 115 square miles
Status: 74 square miles designated wilderness (1964, 1978)
Terrain: Glaciated peak, alpine meadows, forested slopes
Elevation: 1800 feet–11,240 feet
Management: Mount Hood NF
Topographic maps: Mount Hood (Geo-Graphics); Mount Hood Wilderness, PCT Northern Oregon Portion (USFS); Government Camp, Mount Hood (Green Trails, USGS)

Oregon's tallest peak dominates this popular wilderness. Hikers can meet alpine vistas of Hood from every path of the area's well-developed trail network. The dormant volcano's summit, ringed with eleven active glaciers, is the goal of 10,000 climbers a year.

But the peak is not the area's only attraction. The 38-mile Timberline Trail circles the mountain through a succession of stunning alpine meadows filled with flowers. Ramona, Tamanawas, and a dozen other waterfalls grace heavily forested river valleys. Zigzag Canyon is an impressive 1000-foot-deep gorge on the mountain's flank. And 5000-foot Zigzag Mountain, an 8-mile-long western spur of Hood, offers lakes and ridges of its own.

Climate

The area's 150 inches of annual precipitation come largely as snow between October and April. Skiers and snowshoers will find the snow drier, and the skies often bluer, on Hood's east and southeast slopes. Snow melts off lower trails (up to 4000 feet) by

Mount Hood from a ridge near the junction of the Mazama Trail and the Timberline Trail

about June 1 and off higher trails (up to 7000 feet) by mid-July. July and August yield warm days and cold nights. Sudden storms can bring snowfall in any month—a fact that has led to climbing tragedies.

Plants and Wildlife

Dense Douglas fir forests blanket the wilderness' lower areas, with an understory of Oregon grape, huckleberry (ripe in late August), salal, and rhododendron (blooms late May). Higher forests are of mountain hemlock, noble fir, and subalpine fir. Near timberline (6500 feet), gnarled whitebark pines frame meadows of blue lupine, red paintbrush, bear grass plumes, penstemon, purple Cascade aster, and western pasqueflower ("old-man-of-the-mountain"). Profuse displays of white avalanche lilies decorate Paradise Park in July and Cairn Basin in August.

A bird checklist for Hood's south slope notes 132 species, from hummingbirds to bald eagles. Forty species of mammals live on the mountain's slopes, including black bear, mountain lion, and elk.

The whistling, squirrel-like animals often met on Hood's rocky timberline slopes are pikas. Pikas (also known as rock rabbits) are round-eared, apparently tailless animals

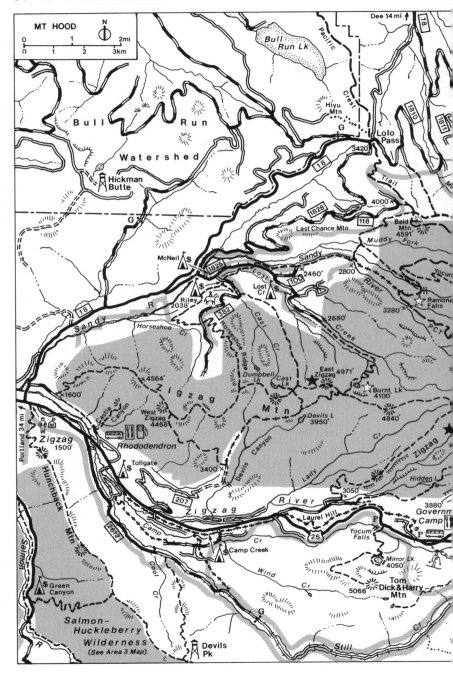

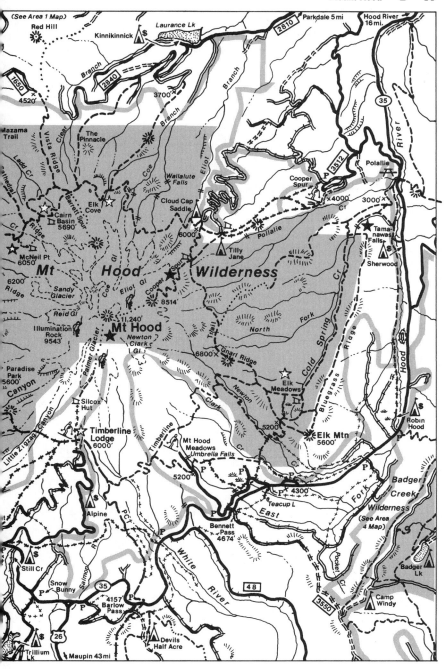

the size of guinea pigs. Colonies of pikas live at higher elevations than any other North American mammal, cutting and sun-drying bushels of grass to last them through nine snowbound months without hibernation. Yellow-bellied marmots also live in rockslides and whistle to each other for warning, but are much larger, resembling bushy-tailed beavers.

Geology

Mount Hood is the most recently active of all Oregon volcanoes. In the 1800s, four minor eruptions of steam, ash, and magma alarmed observers as far away as Portland. In 1907 glowing rock near the summit melted part of the White River Glacier, causing floods. Even today, climbers encounter hot rock, scalding steam vents, and a powerful sulfur smell in the depression south of the summit, between Steel Cliff and Crater Rock.

The volcano itself had its beginnings after the surrounding hills and rivers were in nearly their present form. Lava flows filled nearby river canyons, forcing the rivers aside. When the rivers eroded the softer rock around the hard lava, the original valleys were left as lava-topped ridges—an example of "reverse topography."

Mount Hood reached its greatest height, about 12,000 feet, just before the Ice Age. Then, glaciers removed the crater and much of the north slope. Barrett Spur and Cooper Spur remain to show the mountain's earlier dimensions, indicating the ancient crater was north of the present summit. Crater Rock, south of the summit, was long thought to be a remnant of the volcano's central plug. In fact it is a recent side vent's lava dome, the creation of which smothered the Timberline Lodge area with cinder-and-mud avalanches just 2000 years ago.

History

Spotted in 1792 by Lieutenant Broughton under explorer Vancouver's command, Mount Hood was named for British admiral Lord Hood. In 1845 Sam Barlow laid out Oregon's first toll road around the south base of Mount Hood, leading Oregon Trail wagons from The Dalles to Sandy over Barlow Pass. The route spared settlers the dangers of a raft trip down the Columbia River's rapids but subjected them to the miseries of Laurel Hill, 3 miles west of Government Camp, a slope so steep wagons had to be skidded down with wheels removed.

A 4-mile section of the Barlow Road over Laurel Hill was rebuilt as a hiking and equestrian trail by the Civilian Conservation Corps in 1935. Other Depression-era work projects include the artistically designed Timberline Lodge and the Timberline Trail with its scenic stone shelters.

THINGS TO DO
Hiking

The marvels of Mount Hood are so close to Portland that overuse is a real concern. The many meadows, with their wildflower displays and mountain views, have had to be protected by a complete ban on camping. Backpackers must seek out less fragile sites in forested areas—and even the forested "islands" in Elk Meadows and Elk Cove have been placed off-limits to tents or fires. The small lakes of Zigzag Mountain, popular for their reflections of Mount Hood, are included in a general ban on camping within 200 feet of any lake's or stream's shoreline. Camping is not allowed within 500 feet of popular Ramona Falls, and fires are forbidden within 500 feet of McNeil Point to save the gnarled dead wood at timberline for its own beauty.

This list of relatively crowded areas, however, also reads as a list of the wilderness area's top attractions, worth visiting for day hikers or careful backpackers.

Start with Ramona Falls, a moderate, 7.1-mile loop hike from Road 1825 through the sparse forest along the Sandy River to a mossy, 100-foot falls on a stairstepped cliff of columnar basalt. A comparable, but less well-known day hike on the east side of Mount Hood leads an easy 1.9 miles from the East Fork Trailhead by Sherwood Campground to 100-foot Tamanawas Falls.

The prime hike through Hood's alpine meadows is the 37.6-mile Timberline Trail, a three- to five-day trip usually begun at Timberline Lodge and undertaken clockwise around the mountain, so as to finish up at the showers and swimming pool (suit rentals available) at the classic old lodge. Five unbridged creek crossings on the route can be hazardous in the high water of June and July snowmelt: Zigzag River, Sandy River, Muddy Fork, Eliot Branch, and White River. Water is lower in August and during the mornings.

No fewer than twenty-one trails lead up the flanks of Mount Hood to the Timberline Trail, making all manner of loop hikes and day trips possible. Many of these tributary trails ascend ridges that are scenic in their own right—notably Gnarl Ridge on Hood's east slope, the Zigzag Canyon Trail on the mountain's southwest slope, and the Pacific Crest Trail (PCT), Mazama Trail, and Vista Ridge Trail on Hood's north flank. All make excellent day trips for the fit hiker; distances average 3 to 5 miles one way with 2000-foot elevation gains.

Hikers who shy from such climbs can still sample the Timberline Trail's charms from two high-elevation trailheads. Timberline Lodge, set among wildflowers itself, is a good starting point for an easy 2.2-mile traverse to Zigzag Canyon, an impressive 1000-foot-deep erosional gash into Hood's volcanic scree. On the mountain's northeast flank, Cloud Cap Saddle Campground touches the Timberline Trail amidst 6000-foot-elevation meadows. The popular meadow at Elk Cove is a 4-mile hike west.

The adventurous hiker can climb well above timberline to view Hood's glaciers close-up at several points. By far the highest trail is 8514 feet up Cooper Spur, overlooking Eliot Glacier, 3.9 miles from Cloud Cap Saddle. A trail up from Timberline Lodge passes the Silcox Hut (a European-style hut with café and bunks) before petering out at the 8000-foot level. Yocum Ridge and the McNeil Point shelter are atop other scenic, high trails. Barrett Spur's viewpoint is a cross-country scramble above the Timberline Trail on the less visited north side of Mount Hood. Climbing beyond these points is technical, requiring special gear and climber registration.

West of Mount Hood, Zigzag Mountain is another popular hiking center, with four lakes, two lookout tower sites (West and East Zigzag), and six trailheads. The Devils Canyon Trailhead provides the gentlest grades up to the area's best viewpoints—2.5 miles to West Zigzag and 4 miles to East Zigzag. Even in winter the steep 0.9-mile path to Castle Canyon's rock formations is usually snow free.

A popular 3.4-mile trail up Lost Creek climbs to Burnt Lake, with a ridge-top view 1.2 miles beyond. Use has been so heavy on the trail to Burnt Lake that the Forest Service plans to require permits for day hikers and backpackers alike, starting in 2003. Once this system is in place, you will be able to apply for the free but limited permits online at *www.fs.fed.us/r6/mthood* or from the Mount Hood Information Center on Highway 26 (1-888-622-4822).

East of Hood, Elk Meadows is another popular destination, with its fine mountain view. From Highway 35, reach the meadow's three-sided shelter either up the 3-mile trail from the Hood River Meadows ski area or along the heavily forested 6.2-mile Cold Spring Creek Trail from the Polallie Picnic Area. One of the best hikes for a foggy, viewless day is the 4.1-mile East Fork Hood River Trail, a level forest walk between Robin Hood and Sherwood Campgrounds.

Most equestrian use in the wilderness begins at the horse-loading facilities at Riley Campground, west of Mount Hood. Signs mark the fragile or hazardous trails closed to pack and saddle stock: the non-PCT portion of the Timberline Trail, Mazama Trail, Vista Ridge, Pinnacle Ridge, Elk Cove, Paradise Park Loop, Castle Canyon, Yocum Ridge, Burnt Lake, and the north half of the Ramona Falls Loop.

Climbing

First climbed in 1857, Mount Hood has become the second most-climbed snow peak in the world—after Japan's sacred Mount Fuji. Portland's outdoor club, the Mazamas, was organized in 1894 by 193 climbers who convened on the summit in inclement weather. Hood has been scaled by a woman in high heels, a man with no legs, and a gibbon named Kandy. Climber Gary Leech once raced from Timberline to the summit in 85 minutes.

But Hood is still a technical climb, over crevassed glaciers and loose, rotten rock. Lack of caution, and the area's volatile weather, have given Hood one of the highest accident rates of any peak in the country. An ice ax, crampons, and rope are essential; helmets are recommended. All climbers must register either at Timberline Lodge or at Cloud Cap Inn.

The easiest and most popular route to the top, the "South Side" route, proceeds at a true 5° compass bearing from the Silcox Hut to the Hot Rocks, a geothermal area between Crater Rock and Steel Cliff. A snow hogback north of Crater Rock leads to the summit wall, where a large crevasse must be circumvented before continuing to the summit. The climb takes 4 to 10 hours and is begun in the pre-dawn dark to avoid the afternoon's slushy snow. A descent in poor visibility must be undertaken by compass. The tendency to return "straight down" often leads climbers southwest toward the dangerous chasm of Zigzag Canyon.

The second most common summit route, also rated level I-2, ascends the 45° snow slope above the Cooper Spur viewpoint on the mountain's east face. Avalanches can be a hazard here.

Twelve additional ascent routes vary in difficulty from I-3 to III-5.6.

Illumination Rock, a 9543-foot crag between the Reid and Zigzag Glaciers southwest of Hood's summit, offers some interesting climbing topography. Five level I routes, of classes 4 to 5.4, explore the rock's pinnacles and a summit "skylight" hole.

Winter Sports

Mount Hood offers the largest selection of nordic ski routes in the state. Highways 26 and 35 are plowed in winter, providing access to five developed downhill ski areas and thirteen plowed sno-park lots. All of the downhill areas except Timberline Lodge rent cross-country skis.

From Timberline Lodge, nordic skiers can traverse 2.6 miles to the brink of Zigzag Canyon on the PCT, or choose one of three heavily used routes for the 4-mile glide down to Government Camp. From Government Camp, numerous short trails lace the level area between Multorpor Meadows and the snowed-under Still Creek Campground. More advanced skiers can tackle the 6.3-mile Yellow Jacket Trail, traversing from the junction of Highway 26 and the Timberline Lodge Road to the White River sno-park on Highway 35.

The site of former Snow Bunny Lodge, now a snow play center, is the starting point for the many nordic routes on snowed-under roads around scenic Trillium Lake. The easiest trip is to Summit Meadows, north of Trillium Lake, where the graves of Barlow Road pioneers are marked by white crosses.

The winding, 2.4-mile section of old highway at Barlow Pass makes a pleasant ski route. The Giant Trees loop trail between the old and new highways explores an old-growth grove. Trailless exploration of the scenic White River Canyon is relatively easy from the White River sno-park on Highway 35.

Nordic ski routes from Bennett Pass head southeast along roads toward the Badger Creek Wilderness, crossing a steep slope known as the Terrible Traverse. From the parking lots of the nearby Mount Hood Meadows ski area, Elk Meadows makes a spectacular winter goal, but bring map and compass for safety on the 2.4-mile trail. Robin Hood Campground's sno-park offers level, lower elevation skiing along the East Fork Hood River Trail, as well as on roads to the west, through Horsethief Meadows toward Bluegrass Ridge.

From the Cooper Spur ski area's sno-park, the challenging Cooper Spur Ski Trail climbs 1800 feet in 3 miles to the snowed-under Tilly Jane Campground. A return loop is possible via the 8.6-mile Cloud Cap Road.

Although there are no sno-parks on the west side of Mount Hood, the lower portion of Road 18 is typically snow-free, allowing access to good ski-touring country. Drive to the snow gate at McNeil Campground, then ski 5.7 miles east to beautiful Ramona Falls. Another trip from the snow gate tours 4 miles south up Road 382 into Horseshoe Canyon. In spring, when higher snow levels open Road 18 farther, drive to the snowline and continue on skis along Road 18 to Lolo Pass, where views open up in all directions. For a genuine challenge, ski the 9.2 miles back to McNeil Campground on Road 1828, around Last Chance Mountain.

3 Salmon-Huckleberry and Roaring River

Location: 32 miles southeast of Portland
Size: 164 square miles
Status: 70 square miles designated wilderness (1984)
Terrain: Densely forested river canyons, ridges, lake basins
Elevation: 980 feet–5159 feet
Management: Mount Hood NF
Topographic maps: Salmon-Huckleberry Wilderness (USFS); Mt. Hood Wilderness (Geo-Graphics); Cherryville, Government Camp, Fish Creek Mountain, High Rock, Mount Wilson (Green Trails); Wildcat Mountain, Rhododendron, and five other maps (USGS)

Less than an hour's drive from Portland, this spacious wilderness remains relatively undiscovered. Hidden here are the delightful subalpine lakes of the Rock Lakes Basin and the spectacular Salmon River canyon. Yet the area's greatest charms are subtler: fog-draped ridge crests of ripe huckleberries and lonely white-water canyons lined with mossy maples.

Climate

Trails below 2000 feet are usually snow-free in winter. Ridge trails and the Pacific Crest Trail remain under snow from November to May. Spring and fall rains account for a share of the area's 80-inch annual precipitation. Summers are generally clear and dry.

Plants and Wildlife

Major runs of steelhead, chinook, and coho salmon return annually to the aptly named Salmon River. The Roaring River's thunderous torrent is home to hardy anadromous fish as well, while every stream and lake of size in the area supports brook trout and rainbow trout.

Black bear and mule deer rely on the area's extremely rugged, snowless lower canyons for winter range. The large, trailless upper Roaring River valley shelters several shy wildlife species, including cougar, badger, fisher, and marten. Listen for the flutelike call of the hermit thrush in June and July. Water ouzels whir along streams year round.

The dense western hemlock and Douglas fir forests of the canyon bottoms are interspersed with droopy-branched western red cedar and red alder. Creekside vine maple adds brilliant scarlet foliage in fall. Rare Alaska cedar can be found on the fringes of Salmon River Meadows.

Ridge tops are mostly open, decorated in June with the white plumes of bear grass. The area's famed huckleberries, once the goal of annual harvest treks by Indians and

View across Eagle Creek's canyon to Mount Hood from the trail near Old Baldy

pioneers alike, ripen in late August. The blue fruit is most abundant around Veda Lake, and on Indian Ridge, Huckleberry Mountain, Old Baldy, and Devils Peak.

Geology

The ridges of this area belong to the Old Cascades, a broad volcanic mountain range that erupted 10 million years before the High Cascades, and which now forms the rugged western foothills for those taller, snow-capped peaks. Devils Peak and Salmon Butte are probably remnants of once-tall volcanoes, but the erosive power of water and ice have reduced them to ridges. Broad, U-shaped glacial valleys, now filled with meadows and lakes, are recognizable at Rock Lakes, Squaw Lakes, Plaza Lake, and Serene Lake.

THINGS TO DO
Hiking

Two very easy day hikes with views of Mount Hood are the 1.4-mile trail into Mirror Lake (1 mile west of Government Camp) and the 1.2-mile Veda Lake Trail (8 miles south of Government Camp on Road 2613). The lower Salmon River Trail, paralleling Road 2618 for 2.6 miles, makes another pleasant warm-up trip.

The Salmon River Trail upriver of Green Canyon Campground traces a wilder canyon. The trail ambles amidst massive old-growth trees for the first 2 miles, then

41

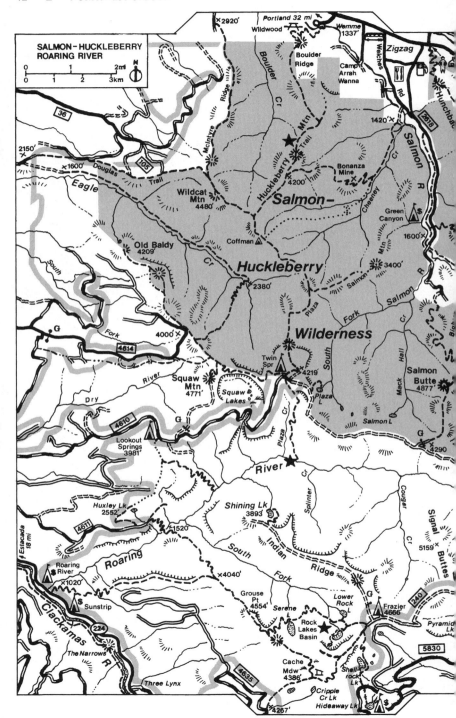

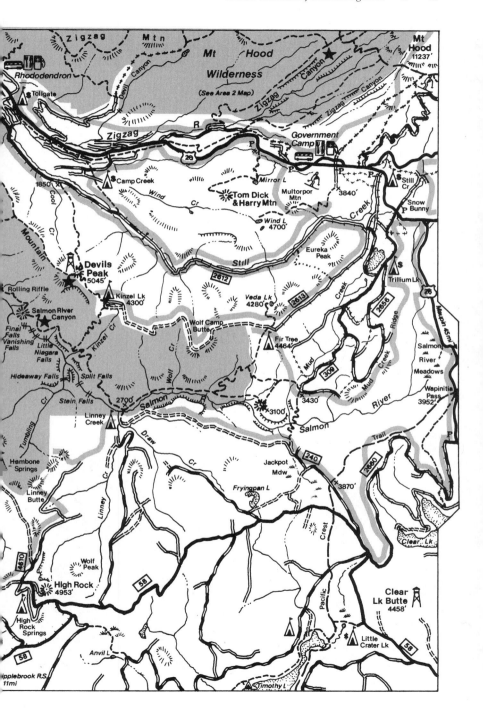

climbs several hundred feet above the river, traversing steep slopes with viewpoints. The roar audible from the second viewpoint (3.8 miles in) is caused by a series of hidden waterfalls, but avoid the dangerous 0.2-mile scramble trail descending toward a slippery viewpoint where a fatal accident occurred. Backpackers can hike onward and upward to other trailheads. (Kinzel Lake is another 4.3 miles; Linney Creek, 5; Fir Tree, 10.7; and Mud Creek Road, 10.6.)

The 7.7-mile Rock Lakes Basin loop trail offers the attractions of a High Cascades hike, without the crowds. The loop passes three subalpine lakes, a cliff-top viewpoint, and the ruin of Cache Meadow's log shelter. Side trails from the loop plunge toward the Roaring River. To reach the trailhead at Frazier Turnaround, take Highway 224 southeast of Estacada 26 miles, turn left just after the bridge at Ripplebrook onto Road 57, turn left again after 7.4 miles onto Road 58, head left after another 6.9 miles onto paved Abbott Road 4610 for 1.3 miles, and then go straight on rough, dirt Road 240 for 4.4 slow miles to its end. From the same trailhead, try the 1.3-mile jaunt down to Shellrock Lake, or drive back 0.2 mile to the primitive Frazier Fork Campground and hike (or bicycle) a scenic abandoned road 4.3 miles to Shining Lake.

The Salmon-Huckleberry Wilderness has no fewer than five panoramic ridges with trails. Most of these hikes begin with long climbs. The closest to Portland is Wildcat Mountain, a 5-mile trip (one way) gradually gaining 1800 feet up McIntyre Ridge to views of Hood. To find the trailhead, drive 11 miles east of Sandy on Highway 26 to the Shamrock Motel and turn right onto East Wildcat Creek Road for 4.1 miles, always keeping to the larger, uphill road at forks.

Two good routes ascend Huckleberry Mountain—the Boulder Ridge Trail from the parking area at the Bureau of Land Management's (BLM) Wildwood Recreation Site, and the Bonanza Trail, which starts along Cheeney Creek and climbs past an old mine

Footbridge across the Salmon River at the Wildwood Recreation Area

tunnel. Park along paved Welches Road and walk across a Salmon River bridge 0.2 mile to the "trailhead," where parking is forbidden.

The panorama from the historic, unstaffed lookout tower on Devils Peak is another worthy hiking goal. It can be reached either by the grueling 4.1-mile Cool Creek Trail from Road 2612, the 5.7-mile Green Canyon Trail from Road 2618, or the 8.1-mile Hunchback Ridge Trail from the Zigzag Ranger Station. Because all these routes gain more than 3000 feet in elevation, it is tempting to take the easy 1.2-mile trail from near Kinzel Lake instead, even though this requires a bone-jarring 10-mile drive to the end of rutted dirt Road 2613.

The views from the open, rocky summit of Salmon Butte are reached by a woodsy 4.4-mile trail climbing 2800 feet from a trailhead near the end of Salmon River Road 2618. The path passes glorious displays of pink rhododendron blooms in June. Another ridge-top trail center is at primitive Twin Springs Campground; drive 6.5 miles southeast of Estacada on Highway 224, then turn left on Road 4610 for 18.4 miles. Twin Springs is atop "The Plaza," a 1-mile-square plateau. Follow the Plaza Trail 1.4 miles north to the Sheepshead Rock viewpoint at the tip of The Plaza, then hike another 3.6 increasingly rugged miles northeast for the view on Salmon Mountain.

Roaring River is one of the wildest and most remote streams in northwest Oregon. Quiet trails switchback down from Twin Springs Campground (2.3 miles) and the end of Road 4611 (1.2 miles). No trails or easy bushwhacking routes follow the river itself through its rugged canyon.

The Eagle Creek Trail follows a rushing stream through a towering old-growth rain forest. A small meadow at 4.7 miles makes a logical stopping point for day hikers. A Mount Hood National Forest map is necessary to locate the trailhead, 19 miles east of Estacada.

Winter Sports

Three excellent cross-country skiing centers border the area. Most popular is the Snow Bunny sno-park on Highway 26, from which a wide variety of tours are possible into the Trillium Lake Basin. Several short trips are described in the Mount Hood entry. Longer tours follow Road 2613 for 5.5 miles to a view on the Veda Lake Trail, or prowl the roads and clearcuts along Mud Creek and Mud Creek Ridge. Numerous loop routes are possible by cross-countrying between roads—remember a compass and topographic map.

The second major nordic skiing area focuses on four sno-parks, located 0.5, 1.5, 2.7, and 4.4 miles south of Wapinitia Pass on Highway 26. The area features road tours around scenic Clear Lake and Frog Lake. A short, often overlooked trip is the 0.5-mile jaunt to spacious Salmon River Meadows, 1.6 miles north of Wapinitia Pass on Highway 26 but hidden from the road by trees.

The high country southeast of Roaring River offers solitude for cross-country skiers. This area begins near the Ripplebrook Ranger Station 26 miles southeast of Estacada on Highway 224. Winter plowing extends as far as the Silvertip Work Center, 3 miles up Road 4630 from Ripplebrook, so after heavy midwinter snows, tours start there. It is 11.4 miles up Road 4635 to Cache Meadow—a worthy overnight trek for the prepared. When the snowline reaches 3000 feet in spring (call Ripplebrook Ranger Station for snow information), skiers can drive 8 miles east of Ripplebrook on Road 57, then turn left on Road 58 for another 3 miles. From that point, tours on Roads 58 and 5830 extend to Shellrock Lake and High Rock.

Badger Creek

Location: 65 miles east of Portland, 44 miles southeast of The Dalles
Size: 45 square miles
Status: 36 square miles designated wilderness (1984)
Terrain: Forested canyons
Elevation: 2100 feet–6525 feet
Management: Mount Hood NF
Topographic maps: Badger Creek Wilderness (USFS); Mount Hood, Flag Point (Green Trails); Badger Lake, Flag Point, Friend (USGS)

Draped across the eastern foothills of Mount Hood, the Badger Creek canyonlands form the remarkable transition zone between High Cascade forest and Columbia Plateau steppe. The area's 80 miles of trails connect with the Mount Hood Wilderness nearby.

Climate

Lying to the east of the Cascade crest, Badger Creek is often sunny when western Oregon suffers from drizzle. Though the area measures just 12 miles end to end, the annual precipitation ranges from 80 inches on the windy western ridges to 20 inches in the dry eastern lowlands. Snows close the lower trails from December to March. The ridges' relatively light winter snowpack melts from the highest trails by mid-June. Afternoon thunderstorms occasionally interrupt hot summer days.

Plants and Wildlife

The higher elevations of Badger Creek share the alpine rock gardens and Hudsonian forests of Mount Hood, but the eastern lowlands are part of a pine-oak biologic zone unique in Oregon wilderness. This open, parklike ecosystem of ponderosa pine and Oregon white oak extends only a short distance north and south of the Columbia River between Hood River and The Dalles.

Nowhere is the pine-oak zone's spring wildflower display as spectacular as on the School Canyon Trail, west from Road 27 over Ball Point. Tall, purple larkspur bloom in mid-April, with pink shooting star in damp areas. By late May, great fields of lupine turn the hillsides blue, splashed yellow in places by balsamroot. By July, white death camas and purple onion remain among yellow, withered grass.

By late July the wildflowers of the pine-oak zone are gone, but the rock gardens of the alpine zone are at their peak. Amble along the Divide and Gunsight Butte Trails for showy penstemon, paintbrush, avalanche lilies, and stonecrop.

The Portland Audubon Society has compiled lists for Badger Creek showing 46 butterfly species, 101 lichens, and 157 birds—surprising diversity for such a compact area.

Geology

Volcanism from Mount Hood provided the raw material for the Badger Creek area. An Ice Age glacier scoured a curving, 2500-foot-deep, U-shaped valley from its cirque at Badger Lake down Badger Creek, leaving the dramatic cliffs below the Divide Trail. A second glacier cut the valley of Boulder Creek; its cirque lake, below Camp Windy, has filled with sediment to become Crane Prairie. Stream erosion since the Ice Age cut the precipitous, narrow gorges of lower Badger Creek and Little Badger Creek, leaving interesting badlands and pinnacles of more resistant rock.

THINGS TO DO
Hiking

The steep 2.4-mile route up from Robin Hood Campground on Highway 35 to Gumjuwac Saddle offers good views of Mount Hood during its 1700-foot climb—and brings the hiker to the intersection of four Badger Creek trails, all suitable for day hikes or longer treks.

Southeast of Gumjuwac Saddle, the Gunsight Butte Trail parallels Road 3550 for

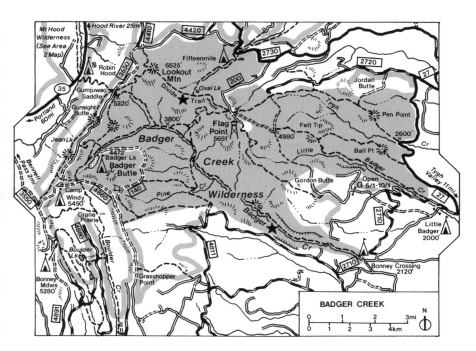

Ponderosa pine tree at the wilderness boundary near Ball Point

4.5 miles to the junction of Road 3550, following a ridge top packed with rock gardens, interesting rock formations, and viewpoints. Due south of Gumjuwac Saddle is the 2.5-mile trail down to Badger Lake.

A trail heading east from Gumjuwac Saddle drops 1300 feet in 2.2 miles to the Badger Creek Trail; from there, Bonney Crossing Campground is an enchanting 9.9-mile backpack downstream past old-growth Douglas fir, green-pooled cascades, and finally, oak-fringed cliffs. Yet another trail from Gumjuwac Saddle climbs 2.2 miles northeast to 6525-foot Lookout Mountain, the finest viewpoint in the area.

It is also possible to drive to the trail crossing at Gumjuwac Saddle via a very rough road. Take Highway 35 around Mount Hood to between mileposts 70 and 71, go 3.8 miles east on Road 44, turn right for 4.7 miles on Road 4410, and turn right on dirt Road 3550 for 3.3 treacherous miles.

The northern portion of the Badger Creek Wilderness features a dramatic 3.7-mile portion of the Divide Trail between Lookout Mountain and Flag Point's staffed fire lookout. The path is a series of cliff-edge viewpoints, rock formations, and wildflower gardens. Reach it by driving as to Gumjuwac Saddle, but at the end of Road 4410 turn left 200 yards on Road 4420. An easy 1-mile abandoned road leads up to the spectacular viewpoint atop Lookout Mountain, and to the Divide Trail.

To reach the trailhead to Crane Prairie, in the lovely valley of Boulder Creek, take Highway 35 to Bennett Pass, drive 4 horribly rough miles on Road 3550, and veer right on Road 4891 for 0.3 mile. Another mile down Road 4891 is Bonney Meadows Campground, which offers several trails, including the pleasant 1.7-mile day hike to Boulder Lake.

On the eastern edge of the wilderness, four trails set out through the unique pine-oak forest. The 11.9-mile Badger Creek Trail to Badger Lake is more than a day hike but worth it. The Little Badger Creek Trail fords its creek four times in the first 3 miles of its rugged canyon; crossings are easy except in early spring. Other trails climb to views at Ball Point and Pen Point. Access to the eastern Badger Creek trailheads is via Highway 197. At milepost 33, near Tygh Valley, turn west on Shadybrook Road for 1 mile. Then turn left on Fairgrounds Road for 1.1 mile, and turn right on Badger Creek Road, which becomes Road 27.

Winter Sports

Cross-country skiers can follow Road 3550 from the sno-park at Bennett Pass toward a number of destinations: Bonney Meadows (5.8 miles), Gunsight Butte (7.2 miles), and Badger Lake (7.4 miles via the trail at Camp Windy). All of the routes cross a frightening slope known as the Terrible Traverse.

5 Table Rock

Location: 19 miles southeast of Molalla, 50 miles south of Portland
Size: 9 square miles
Status: 9 square miles designated wilderness (1984)
Terrain: Forested ridges
Elevation: 1300 feet–4881 feet
Management: Salem District BLM
Topographic maps: Rooster Rock, Gawley Creek (USGS)

This pocket wilderness offers surprisingly quiet forest trails within a short drive of the populous Willamette Valley. Table Rock's basalt mesa is the area's high point, with a view worth the climb.

Climate

Summers are sunny, while other seasons are mild and wet (100 inches annual precipitation). Winter snows cover trails above 3000 feet from December to May.

Plants and Wildlife

The forests here are Douglas fir and western hemlock, with noble fir at higher elevations. Pink-blossomed rhododendron crowd upper slopes. The small, sparsely petaled Gorman's aster found on rock slides is a federally listed endangered species, as is Oregon sullivantia, a saxifrage of cliff seeps. White Clackamas iris, showy Washington lilies, and delicate calypso orchids are endangered primarily by indiscriminate flower pickers.

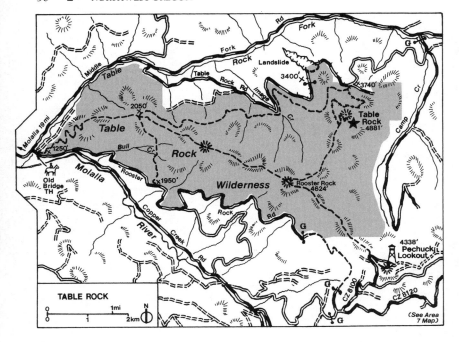

Geology

Fortress-shaped Table Rock is the remnant of a hard basalt lava flow that once capped the entire area. All local rocks date from the Old Cascades' eruptions 16 to 25 million years ago.

History

Table Rock was in the hunting grounds of the Northern Molalla, a small tribe confined to the rugged foothills between the Willamette Valley and the High Cascades. Because the Molalla spoke a Shahaptian language similar to that of the Nez Percé, they are thought to have been driven from an eastern Oregon homeland centuries ago to this unlikely range.

The east–west trail from the Molalla River to Pechuck Lookout is a remnant of a Molalla trail leading from the lowlands to Bull of the Woods and the High Cascades. Three archaeological sites—evidently Molalla camps—have been identified in the area.

THINGS TO DO
Hiking

Start with a 3.6-mile hike that gains 1500 feet to a sweeping wilderness viewpoint atop Table Rock's cliff. From the landslide on Table Rock Road, the route follows the closed road 1.3 miles. From there a trail heads into the woods, winds about the impressive columnar basalt cliffs of Table Rock's north face, and switchbacks up the gentler

Columnar basalt in Table Rock's cliff

west slope. The panorama extends from Mount Rainier to the Three Sisters, including views into the Bull of the Woods Wilderness and the Willamette Valley.

Rooster Rock, an additional 1.4 miles by trail from Table Rock, affords similar views and protrudes from a scenic heather-topped ridge. The hiker who has planned a car shuttle can continue past Rooster Rock on this ridge to the Old Bridge Trailhead on the Molalla River—an 8.8-mile trip in all. Pechuck Lookout, a rare two-story stone structure from 1932, is another interesting goal.

There are no reliable water sources on the area's trails. Equestrians will want to avoid the rough rock talus slope directly north of Table Rock.

All trailheads are reached via the town of Molalla, 30 miles south of Portland. Take Highway 211 for 0.5 mile east of Molalla, turn south onto South Mathias Road for 0.3 mile, turn left on South Feyrer Park Road for 1.6 miles, and then turn right onto South Dickey Prairie Road. Follow this road past several jogs 5.3 miles to a poorly marked junction with South Molalla Forest Road. Turn right on a bridge across the Molalla River, and follow the paved road 12.8 miles to a junction with Middle Fork Road. The low-elevation Old Bridge Trailhead is a stone's throw to the east. To find the upper trailhead, veer left onto gravel Middle Fork Road for 2.6 miles, and turn right on Table Rock Road for 4.4 miles to a landslide, the current trailhead. There are no parking fees.

Winter Sports

From December through March it is pleasant to drive to snowline on Table Rock Road, park to one side, and ski up the road and Table Rock Trail to the base of Table Rock's ice-encrusted cliffs for the view. The distance varies from 3 to 4 miles, depending on the road's snow level.

6 Silver Falls

Location: 26 miles east of Salem
Size: 13 square miles
Status: State park
Terrain: Forested gorge, waterfalls
Elevation: 760 feet–2400 feet
Management: Oregon Parks and Recreation Department
Topographic maps: Silverton, Scotts Mills, Stayton Northeast, Drake Crossing (USGS)

Waterfalls are the specialty of Oregon's largest state park, visited by a million people each year. Trails lead through a steep-sided, scenic canyon past ten falls, five of which are more than 100 feet tall. In three cases, trails actually lead through mossy caverns *behind* waterfalls.

Climate
The mild, wet weather of this relatively low elevation park allows hiking in any season. In fact, the falls are most spectacular in winter, when silvery icicles and snow add a delicate beauty missed by the summer crowds.

Plants and Wildlife
Dense Douglas fir forests and streambank maples shelter a lush undergrowth of ferns, Oregon grape, salal, and many forest wildflowers. Though most wildlife species shy away from the park's populous trails, look for robin-sized water ouzels dipping or flying along the creek. Hikers often marvel at the area's spectacular anthills, some 4 feet tall.

Geology
Silver Creek Canyon's cliffs are part of the Columbia River basalt flows that inundated this area about 15 million years ago from vents near Hells Canyon. The lava was following the ancestral Columbia River channel west to the ocean shore, then located near Stayton. Displaced by the lava, the Columbia moved north. When this area later tilted upward with the rising Cascade Range, Silver Creek cut through the resistant basalt. The basalt now forms the lips of the waterfalls. Many of the waterfalls' splash pools have eroded caverns into the soft rock beneath the basalt. Cylindrical indentations in the roofs of these canyons are "tree wells" left when the Columbia River lava flows surrounded tree trunks, which then burned.

Another feature of the basalt is its interesting six-sided columnar jointing. When basalt cools slowly, it cracks into a honeycomb of pillars perpendicular to the cooling surface. Look for these pillars in the cliffs.

History

The Silverton Fire, largest in Oregon history, burned this area in 1865. Silver Falls City, on the site of the present South Falls picnic area, was founded as a logging camp in 1888. Stumpfields left by early logging caused the area to be rejected for national park status in 1926. The private entrepreneur who owned South Falls in the 1920s charged picnickers ten cents to watch junk Model T Fords float over the brink. He hired daredevil Al Faussett to canoe over the 177-foot falls in 1928; Faussett survived with severe injuries. The area became a state park in 1931. The canyon trails, lodge, shelters, and highway overlooks were built by Civilian Conservation Corps employees stationed near North Falls from 1935 to 1942.

THINGS TO DO
Hiking

Long, graceful waterfalls appear at nearly every bend along the beautiful 4.5-mile canyon trail from South to North Falls. Side trails create loop hike possibilities ranging in length from 0.7 to 7 miles. Dogs on short leashes are tentatively being permitted on the canyon trails. A $3-per-car fee is charged throughout the park.

Most loop hikes begin at 177-foot South Falls, the tallest and most popular of the cascades. A paved, heavily used 0.7-mile loop winds through the cavern behind the waterfall, crosses a footbridge, and returns to the South Falls picnic area. A quieter 2.4-mile

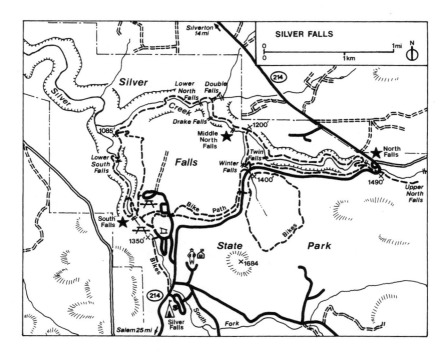

loop extends the shorter hike down the canyon past 93-foot Lower South Falls.

A 5.1-mile circuit of the canyon continues past Lower South Falls to Lower North, Double, Drake, and 106-foot Middle North Falls before crossing a footbridge and climbing to the Highway 214 parking area above Winter Falls. From there a 1.6-mile hiking trail through a large Douglas fir forest parallels the highway back to the South Falls picnic area. The longest loop hike, 7 miles, follows the canyon from South Falls to 136-foot North Falls and returns on the trail near the highway.

A paved 4-mile bicycle path begins at Silver Falls Campground, passes near the lodge at South Falls, and then prowls the forest on a loop above Winter Falls. Another 12.2 miles of hiking and equestrian trails begin at the hitching rails and horse loading

Lower South Falls

ramp at the southwest park entrance on Highway 214. This trail network consists primarily of old logging roads maintained for recreation.

The most remote portion of the park is the lower 2.5 miles of Silver Creek Canyon, a trailless gorge with four rarely visited waterfalls.

Opal Creek and Bull of the Woods

Location: 68 miles southeast of Portland, 64 miles east of Salem
Size: 80 square miles
Status: 54 square miles designated wilderness (1984)
Terrain: Densely forested mountain ridges, valleys
Elevation: 2000 feet–5710 feet
Management: Mount Hood NF, Willamette NF
Topographic maps: Bull of the Woods Wilderness (Geo-Graphics); Battle Ax (Green Trails)

Hidden high in the Cascade foothills, these adjacent wilderness areas feature ancient forests, subalpine mountains, wild rivers, and a dozen lakes. In the west, the popular Opal Creek Trail, open all year, visits towering stands of giant trees. To the east, the Bull of the Woods' extensive trail network centers on the Bull of the Woods lookout tower, elevation 5523 feet, with a sweeping view of the high country from Mount Hood to Mount Jefferson. The rustic, free bathhouse at Bagby Hot Springs, with its cedar-log tubs, provides a relaxing trailside stop.

Climate
Only the Opal Creek Trail is usually open all winter. Other trails below 3000 feet are generally snow-free from April into December, and the highest trails are clear from June through October. Despite more than 100 inches of annual precipitation, summers are sunny.

Plants and Wildlife
This area is one of the last great old-growth forest reserves of western Oregon. Towering Douglas fir, western hemlock, and western red cedar remain in the valleys, with a complex ecosystem of lichens, birds, insects, and mosses. Elegant white trillium and yellow-clustered Oregon grape bloom in the deep forest in April. Tangles of rhododendrons erupt in pink blossom in June.

Here the patient observer may sight a northern spotted owl, the huge, shy bird threatened by reductions in its old-growth habitat. By day the owl remains in its nest, high in the resprouted top of a broken conifer—or it may perch like an 18-inch-tall, earless statue on a branch near the trunk, where the owl's mottled, white-spotted feathers camouflage it perfectly against the tree's bark. At night, however, this owl glides through the forest on its 3.5-foot wingspan, catching wood rats, mice, and flying squirrels. In the dark it answers readily to its own recorded call, a high-pitched "hoo, hoo-hoo" (a human imitation will do). Then a flashlight held at the observer's eye level will reflect off the owl's dark eyes, revealing its location.

Five other species of owls share the area: the larger, ear-tufted great horned owl, the robin-sized screech owl, the day-hunting pygmy owl, the small saw-whet owl, and the dark-eyed flammulated owl. A good range for owling indeed!

Geology

Erosion has uncovered quartz veins containing small amounts of copper and silver in this section of the 16- to 25-million-year-old "Old Cascades." A relic of the Elkhorn Mining District, which once brought a rush of prospectors to the area, survives in the historic Jawbone Flats mining camp along Opal Creek. In the northern end of the wilderness, pioneer miner Robert Bagby blazed a trail from Bagby Hot Springs to his Pansy Blossom Mine, named for its colorful ore. The mine entrance is still visible above Pansy Lake.

Ice Age glaciation carved the area's many bowl-shaped lake valleys. A vanished Ice Age glacier carved Elk Lake's basin and polished the smooth bedrock visible along the trail on the eastern slope of Battle Ax.

THINGS TO DO
Hiking

This wilderness has ample room for satisfying two- and three-day backpacking trips, yet it is small enough to be explored by day hikers as well.

Start with a stroll into the Opal Creek Wilderness from the locked gate on Road 2209, following an old mining road (now a broad trail) amid giant, 400-year-old Douglas firs. After 2 miles pass Merten Mill, a defunct sawmill site with a campable meadow and a deep, swimmable pool at the base of a broad waterfall. For a 7.1-mile loop, continue 0.2 mile past Merten Mill, keep right at a fork in the road, cross the river, and take the Opal Creek Trail 1.4 miles to an overlook of Opal Pool's scenic gorge. Then keep left to cross a footbridge and return on an old road through Jawbone Flats. The rustic collection of private cabins here, built 1929–32, is now an old-growth study center for the Friends of Opal Creek. For a longer hike up Opal Creek, continue upstream from Opal Pool 1.5 miles to Beachie Creek, just beyond a grove of ancient cedars. The trail peters out here, but a more extensive trail network is planned.

To find the Road 2209 trailhead for Opal Creek, drive east of Salem 23 miles on Highway 22 to Mehama's second flashing yellow light, and turn left on Little North Fork Road for 15 paved miles and an additional 1.3 miles of gravel. At a fork, veer left on Road 2209 for 6 miles to the gate.

In the adjacent Bull of the Woods Wilderness, the most popular day trip is the easy, 1.5-mile hike through a huge, old-growth forest to Bagby Hot Springs. Although the hot springs' shake-roofed bathhouse burned in 1979 when night bathers left a candle lit, the 8-foot cedar log tubs were too waterlogged to burn and have been installed in an even larger bathhouse, built by volunteers. A resident ranger enforces a ban on camping extending from the trailhead to a quarter mile beyond the springs. Visit in midweek to avoid crowds.

To reach the hot springs' trail from Estacada, drive Highway 224 southeast 26 miles to the bridge by Ripplebrook Campground, veer right onto Road 46 for 3.6 miles, continue to the right on Road 63 another 3.5 miles, then turn left on Road 70 for 6 miles. Break-ins are not uncommon for cars left at this trailhead.

Pansy Lake is another rewarding, easy goal. A 1.2-mile trail traverses a towering grove of Douglas fir on the way to the swimmable lake in a forested cirque. The drive starts out the same as to the hot springs, but follows Road 63 for 5.6 miles before turning left onto Road 6340 for 7.8 miles; then turn right onto Road 6341 for 3.5 miles.

Several outstanding, but more strenuous, day hikes seek out viewpoints. Chief among these is Bull of the Woods, the only area peak still topped by a lookout tower. Here the view across bear grass–dotted meadows stretches from Mount Rainier to the Three Sisters. Staffed only in times of extreme fire danger, the tower also serves as an emergency shelter. The Pansy Basin Trail extends to the Bull of the Woods lookout—a 3.8-mile route in all—but the Bull of the Woods Trail from Road 6340 (past the Dickey Peaks) climbs 1200 feet less and is 0.5 mile shorter.

Two craggy peaks contend for the title of best viewpoint in the southern end of these wilderness areas: Battle Ax and Mount Beachie. To reach either, drive Highway 22 to Detroit, turn north for 4.4 miles on Breitenbush River Road 46, turn left onto Road 4696 for 0.8 mile, turn left onto Road 4697 for 4.7 steep miles, and turn left for 2 miserably rough miles to the Elk Lake Campground entrance. The 1-mile dirt track

Sawmill Falls on the Little North Santiam River near Opal Creek

from the campground to the trailheads at Beachie Saddle is too rough for most vehicles. Park and walk.

To the north from Beachie Saddle, a 1.6-mile trail switchbacks up to the cliff-top views at Battle Ax's old lookout site, gaining 1200 feet elevation. The lookout's old water trail continues north, making a loop trail possible back to the Elk Lake Campground—a pleasant 6.5-mile hike in all.

To the southwest from Beachie Saddle, a 5.6-mile trail traverses a lovely ridge topped by Mount Beachie, gaining just 900 feet to reach views of Elk Lake, Mount Jefferson, and beyond.

Whetstone Mountain, a former lookout site in the seldom visited northwest edge of the wilderness, is the quietest viewpoint of all. The easiest route up, a 2.4-mile trail on the mountain's north flank, begins on Road 7020, 9 miles south of the Bagby Hot Springs Trailhead.

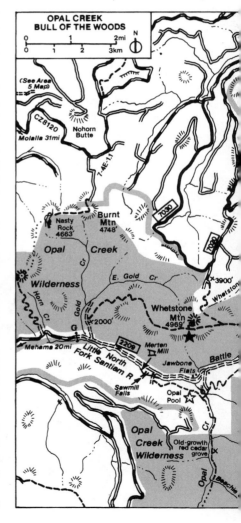

A much more arduous trail up Whetstone Mountain—gaining 3000 feet in 4.5 miles—is the route of choice for some hikers because of its easier trailhead access from Salem. From the gate on Road 2209, hike 0.5 mile up the old mining road toward Jawbone Flats and turn left up a spur road along Gold Creek 0.5 mile to the trail.

Another good old-growth forest walk follows an easy 4-mile trail from Elk Lake to the site of the former Battle Creek shelter, where two woodsy streams join.

Most of the small, scenic lakes in the Bull of the Woods Wilderness are just far enough from trailheads to be the destinations either of very challenging day hikes or pleasant overnight trips. For instance, the Welcome Lakes are 5 miles in and 2000 feet up from the Road 6380 trailhead—a rugged 10-mile day hike through old-growth forest. But backpackers can pitch a tent near Upper Welcome Lake and still have energy left to hike another mile up to the Bull of the Woods lookout, or to prowl the interesting ridges and meadows along nearby trails.

Likewise, Big Slide Lake is 5.5 miles

in and 2300 feet up the rhododendron-lined Dickey Creek Trail from Road 6340-140. A base camp at the lake allows backpackers to continue out Big Slide Mountain's ridge to Lake Lenore's cliff-top cirque.

Another pretty lake destination is Silver King Lake. It is a 5.6-mile hike from Road 7020 along the Whetstone Mountain Trail's scenic ridge top. Those who can arrange a short car shuttle can camp at the lake, then hike 7.7 miles down the Bagby Trail the second day through old-growth forest to Road 70, stopping at the hot springs for a dip on the way.

The Twin Lakes make a good hiking goal. Start out from Road 4697 near the Elk Lake Campground, climbing to a scenic ridge-top trail north of Battle Ax. Camp after

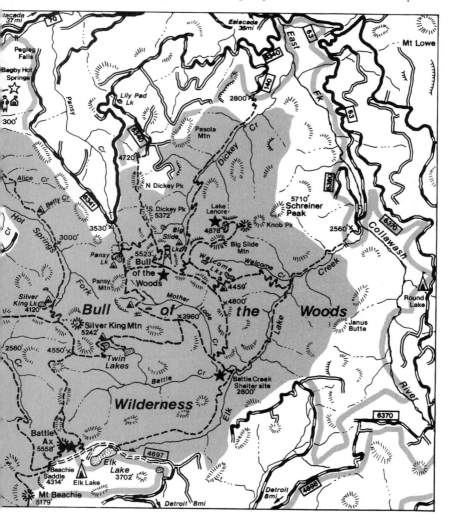

6.2 miles at Lower Twin Lake. The second day, stroll 5.3 miles to an easy camp at the site of the former Battle Creek shelter; then hike 4 miles farther to complete a loop back to Elk Lake.

Only the most determined bushwhackers can follow Opal Creek for 2 rough, trailless miles from Beachie Creek up to Opal Creek's headwaters at Opal Lake (not shown on the map), climbing around a spectacular waterfall below the lake's outlet. However, a much easier, 0.5-mile route to the marshy-edged lake follows a small trail down from gravel Road 2207. From Detroit, take French Creek Road 2223 for 4.2 miles and turn right on Road 2207 for 5 miles.

Climbing

Nasty Rock and a small unnamed pinnacle to the southwest offer some technical rock pitches. Many of the routes on these remote volcanic crags are untested. The rugged, up-and-down, 4-mile trail route to Nasty Rock begins off Road 2209 a mile before the road's gate.

Winter Sports

Though roads are unplowed in winter, skiers park at snow line on Road 4697 and ski to Elk Lake. In spring the trip is usually 3 to 4 miles one way, with Beachie Saddle a tempting additional 1.5-mile climb.

8 Olallie Lake

Location: 80 miles southeast of Portland, 69 miles east of Salem
Size: 36 square miles
Status: 17 square miles Forest Service scenic area, 14 square miles Indian reservation
Terrain: Forested, lake-dotted plateau
Elevation: 2100 feet–7215 feet
Management: Mount Hood NF, Confederated Tribes of Warm Springs
Topographic maps: Olallie Scenic Area, PCT Northern Oregon Portion (USFS); Olallie Butte (USGS); Breitenbush (Green Trails)

In the shadow of Mount Jefferson, this forested plateau of 200 lakes and ponds is one of the more accessible portions of the Cascade's high country. Short, nearly level trails from seven developed campgrounds along Skyline Road 4220 lead to the larger lakes, while the open, lodgepole pine forests invite easy cross-country hikes to more remote lakeside campsites.

Climate

A very heavy winter snowpack keeps most trails, and Road 4220, closed from about mid-October to July 1. As lingering snow melts during the peak wildflower month of July,

Olallie and Monon Lakes from Olallie Butte

mosquitoes are so profuse that headnets are advisable. By late summer, cross-country hikers may stumble on ground-nesting yellow jackets.

Plants and Wildlife
Low huckleberry bushes provide a carpet beneath the forests of lodgepole pine and mountain hemlock. Watch for mink, otter, and eagles at the many fish-filled lakes.

Geology
This Cascade Range upland has been dotted by geologically recent cinder cones such as Olallie Butte and Potato Butte. A broad Ice Age glacial ice sheet left the many shallow lake basins. Look for glacier-polished bedrock at the north end of Monon Lake and along the Pacific Crest Trail (PCT) near Olallie Lake.

History
The Indians who once trekked here each fall to hunt deer and gather the abundant huckleberries named the largest lake *Olallie*—the Chinook jargon word for "berry." Seven bands of central Oregon Indians were granted the eastern portion of this area when an 1855 treaty created the Warm Springs Indian Reservation.

THINGS TO DO
Hiking
Short trails and frequent lakes make the area well-suited for beginning backpackers and families with young hikers. A good day hike for children is the 0.8-mile Russ Lake Trail from wildflower-filled Olallie Meadows. Hiking the shore trails around Olallie or Monon Lakes is also fun with children and yields first-rate views of Olallie Butte and Mount Jefferson. It is 2.9 miles around Monon Lake (with 0.3 mile on a road) and 4.6 around Olallie Lake (including 1.6 miles along a road).

The pleasant 2.8-mile trail from Si Lake past cliff-rimmed Fish Lake and 73-foot-deep Lower Lake climbs 700 feet on its way to the Lower Lake Campground.

Good camping lakes appear at nearly every bend in the 5.7-mile Red Lake Trail between Road 380 and Olallie Lake. Worthwhile side trips to this east–west route are trails that climb to viewpoint peaks. It is 0.7 mile from Sheep Lake to the top of Potato Butte and 1.2 miles from Top Lake to Double Peaks.

The most interesting section of the PCT here is the 6.3 miles between Olallie Lake Guard Station and the PCT Trailhead near Breitenbush Lake. At either end, this section follows cliffs and ridges with good views.

Olallie Butte has the best view of all, atop a trail climbing 2600 feet in 3.8 miles from an unmarked trailhead under the southernmost of three sets of powerlines. This is Indian land, so disturb nothing along the route. The former lookout site not only overlooks the entire Olallie Lake area but it also offers an eye-level view of Mount Jefferson and a long look into Central Oregon.

Cross-country hiking to trailless lakes avoids the crowds of the best hiking months, August and September. Beginners in the art of routefinding can practice their map and compass skills by bearing south from crowded Lower Lake to quiet Gifford Lake, or from Timber Lake to View Lake (the view is of Olallie Butte). Then try bushwhacking on compass bearings along the string of small lakes that form a 1-mile-diameter circle about the northern base of Double Peaks. It is difficult to become hopelessly lost

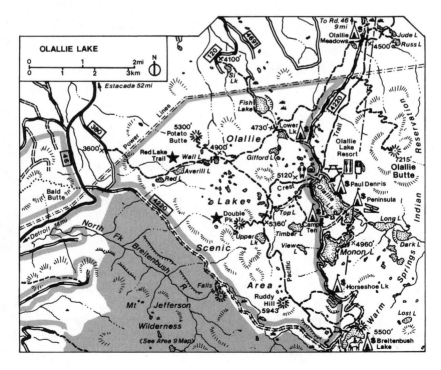

Olallie Butte from Top Lake

anywhere in the area, because a trail or road is never more than a mile away.

Camping is prohibited within the Warm Springs Indian Reservation, except specifically at Breitenbush Lake. Anglers on reservation lands must have a state fishing license, a tribal fishing permit, and a copy of the Warm Springs fishing regulations. Violators are subject to a $200 fine or ninety-day imprisonment.

To reach the Olallie Lake area from the north, follow Highway 224 and then paved Road 46 a total of 47.5 miles past Estacada. Turn left on paved Road 4690 for 8 miles, then turn right on gravel Road 4220 for 6 miles to Olallie Lake. Beyond Horseshoe Lake, Road 4220 becomes a very slow, badly rutted track, unsuited for trailer travel. The Fish Lake Trailhead is only 6 miles from Highway 46; drive 3.4 miles up Road 4690, turn right on Road 4691, and follow signs.

Drivers approaching from Salem can take Highway 22 to Detroit, follow paved Road 46 for 17 miles, then turn right on treacherously rutted Road 4220 for 7.5 miles to Breitenbush Lake. Those without four-wheel drive should continue on paved Road 46 another 7 miles before turning right on Road 4690 toward Olallie Lake.

Winter Sports

Road 46, plowed in winter, allows cross-country ski access to the area's lakes via snowed-under Roads 4220 and 4690. Snowmobiles are allowed on these routes. The 7.5-mile distance to Breitenbush Lake makes an overnight trip in order, perhaps to one of the two shake-roofed, stone shelters beside the lake.

Boating

A small resort at Olallie Lake rents rowboats, and Peninsula Campground offers a boat ramp. Canoeing is excellent because motors are prohibited on all of the area's lakes.

9 Mount Jefferson

Location: 64 miles east of Salem, 37 miles northeast of Bend
Size: 273 square miles
Status: 174 square miles designated wilderness (1968, 1984)
Terrain: Glaciated peak, forested ridges, lake basins
Elevation: 2400 feet–10,497 feet
Management: Willamette NF, Deschutes NF, Mount Hood NF, Confederated Tribes of Warm Springs
Topographic maps: Mount Jefferson, Santiam Pass Winter Recreation (Geo-Graphics); Mount Jefferson Wilderness, PCT Northern Oregon Portion (USFS); Mount Jefferson, Whitewater River (Green Trails)

Mount Jefferson ranks as Oregon's second highest peak (after Mount Hood) and forms the centerpiece of Oregon's second most visited wilderness (after the Three Sisters).

The top attractions are 150 mountain lakes, ranging from heavily visited, half-square-mile Marion Lake to the delicate tarns of Jefferson Park's popular alpine wild-flower meadows. Three Fingered Jack, an impressive 7841-foot crag, dominates the southern end of the wilderness with its own collection of alpine lakes and meadows.

Climate

Winter snows start early in November and total from 20 to 58 feet at Santiam Pass. The spring melt typically opens trails up to 3500 feet by mid-May, up to 4500 feet by mid-June, up to 5500 feet by mid-July, and up to 6500 feet by August 1. Mosquitoes are troublesome for two to three weeks following the final snow melt in each region.

Storms occasionally interrupt clear, dry summer weather. The eastern slopes, with 40 inches annual precipitation, are often sunny even when the western slopes, with 100 inches precipitation, are lost in clouds.

Plants and Wildlife

Deer, elk, black bear, and coyotes are numerous enough to be seen frequently. Bald eagles can be spotted fishing in the lakes.

The area's lower western valleys shelter old-growth Douglas fir forests. Spire-shaped subalpine fir and mountain hemlock cluster at higher elevations. Descending the area's drier eastern slopes is a remarkably compact sequence of forest zones, from mountain hemlock to lodgepole pine, and finally to the long-needled ponderosa pine of the Metolius Valley.

Fields of blue lupine and red paintbrush attract day hikers to Canyon Creek Meadows, Jefferson Park, the Eight Lakes Basin, and Santiam Lake area in late July.

Also in July, the white, 4-foot-tall plumes of bear grass may be profuse along ridges, on slopes, and in lodgepole pine forests. This bunchgrasslike plant fills the wilderness with its fragrant blooms every second or third year, mysteriously choosing not to flower at all in other years. An unlikely looking lily family member, bear grass has blooms consisting of hundreds of tiny, six-petaled flowers. Bears unearth and eat the plant's succulent root, which, when boiled, is said to make a substitute for soap. Indians gathered the plant's 2-foot-long leaves and wove them into useful baskets—a craft that wilderness hikers today can practice to while away an evening.

Geology

Mount Jefferson and Three Fingered Jack are both heavily eroded remnants of apparently extinct volcanoes. On Three Fingered Jack, only the hard lava plug, or central core, survives, flanked by ridges of the old volcano's subsidiary lava dikes. Mount Jefferson is also topped by a lava spire, but it is not the mountain's ancient plug. Glaciation has removed the western third of the mountain, including the ancient summit. The current summit rock was once a flank lava flow.

Geologically recent cinder cones (including Pyramid Butte, South Cinder Peak, and Maxwell Butte) and two large 6500-year-old lava flows 6 miles southeast of Mount Jefferson prove that the area is not volcanically dead.

History

Lewis and Clark sighted Mount Jefferson from the mouth of the Willamette River in 1806 and named it after the president who had sent them on their expedition. Three Fingered Jack apparently won its name because its summit spires reminded pioneers of a renowned, mutilated cohort of California Gold Rush bandit Joaquin Murietta.

Two failed transportation routes across the Cascade Range left their mark on the wilderness here. Minto Mountain and Minto Lake recall Salem pioneer John Minto, who urged in vain that a wagon road be built over Minto Pass in the 1870s.

The designated wilderness boundary between Santiam Pass and Lost Lake follows

Mount Washington from Rockpile Lake, on the Pacific Crest Trail

a bit of railroad grade built in 1888 by entrepreneur Colonel T. Egenton Hogg. Hogg dreamed of a transcontinental line from Corvallis east, but his London financiers doubted a crossing of Santiam Pass was feasible. Undaunted, he ordered Chinese laborers to build 11 miles of grade, lay 300 feet of track, and pack a disassembled boxcar to the site. Mules pulled the car across the pass, allowing Hogg to tell his investors, straight-faced, that his train already had crossed the Cascades. The grade is still hikable from Santiam Lodge part way around the sheer cliffs of Hogg Rock.

THINGS TO DO
Hiking
With 200 miles of trails, the Mount Jefferson area has room for plenty of day hikes and even week-long backpacking trips. The open high country and many off-trail lakes invite cross-country exploration as well—the surest way to find solitude.

At the most popular lakes, camping is permitted only at designated sites marked with a post. This restriction affects Square Lake, Duffy Lake, Pamelia Lake, and all the lakes in Jefferson Park. No campfires are permitted in Jefferson Park. Camping is banned altogether on Marion Lake's northwest peninsula, on the peninsulas of Scout and Bays Lakes, and within 100 feet of the high watermark of Marion, Pamelia, Hanks, and Hunts Lakes. Campfires are banned within 100 feet of any water source. Livestock may not be tethered or picketed within 200 feet of any body of water. Wilderness rangers patrol the area. Camping is also banned within the Warm Springs Indian Reservation except at Breitenbush Lake. Hikers entering the reservation need written permission from the Confederated Tribes.

Among the easiest and most rewarding day hikes is the 2.2-mile trail from Road 2246 along a splashing creek under towering Douglas firs to Pamelia Lake. Because this trip is so popular, this is the only part of the wilderness where *visitors must obtain an entry permit in advance from the Detroit Ranger Station* (call 503-854-3366 for details). Only twenty groups are issued permits for each day for the Pamelia Lake–Hunts Cove area, so plan ahead for summer weekends. In early June the lake is ringed with pink rhododendron blooms. The area's best mountain view is 2.8 miles beyond the lake, at the old lookout site atop Grizzly Peak, 1900 feet above the lake and breathtakingly close to Mount Jefferson.

Marion Lake is an easy 2.5-mile walk from Road 2255 along a wide and occasionally dusty path. Hikers can pack in inflatable boats or light canoes to sail the 360-acre, 180-foot-deep lake. Fishing is prohibited in inlet streams and in the outlet creek.

Square Lake, nestled in the forest at the foot of Three Fingered Jack, is an easy 2.2-mile day hike either from the Pacific Crest Trail's (PCT) Santiam Pass Trailhead on Highway 20 or from the Round Lake Campground.

Wildflowers and a close-up view of Three Fingered Jack highlight the easy 4.5-mile loop to Canyon Creek Meadows from the primitive Jack Lake Campground at the end of Road 1234. To limit encounters on this popular trail, hikers are encouraged to hike the loop clockwise, returning past Canyon Creek's beaver ponds and a pair of 20-foot waterfalls. From the meadows, an additional 1.5-mile track leads steeply up a glacial moraine, past an ice-filled cirque lake, to a viewpoint saddle overtowered by Three Fingered Jack's summit pinnacles. A different side trip from the loop leads 0.7 mile from Canyon Creek's waterfalls to Wasco Lake.

The fire lookout structures that once topped five peaks in this wilderness have been removed, but their panoramic views remain as enticing goals for invigorating day hikes. Bear Point's view of Mount Jefferson is 3.8 miles away, and 2900 feet up, from Road 4685, which joins Road 46 a mile east of Breitenbush Hot Springs.

Triangulation Peak is surrounded by several interesting rock spires and a cave. The huge mouth of Boca Cave, a protected archaeological site, can be reached by scrambling several hundred yards down the rugged east side of the summit. Triangulation Peak is an easy 2.1-mile walk through the woods from the junction of Roads 2233 and 635. Some stout-hearted hikers prefer to start at the Cheat Creek Trailhead on Whitewater Creek Road 2243 instead. The trail that begins there gains 2500 feet in 6.3 miles, passing a lovely meadow and a scenic ridge en route to Triangulation Peak.

Marion Mountain, the area's lowest lookout site, is a 2.8-mile side trip up from Marion Lake, or a 4.2-mile hike from the Camp Pioneer trailhead on Road 2261. Maxwell Butte, a cinder cone overlooking the Santiam Pass area, is 4.8 miles up from Road 080, off Highway 22 at the Maxwell Butte sno-park. At the dry trail's midpoint, Twin Lakes offer an irresistible swimming opportunity.

Another viewpoint worth the hike involves following the PCT 5.3 miles from Santiam Pass to Three Fingered Jack. After a 1600-foot climb the PCT crests a ridge with views south along the Cascades, then traverses almost directly below Three Fingered Jack's sheer west face.

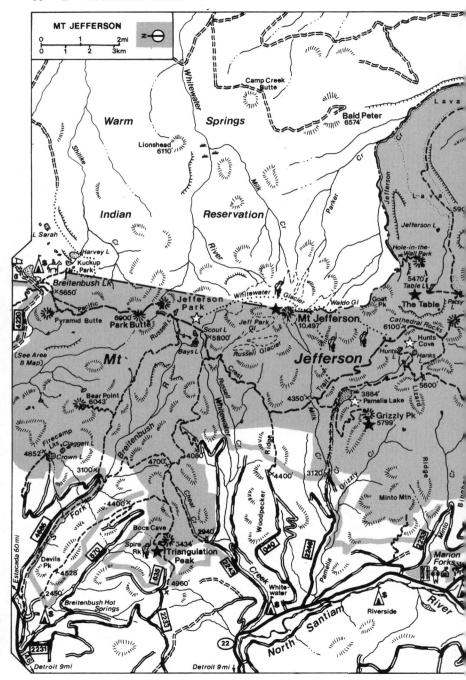

MT JEFFERSON

0 1 2mi
0 1 2 3km

z

Camp Creek Butte

Bald Peter 6574'

Whitewater

Warm Springs

Lava

Lionshead 6110'

Milk

Parker

Cr

Cr

Jefferson

Lava

590

Indian Reservation

River

Jefferson L

L Sarah

Shitike

Cr

Jefferson L

Harvey L

Kuckup Park

Hole-in-the-Wall Park

5470' Table LL

The Table

Patsy

Breitenbush Lk ×5650

Whitewater Glacier

Jefferson Park

Waldo Gl

Goat Pk

Cathedral Rocks

4420

Pyramid Butte

Pacific

6900 Park Butte

Russell L

Scout L ×5800'

Jeff Park Gl

Mt Jefferson 10,497'

6100'

Hunts Cove

(See Area 8 Map)

Mt

Bays L

Russell Glacier

Jefferson

Hunts L

Hanks

5600'

Bear Point 6043'

Crest

Russell R

Whitewater

Trail

Milk

4350×

3884'
Pamelia Lake

5600'

Firecamp Lks

Claggett L

4852× Crown L

Breitenbush R

Ridge

Cr

Grizzly Pk 5799'

Ridge

Blanket

3100×

4700'

4080

4400'

3120×

Grizzly Cr

Minto Mtn

Minto

4400×

4405

S

Fork

Cheat Cr

Woodpecker

940

2246

2253

Marion Forks

Boca Cave

2940

Devils Pk

670

Spire Rk

3434
Triangulation Peak

535

243

Pamelia

S

4528

4960'

Creek

White-water

S

Riverside

2450

Breitenbush Hot Springs

2233

North Santiam

River

2231

22

26

Detroit 9mi

L Estacada 60mi

Detroit 9mi

Many of the wilderness' most spectacular areas are reached either by very long day hikes or by leisurely backpacking trips. The best example is Jefferson Park, a square-mile plain of lush wildflowers and swimmable alpine lakes set so close to Mount Jefferson that the snowy mountain seems to fill the sky.

Three routes reach Jefferson Park. The easiest trail climbs 5.1 miles from Whitewater Creek Road 2243 along a pretty ridge. The PCT also climbs to Jefferson Park, crossing 6900-foot Park Ridge along the way. That 5.6-mile route begins at the Skyline Road 4220 near Breitenbush Lake. A third, less-used route to Jefferson Park climbs 6.2 miles along the South Breitenbush Trail from Road 4685.

Hunts Cove is a similar but much smaller alpine basin on the south side of Mount Jefferson. The two main lakes, Hunts and Hanks, are 6.2 miles up from Road 2248 via Pamelia Lake. Hunts Cove is part of the Pamelia Lake limited entry area, so permits must be obtained in advance from the Detroit Ranger Station. Call (503) 854-3366 for details. Backpackers based at Hunts Cove can climb to the PCT and prowl the interesting crags of Cathedral Rocks.

Duffy, Mowich, and Santiam Lakes lie in a plateau of open lodgepole pine forests and small wildflower openings at the foot of Three Fingered Jack. From Road 2267 a 3.5-mile trail through the dry forest along the North Fork Santiam River reaches Duffy Lake. Mowich Lake, with its large island, is another mile beyond. Santiam Lake is a 5.1-mile walk from Highway 20 at Santiam Pass.

Just 1.8 miles past Mowich Lake is the Eight Lakes Basin, a patchwork of meadows and forest renowned for its wildflowers, pretty lakes, and July mosquitoes. The five nearest trailheads are from 6.8 to 8.6 miles distant. If you arrange a car shuttle, you can see a different trail on the trip out.

Trails on the east side of the wilderness are often sunnier. They are also much less used because of the longer gravel road access. From the Bear Valley Trailhead at the end of Road 1235, keep right on the Two Springs Trail to gain 2100 feet in 5.4 miles to the PCT at Rockpile Lake, a lovely little pool with views and alpine rock gardens. For a 13.4-mile loop, return from the lake by heading south on the PCT 2.9 miles and keeping left.

Carl Lake, a forest-rimmed rock basin, is 4.7 miles up the Cabot Creek Trail from Road 1230. Hike 2 miles past Carl Lake to reach the sweeping viewpoint atop South Cinder Peak.

Table Lake lies at the center of a fascinating, rarely visited landscape of wildflower-filled mesas, sudden canyons, cinder cones, and lava flows. Backpack to Table Lake via Carl Lake (10 miles from Road 1230), via the long uphill climb of Sugarpine Ridge (10.5 miles from Road 1292), or on the Jefferson Lake Trail, skirting a lava flow (10.1 miles from Road 1292).

Another rewarding, longer backpack is the 20-mile circuit around Three Fingered Jack, following the PCT from Santiam Pass and returning via Jack and Square Lakes. Plan to take three days.

For an even greater challenge try the 36-mile stretch of the PCT from Breitenbush Lake to Santiam Pass. After crossing Jefferson Park and skirting half way around Mount

Jefferson, the wide, well-graded PCT follows a high, scenic ridge crest south 10 miles to Minto Pass, passing lots of viewpoints, but no water. Then the PCT climbs high along the side of Three Fingered Jack before dropping to Santiam Pass. A spectacular three- to six-day hike.

Climbing

Mount Jefferson is the most difficult to scale of Oregon's Cascade peaks, both because of the relentless, 4000- to 6000-foot elevation gains required from base camps and because of the 400-foot summit pinnacle of crumbly lava, a class 4 climb in itself.

A dozen routes ascend as far as the summit pinnacle, with difficulties ranging from I-2 to III-5.2. The three easiest are from Jefferson Park across Whitewater Glacier to the ridge south of that glacier, from Pamelia Lake straight up the mountain's southwest ridge, and from the PCT above Hunts Lake directly toward the summit.

In the nineteenth century Mount Jefferson was believed unclimbable. A reputed "first ascent" in 1888 probably did not reach the summit. When a group led by Salem lawyer Charles E. Robin really did scale the peak in 1899—but found that their photographer had put in his film backwards—skeptics drove Robin to climb it again a week later.

Three Fingered Jack, though much lower and easier, was first climbed on Labor Day, 1923, by six Bend boys, four of whom had been first to the top of Mount Washington the previous weekend.

A popular, level I-4 route follows a well-defined climbers' trail up the south ridge, passes to the east of a gendarme spire at 7600 feet, and continues 300 feet to a rough, 40-foot recessed wall in the summit block.

The West Face Direct route is a level II-5.6-A1 climb, while a northeast route, above Canyon Creek Meadows, is rated III-5.4. Both cross dangerously rotten rock.

Winter Sports

Santiam Pass typically has enough snow to ski by late November. Starting from the Santiam Pass sno-park opposite Hoodoo Ski Area's entrance road, a marked trail leads 1 mile east through the woods to the snowed-under PCT Trailhead. Following the PCT into the wilderness, you have three choices. If you veer right on the Square Lake trail, you will reach that lake in 2.4 miles, where views of Three Fingered Jack emerge. If you continue straight on the PCT itself, you will climb steadily up a forested ridge 3 miles to increasingly nice views that stretch from the Three Sisters to Three Fingered Jack. The return trip requires downhill skiing skills. If instead you veer left on the old Skyline Trail, you will traverse across pleasant, rolling terrain for 3.3 miles to Lower Berley Lake.

Map and compass are essential on all wilderness trail routes. Consult the Mount Washington entry for ski tours south from Santiam Pass.

The Mountain View Shelter, a free, heatable cabin that sleeps fifteen (no reservations required) is the goal of a 4.8-mile loop from the Maxwell sno-park on Road 080. Another option is the level trail 1.3 miles to Fay Lake (which passes Big Meadows, a large open area good for exploring). Only the hardy tackle the tough, unmarked route up through a forest of snow wells to the views on Maxwell Butte.

After December, routes lower in the North Santiam River canyon become skiable. Marion Lake and Pamelia Lake are both dramatic goals. In midwinter, when the access roads are snowed in all the way down to Highway 22, Pamelia Lake is 6 miles and Marion Lake is 8. Most skiers turn back halfway to the lakes at viewpoints along the snowed-under access roads. By late March the snow melts off these access roads and shortens the ski trip to the lakes. Spring brings corn snow with sunny, shirt-sleeves skiing weather.

Mount Washington

Location: 70 miles east of Eugene, 31 miles west of Bend
Size: 111 square miles
Status: 82 square miles designated wilderness (1964, 1984)
Terrain: Lava plains, high forest, peak
Elevation: 2800 feet–7794 feet
Management: Deschutes NF, Willamette NF
Topographic maps: Mount Washington, Santiam Pass Winter Recreation (Geo-Graphics); Mount Washington Wilderness, PCT Northern Oregon Portion (USFS)

Sometimes called the "Black Wilderness" because of its 38 square miles of rugged lava flows, the Mount Washington area also features sweeping forests and scores of small lakes. Mountain vistas are everywhere, not only of Mount Washington's craggy spire, but of a half dozen snowpeaks in the adjacent Three Sisters and Mount Jefferson areas.

Climate
Santiam Pass, with an average snowfall of 20 to 58 feet, is plowed throughout winter. Highway 242 over McKenzie Pass is closed from November or December to May or June. Trails are clear of snow from mid-June to mid-October. Summers are warm and dry.

Plants and Wildlife
The barren lava fields support little more than an occasional, bonsaied whitebark pine. But the high plains surrounding the lava are evenly covered by mountain hemlock and true fir on the west and by lodgepole and ponderosa pine on the east. Black-tailed deer wintering in the Old Cascades and mule deer wintering in the Metolius Valley often make Mount Washington their summer range.

Geology
At least 125 eruptive centers have produced cinder cones and basalt lava flows in this area since the Ice Age—an average of one major eruption every century. The most recent

flow, 1300 years old, streamed 12 miles from Belknap Crater's flank to divert the McKenzie River south of Koosah Falls.

Clear Lake formed 3000 years ago when a lava flow from a cone south of Sand Mountain dammed the McKenzie River and drowned a forest. The lake's water is so cold and clear that the unpetrified, branchless trees are still there and can be seen as much as 100 feet below the lake surface—a source of fascination for boaters (no motors permitted) and wet-suited scuba divers.

The surface of the area's lava flows is intensely jumbled and almost uncrossable. As the crust of the flows cooled, it was broken up by the liquid lava that continued to flow underneath. Where molten lava flowed out from under an intact crust, lava tubes formed, such as Sawyer's Cave and Skylight Cave. Permanent ice and smooth lava stalactites can be seen in these long caves and in the collapsed lava tubes filling the summit crater of Little Belknap.

Though at least 100,000 years older than Belknap Crater, Mount Washington began as a similarly broad shield volcano. It went on to add a cone as large and symmetrical as any of the Three Sisters, but then was stripped to its central lava plug by glaciation.

History
The Santiam Wagon Road, built in 1866 to allow the grazing of Willamette Valley livestock in central Oregon, has been reopened as a trail through the South Santiam's canyon and survives as a rugged track along the north edge of the Mount Washington Wilderness, between Fish Lake and the 1896 Cache Creek Toll Station site.

On a cinder cone along that route, the Sand Mountain fire lookout tower burned in 1968. The lookout was rebuilt in 1990 by volunteers who staff the tower in summers and welcome visitors. A 1.3-mile loop trail passes the tower and tours the cinder cone's rim.

In 1871–72, John Templeton Craig built a wagon route over McKenzie Pass, arduously chipping and leveling a lava roadbed still visible in the rugged basalt flows around Hand Lake and near Dee Wright Observatory at McKenzie Pass. Craig contracted to carry mail across his wagon road through the winter on skis. In an 1877 storm he froze to death in a cabin at Craig Lake. Since the 1930s, an annual John Templeton Craig ski tour and ski race has carried specially marked mail on the 22-mile route across McKenzie Pass each April.

THINGS TO DO
Hiking
One of the most popular day hikes near McKenzie Pass is the 0.5-mile walk from Highway 242 through pine woods to the wildflower meadow at the Hand Lake shelter. For a longer hike, circle the lake on a 1-mile stroll alongside a lava flow.

Another very heavily used trail climbs 400 feet in 1.4 miles from photogenic Scott Lake (where you will find a primitive campground and excellent reflections of the Three Sisters) to Benson Lake, a deep blue jewel partly rimmed by cliffs. Beyond Benson

Lake 1.1 miles are the similarly scenic and popular Tenas Lakes. Hikers seeking solitude should bring a compass and head for one of the many off-trail lakelets in this area. Because the entire Mount Washington Wilderness lacks running water most of the year, campers should bring an approved filter to purify lakewater. For a panoramic viewpoint, continue on the main trail past the Tenas Lakes 1.6 miles to the summit of Scott Mountain, a former lookout site.

The Patjens Lakes, with wildflower meadows and reflections of Mount Washington, are on a 6-mile loop through rolling forest from the end of paved Road 2690 at Big Lake. An equally swimmable, but far less visited lake is Robinson Lake, on an easy 0.3-mile trail from Road 2664.

Day hikers often follow the Pacific Crest Trail (PCT) south from Lava Camp Lake Campground to South Matthieu Lake, then take the abandoned Skyline Trail back via North Matthieu Lake—a 6-mile loop through both lava and forest.

The lava fields at McKenzie Pass are so impressively rugged that many visitors only hike the paved 0.5-mile Lava River nature trail around the Dee Wright Observatory's basalt-block hut. But the PCT climbs on a very good grade from a nearby trailhead through the heart of the lava's spectacular barrens. The panoramic view atop Little Belknap is 2.6 miles via a short spur trail that passes three small lava caves. From the spur trail, Belknap Crater's three distinct summit craters are an additional 0.7-mile cross-country climb, mostly slogging up a cinder slope.

The view from Belknap Crater is good, but the best view of the Three Sisters is atop Black Crater, on a trail that climbs 2500 feet in 3.7 miles from Highway 242.

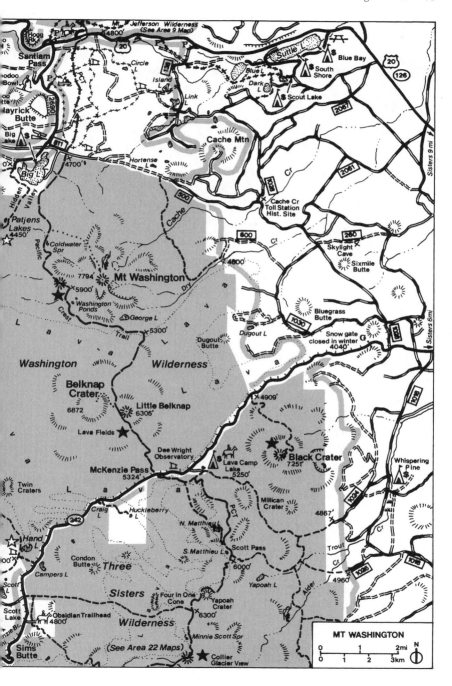

MT WASHINGTON

0   1   2mi
0   1   2   3km

Scott Mountain from Benson Lake

The PCT leads to views up and down the Cascades from wildflower meadows on Mount Washington's shoulder. Carry water on this dry, 12.4-mile section of the PCT north from McKenzie Pass to Road 811.

Cross-country hiking, though impractical on lava, is pleasant both through the open forest and along the beachlike cinder strips separating lava flows from forest.

Climbing

Mount Washington's eroded lava plug offers several technical climbs. To take the level I-4 North Ridge route, pioneered by six boys from Bend in 1923, follow the PCT 2 miles south of Road 811. Follow tree blazes cross-country to the mountain's north ridge, then hike up the ridge to a small saddle at the base of the summit pinnacle. West of the saddle 25 feet ascend a 30-foot chimney, then climb 30 feet upward and to the left on the rough, rotten rock of the "nose." Atop the nose, a steep hike leads to an additional 20-foot chimney and the summit.

A dozen additional climbing routes increase in difficulty to the foolishly dangerous, level III-5.7 East Face Direct and the west face's level II-5.8 Chimney of Space.

Winter Sports

Santiam Pass is a major nordic skiing center, while McKenzie Pass offers a few longer, more remote trips. See Area 9, Mount Jefferson, for routes north of Santiam Pass.

Santiam Pass' largest network of marked cross-country ski trails converges at the Ray Benson sno-park near the Hoodoo Ski Area on Big Lake Road 2690. Three rustic, open-sided shelters make easy goals in the rolling terrain, with mountain views from sparsely forested areas hit by a 1967 fire. Bear left for 1.8 miles to the North Blowout

Shelter, bear right for 2.7 miles to the better view at the Brandenburg Shelter, or head east for 3.3 miles to the Island Junction Shelter. Nordic routes occasionally cross or parallel marked snowmobile routes. Cross-country ski rentals, lessons, and groomed trails are available for a fee at Hoodoo Ski Area nearby.

Another marked nordic route climbs 1000 feet along a snowed-under road in 1.9 miles from the Road 830 sno-park near Lost Lake to the view atop Potato Hill. For a 3.8-mile loop with less of a climb, turn right off the Potato Hill route onto the Hash Brown Trail through the woods.

The generally unplowed side roads from Highway 126 are skiable, especially Road 2664 to Robinson Lake (4 miles one way) and Road 2649 to Melakwa Lake (10 miles one way).

McKenzie Pass is typically plowed only a week or so past the first snowfall, usually in November. Once the snow gates are closed, tourers must hike and/or ski 7 miles from the east gate and a full 15 miles from the westside gate at White Branch camp. Those prepared for a snow camp will find the 18-mile crossing of McKenzie Pass unparalleled in scenic splendor.

11 Old Cascades

Location: 45 miles east of Albany
Size: 74 square miles
Status: 8 square miles designated wilderness (1984)
Terrain: Densely forested ridges, ridge-top meadows, rock pinnacles
Elevation: 1230 feet–5830 feet
Management: Willamette NF
Topographic maps: Menagerie Wilderness (USFS); Upper Soda, Harter Mountain, Echo Mountain, Cascadia (USGS); Bull of the Woods, Santiam Pass Winter Recreation (Geo-Geographics)

Six separate roadless areas along Highway 20 remain to show the scale of the wild forests that once blanketed the western foothills of the Cascade Range. Here are broad ridges, subalpine meadows, and views of the High Cascades' snowpeaks, all within an hour's drive of the Willamette Valley.

Climate
The area's 80 annual inches of precipitation come as snow from December through March and rain in spring and fall. Trails up to 4000 feet are usually clear of snow by May.

Plants and Wildlife
The Old Cascade's remarkable botanical diversity is best seen in early summer on the Echo Mountain–Iron Mountain ridge. A study of this site found sixty plant species

that are rare or unusual in the western Cascades, including spectacular penstemon and other wildflowers. Nowhere in Oregon are there more varieties of conifers in such a compact area—seventeen species, from water-loving western red cedar to drought-tolerant juniper and rare alpine Alaska cedar.

Lower elevation areas of the Old Cascades include pockets of old-growth western hemlock and Douglas fir. Higher elevations are dominated by flexible-limbed, snow-resistant Pacific silver fir and noble fir. Stumps in a 1986 clearcut 3 miles south of House Rock Campground indicate the area held Oregon's oldest trees.

Fishing is banned in Hackleman Creek to protect that stream's unique strain of cutthroat trout.

Geology

The Old Cascades are a chain of volcanoes predating the peaks of the High Cascades by 10 million years. It was the Old Cascades that originally made eastern Oregon the semiarid area it is today and that filled ancient inland seas with rhyolite ash, preserving the John Day area's famous fossils.

Time and erosion have reduced the Old Cascades' once-tall volcanic cones to a dissected canyonland, studded with the cliffs and pinnacles of resistant lava intrusions. The Menagerie is a collection of two dozen such rock spires, including three natural arches and a 300-foot tower called Turkey Monster.

History

The Santiam band of Kalapuya Indians once had a summer hunting and gathering camp at House Rock. White settlers built the Santiam Wagon Road through the area between Albany and central Oregon in 1864–65. The state purchased the heavily used toll route by 1925. Construction of Highway 20 largely bypassed the old wagon route in 1939, but it has now been reopened as a recreation trail.

THINGS TO DO
Hiking

All six of the Old Cascades' roadless areas have good hiking trails. In the east, follow the Old Cascades Crest Trail 1.1 easy miles from Road 508 to Maude Creek, a good turnaround point for hikers with small children. For a longer hike, continue 3.2 miles up across broad, grassy slopes of alpine wildflowers to the

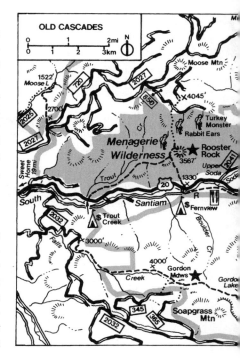

viewpoint atop Crescent Mountain, gaining 2200 feet of elevation. The Old Cascades Crest Trail continues a total of 27 miles, passing the Three Pyramids en route to the Middle Santiam Wilderness (see Area 12).

The area's most popular trail climbs 1.7 miles past wildflower slopes to the historic lookout atop Iron Mountain, gaining 1400 feet. After a 1976 winter storm blew off the original 1933 lookout building, the Forest Service used a helicopter to replace it with a similar structure from another peak. Park at the Iron Mountain Trailhead just west of Tombstone Pass on Road 15 and hike up to the lookout. To return on a 6.6-mile loop, keep right on the Cone Peak Trail, traversing even more spectacular wildflower fields on a gentler grade 3.3 miles down to Highway 20. Cross the highway and take the Tombstone Nature Trail 0.6 mile to the Tombstone Pass sno-park, where the Santiam Wagon Road leads 0.3 mile to your car. For a scenic cross-country side trip, leave the trail at Cone Peak and follow the open ridge east past Echo Mountain to North Peak.

Two trails lead to the fern meadows of Browder Ridge—the 4.5-mile Browder Ridge Trail from Road 080 and the lovely 3.1-mile Gate Creek Trail from Road 1598. Where the routes join, take a faint spur trail 1 mile north and bushwhack up a meadow to the ridge's panoramic high point.

A portion of the historic Santiam Wagon Road has been reopened as a trail for hikers, bikers, and equestrians. The 19.5-mile trail begins opposite the Mountain House

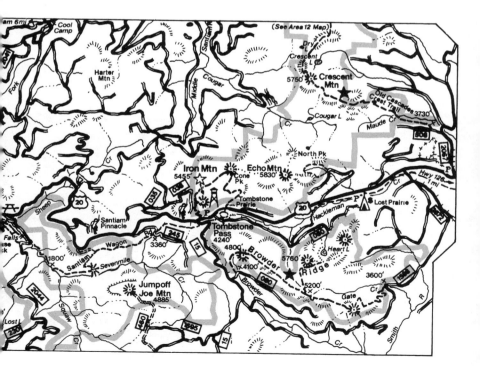

restaurant at Upper Soda, passes House Rock Campground, crosses Tombstone Pass, and continues to Highway 126 at the Fish Lake guard station. An interesting 0.8-mile loop sampling the historic wagon route starts at House Rock Campground, crosses the river, and passes a house-sized cave and a waterfall. For a longer hike, continue up from the waterfall 3.4 miles to a switchback near the 5-mile marker post, where a knoll overlooks the Sevenmile Creek.

The weird rock pinnacles of The Menagerie can be reached by two trails from Highway 20, both of which climb 2200 feet through Douglas fir forests. The 3.3-mile Trout Creek Trail begins near the Trout Creek Campground entrance, while the steep, 2.1-mile Rooster Rock Trail starts near Fernview Campground's entrance. From the viewpoint beside Rooster Rock's spire, a rough climber's path contours onward to Rabbit Ears' twin towers.

The wildflowers of Gordon Meadows are a good hiking goal. The brushy meadows are 4.3 miles through the old-growth forests of the Falls Creek Trail from Road 2032, or 3.6 miles from Road 230, past scenic Gordon Lakes and the cliffs of Soapgrass Mountain.

Moose Lake, snow-free most winters, is particularly pretty in spring, when the moss of Moose Creek's boulder-strewn rapids glows a brilliant green. Reach the steep, rough, faint,1-mile scramble route to Moose Lake by turning off Highway 20 onto the Moose Creek Road, 2.5 miles east of Cascadia. Promptly turn right on Road 2027 for 5.5 miles, fork left onto Road 720 for 0.2mile, and park at a wide spot in the road.

Climbing

The two dozen spires of The Menagerie provide popular technical climbing challenges. Rooster Rock's old lookout site can be reached with class 5.4 skills. Three other routes

Meadows on Crescent Mountain, with Mount Washington on the horizon

up that crag range in difficulty to level II-5.8. Nearby are Roosters Tail, Chicken Rock, and Hen Rock, with routes of similar difficulty.

Clustered a mile north of Rooster Rock, but composed of slightly lower-quality rock, are two natural arches (Big Arch is a level II-5.7-A1 climb) and six additional spires, including 265-foot South Rabbit Ear (a III-5.7 climb) and North Rabbit Ear (III-5.7-A2). A climbers' trail accesses all of these destinations from a gravel road on the ridge above the Wilderness. Because the end of Road 850 has been closed, drive straight on Road 857 and then keep left at junctions to find the new trailhead at the end of Road 856.

A dozen other crags and spires dot the slope above Keith Creek, 0.5 mile east of Rabbit Ears. The first of these is Turkey Monster, unclimbed until 1966. This 300-foot column has level III-5.6-A3 and IV-5.7-A3 routes. Other difficult spires include The Porpoise (I-5.8) and The Bridge (II-5.9).

Elsewhere in the area, the Santiam Pinnacle, above Highway 20, offers four routes of level I-4 to II-5.6 difficulty. Although a trail ascends Iron Mountain's west slope, the 400-foot cliff on the south face is a level I-5.6 climb.

Winter Sports

Plowed Highway 20 provides access to cross-country ski opportunities on trails and side roads in the Tombstone Pass area, notably the old Santiam Wagon Road to the east of the Tombstone Pass sno-park. Skiable snow can be expected from January to mid-March. Beginners often practice on Tombstone Prairie. A small pullout with a snowed-under spur road a mile east of Tombstone Pass is the starting point for adventurous tours of Cone Peak's scenic ridge-top meadows. Sno-parks at Lost Prairie and Lava Lake Road 2067 provide a half dozen marked tours and loops.

12   Middle Santiam

Location: 56 miles east of Albany
Size: 40 square miles (including the Pyramids)
Status: 13 square miles designated wilderness (1984)
Terrain: Densely forested river valley, rocky peaks
Elevation: 1300 feet–5618 feet
Management: Willamette NF
Topographic maps: Bull of the Woods Wilderness (Geo-Graphics); Chimney Peak, Coffin Mountain, Echo Mountain, Harter Mountain, Quartzville (USGS); Detroit (Green Trails)

One of Oregon's largest low-elevation, old-growth forests lies hidden along the remote headwaters of the Middle Santiam River, surprisingly close to the Willamette Valley. Great Douglas firs, western hemlocks, and western red cedars rise from the steep, mist-shrouded Middle Santiam canyon, where the green-pooled river cascades between mossy banks.

Climate

Though the river's canyon seldom sees snow, access roads and trails cross higher elevations and are blocked from about December through March. Annual rainfall averages 80 inches. Only summers are reliably dry.

Plants and Wildlife

Pockets of extremely old forest (over 450 years) throughout the area form a spectacular 200-foot-high canopy above a shady world of rhododendrons, lichen-covered snags, and huge rotting logs. Old-growth forests, now rare in Oregon, are the optimum habitat for 137 vertebrate species, including the spotted owl and 85 other types of birds.

Fallen old-growth trees across the Middle Santiam River create the river's silt-free, gravel-bottomed pools—the spawning sites of a third of the Santiam drainage's chinook salmon.

The Three Pyramids host higher-elevation plant species: wildflowers in subalpine meadows and old-growth noble fir.

Geology

In the east, the Three Pyramids are relatively recent volcanoes associated with the High Cascades. The remainder of the area consists of ancient, heavily eroded Old Cascades volcanics. Chimney Peak is an Old Cascades lava plug. Traces of gold and silver brought prospectors to Quartzville Creek in the nineteenth century.

Cliffs left by immense landslides extend from Scar Mountain to Knob Rock. One of these ancient slides dammed Donaca Lake. The area's steep, unstable clay soils made road construction so expensive that many of the unroaded old-growth forests could only be cut at a net loss. The southeast edge of the wilderness is rimmed with a moonscape of landslides triggered by the Forest Service's abortive effort to punch logging roads into the area before wilderness designation in 1984. Adventurous hikers can follow an abandoned portion of Road 2041 past a half-mile landslide and the washed-out ruin of the road's bridge across Pyramid Creek.

Blue huckleberries

THINGS TO DO
Hiking

In the east, forest-rimmed Daly, Parrish, and Riggs Lakes are each at the end of easy half-mile trails suitable for day hikes with children. Drive Highway 22 north of the Santiam Y junction toward Salem 7.5 miles to milepost

Shelter Falls on the Middle Santiam River

74 and turn west on Parrish Lake Road 2266 for 4.6, 5, or 6.5 miles, depending on which lake's trailhead you prefer.

Viewpoints and alpine rock gardens at the summit of Middle Pyramid climax a more challenging 2-mile trail that gains 1800 feet of elevation from Road 560. Drive Highway 22 north of the Santiam Y junction with Highway 20 for 4.8 miles. Between mileposts 76 and 77, turn west on Lava Lake Meadow Road 2067 for 1.9 miles, and turn right on Road 560 for 3.5 miles to its end. The Middle Pyramid Trail serves as a link in the 27-mile Old Cascades Crest Trail. Backpackers or equestrians can continue south to Crescent Mountain (see Area 11) or north past Scar Mountain and Knob Rock to the Middle Santiam Wilderness.

Chimney Peak, site of a former fire lookout, commands views across valley after valley of old-growth forest. The 6.1-mile McQuade Creek Trail leads to the peak, through deep forest and past a collapsed shelter. The trail ends 100 yards below the summit. The final climb is a tricky scramble requiring caution and both hands. To find the McQuade Creek Trailhead, turn north from Highway 20 onto the Quartzville Road 4 miles east of Sweet Home. After 24.7 miles, cross a bridge to a three-way fork. Keep right on Road 11 for 2.6 miles and turn right on Road 1142 for 4 miles.

The best sampler of the Middle Santiam, however, begins off Road 2041 with an

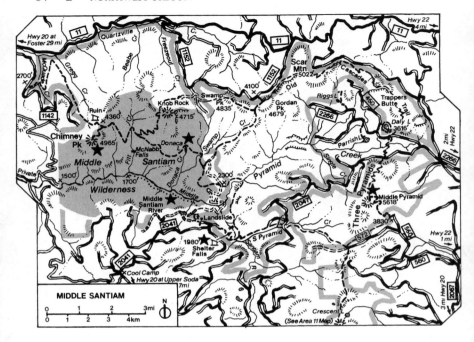

MIDDLE SANTIAM

0   1   2   3mi
0 1 2 3 4km
N

easy 0.7-mile hike down to the rustic, rain-proof Shedd Camp Shelter, near a spectacular blue-green pool fed by a 20-foot waterfall. A pebbly beach here invites swimmers to a chilly dip. The main trail crosses the 30-foot-wide Middle Santiam River just upstream, without a bridge. By late summer, expert rock-hoppers can avoid wading. On the far shore, the trail climbs 0.3 mile to a fork. To the right, the South Pyramid Creek Trail climbs 5.4 miles to the Old Cascades Trail at Road 572. To the left, the trail contours above the river 2 miles, fords Pyramid Creek, climbs 0.8 mile to an abandoned portion of Road 2041, and continues 2.7 miles to little, blue-green Donaca Lake. Backpackers will be able to camp at the lake and continue 6.2 miles to Chimney Peak, or perhaps take side trails up to Gordan Peak or the viewpoint at Knob Rock.

To find the trailhead off Road 2041, drive Highway 20 east of Sweet Home 24 miles. Just before the Mountain House restaurant (and after milepost 52), turn left on Soda Fork Road 2041 for 0.9 mile, and keep left at a fork for 7.1 miles to a six-way intersection in Cool Camp's pass. Go straight on 2041 for 4.5 miles to a three-way fork, and take the middle route (Road 646) for 0.6 mile to its end.

A cross-country route to the Middle Santiam River begins at the landslide that now ends Road 2041. Adventurers can bushwhack from the bottom of the slide down to the river and follow the river's south bank downstream 3 miles. Flats along the river feature towering Douglas firs, mossy bigleaf maples, and frequent glimpses of Chimney Peak and the Pyramids. West of Fitt Creek the canyon becomes too narrow even for bushwhackers.

Crabtree Valley

Location: 42 miles east of Albany
Size: 2 square miles
Status: Outstanding natural area, area of critical environmental concern
Terrain: Old-growth forest valley
Elevation: 2850 feet–4443 feet
Management: Salem District BLM
Topographic map: Yellowstone Mountain (USGS)

Oregon's oldest trees—perhaps 1000 years old—grow undisturbed in this secluded Western Cascades valley.

Climate
Snow typically blocks the roads from December to April. Annual precipitation is 100 inches.

Plants and Wildlife
Crabtree Valley's claim to Oregon's oldest trees remains unproven, because the very largest trunks are too wide for growth rings to be counted by the usual method—drilling out a core sample with an incremental borer. King Tut, a monumental Douglas fir, is a prime suspect for 1000-year honors. The majority of the Douglas fir, western hemlock, and western red cedar forming a canopy across the valley are 500 years old.

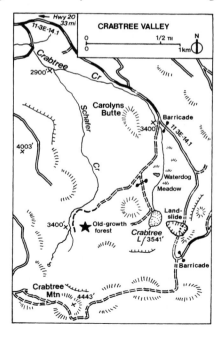

Even before the advent of logging, Western Cascades forests rarely lived 200 years before being overswept by fire. But Crabtree Valley's ring of glacier-carved palisades has served as a natural firebreak. The valley was preserved from logging when a 1985 land swap transferred a square mile of private land to the Bureau of Land Management (BLM).

THINGS TO DO
Hiking
The valley lends itself to short, cross-country trips. Crabtree Lake, Waterdog

Old-growth forest

Meadow, or cascading Schafer Creek may be the destinations, but the huge old-growth forests on either hand are always the real goal. Fall mushrooms provide another good excuse to roam these grand woods.

Although it is possible to drive directly from Lacomb to Crabtree Valley via Road 11-3E-14.1, this western route traverses a maze of logging roads, many of them unmarked and private. Public access to Crabtree Valley is from the southeast, but this route is also confusing and can change without notice. The BLM recommends you call their local specialist Laura Graves at the Salem District office (503-315-5908 or 503-375-5646) for detailed directions. To begin the public route, drive 4 miles east of Sweet Home on Highway 20, turn north at a sign for Quartzville, and drive 20.5 paved miles on what becomes Quartzville Access Road 11 along Green Peter Reservoir. Three miles past the reservoir's end, turn left onto Yellowstone Access Road (11-3E-35.1) to enter the BLM's labyrinth of gravel roads. After 11 miles and many junctions, park where the road is blocked. Then hike a mile down to Crabtree Lake, crossing the landslide that obliterated this final part of the road.

The BLM's Salem District *Cascades Resource Area–South Part* transportation map, showing the maze of logging roads around Lacomb and Crabtree Valley, is a good investment.

14 Saddle Mountain

Location: 73 miles northwest of Portland, 21 miles east of Seaside
Size: 4 square miles
Status: State park
Terrain: Meadow-topped mountain
Elevation: 900 feet–3283 feet
Management: State Parks and Recreation Department
Topographic map: Saddle Mountain (USGS)

From the summit of this saddle-shaped mountain, the highest point in the northern Oregon Coast Range, views sweep from Mount Rainier to the mouth of the Columbia River.

Climate

The area's mossy rain forest thrives on the area's 120 inches of annual precipitation. Storms briefly cover the peak with snow and treacherous ice in midwinter, but the trail is otherwise open year round.

Plants and Wildlife

Saddle Mountain harbors an astonishing 301 identified species of flora, some of which have chosen this singular, tall peak as their sole Coast Range habitat. Trilliums and pink coast fawn lilies spangle the lower slopes in April and May. Summit wildflower displays peak in mid-June. Patterson's bittercress, a delicate, pink-petaled mustard, is known only from Saddle Mountain and nearby Onion Peak.

Herds of up to seventy elk have been sighted on the peak. The Sitka spruce and western hemlock rain forest around the mountain's base is regrowing from 1920s logging and fires in 1936 and 1939.

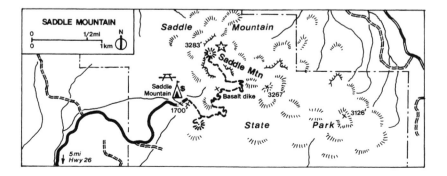

The trail near Saddle Mountain's summit

Geology

The massive basalt lava forming Saddle Mountain erupted from fissures 300 miles away near Idaho. When Columbia River basalt floods were inundating most of eastern Oregon and Washington 15 million years ago, a tongue of the lava spilled through the Columbia Gorge and puddled up here 1000 feet deep in what was then a seashore bay. Neahkahnie Mountain and Mount Hebo were formed by the same lava, characterized by lumpy "pillow basalt" typical of underwater flows. Here the lava was so heavy that it squirted into cracks in the soft, underlying rock, creating resistant, wall-like dikes. One dike along the summit trail fractured hexagonally due to slow cooling and now resembles an immense stack of cordwood. As the Coast Range gradually rose, the softer, surrounding rock eroded away, leaving the hard basalt lava as a mountain, an example of reverse topography.

THINGS TO DO
Hiking

The exhilarating 2.6-mile summit trail traverses through dense forest, then switchbacks up to a cliff-edged saddle before crossing meadows to the taller of the mountain's two peaks, the former site of a fire lookout cabin. Bring binoculars to spot the Olympic Mountains and Astoria's Columbia River Bridge.

The park's paved 7-mile access road turns off Highway 26 near milepost 10, west of Portland 66 miles or east of Seaside 10 miles.

15 Mount Hebo

Location: 20 miles south of Tillamook, 26 miles north of Lincoln City
Size: 24 square miles
Status: Undesignated wilderness
Terrain: Flat-topped mountain, steep forested flanks, lakes
Elevation: 200 feet–3176 feet
Management: Siuslaw NF
Topographic maps: Niagara Creek, Hebo, Blaine, Beaver (USGS)

The mossy forests ringing this broad peak harbor a pair of waterfalls and three lakes—rarities in the Coast Range.

Climate
More than 100 inches of annual precipitation sustain Mount Hebo's rain forest. Snow caps the summit briefly after winter storms.

Plants and Wildlife
Early summer wildflowers, thimbleberry, and bracken fern carpet the summit meadows, home to the rare silverspot butterfly. At lower elevations, Douglas fir, Sitka spruce, and alder dominate a green world of moss, sourgrass, sword fern, and trilliums.

Geology
Mount Hebo's flat top is a remnant of a Columbia River basalt lava flow that erupted 15 million years ago near Idaho, poured west through the Columbia Gorge, and

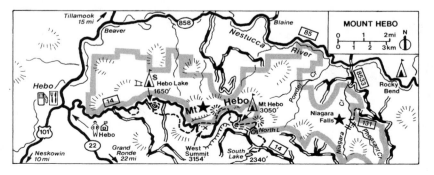

puddled up in a seashore bay here. Subsequent uplifting of the Coast Range made this erosion-resistant basalt a plateau.

History

Tillamook settlers seeking a route to the Willamette Valley used an Indian trail across Mount Hebo from 1854 to 1882. A portion of the route was restored in 1984 as the Pioneer–Indian Trail. Following massive fires in 1853 and 1910, the Forest Service replanted 12 square miles with Douglas fir in 1912. One of the earliest Oregon refor-estation projects, the forest has grown slowly because the Douglas fir seedlings were imported from the Rocky Mountains and were not adapted to the coastal climate. A World War II radar installation was removed from the west summit in the 1980s, but a small military reservation remains on the slightly taller east summit, near primitive Mount Hebo Campground.

THINGS TO DO
Hiking

A 1-mile trail descends from Road 131 to a footbridge at the base of two waterfalls, Niagara Creek's 100-foot plunge and neighboring Pheasant Creek's 80-foot fan.

An even easier, all-accessible path loops 0.5 mile around Hebo Lake from the Hebo Lake Campground, just off Road 14. The campground itself is gated closed for cars from November to mid-April, adding 0.2 mile to the hike.

For a more substantial hike, try the 8-mile Pioneer–Indian Trail. Starting at Hebo

Trail around Hebo Lake

Lake, this route climbs 1200 feet in 2.9 miles to a crossing of paved Road 14. At this point an unofficial side trail to the right climbs steeply 0.2 mile to a panoramic view atop Mount Hebo's west summit. The main trail contours 2.4 miles through meadows to a junction near Mount Hebo Campground, switchbacks 1 mile down to brush-lined North Lake, and ambles 1.7 miles to a campsite at South Lake.

A new network of loop trails, designed primarily for equestrians, branches off the Pioneer–Indian Trail near Hebo Lake. The Hebo Plantation Trail, a 0.7-mile loop from Road 14 west of Hebo Lake, was built by the Civilian Conservation Corps in the 1930s to showcase reforestation methods.

16 Cascade Head

Location: 7 miles north of Lincoln City, 56 miles west of Salem
Size: 10 square miles
Status: Scenic-research area; islands are designated wilderness
Terrain: Cliff-top meadows, rain forest
Elevation: 0 feet–1783 feet
Management: The Nature Conservancy, Siuslaw NF
Topographic map: Neskowin (USGS)

Surf-pounded cliffs surround the wildflower meadows on Cascade Head's steep headland. Craggy islands crowded with birds dot the sea. On either hand, 20 miles of beaches and headlands diminish into blue silhouettes. Yet just behind the meadows lie dark green rain forests of dense salal and Sitka spruce, where it is easy to imagine yourself far from the ocean.

Climate

Rain falls at Cascade Head on more than 180 days of the year. Cool fog shrouds the headland most of the summer, particularly when temperatures in the Willamette Valley are high. Fog drip brings the annual precipitation to more than 100 inches in the forests, although rainfall totals only 69 inches on the beach. Winters are snowless. Fall and spring have the most clear days.

Plants and Wildlife

The area's many offshore crags, roosting sites for a multitude of seabirds, are part of the Oregon Islands Wilderness (see Area 40). Hundreds of Steller sea lions lounge on the inaccessible beaches below the cliffs of Harts Cove. Cascade Head is also an ideal lookout from which to spot the spouts of migrating gray whales from December to May. Cascade Head's meadow is one of only three locations worldwide that supports a stable population of the threatened, orange-and-brown mottled, Oregon silverspot butterfly.

The headland meadows are filled with summer asters and paintbrush reminiscent of an alpine environment. Several species of these wildflowers grow only in the windswept meadows of coastal headlands. Wind has sculpted the oceanfront Sitka spruce into a waist-high mat, but only a short distance inland, Sitka spruce grow as much as 7 feet thick and 240 feet tall. The mossy western hemlock and Sitka spruce rain forest has one of the fastest growth rates and one of the highest biomass-per-acre ratios of any area in the world. At its densest, the forest has 24 square meters of leaf surface for every square meter of sunlight.

The Cascade Head Experimental Forest, a research facility overseeing National Forest land on the headland, pioneered many of the devastating clearcutting and herbicide-spraying techniques that dominated Northwest forestry in the late 1900s.

Geology

As at most coastal headlands between Astoria and Newport, the massive basalt forming Cascade Head is the tip of a 300-mile-long Columbia River basalt lava flow that erupted near Idaho about 15 million years ago and puddled up at the seashore here. Subsequent uplifting of the Coast Range has worn away the softer, surrounding rock.

CASCADE HEAD

History

Cascade Head won its name when sailors noticed a waterfall cascading directly into the ocean. Chitwood Creek's waterfall is still visible from ships and from the Harts Cove Trail. In 1967, when Cascade Head's panoramic, bluff-top wildflower meadows were threatened by commercial development, fans rallied to purchase 300 acres of the headland's fragile tip and donate it to the nonprofit Nature Conservancy.

THINGS TO DO
Hiking

The most popular trail is the Nature Conservancy path that gains 1100 feet in 1.7 miles to a viewpoint atop Cascade Head. After a mile through a lush forest of gnarled spruce, sword ferns, salmonberry (edible orange berries in June), and red alder, the route breaks

Harts Cove

out into steep meadows with breathtaking views across the Salmon River estuary and offshore islands. Dogs are not allowed on this trail and hikers are strictly forbidden from leaving the path. Even spreading out a picnic may inadvertently trample the meadow's rare checkermallows (five-petaled pink wildflowers) or the rare violets that serve as the only food source for caterpillars of the threatened Oregon silverspot butterfly.

To find the Nature Conservancy Trailhead, drive 1 mile north on Highway 101 from the junction with Highway 18. Turn left on the paved Three Rocks Road for 2.2 miles, and turn right on Savage Road for 0.5 mile to a wooden sign on the right. Parking is limited here to ten cars; others must park 0.6 mile back down the road at a county boat ramp.

An easier, upper trailhead for the same trail is closed by the Forest Service each year from January 1 to July 15 to protect the rare butterflies. This path ambles 1 mile through a hemlock forest to the viewpoint atop Cascade Head. Get there by driving 4 miles north of the Highway 18 junction on Highway 101. Just before the crest of a hill, turn left on Cascade Head Road 1861 for 3.3 miles, and park at a guardrail on the left.

Harts Cove is a cliff-rimmed bay where the crashing of the surf competes with the barks of sea lions, the cries of gulls, and the rush of Chitwood Creek's waterfall. The 2.7-mile downhill trail to the meadow overlooking the cove begins at the end of Road 1861. After wet weather, the path can be too muddy for tennis shoes. Like the upper Cascade Head trail, this path is closed January 1 to July 15 by a gate on Road 1861. Hikers who violate the closure are issued $100 fines.

For a woodsy hike that is open all year, but away from the roar of the sea, try the "other" Cascade Head Trail (not shown on map) that crosses this headland a few miles inland, through a dense forest with few views. A valuable link in the Oregon Coast Trail, this path starts at the junction of Three Rocks Road and Highway 101, climbs 1200 feet in 3.6 miles to a crossing of Road 1861, and descends 2.4 miles to a marked Highway 101 pullout, 1 mile south of Neskowin. Horses are allowed on this trail, but camping is banned everywhere on Cascade Head, and all trails are closed to bicycles.

17 Drift Creek

Location: 12 miles east of Waldport, 57 miles west of Corvallis
Size: 18 square miles
Status: 9 square miles designated wilderness (1984)
Terrain: Steep valleys, rain forest
Elevation: 80 feet–2100 feet
Management: Siuslaw NF
Topographic maps: Tidewater, Hellion Rapids (USGS)

Drift Creek features the Coast Range's largest remaining stands of old-growth rain forest. The rock-strewn creek's steep-sided canyon gives the area a mountainous feel, although it is actually close to tidewater.

Climate
Temperatures are mild year round. Heavy rainfall can be expected from fall through spring (74 inches annually in the west, 120 inches at Table Mountain). Winter snow is rare even at high elevations.

Plants and Wildlife
Sitka spruce and western hemlock trees grow 7 feet thick in many places in the area, particularly along the northern portion of the Horse Creek Trail. Creekbanks are over-hung with bigleaf maple trees, their spreading branches cushioned by a 6-inch-deep layer of moss and licorice ferns.

In summer look for edible berries in the rain forest undergrowth: orange salmon-berry, red thimbleberry, blue and red huckleberry, and dark blue salal. Sourgrass, or oxalis, is edible in small quantities and tart as a lemon. Its shamrock-shaped leaves often carpet the forest floor. Swampy areas brighten in April with the huge yellow spathes of skunk cabbage. Disturbed hillsides sprout 6-foot-tall spires of red and white foxglove throughout summer.

Several pairs of northern spotted owls and bald eagles, both endangered in Oregon, nest in the old-growth forest. It is not uncommon to find evidence of Roosevelt elk or black bear.

Drift Creek

Though Drift Creek is not ranked as a river, it supports river-sized runs of native fish. Chinook salmon, coho salmon, steelhead, and cutthroat trout return each fall, while a much smaller chinook run comes in spring. Hatchery fish have never been stocked.

Geology

This area's crumbly sandstone and siltstone weather to slippery clay, making roads and trails susceptible to landslides. The rock began as oceanic deposits of mud and sand. The rise of the Coast Range lifted this section of sea floor from the waves about 15 million years ago.

History

Drift Creek was once the hunting and gathering grounds of the Waldport Bay–based Alsea Indians. The creekside meadow on the Harris Ranch Trail is an abandoned homestead from the 1920s.

THINGS TO DO
Hiking

Three paths descend through forest to the shady, green banks of Drift Creek. The trails can be connected by wading 20-foot-wide Drift Creek. By late summer, expert rock-hoppers can sometimes accomplish the crossings dry-footed. Rarely, after midwinter rains, the fords are not passable at all.

The easiest route to the creek, the Harris Ranch Trail, starts out along a closed road for 0.8 mile and then descends 1200 feet in 2.2 miles to a large, campable meadow in a bend of Drift Creek. The exposed rock creekbanks here are great for sunbathing or wading. Red crawdads crawl in the shallows. To return on a different trail, wade knee-deep across the creek, follow the trail upstream 1 mile, cross the creek again (often passable at this point without wading), and climb 4 miles up Boulder Ridge to the southern Horse Creek Trailhead. The final 1.6 miles of this route follows an abandoned road, and if you haven't left a shuttle car or bicycle at the southern Horse Creek Trailhead, you will have to trudge an additional 3.1 miles along Road 3446 to complete the loop back to your car.

To find these trailheads, drive Highway 34 east of Waldport 6.9 miles (or west of

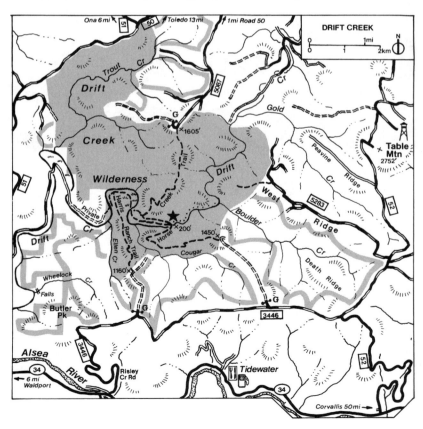

Corvallis 57 miles) to an Alsea River bridge, and turn north on Risley Creek Road 3446, always taking the larger fork at junctions. You'll reach the Harris Ranch Trailhead after 4.1 miles and the southern Horse Creek Trailhead after 7.2.

The third route to Drift Creek, the 3.6-mile-long northern portion of the Horse Creek Trail, descends 1400 feet through spectacular old-growth forest. Hikers starting on this trail usually return the way they came, because a car shuttle to the other side of the wilderness requires a 33-mile drive on twisty backroads.

A very rough angler's trail scrambles along the north bank of Drift Creek from the Horse Creek Trail crossing as far as a campable site across from the mouth of Boulder Creek. Bushwhacking along other creeks and ridges is difficult enough to ensure solitude.

To find the northern Horse Creek Trailhead, drive Highway 101 north of Waldport 7 miles to Ona Beach State Park, turn inland on North Beaver Creek Road 1 mile, fork left for 2.7 miles, turn right onto paved North Elkhorn Road for 5.8 miles, turn left on Road 50 for 1.4 miles, and fork right onto gravel Road 5087 for 3.4 miles.

18 Cummins Creek and Rock Creek

Location: 15 miles north of Florence
Size: 26 square miles
Status: Designated wilderness (1984)
Terrain: Steep valleys, coastal rain forest
Elevation: 0 feet–2300 feet
Management: Siuslaw NF
Topographic maps: Yachats, Heceta Head, Cummins Peak, Cannibal Mountain (USGS)

On this wild stretch of coast, pristine rain forest canyons pour half a dozen clear creeks between the cliff-tipped headlands of 2000-foot-tall ridges. Here, hikers can prowl an old-growth forest, study tide pools, or picnic on a secluded beach.

Climate
Rainfall varies from 80 inches annually on the beach to more than 100 inches in the interior. Cool fogs line the coast and fill the valleys most of summer. Winters are snowless. Fall and spring have the most clear days.

Plants and Wildlife
The ridge between Rock Creek and Big Creek is one of only three locations worldwide to support a stable population of the threatened, orange-and-brown mottled Oregon silverspot butterfly. Cape Perpetua is a popular lookout from which to spot the spouts of migrating gray whales from December to May. Low tides expose sea urchins, sea

Giant Sitka spruce on Cape Creek near Cape Perpetua

anemones, and other marine tidepool life on the rocky coastline between the Devils Churn and Gwynn Knoll.

Sitka spruce as large as 9 feet in diameter dominate the valley slopes within 2 miles of the ocean. Farther inland the forest gradually shifts to old-growth Douglas fir. The undergrowth of rhododendron (blooms in May), salal, sword fern, and salmonberry is so dense that even shade-tolerant western hemlock seedlings often must sprout atop rotting old-growth "nursery logs" to survive. Creeks are overhung with red alder, mossy bigleaf maple, and autumn-reddening vine maple. Wildflowers include yellow monkeyflower, purple aster, white candyflower, and the tall red spires of foxglove. Wild lily-of-the-valley carpets the forest with heart-shaped leaves.

The area supports larger native runs of salmon, steelhead, and cutthroat trout than any other similar-sized watershed in Oregon. Although runs have since declined here and statewide, a fish count in 1979 found an average of 50 coho salmon per 100 feet on the lower 2 miles of Cummins Creek in late June.

Geology

The area's basalt bedrock began as undersea lava flows. As upfaulting lifted the Coast Range from the ocean, creeks eroded the face of the fault block into steep, shallow-soiled canyons. Small oceanfront fractures have been widened by wave action into slot-shaped spouting horns and the Devils Churn.

History

Excavation of middens (shell piles) near the cape's tide pools show that humans have camped here to gather mussels for 6000 years—a tradition carried on by the Alsea tribe until the 1870s.

Explorer Captain Cook, sailing against stormy seas near here on March 11, 1778, complained that the same cape had been in sight to the north for five days. He named the perpetual landmark Cape Perpetua, in part because March 11 is the holy day of St. Perpetua, a faith-tested martyr.

THINGS TO DO
Hiking

Five trails suitable for day hikes begin at the Cape Perpetua Visitor Center. The most heavily used of these are paved, and several are equipped with interpretive signs. An 0.8-mile loop ducks through a tunnel under Highway 101 to visit tide pools, shell middens, and Cook Chasm's spouting horn (an optional 1-mile loop continues north to the Devils Churn). A different 1.5-mile trail from the visitor center crosses Cape Creek and climbs 700 feet to a spectacular viewpoint at a 1933 stone shelter atop Cape Perpetua. A 1-mile trail follows the south bank of Cape Creek, past the Perpetua Campground, to a giant spruce tree 15 feet in diameter. A more ambitious 5.8-mile loop starts from the visitor center's upper parking lot, climbs 2.3 miles along the Cooks Ridge Trail amid old-growth spruce, turns right to descend the Gwynn Creek Trail 2.5 miles, and then follows the Oregon Coast Trail right 1 mile along a pioneer wagon road to complete the loop.

A lovely, unofficial trail along Cummins Creek emerges at intervals from lush, valley-bottom rain forest to pass creekside gravel bars ideal for picnics. To start, turn

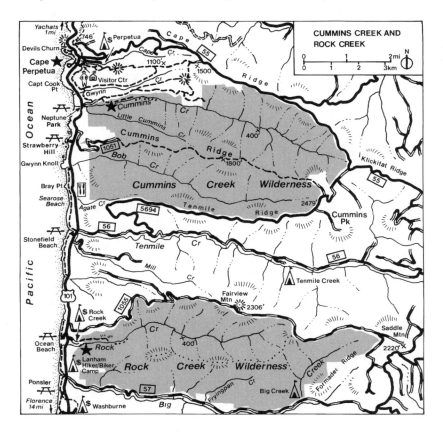

off Highway 101 immediately north of Neptune State Park at a sign reading, "Cummins Creek Trailhead ¼ mile." The trailhead is a barricade blocking Road 1030. Hike up the abandoned road 300 yards and take an unmarked spur to the right. This rough path follows the creek 0.6 mile to a small creekside gravel bar.

To hike the official Cummins Creek Trail (and to make a 7.4-mile loop), walk up abandoned Road 1030 through deep forest for 1.4 miles. Turn left here on a trail that

A stone shelter from the 1930s overlooks Cape Perpetua's rugged coastline

climbs to a ridge crest with occasional ocean views. Keep left at all trail junctions to return down Gwynn Creek and a portion of the Oregon Coast Trail to your car.

A 6-mile trail exploring the old-growth Sitka spruce forest on Cummins Ridge begins at the barricaded end of Road 1051. Hike the abandoned road 3 miles along the ridge top to a cairn and veer right onto a ridge crest trail to Road 515, a short spur of Road 5694.

Hikers heading up Rock Creek start at the Rock Creek Campground and walk east along a short Forest Service road and through a meadow that was once the site of a homestead. The impromptu trail quickly becomes a bushwhacking route. To continue, wear tennis shoes and walk up the middle of the chilly (average 56° F) creek.

A 5-mile-long elk trail traces the Rock Creek–Big Creek Divide from a saddle on Road 1055. Ridge-top meadows allow views of the valley forests on either hand.

The Oregon Coast Trail is being developed along the length of this shore. A new 1.7-mile section of this trail descends from Cape Perpetua's stone shelter toward Yachats. Another nice section is farther south. A path from Washburne State Park's campground extends 1.7 miles south to a crossing of Highway 101 at a parking pullout. From there, a scenic 1.3-mile segment of the Oregon Coast Trail leads onward to the Heceta Head lighthouse.

19 Lower Deschutes River

Location: 14 miles east of The Dalles
Size: 38 square miles
Status: Federal wild and scenic river
Terrain: Rimrock-lined river canyon
Elevation: 150 feet–2500 feet
Management: Prineville District BLM, Oregon Parks and Recreation Department
Topographic maps: Wishram, Emerson, Locust Grove, Erskine, Summit Ridge, Sinamox, Sherars Bridge, Maupin (USGS)

Roaring white water and cliff-rimmed canyons highlight the final 51 miles of the Deschutes River, popular for two-day float trips.

Climate

With just 10 inches of annual precipitation, this canyon boasts reliable sunshine. Summers are hot, but frost is common at night and throughout winter.

Plants and Wildlife

Sagebrush dominates this canyonland. Mule deer, coyotes, and rattlesnakes are common. The river's famous steelhead include a native Deschutes strain (6 to 8 pounds), which swim up the river from June to September, and a Clearwater River strain (up to

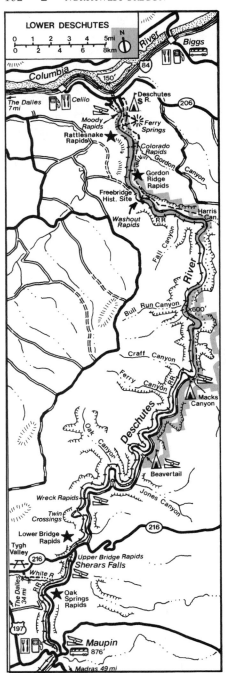

LOWER DESCHUTES

22 pounds), which visit the cool Deschutes seeking respite from the warmer Columbia River on their way to spawning grounds in Idaho.

Geology

The canyon walls are layered with 25- to 100-foot-thick lava flows belonging to the 13- to 16-million-year-old Columbia River basalts.

History

Warm Springs Indians maintain a centuries-old tradition by dipnetting migrating salmon each spring and fall from rickety wooden platforms overhanging 15-foot Sherars Falls. Explorer Peter Skene Ogden lost five horses through an Indian bridge at the falls in 1826. A toll bridge built there in 1860 connected The Dalles with the rich Canyon City gold fields in central Oregon. The old county bridge at Freebridge was apparently dynamited in 1912 by competing toll-bridge owners.

Although an 1855 Army engineering survey reported that a railroad grade was impossible along the lower Deschutes, rivalry between railroad magnates James Hill and Edward Harriman resulted in two rail lines being built up the "impossible" canyon to Bend in 1909–11. Hill's Oregon Trunk Railway remains on the west bank; track has been removed from the east-bank grade, now a bike path.

THINGS TO DO
Hiking

The best trails start at Deschutes River State Park. For a 4.2-mile loop, hike

Bicyclists on the converted railroad grade along the Deschutes River

the riverbank path to Moody Rapids, climb to a viewpoint at Ferry Springs, and return on a portion of a historic wagon road. Also from the park, the old railroad grade, converted to a mountain bike path, leads 12 miles to Harris Canyon, and continues as an undeveloped route to Macks Canyon Campground. Backpacking campsites are plentiful along the river, but stays are limited to four nights; campfires are all but prohibited; and private land can block access, especially south of Freebridge (on the west bank) and Harris Canyon (on the east). Anglers are urged to use barbless hooks and to release all native fish.

An easy 0.3-mile trail from the Tygh Valley picnic area on Highway 216 visits three colossal White River waterfalls. A bushwhacking route continues downstream 2.2 miles to the Deschutes, but expect lush poison oak along the way.

Boating

The popular 51-mile drift trip from Maupin to the Columbia River encounters three thrilling class 4 rapids, dozens of lesser riffles, and one impassable falls.

Four miles below the Maupin City Park boat ramp, class 4 Oak Springs Rapids split the river into three channels; stop to look it over, then avoid the right-hand channel. After another 3.5 miles, all craft must portage around unnavigable Sherars Falls. Just 150 yards beyond the portage, boaters are faced with class 3 Upper Bridge Rapids, and, in another 0.2 mile, the dangerous Lower Bridge Rapids. Scout this class 4+ white water from the right bank, then paddle hard to stay in the smaller, right-hand channel.

The Lower Deschutes River from Ferry Springs

Downriver 3.6 miles, class 3 Wreck Rapids introduce a 34-mile stretch of calmer water with a steady 5-mile-per-hour current, past some of the canyon's most spectacular basalt rimrock.

The pace picks up for the river's final 7 miles. First comes Washout Rapids, an unrated boulder field created when a late 1990s flash flood blasted rocks out of a side creek's twin culverts. A mile later is Gordon Ridge Rapids, a long, class 2+ ride with outcroppings of columnar basalt in midriver. Scouting is required. A mile and a half downstream comes class 3 Colorado Rapids, with a treacherous standing wave and suckhole on the left-hand side. Class 4 Rattlesnake Rapids are only 1.2 miles farther. Three drownings testify to the danger of this narrows, where boaters must thread their way between rocks on the river's left side and a gigantic suckhole in the river's middle. Two miles farther on, the class 2 Moody Rapids delivers boaters to the backwater of The Dalles Dam.

All boaters must carry a Deschutes River Boater Pass, available at local sporting goods stores. Fishing is prohibited from any floating device in the river. Campfires are permitted only in firepans and only from October 16 to May 31. Campsites between

Macks Canyon and the Deschutes River State Park campground have a four-night stay limit, and maximum group size is sixteen. No camping is allowed on islands. Boaters can recognize the beginning of private, off-limits shorefront by watching for posts marked with circles; posts with triangles signal the return to public lands.

Lower Deschutes float trips are often coupled with the two-day, 45-mile drift of the central Deschutes River, from the Highway 26 bridge near Warm Springs to the boat landing at Maupin. Jet boats and motors are banned on the portion of the river bordering the Warm Springs Indian Reservation and are restricted elsewhere.

 Deschutes Canyon

Location: 32 miles north of Bend
Size: 29 square miles
Status: Undesignated wilderness
Terrain: Cliff-lined canyons, desert plateaus
Elevation: 1945 feet–2950 feet
Management: Crooked River National Grassland
Topographic maps: Central Oregon (BLM); Steelhead Falls, Squaw Back Ridge, Round Butte Dam (USGS)

The Deschutes River roars through this seldom-visited, 700-foot-deep canyon, beneath sagebrush mesas with views of the High Cascade snowpeaks.

Climate
Sunshine is the rule in this steppe, which gets less than 10 inches of annual rainfall. Summers are hot, but frost is common at night and in winter.

Plants and Wildlife
Heavy grazing on the tablelands has converted a historic bunchgrass steppe to sagebrush, cheat grass, and tumbleweed. The steep canyons and The Island north of Cove Palisades Park, however, preserve native bunchgrasses and the original "desert crust," a complex ground cover of lichens and mosses. The river itself creates a narrow oasis dotted with ponderosa pine and vine maple. Coyote and mule deer abound.

Geology
The canyon's layer cake–style cliffs consist mostly of 5- to 25-million-year-old basalt lava flows from the Cascade Range. The Island, however, and certain other terraces halfway up the cliffs, are remnants of the Intracanyon Basalt, a more recent flow that began 60 miles away at Newberry Volcanic National Monument. Slow cooling allowed many of the basalt layers to fracture into a distinctive pattern of hexagonal pillars. The

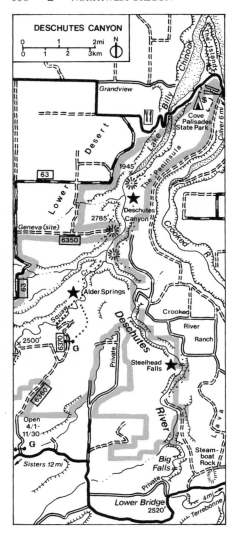

slopes between cliff layers, sometimes eroded into multicolored pinnacles, are composed of volcanic ash, gravel, and soil that accumulated between the devastating basalt floods, which were often 100,000 years apart.

THINGS TO DO
Hiking

The area's only official path, the Tam-a-lau Trail, gains 550 feet in 1.3 miles from the far west end of the Cove Palisades campground to The Peninsula. From there, a 3.6-mile loop trail skirts the edge of this arid mesa, passing excellent views of the Billy Chinook Reservoir.

To the south, massive Steelhead Falls is a 0.5-mile hike from poorly marked dirt roads. Roads in the extensive Crooked River Ranch subdivision north and east of Steelhead Falls are open to public use.

To the southwest, dirt Roads 6360 and 6370 descend to Squaw Creek, a linear oasis of quaking aspen and wildflowers in a cliff-rimmed canyon. To protect Roads 6360 and 6370 from tire damage, they're closed by gates during the wetter winter months, December 1 to March 31.

A rewarding 2.2-mile walk from Road 6370 follows Squaw Creek to the hidden natural amphitheater at Alder Springs, walled with striped cliffs. At the remote canyon abyss where Squaw Creek and the Deschutes River join lies a difficult 1.5-mile scramble downstream. While Squaw Creek can be forded nearly everywhere, the raging Deschutes River is nowhere crossable.

To find Squaw Creek from Sisters, drive 4.5 miles east on Highway 126 toward Redmond, turn left on Goodrich Road for 8 miles, turn left on Road 6360 for 3.4 miles, turn right on Road 6370 for 0.8 mile, and park at a gate. Beyond this point the road has been churned up to return the area to its natural state. When the private ranch that once was here proved to be hiding a methamphetamine laboratory, officials

The Island from The Peninsula in Cove Palisades State Park

demolished the house, confiscated the property, and turned it over to the Crooked River National Grassland. Follow the old roadbed downhill 1 mile (keeping left at forks), cross the creek, scramble up the far shore, and hike right 1.2 miles to Alder Springs' riverbend oasis.

Another cross-country hiking option is to drive Road 6360 to its ford of Squaw Creek and to hike 2.5 miles upstream to the end of public land. This canyon route requires some wading but features pictographs (don't touch!) and caves.

To explore The Island's otherworldly, 2.4-mile-long plateau, park at the Crooked River Petroglyph pullout at a pass in Cove Palisades Park, cross the road to the park's dump, and take an unmarked path up to the right. Because The Island is a botanical study area, however, this path is often closed to the public.

Boating

Big Falls and Steelhead Falls stop all white-water boating on the Deschutes. Kayaks carried to the base of Steelhead Falls face 7.5 miles of apparently runnable rapids.

21 Metolius River

Location: 45 miles north of Bend, 32 miles west of Madras
Size: 17 square miles
Status: Undesignated wilderness
Terrain: Steep, forested river canyon
Elevation: 2000 feet–5050 feet
Management: Deschutes NF
Topographic maps: Whitewater River (Green Trails); Shitike Butte, Prairie Farm, Fly Creek (USGS)

The Metolius is the most magical of all Oregon rivers. From the arid base of Black Butte it springs fully grown, at an identical temperature and volume year round, then slides swiftly through 29 miles of rugged canyons before vanishing into the back-waters of the Lake Billy Chinook reservoir. The remote lower river twists through a wilderness canyon bend called the Horn of the Metolius.

Climate
Though mostly sunny and dry (20 inches annual precipitation), the area receives snow from about December to February. Snow lingers on Green Ridge until April.

Plants and Wildlife
Orange-trunked ponderosa pine and autumn-red vine maple flank the river. Bitter-brush and rabbitbrush (bright yellow blooms in fall) form a sparse ground cover. On the eastern ridges, gnarled juniper are the only trees.

The river's name comes from the Warm Springs Indian *Mpto-ly-as,* "white fish." The light-fleshed salmon that prompted this name are gone; however, introduced ko-kanee salmon and abundant hatchery trout attract eagles, bears, and other anglers.

Geology
Green Ridge, a 16-mile-long, 2500-foot-tall fault scarp, gave rise to Black Butte's vol-canic cone on the south and displaced the Metolius River to the north. Later basalt lava flows from the Cascade Range created the adjacent Metolius Bench tablelands, with their dramatic rimrock.

THINGS TO DO
Hiking
The 1.5-mile Shut-in Trail traverses a dense forest along the rushing Metolius River in a remote canyon called the Horn of the Metolius. But now that cars have been banned from 14.9 miles of the trail's badly rutted access roads, hikers, equestrians, and bicyclists

can tour along the wild river undisturbed for a total of 16 miles from Lower Bridge Campground to Monty Campground.

The route's eastern trailhead at Monty Campground is reached by driving west from Madras through Cove Palisades State Park and Grandview to the gated end of Road 64. If you are coming from Sisters, drive 5 miles west on Highway 20, turn north onto Road 11 for 18 miles, turn right onto Road 1170 for 5 miles, and then take Road 64 to the left for 8 miles to Monty Campground. Park at the gate and hike (or bicycle) the old road 4 miles to the Shut-in Trail.

To find the route's western trailhead, take Highway 20 east of Santiam Pass 10 miles and turn north on paved Road 14 through Camp Sherman, passing many campgrounds, for a total of 13 miles to Lower Bridge Campground. From the campground, hike (or bicycle) down a gated road along the river for 9.4 miles to the Shut-in Trail.

The Metolius River forms the southern boundary of the Warm Springs Indian Reservation. Entry to tribal lands is completely prohibited here.

Excellent views of Mount Jefferson, craggy Castle Rock, and Five-Fingered Sentinel await cross-country hikers willing to scale the persistent slopes of Green Ridge. The open forest presents no obstacle.

A nice hike in the east of the area follows an unmarked 0.5-mile-long trail up Street Creek. To find Street Creek, drive 2 miles past Perry South Campground on Road 64 to a sign reading "Monty Campground 3 miles." From here the trail follows

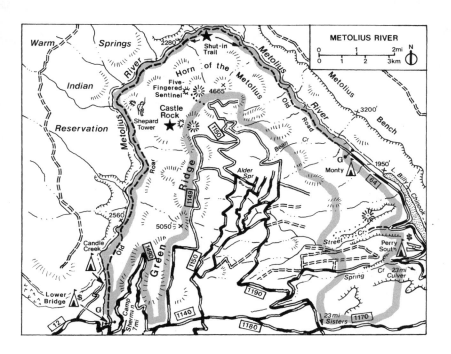

The Metolius River

the creek's north bank. At trail's end, adventurous hikers can bushwhack another 1.5 miles upstream past ash formations and a cave, hike north up a side canyon, and walk east along the rimrock's edge to a viewpoint.

The East Metolius Trail, open to hikers only, continues 10.2 miles upstream from Lower Bridge Campground to Riverside Campground, near the river's source at the Head of the Metolius' massive springs. This less wild hiking route (not shown on map) traverses seven car campgrounds along the way.

Climbing

Shepard Tower of the Metolius, 0.5 mile uphill from the road/trail along the Metolius River (6.5 miles from the Lower Bridge Trailhead) offers four routes via chimneys and ledges. Difficulty levels are I-3 to I-5.4.

Boating

Clear, deep, and cold (46° F year round), the Metolius races along at between 5 and 10 miles per hour, providing plenty of white-water thrills. In 26 miles of free-flowing water between Riverside Campground (1.5 miles south of Camp Sherman) and Lake Billy Chinook, the only unnavigable hazard is at Wizard Falls, 6.5 miles from the start. The "falls" itself is merely a reeflike ledge, but the dangerously low bridge beyond it requires a portage. The last bridge across the river, Lower Bridge, is at river mile 9. The Confederated Tribes of Warm Springs discourage boating beyond this point because the river borders the reservation here. To avoid trespassing and possible arrest, do not land on the left bank. Those who continue usually take out at Monty Campground, because the next public boat landing (at Perry South Campground) requires a 3.5-mile paddle across the reservoir.

Smith Rock

Location: 9 miles north of Redmond
Size: 1 square mile
Status: State park
Terrain: River peninsula with rock formations
Elevation: 2620 feet–3500 feet
Management: Oregon State Parks and Recreation Department
Topographic maps: Redmond, Opal City, O'Neil, Gray Butte (USGS)

The orange rock walls and pinnacles of Smith Rock tower above an oasislike riverbend at the edge of central Oregon's sagebrush plains. The spectacular formation is both a reliably rainless hiking destination and the best technical rock climbing site in Oregon. An automat accepts bills or change for the park's special $3-per-car parking fee.

Climate
With just 8.5 inches of annual precipitation, Smith Rock is usually sunny even when the trails of the High Cascades are beset with rain or snow. Midwinter brings a few dustings of snow, and midsummer brings blazing heat.

Plants and Wildlife
Visit in spring for high desert wildflowers. Admire but do not pick the riverbank's wild asparagus and wild onions. Climbers should take pains not to disturb birds of prey nesting on the crags.

Geology
The western vanguard of the Ochoco Mountains, Smith Rock is formed of welded rhyolite ash. This ash erupted from the Old Cascades, settled in a large inland sea, and fused to form rock by heat and pressure. More recent lava flows pushed the Crooked River up against Smith Rock and left the basalt rimrock of the river's south shore.

THINGS TO DO
Hiking

Start by hiking from the picnic area down a service road 0.4 mile to a footbridge over the Crooked River. Cross the bridge and turn left on a delightful riverbank trail that skirts below orange cliffs. After 2 miles along the river you will approach the base of Monkey Face, a 350-foot rock monolith topped by a remarkable natural sculpture of a monkey's head. If you scramble up to the actual base of the tower, you will find a trail that winds steeply uphill to a ledge near the monkey's head, where views extend across central Oregon to the Cascade snowpeaks. Continue across the upland area to find a staircase down Misery Ridge to the Crooked River footbridge, completing a 4-mile loop.

For a more challenging, 6.3-mile loop, follow the river trail 0.2 mile past Monkey Face to a house-sized boulder, veer right on a path up a steep rock gully, and turn left along a ridge-crest path for a mile to Burma Road. Turn right at this dirt track 0.7 mile to the start of a canal, and then take a side path back down to the Crooked River. Mountain bikes and horses are not allowed on park trails.

To reach the park, turn east off Highway 97 at Terrebonne, 6 miles north of Redmond, and follow state park signs 3 miles, past Juniper Junction, a shop known

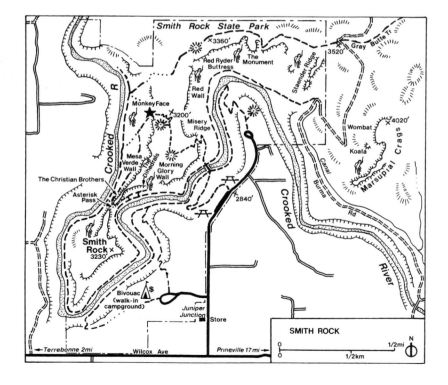

The Crooked River at Smith Rock State Park

for its refreshing huckleberry ice cream.

The 5.8-mile Gray Butte Trail joins the Burma Road track at the top of Smith Rock's ridge, providing a quieter, back-door route to this popular park. The two Gray Butte trailheads charge no parking fee and are open to bicyclists and equestrians. To find the trailheads, turn off Highway 97 at Terrebonne onto Smith Rock Way, but then stick to this paved road 5.9 miles, ignoring signs that point left to the park. At a T-shaped junction, turn left on Lone Pine Road for 3.4 miles, and then turn left across a cattle guard onto gravel Road 5710 for 1.1 mile. For the Gray Butte Saddle Trailhead, turn left on Road 5720 for 1.6 miles. For the McCoin Orchard Trailhead, continue straight on Road 5710 another 1.4 miles and turn left on Road 57 for 0.7 mile.

Climbing

With more than 3 miles of rock faces and nearly 1000 named routes, Smith Rock ranks first among Oregon's technical climbing sites, with routes to level IV-5.12 and beyond. Good weather and easy access add to the area's popularity.

Heavy use, however, has necessitated several rules. Stay on established trails as much as possible. Add no permanent anchors. Camp only in the designated bivouac area. Campfires are prohibited.

Large climbing classes and search-and-rescue practice groups should strive to minimize their impact by climbing in beginner areas. The 30-foot basalt rimrock cliffs on the opposite shore of the river from The Monument are easily accessible and offer technical pitches. Beginners intent on trying rhyolite will find a good practice boulder (named "Rope de Dope") on the riverbank opposite Morning Glory Wall.

The area's most spectacular challenge is Monkey Face, a 350-foot tower overhanging on all sides, first climbed on January 1, 1960. There are 27 routes and variations, including the level II-5.11 Monkey Space route behind the monkey's head, and the level II-5.7-A1 Pioneer Route past Panic Point, on the monkey's Mouth Cave.

Other major climbing areas include Picnic Lunch Wall (24 routes), Morning Glory Wall (56 routes), The Dihedrals (52 routes), The Christian Brothers (43 routes), Smith Rock Promontory (43 routes), Mesa Verde Wall (23 routes), Red Wall (26 routes), Red Ryder Buttress (6 routes), Staender Ridge (6 routes), and Marsupial Crags (31 routes).

Opposite: *Salt Creek, the outlet of Gold Lake (Area 24)*

chapter 2 **Southwest Oregon**

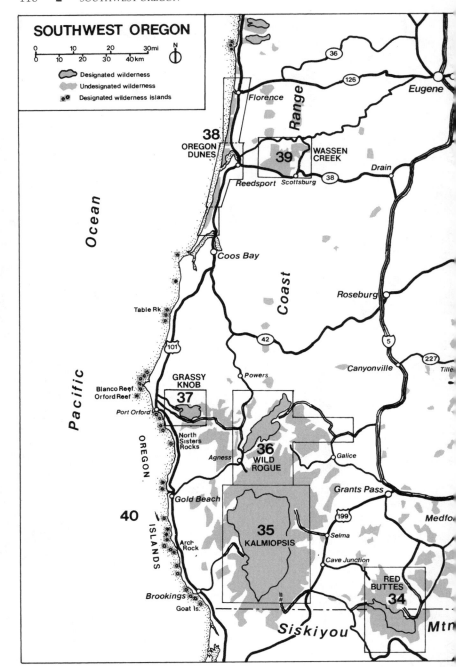

SOUTHWEST OREGON

0 10 20 30mi
0 10 20 30 40km
N

Designated wilderness
Undesignated wilderness
Designated wilderness islands

Florence

Range

36

126

Eugene

38
OREGON
DUNES

39

WASSEN
CREEK

Drain

Reedsport Scottsburg

38

Ocean

Coos Bay

Coast

Roseburg

Table Rk

42

101

5

227

Tille

Canyonville

Pacific

GRASSY
KNOB

Powers

Blanco Reef
Orford Reef

37

Port Orford

North
Sisters
Rocks

Agness

36
WILD
ROGUE

Galice

OREGON

Gold Beach

Grants Pass

40

199

Medfo

ISLANDS

Arch
Rock

35
KALMIOPSIS

Selma

Cave Junction

RED
BUTTES

34

Brookings

Goat Is.

Siskiyou

Mtn

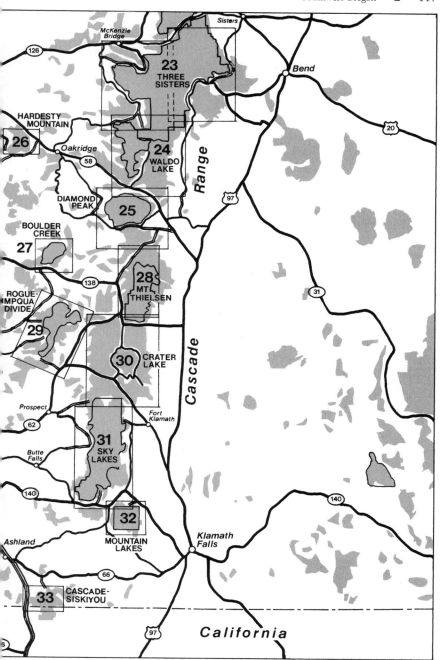

23 Three Sisters

Location: 52 miles east of Eugene, 26 miles west of Bend
Size: 572 square miles, including Century Lakes, Chucksney Mountain, and Macduff Peak
Status: 443 square miles designated wilderness (1964, 1978, 1984)
Terrain: Snowpeaks, lava, forests, lakes, valleys
Elevation: 1850 feet–10,358 feet
Management: Deschutes NF, Willamette NF
Topographic maps: Three Sisters (Geo-Graphics); Three Sisters Wilderness, PCT Northern Oregon Portion (USFS)

A cluster of glacier-clad volcanoes highlights Oregon's most visited wilderness. This large area contains four very different geographic zones.

In the alpine region ringing the Three Sisters and craggy Broken Top, wildflower meadows alternate with lava formations. But to the south, the Cascade crest is a rolling forest of pine and mountain hemlock with hundreds of lakes. To the west, foggy, low-elevation canyons brim with old-growth Douglas fir. To the southeast, sparse forests of lodgepole pine and bear grass carpet arid lands beyond the Century Lakes.

Climate

Winter snow in the uplands drifts to depths of up to 20 feet. In the east the snow falls dry, providing some of the state's best powder skiing. Even the lowest trails remain blocked by snow until May. Trails up to an elevation of 5000 feet are clear by about mid-June and trails at 6500 feet are usually clear by August, though snowstorms can occur in any month.

The area's western slopes receive 90 inches of annual precipitation, but the eastern slopes receive just 20 inches a year. The Mink Lake and Horse Lake basins especially are plagued by mosquitoes in July and early August.

Plants and Wildlife

The area's size makes it a refuge for large, shy animals such as wolverine, mink, cougar, and bald eagle. Geographic diversity makes the area home to more plant species than any other Oregon wilderness.

Subalpine wildflower displays in July and early August include blue lupine and red paintbrush. Snowmelt zones teem with white avalanche lily, marsh marigold, and fuzzy pasqueflower. Wet areas have red elephanthead, shooting star, yellow monkeyflower, columbine, and larkspur. Drier fields host fuzzy cat's-ears and wild sunflower.

Pink rhododendron displays brighten the lower western slopes in early June. Ripe wild huckleberries line forest trails in the 5000- to 6500-foot elevation range in late August.

South Sister from the Chambers Lakes trail in April

Geology

Although a 1925 theory claimed the taller peaks were remnants of an exploded super-volcano, "Mount Multnomah," more recent study shows the mountains formed separately, all within the past 100,000 years, along the High Cascades fault zone.

Oldest peaks in the group are North Sister, which has lost a third of its bulk to glacial erosion, leaving its central plug as a summit spire, and Broken Top, eroded so severely it offers a good cut-away view of a composite volcano's interior structure—alternating red and black bands of cinder and lava. Broken Top's violent past has left the area strewn with interesting, drop-shaped "lava bombs," football-sized bits of exploded magma that cooled in flight.

Middle Sister's Collier Glacier was once the state's largest, but a 1-mile retreat since 1900 has transferred the honor to South Sister's Prouty Glacier. South Sister is geologically "young" enough to have kept its uneroded conical shape. Its summit crater cups the state's highest lake, Teardrop Pool. Mount Bachelor, another "youthful" volcano, harbors inner fires that create small snow wells on the mountain's north slope, a hazard for skiers.

Collier Cone erupted some 15,000 years ago directly in the path of the mighty

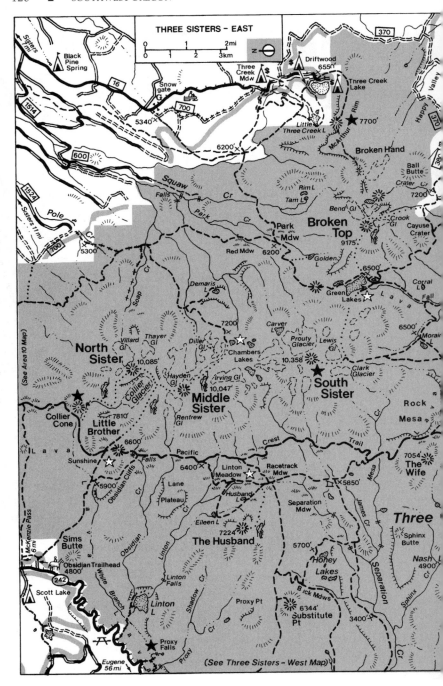

THREE SISTERS - EAST

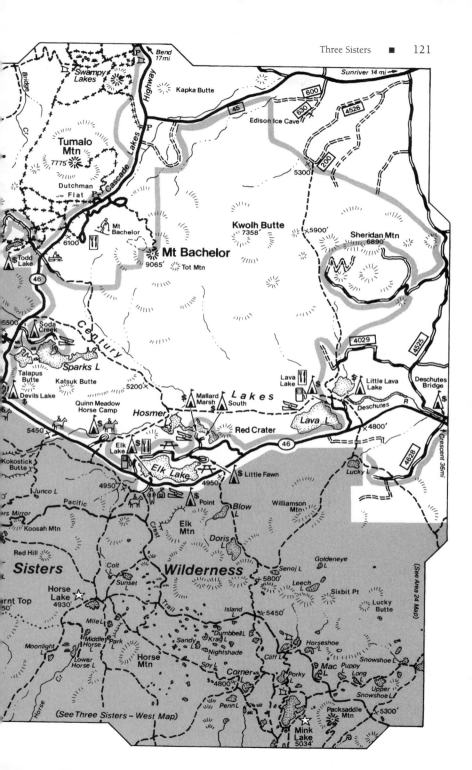

Collier Glacier, commencing a battle of fire and ice. One of the cone's fresh-looking lava flows traced the White Branch valley for 8.5 miles, damming Linton Lake.

Flows of glassy, black obsidian are exposed both below Sunshine, near North Sister, and at Green Lakes, near South Sister. Another kind of high-silica-content eruption formed the frothy, lighter-than-water pumice of Rock Mesa. A California company's mining claim on Rock Mesa's pumice, which would have converted this prominent wilderness feature to cat litter, ended with a $2 million buyout by Congress in 1983.

Ice Age glaciers formed the steep, U-shaped valleys of the South Fork McKenzie River and Separation Creek. Sand-pile moraines left by retreating glaciers dammed most alpine lakes.

History

Once a popular autumn camp for Indians, the area provided huckleberries, venison, obsidian for arrowheads, and bear grass for basketry. Antler-shaped pictographs across the Cascade Lakes Highway from the east end of Devils Lake are federally protected.

Many place names in the area recall Chinook jargon, an Indian trade language once widely used by Indians and settlers of the Oregon frontier. Hikers can cross Skookum ("powerful") Creek, camp in Olallie ("berry") Meadows, climb Koosah ("sky") Mountain, and spot Cultus ("worthless") Lake.

Visitors to the area sometimes smile at the Three Sister's "family" of lesser peaks—Little Brother, The Husband, and The Wife. Few realize there are also a Chinook aunt and uncle (Kwolh Butte and Tot Mountain) hiding behind Mount Bachelor. Other Chinook names in the area are Tipsoo ("grassy") Butte, Hiyu ("big") Ridge, Moolack ("elk") Mountain, Kokostick ("woodpecker") Butte, Talapus ("coyote") Butte, and Sahalie ("upper") Falls.

THINGS TO DO
Hiking (East Map)

Free wilderness entry permits can be filled out conveniently at all of the trailheads except the Obsidian Trailhead, near North Sister's Sunshine area. To limit crowds in that popular area, permits are issued for only twenty groups a day, and the permits must be reserved in advance from the McKenzie Ranger Station. Call (541) 822-3381 for details.

The Three Sisters' popularity has brought other restrictions as well. In the Sunshine area, where several square miles of alpine meadows spread below North Sister, all campfires are banned and tents must be more than 100 feet from any water source or trail. Campfires are likewise taboo within a quarter mile of Husband or Eileen Lakes and within 0.5 mile of other popular pools: Camp Lake, the three Green Lakes, the four Chambers Lakes, and Moraine Lake. At the Green Lakes, and at several other popular destinations, camping is allowed only at sites marked by a post. To avoid crowds, plan to visit in fall or in the middle of the week, or try striking off cross-country by compass; it is not hard through the high country.

Two of the area's easiest hikes are the 1-mile loop to feathery Proxy Falls and the

1.4-mile, relatively level trail to Linton Lake. Both paths start from the scenic, historic Highway 242 west of McKenzie Pass. Several other hikes in the dramatic McKenzie Pass area are described in Area 10. For an easy hike near Sisters, take the 1.5-mile trail to 30-foot Squaw Creek Falls from a spur of Road 1514.

Special permits are required for the very popular 4.8-mile, uphill path to Sunshine Meadow that begins at the Obsidian Trailhead on Highway 242. Day hikers should not miss the loop past Obsidian Cliffs and Obsidian Falls. Following the Pacific Crest Trail (PCT) in either direction from Sunshine makes for memorable backpacking trips. Two miles north, the PCT crosses a lava flow to Collier Cone and a viewpoint of the huge Collier Glacier. Five miles south of Sunshine, side trails of the PCT reach Linton Meadow, nestled between Middle Sister and the crags of The Husband.

The 7000-foot-high Chambers Lakes, surrounded by the glaciers of Middle and South Sister, often have drifting ice throughout summer. Wind-gnarled whitebark pines are the only trees. The dramatic lakes are 7.1 miles from the Pole Creek Trailhead at the end of Road 1524. From the town of Sisters, drive west 1.4 miles on Highway 242, then turn left onto Road 15 for 5 miles to Road 1524.

Park Meadow features views of four mountains. Nearby, easy cross-country hikes lead to Golden Lake and other wildflower havens higher on the slopes of Broken Top and South Sister. Park Meadow is an almost level 4.9 miles from the end of pavement on Road 16, a road that begins as Elm Street in downtown Sisters.

Cliff-edged Tam McArthur Rim rises from the lodgepole pine forests of central Oregon. A 2.5-mile trail climbs from the turnoff to Driftwood Campground on Road 16 to a dramatic rim viewpoint, where snow lingers through August. From there, the rim's above-timberline crest lures hikers on toward Broken Hand and increasingly grand views.

A dozen popular campgrounds and trailheads line the Cascade Lakes Highway. Opposite the turnoff to Mount Bachelor on this route is the trail to Tumalo Mountain, a 1.4-mile path climbing 1400 feet up the conical, sparsely forested butte to a former fire lookout site.

The most heavily used trail in the area, and one of the most scenic, climbs 4.2 miles from Sparks Lake to the Green Lake basin at the foot of South Sister. The route follows rushing Fall Creek around a blocky lava flow to the high lakes—which really are green, colored by finely ground silt from nearby Lewis Glacier. Campfires are banned within 0.5 mile of Green Lakes.

A more nearly level route into the Green Lakes is available by the start of August when snowmelt opens Road 370 from Todd Lake to the Crater Ditch Trailhead. The 4.8-mile Ditch Trail from spur Road 380 contours around Broken Top, offering viewpoints at every turn. A worthwhile cross-country trip from the same trailhead follows Crater Creek up to its head at an ice-filled lake inside Broken Top's ruined crater.

Scaling South Sister may sound too ambitious for a hike, but in fact Oregon's third-tallest mountain requires no technical climbing skills or equipment. The hike gains 4900 feet in 5.5 miles to the view of a lifetime. Begin at the Devils Lake Campground and head directly for the summit. The unofficial trail peters out at the edge of Lewis

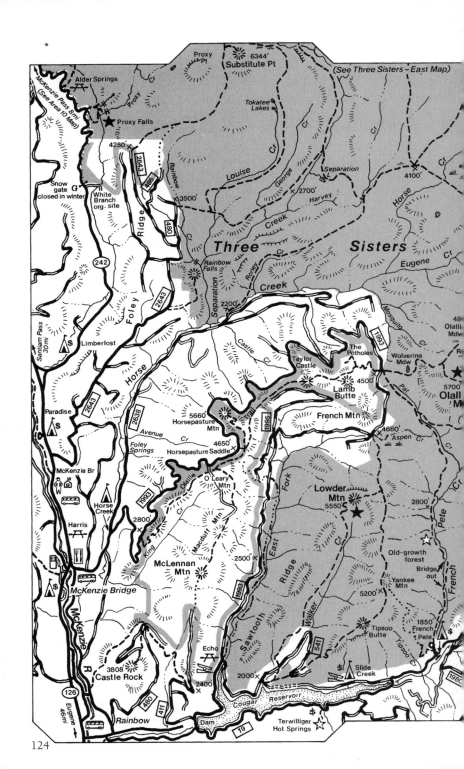

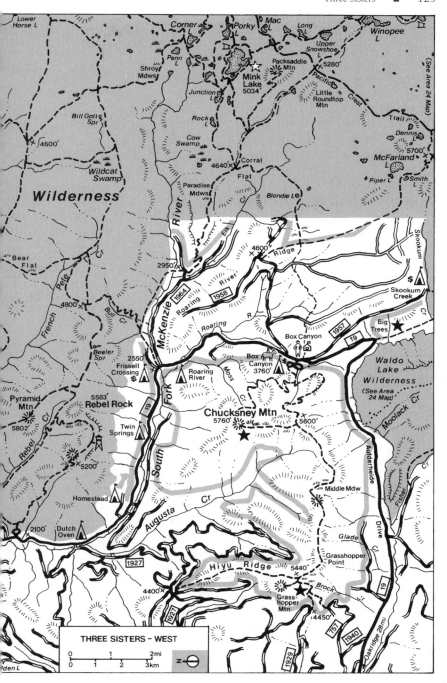

THREE SISTERS - WEST

0   1   2mi
0   1   2   3km

Glacier, but hiking is easy on snow and steep cinder slopes from there to the summit. Do not attempt the trip in anything less than perfect weather. A good consolation goal is Moraine Lake, surrounded by an ancient, sandy glacial terminus.

South Sister rises like a wall from the edge of Wickiup Plain, a square mile of cinders and bunchgrass located 2 miles by trail from Devils Lake. LeConte Crater, a perfect little cinder cone at the plain's upper edge, makes a fun climb. The scenic plain has no water, so the meadows a mile farther west, at Sisters Mirror Lake, see heavy camping use. This area is quite fragile; explore the interesting surrounding terrain for campsites well away from trailside lakes.

Horse Lake, an easy 3.3-mile hike west of the Cascade Lakes Highway at Elk Lake, is the most heavily visited of a broad basin of lakes. Trails radiate from Horse Lake toward dozens of more peaceful lake destinations, although the forested lakeshores in this area lack views of snowpeaks.

Mink Lake is the largest of another cluster of forest-rimmed lakes. A popular 8.6-mile route to Mink Lake begins a mile south of Elk Lake. Expect crowds at the narrow gravel beach of Blow Lake, 1 mile along this trail, and at 90-acre Doris Lake, 1.4 miles

South Sister from the Green Lakes

farther. At a junction 5.4 miles from the trailhead, the PCT leads to other heavily used lakes: Mac, Horseshoe, Cliff, Island, and Dumbbell. Lake lovers can easily find solitude at the hundreds of quieter lakes nearby.

Equestrians should keep in mind that pack and saddle animals are not permitted within 200 feet of any lake in the designated wilderness except for watering, loading, or traveling on established trails.

Trails in the Century Lakes area, often used by equestrians, are also suitable for hikers. The 8-mile route from the Quinn Meadow Horse Camp to Soda Creek Campground passes Hosmer Lake, then dives back into the dry, lodgepole pine forest toward Sparks Lake. Trails from Hosmer Lake to Lava Lake, and from Lava Lake east, traverse unbroken forests of lodgepole pine, bear grass, and cinders. Carry water. Even the briefest cross-country travel in this 54-square-mile roadless area provides complete solitude. Explorers may search here for undiscovered lava tube caves.

The PCT offers a long-distance route the length of the Three Sisters Wilderness—52 miles from McKenzie Pass to Taylor Burn Road 600. Another rewarding long-distance challenge is the 44.1-mile hike around the Three Sisters, which follows 19.1 miles of the PCT's most scenic section.

Hiking (West Map)

An often overlooked hike in this area is the 1-mile Rainbow Falls Viewpoint Trail. To find it, drive 3 miles east of the McKenzie Bridge Ranger Station on Highway 126 and turn right on Road 2643 for 6.5 miles.

Substitute Point's abandoned lookout site is the goal of another good viewpoint hike, through 5 miles of forest from the Foley Ridge Trailhead. Linton Meadows and the PCT are 4.5 miles past Substitute Point (Buck Meadows and the Honey Lakes are even closer), offering good backpacking goals. To start, drive 4.8 miles past Rainbow Falls to the end of Road 2643.

Several day hikes in the Olallie Ridge Research Natural Area begin at Horsepasture Saddle. To find the trailhead, drive to the east end of the bridge in McKenzie Bridge, turn onto Horse Creek Road for 1.7 miles, and turn right onto Road 1993 for 8.6 paved miles. A path east from the saddle climbs 910 feet in 1.4 miles to a first-rate viewpoint atop Horsepasture Mountain. A 5-mile trail northwest from the saddle follows a ridge down 1800 feet before rejoining Road 1993. A 4.5-mile hike west from the saddle traverses the ridge-top meadows of Macduff Mountain. Finally, a delightful 6-mile segment of the Olallie Trail leads southeast from Horsepasture Saddle, past viewpoints at Taylor Castle and Lamb Butte, to Road 1993 near Pat Creek.

The abandoned, unlocked 1930s lookout building atop Olallie Mountain has a front-row view of the Three Sisters and eight other snowpeaks. From the Pat Saddle Trailhead on Road 1993, follow the Olallie Trail south 2.1 miles, then turn right on a path through bear grass meadows 1.5 miles to the summit. If instead you continue on the Olallie Trail 0.9 mile you will reach the ruin of the 1930s Olallie Meadows Guard Station, crushed by falling trees in 1996. Horse Lake is another 10.8 miles along the trail.

Castle Rock, an abandoned fire lookout site, has a panoramic view of the McKenzie

Valley. Depending on the trailhead you choose, you will either climb 630 feet in 1 mile to the top or 2600 feet in 5.7 miles. Both routes are open to mountain bikes. The short route begins at the end of gravel Road 480. The longer route begins from paved Kings Road 2639.

The meadow on Lowder Mountain's tablelike summit offers eye-level views of the High Cascades. Several trails lead there. The 2.8-mile route from Road 1993 is easiest. The Walker Creek Trail is a 6.5-mile climb.

Terwilliger Hot Springs (also known as Cougar Hot Springs) is a good place to wash off trail dust. An easy 0.5-mile path leads to an old-growth forest canyon with a string of crowded natural hot pools (closed after dark). Expect a $3-per-person fee at the well-marked trailhead beside Cougar Reservoir on the paved Aufderheide Drive (Road 19).

The popular French Pete Creek Trail winds through a forest of massive old-growth Douglas fir. Day hikers starting from the French Pete Trailhead on Road 19 usually turn back at the 1.7-mile mark, where the first of two missing bridges demands a cold wade or an iffy crossing on wiggly logs. A car-shuttle option is to start at Road 1993 and descend Pat and French Pete Creeks 9.8 miles to Road 19.

The Rebel Rock Trail climbs 3200 feet in 4.8 miles from Road 19 to a viewpoint and a cliff-edge lookout building (which is actually located 1 mile west of Rebel Rock's trailless summit). An easier trip is the 1.1-mile walk up the adjacent Rebel Creek Trail to its second bridge amid 400-year-old Douglas firs. Or connect both trails with a strenuous 12.3-mile loop.

Two 7.8-mile routes lead backpackers into the popular Mink Lake area from the west. The heavily used Elk Creek Trail switchbacks uphill 1700 feet in its first 2 miles from Road 1964. The lesser-known Crossing Way Trail, along Roaring River Ridge from Road 1958, avoids the initial, grueling climb. The two trails join at Corral Flat.

Chucksney Mountain boasts long ridge-top meadows with sweeping views. A 10.3-mile loop trail along this scenic ridge crest climbs 2000 feet from Box Canyon Horse Campground on Road 19. The trip is popular with equestrians and mountain bikers as well as hikers. With a car shuttle, it is possible to continue 5 easy miles from the end of the loop to Grasshopper Mountain's meadows.

Grasshopper Mountain can also be the goal of two shorter hikes, either along Hiyu Ridge 4 miles from Road 1927, or up the 1.4-mile trail from Road 1929. To reach the Road 1929 trailhead, drive 13 miles from Westfir (near Oakridge) on Road 19, turn left on Road 1926 for 3 miles, then turn right on Road 1927 for 2.1 miles, and finally turn right on Road 1929 for 5.5 miles.

Climbing

The Three Sisters and Broken Top are popular with climbers chiefly because of the very scenic setting. The rock itself is crumbly and the technical challenge is not great. Solo climbers have scaled all four peaks consecutively in a single day. The area's changeable weather and the large number of novice climbers account for an above-average mountain rescue rate.

North Sister is by far the most dangerous, both because of the exposure and because the rotten rock is only completely stable after ice storms. For the easiest route (level I-4), hike from Sunshine to the col between Middle and North Sister. Follow the ridge toward North Sister, passing several gendarmes on the west at the 9500-foot-level. Skirt steep scree and snow slopes to the western base of the crown-shaped summit pinnacle, then scramble up a steep chute to the top.

Of North Sister's eight additional routes, the two most difficult (levels II-5.2 and III-5.2) ascend the east face's couloir and arête. They have only been done in winter.

Middle Sister is frequently climbed from Sunshine. A trail from the meadow at Sunshine leads toward the col between North and Middle Sister, where climbers turn south and scramble to the top. An equally easy (I-2) route ascends the southeast flank's scree slopes. Climbers usually hike 4.6 miles from the Pole Creek Trailhead toward the Chambers Lakes, but then follow North Fork Squaw Creek to Middle Sister's southeast flank. Level II-5.2 and II-5 routes scale the east face glaciers' headwalls.

Broken Top is a level I-3 climb, either from Green Lakes (via the peak's northwest ridge to a crumbly pinnacle) or from Crater Creek Ditch (ascending the Crook Glacier to the crater rim's lowest notch). The north face requires level II-5.2 skills.

The Husband, via the south ridge, is a I-3 climb.

Winter Sports

Powder snow and panoramic scenery make the Dutchman Flat–Swampy Lakes area near Mount Bachelor ideal for nordic skiing. Highway 46 is plowed in winter to the Mount Bachelor ski resort, where cross-country ski rentals are available. Just across the highway, the Dutchman Flat sno-park has an extensive network of easy, marked trails through meadow and forest. Loop trips range from 1.4 to 8 miles. Snowmobiles are allowed in certain areas, notably Road 370 and the unplowed portion of the Cascade Lakes Highway.

Closer to Bend on the Cascade Lakes Highway, the Swampy Lakes and Meissner sno-parks access an even larger nordic ski trail network, with eight rustic shelters serving as fun destinations and emergency refuges.

Popular trips from the Swampy Lakes sno-park include the easy 4.4-mile loop to the Swampy Lakes Shelter, the 6.2-mile Emil Nordeen Shelter loop, and a 9-mile loop to the Swede Ridge Shelter. The South Fork Trail descends to the Skyliner sno-park, a smaller nordic center accessed by driving west of Bend on Galveston Street. An 8-mile trail connects the Dutchman Flat and Swampy Lakes sno-parks, climbing through forest behind Tumalo Mountain.

Skiers and snowshoers can climb 1400 feet up Tumalo Mountain to an outstanding view. Ski directly up the cone-shaped mountain—any side will do, but Dutchman Flat is the usual starting point—and telemark down through the sparse forest. The open, high country between Broken Top and Tam McArthur Rim invites longer, cross-country tours. From the Dutchman Flat sno-park, Broken Top's spectacular crater is 6 miles via the snowed-over Crater Creek Ditch. McArthur Rim is 8 miles. The Green Lakes are 9 miles. Carry a compass and emergency gear.

Paved Road 16 from Sisters is plowed in winter to the Three Creek sno-park. From there, a 4.9-mile ski tour reaches scenic Three Creek Lake. Very strong skiers can climb onward to astonishing views on the Tam MacArthur Rim Trail.

From mid-April to June, cars can drive from Sisters up unplowed Roads 15 and 1524 to the Pole Creek Trailhead, where dramatic (but unmarked) ski tours to Soap Creek's meadows below North Sister begin. Expert backcountry skiers can tackle a stupendous three-day tour that traverses south from Pole Creek via the Chambers Lakes and the Green Lakes to a shuttle car at the Dutchman Flat sno-park at Mount Bachelor.

Ski tours in the McKenzie Pass area are described in Area 10, but the Three Sisters maps cover two additional, easy trips on Highway 242. Park at the White Branch snow gate, where plowing ends, and ski 2.5 miles to see the ice cascades of the 1-mile Proxy Falls loop trail, or ski 4 miles to the 1.4-mile Linton Lake Trail.

 Waldo Lake

Location: 59 miles southeast of Eugene, 43 miles southwest of Bend
Size: 148 square miles, including Maiden Peak
Status: 58 square miles designated wilderness (1984)
Terrain: Lake-dotted upland forests
Elevation: 2480 feet–7818 feet
Management: Deschutes NF, Willamette NF
Topographic maps: Waldo Lake Wilderness, PCT Oregon Central Portion (USFS); Three Sisters, Willamette Pass X-C Ski Trails (Geo-Graphics)

Sailboats ply Oregon's second-largest natural body of water, a brilliant blue lake so pure and clear that fish are visible 100 feet below the surface. The forests rimming Waldo Lake shelter hundreds of smaller lakes and a thorough trail network.

Climate

Snowfall from November to April accounts for most of the area's 60 to 75 inches of annual precipitation. Trails are generally clear of snow in late June. Headnets or repellent are necessary from early July to early August, when mosquitoes are plentiful.

Plants and Wildlife

Very few species live in Waldo Lake's renowned clear water, largely because the lake has no year-round inlet to bring nutrients for plant life.

The Charlton Butte–Cultus Lake area is frequented by bald eagles and the osprey that often roost at Crane Prairie Reservoir (a viewing blind is near Quinn River Campground). The Maiden Peak area, with the Pacific Northwest's largest stands of mountain hemlock, provides known habitat for the shy wolverine, threatened in Oregon. The meadows and high ridges west of Waldo Lake support a large Roosevelt elk herd. Black bear, cougar, bobcat, fisher, and marten are found throughout the area.

Sheepmen torched the forests of the Taylor Burn area around 1900 to encourage grass growth, but the result was a vast, even-aged stand of fire-resilient lodgepole pine.

Geology

During the Ice Age, sheet glaciers covered the entire Cascade crest here, creating the many lake basins. Maiden Peak, Charlton Butte, The Twins, and Cultus Mountain are the largest of the many geologically recent volcanoes in the area. Irish Mountain is an older, heavily eroded volcanic plug.

History

In 1888, Salem Judge John B. Waldo (1844–1907) and four companions were the first white men to travel the length of Oregon's Cascade Range from Willamette Pass to Mount Shasta. Klovdahl Bay is named for an engineer who built a tunnel there in 1912–14 to tap Waldo Lake for irrigation and power, but the tunnel failed to work properly.

In the 1970s the Forest Service paved the lake's access roads and built large campgrounds with giant boat ramps to attract motorized recreation to Waldo Lake, then considered one of the purest lakes of its size in the world. Later studies showed the lake's clarity slowly decreasing, evidently because of fuel spills, campground runoff, and attempts to stock the lake with fish (at times dropped from aircraft). Motorboats are now limited (and may be banned), pit outhouses have been removed, and fish stocking has ceased.

Trees bent with winter snow

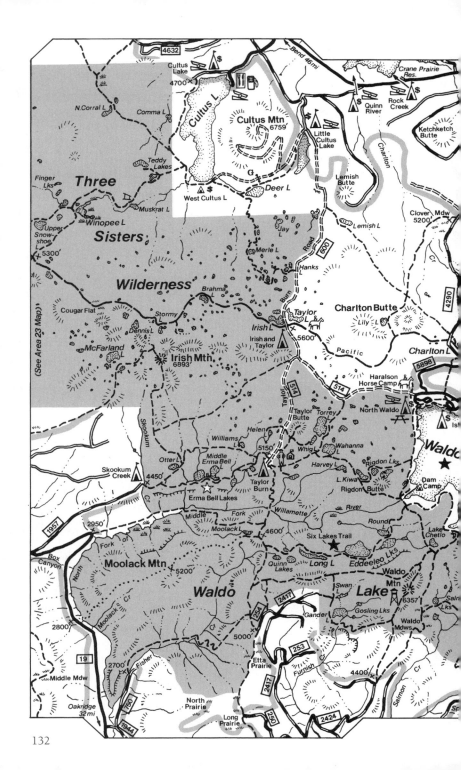

132

WALDO LAKE

The Maiden Peak Shelter on the Pacific Crest Trail

THINGS TO DO
Hiking

Two of the most popular 0.5-mile hikes are to Betty Lake (from Waldo Lake Road 5897) and to Upper and Lower Marilyn Lakes (via any of four paths off Road 500). Both trips lead to views of Diamond Peak across the lakes.

The three Rosary Lakes nestle in a forest basin between Pulpit Rock's crag and the broad cone of Maiden Peak. A 2.7-mile section of the Pacific Crest Trail (PCT) from Willamette Pass leads to large Lower Rosary Lake, traversing an old-growth subalpine fir and mountain hemlock forest with glimpses of Odell Lake. Overuse has stripped ground cover from several large campsites and much of the first Rosary Lake's shore.

Several short hikes sample Waldo Lake's shoreline. It is 1.7 miles from Shadow Bay Campground to a meadow by the rustic, three-sided South Waldo Shelter. From North Waldo Campground, a 3-mile hike reaches the lake outlet, source of the North Fork Middle Fork Willamette River. The trail traverses miles of blackened snags from a 1996 fire, but huckleberry bushes and some wildflowers are returning. After 2.3 miles, a sandy beach on the left invites swimming, though the water is chilly. Camping is banned on Waldo Lake's north shore except at the lake outlet. For an 8-mile loop, return via the Rigdon Lakes. They are flanked by a little rocky-topped butte with a good view.

Lily Lake is an easy 2.4 miles, mostly on the PCT, from Road 4290. The route passes lily pad ponds in the lodgepole forest below Charlton Butte. Minimally maintained trails east of the butte provide a loop trip option.

Cultus Lake is big, but you can hike half way around it as a day trip. It is 3.7 miles from Cultus Lake Campground to the West Cultus Lake camp. Those who plan a boat shuttle need only hike one way.

A waterfall connects popular, huckleberry-rimmed Middle Erma Bell Lake with its deep blue partner, Lower Erma Bell Lake. They are 1.7 and 2.1 miles along a nearly level, all-accessible trail from Skookum Creek Campground. Road access is via Oakridge; drive to Westfir and 32 miles beyond on Road 19 to the Skookum Creek turnoff.

Gander Lake, appropriately, is near Swan Lake and the Goslings. The downhill 1.2-mile trail to Gander Lake begins at the end of Road 2417. Follow paved Salmon Creek Road 24 east of Oakridge for 11 miles and fork left onto Road 2417 for 7.2 miles.

Waldo Mountain's fire lookout and viewpoint are the climax of a 2.9-mile trail that climbs 1900 feet. Drive to the trailhead as for Gander Lake, but turn off Road 2417 after 6 miles onto Road 2424. From the same trailhead, a much less strenuous 2.5-mile path leads to Waldo Meadows' wildflowers and the nearby Salmon Lakes. For a loop trip, connect the two hikes on a 8.5-mile circuit.

Black Creek's impressive, 2000-foot-deep canyon is the start of a day hike with variety. After climbing past Lillian Falls, the 3.8-mile Black Creek Trail takes hikers to a good picnic spot on Waldo Lake's Klovdahl Bay. To reach the trailhead follow Salmon Creek Road 24 from Oakridge for 14.2 miles, then continue straight on Road 2421 for 8.2 miles to its end.

Interesting cinder formations and a view from Mount Hood to Mount Thielsen are the rewards at the former lookout site atop conical Maiden Peak. The 5.8-mile trail gains 2800 feet at a good grade from Road 500, 0.5 mile south of Gold Lake Campground. A next-best viewpoint hike, atop The Twins' double summit, requires only a 3.3-mile hike (one way), gaining 1600 feet from paved Waldo Lake Road 5897.

Fuji Mountain is a cliff-topped old lookout site with an impressive view. A 1.5-mile trail reaches the peak from gravel Road 5883 (which joins Highway 58 east of Oakridge 15 miles), but many hikers prefer the 5.6-mile Fuji Mountain Trail from paved Waldo Lake Road 5897 near Gold Lake.

Two loop hikes prowl the forest east of Fuji Mountain, starting at paved Road 5897: the 9.7-mile trip from Gold Lake to Island Lakes, and the 9.5-mile circuit of Mount Ray past the South Waldo Shelter.

Irish Mountain has no trail to its summit, but the PCT skirts the small lakes around its base. The foot of the mountain is a 4-mile day hike on the PCT from the Taylor Burn Road.

Extending deep into the wilderness, the Taylor Burn Road (numbered 600 and 514) is a series of deep mudholes when wet and a rugged, high-centering track when dry. Vehicles able to survive 7 miles on this road can reach Taylor Burn Campground. From there, short hikes through the lodgepole pine forest lead to Wahanna, Upper Erma Bell, and half a dozen other lakes.

Many people enjoy hiking—or jogging or mountain biking—the demanding but scenic 20.2-mile trail around Waldo Lake in a single day. If 14.6 miles sounds better, plan a car shuttle between Shadow Bay and the North Waldo Campground. Shorten the trip further by arranging to meet a boat at Klovdahl Bay or the lake's outlet.

The Six Lakes Trail leads through deep woods to the two Quinn Lakes, Long Lake, and the three Eddeeleo Lakes. Expect rhododendron blooms in June, mosquitoes in July, and huckleberries in August. From Road 254, it is 2 miles to the first lake and 6 miles to the last. Backpackers can continue to Waldo Lake and the Rigdon Lakes. From Oakridge, drive Salmon Creek Road 24 for 11 miles, veer left onto Road 2417 for 10.9 miles, and turn left onto Road 254 for 0.3 mile to a wide spot on the right.

Winter Sports

Though snow at Willamette Pass is often wet, an abundance of trails and scenery make the area very popular. The Willamette Pass ski resort offers ski rentals and groomed trails for a fee, but the free trails to six nearby ski shelters provide more interesting goals. All of the shelters have woodstoves and are available free, without reservations, for overnight use, but only the Maiden Peak Shelter is fully enclosed and heatable.

Start at the Gold Lake sno-park on Highway 58, 0.5 mile west of Willamette Pass. On weekends, nordic ski patrol volunteers staff a little log cabin here, doling out advice, help, and sometimes even hot chocolate. For the easiest ski trip, start at the far right-hand end of the sno-park, ski along a snowed-under road, and keep left at junctions for 0.7 mile to the Westview Shelter. If you would rather ski to the Bechtel Shelter (2.1 miles from the Gold Lake sno-park) start out along the same snowed-under road, but keep right at junctions instead.

The very popular, easy 2.2-mile ski trail to Gold Lake (and yet another three-sided log shelter) begins across the highway from the entrance to the Gold Lake sno-park. Intermediate skiers can return from Gold Lake on side trails past the Marilyn Lakes.

The Salt Creek Falls sno-park is at the top of a 286-foot waterfall, Oregon's second tallest. From here, ski 0.3 mile back to Highway 58, cross it, and climb 1500 feet in 4 miles on Road 5894 to the Fuji Mountain Shelter, with its grand view of Diamond Peak.

The scenic basin of the Rosary Lakes is 2.8 miles from Willamette Pass, climbing gently on the PCT. Strong skiers with good routefinding skills can continue 3.7 miles on the PCT to the Maiden Peak Shelter, a fully enclosed, octagonal log cabin that sleeps fifteen (GPS location N43°37.931' W122°00.202'). Riding the ski area's chairlift to the top of Eagle Peak shortens the trek by half. The shelter serves as base camp for the challenging snowshoe or ski trek to the panoramic summit of Maiden Peak, gaining 1750 feet in 2.7 miles.

Snowmobiles are allowed on the snowed-under Waldo Lake Road 5897, but use is low enough that skiers are rarely disturbed on the demanding 8.9-mile trek to the South Waldo Shelter and the wilderness beyond.

Tours into the Diamond Peak Wilderness are discussed in that area's description (see Area 25).

Boating

In the still of the morning, canoeists can watch fish as much as 100 feet below the surface of 417-foot-deep, 10-square-mile Waldo Lake. From about 11 A.M. to sunset, a steady southwest wind fills the sails of sailboats and creates sizable waves that keep canoeists close to shore. Note that dangerous rock reefs near North Waldo and Shadow Bay can be obscured by choppy water.

Waldo, Davis, Odell, and Little Cultus Lakes have 10-mile-per-hour limits for power boats; motorized trolling is banned on Davis Lake. Cultus Lake, with no speed limit, is abuzz with waterskiers. Motors are prohibited on all other lakes.

25 Diamond Peak

Location: 62 miles southeast of Eugene, 64 miles southwest of Bend
Size: 126 square miles, including Cowhorn Mountain
Status: 82 square miles designated wilderness (1964, 1984)
Terrain: Snowpeak, forested uplands, lakes
Elevation: 4240 feet–8744 feet
Management: Deschutes NF, Willamette NF
Topographic maps: Diamond Peak Wilderness, Willamette Pass X-C Ski Trails (Geo-Graphics); Diamond Peak Wilderness, PCT Central Oregon Portion, Rogue-Umpqua Divide and Oregon Cascades Recreation Area (USFS)

Diamond Peak is not the only summit rising above this area's broad forests. Four other less-well-known crags top 7000 feet, each surrounded by its own scenic lakes and trails.

Climate

Snowfall from November through April accounts for much of the area's annual precipitation, which totals 80 inches in the west and 40 inches in the east. Most trails are snow-free by July 1, but hikers must cross snowfields on the Pacific Crest Trail (PCT) over Cowhorn Mountain and Diamond Peak until about August 1. Mosquitoes are a quite a problem from early July to early August.

Plants and Wildlife

Alpine scree slopes are habitat for pikas and marmots. They also provide footholds for lupine, penstemon, and heather. Dense mountain hemlock forests surround the peaks, leaving few openings for meadows. Lower forests are dominated by lodgepole pine

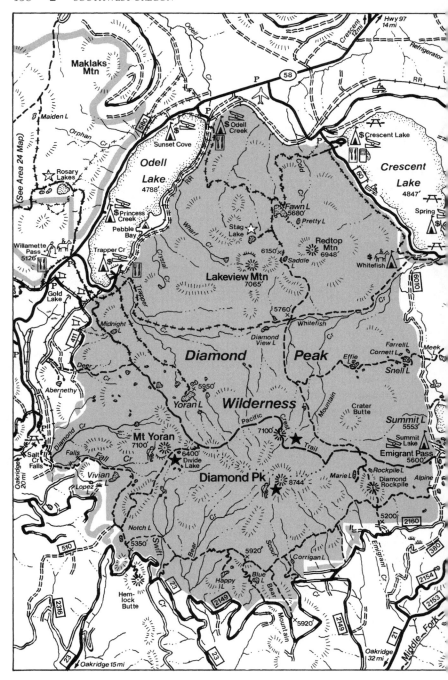

DIAMOND PEAK

0   1   2mi
0 1 2 3km

and bear grass in the east, and by Douglas fir, rhododendrons, and huckleberries in the west. Roosevelt elk are frequent until the first snows.

Geology

The tallest peaks are the eroded remnants of extinct volcanoes. Odell Lake and Crescent Lake fill the U-shaped gouges left by vanished Ice Age glaciers. The lakes prove the ancient glaciers were several miles wide, flowing east from the Cascade passes.

History

John Diamond first climbed and named Diamond Peak in 1852 while leading an exploration party from Eugene that hoped to survey an Oregon Trail shortcut across the Cascades. Misled by word that the proposed shortcut was complete, 1500 people with 650 wagons left the usual Oregon Trail route in Idaho and followed Elijah Elliott through the desert to central Oregon. There the "Lost Wagon Train" had trouble deciding which of the Cascade peaks was Diamond's landmark. They followed his sporadic blazes to Emigrant Pass at Summit Lake, arduously hewing a wagon route from the dense forest. In mid-October, the starving pioneers finally abandoned their wagons in despair. A rescue party found them on the Middle Fork Willamette River and led them down to the Willamette Valley, where they doubled Lane County's population.

THINGS TO DO
Hiking

For a waterfall hike, start at the Salt Creek Falls picnic area off Highway 58, west of Willamette Pass 5 miles. Oregon's second-tallest cascade, Salt Creek Falls, drops 286 feet from the picnic area. Cross a footbridge

Mount Yoran from Divide Lake

and take a 3.4-mile loop trail to lacy, 100-foot Diamond Creek Falls. For a longer hike, continue up the Vivian Lake Trail past several more falls for 2.3 miles to huckleberry-rimmed Vivian Lake, with a reflection of Mount Yoran's monolith.

From Willamette Pass, an easy, 3.3-mile segment of the PCT leads through old-growth forest above Odell Lake to tree-rimmed Midnight Lake. Nearby, a trailhead opposite the Trapper Creek Campground serves as a starting point for two popular, ambitious day hikes to lakes with fine views of Diamond Peak. Yoran Lake is 5 miles on a steady uphill grade through forest, and Diamond View Lake is 5.4 miles up the Trapper Creek Trail.

Fawn Lake is also a popular destination, 3.8 trail miles from Odell Lake Lodge or 3.4 trail miles from the Crescent Lake Campground entrance. Worthwhile side trips lead 1.4 miles to shallow Stag Lake, at the foot of Lakeview Mountain's impressive cliffs, and 1.8 miles up to little Saddle Lake.

Trails fan out from Crescent Lake and Summit Lake to dozens of quiet lakes among the pines. The Windy Lake group is 3.9 miles from Road 60 at Crescent Lake; the Bingham Lake cluster is 3 miles from Road 60.

The PCT climbs unusually high over Diamond Peak and Cowhorn Mountain to sweeping vistas on above-timberline slopes. On Cowhorn Mountain, the PCT comes within an easy 0.4-mile scramble of the craggy summit, 3.5 miles from Windigo Pass. The PCT's best viewpoints on Diamond Peak are 6 miles from Emigrant Pass—a long but rewarding day hike. Really energetic hikers can follow the PCT to timberline, then climb Diamond Peak's smooth southern ridge cross-country to the exhilarating summit view. The 12-mile round-trip climb requires no technical skills, only stamina.

Sawtooth Mountain overtowers a scenic, less-visited network of trails. From Timpanogas Campground, hike 1.9 miles to a backcountry campground at Indigo Lake, directly below the mountain's cliffs. For a 9.2-mile loop around Sawtooth Mountain, turn left just before Indigo Lake and then keep right; this sometimes faint loop comes within an easy 0.4-mile bushwhack of the mountain's panoramic summit.

For a backpackable 9.9-mile loop from the Timpanogas Campground, hike left halfway around Timpanogas Lake, climb 1.1 mile to the Windy Pass Trail, and keep right at all junctions, returning past Indigo Lake. A 1-mile side trip from this loop climbs 0.3 mile to the PCT, follows the PCT south 0.3 mile to the trail's high point, and then scrambles left along a ridge to Cowhorn Mountain's summit.

To reach the Sawtooth Mountain area from Oakridge, follow Highway 58 a mile east of town, turn right at a sign for Hills Creek Reservoir, follow paved Road 21 for 31.2 miles, head left on Road 2154, and follow signs for Timpanogas Lake 9.3 miles.

Hidden on the less-visited west side of Diamond Peak are a collection of good day hikes—and prime huckleberry picking in late August. Some of the area's best wildflower meadows border Blue Lake (1 mile) and Happy Lake (3 miles) along an up-and-down trail from Road 2149.

The former lookout site atop Hemlock Butte offers a panoramic view of Mount Yoran and Diamond Peak and requires only a 0.5-mile hike from Road 2145. But for mountain views, few trails can match the 4-mile path from Road 23 to Divide Lake. The route passes narrow Notch Lake in a forest, then switchbacks up a ridge to a timberline valley of tiny lakes below Mount Yoran's sheer face.

Trailheads on the west side of Diamond Peak are reached via Oakridge. Follow Highway 58 a mile east of town, turn right at a sign for Hills Creek Reservoir for 0.5 mile to an intersection, and go straight on Road 23.

Long-distance hikers often choose the scenic, 28.7-mile section of the PCT from Willamette Pass to Windigo Pass, but there are other good routes as well. Most spectacular is the 29-mile circuit of Diamond Peak, passing Divide Lake and Diamond Rockpile.

Cross-country hiking is not difficult in the high, open forests, and is particularly worthwhile in the lake-dotted forests between Yoran Lake and Willamette Pass, because the lakes directly along the PCT are overused.

Climbing

Diamond Peak's smooth scree ridges make it a hike rather than a technical climb. Likewise, hikers hardly have to use their hands to summit Cowhorn Mountain and Sawtooth Mountain. Mount Yoran is a bit harder, requiring level I-3 skills.

Diamond Creek Falls, on a 3.4-mile loop trail from Salt Creek Falls

Winter Sports

A network of cross-country trails centers on the nordic ski patrol shelter at the Gold Lake sno-park. Tours north of this area are described under Area 24. To the south, the well-traveled PCT leads 2.7 miles at a modest grade through forest to Midnight Lake. Returning on a loop past the Bechtel Shelter is not much longer. The unmarked 6.3-mile trail to Yoran Lake and the 7.1-mile trail to Diamond View Lake are for skiers with routefinding skills and emergency gear.

Fawn Lake is a very popular, intermediate-level goal. One trail there climbs 3.8 miles from Odell Lake Lodge (ski rentals available). A slightly easier route from the

Crescent Lake sno-park makes the climb in 3.4 miles. The additional side trip to Stag Lake is worth the extra 1.4 miles.

Redtop Mountain makes an excellent cross-country goal for advanced skiers willing to gain 2100 feet in 4 miles. The summit has a panoramic view of Diamond Peak, and the open, upper slopes are often draped with dry powder snow. From the Crescent Lake sno-park, ski 0.5 mile toward Fawn Lake and then follow a compass bearing due east up through the woods.

Skiers should avoid the tempting railroad grade along Odell Lake because of frequent high-speed trains. Safer tours along Odell Lake follow forest roads above Sunset Cove.

Boating

High-elevation, 500-acre Summit Lake not only has a postcard view of Diamond Peak but it also offers reliable afternoon breezes for sailboaters and an interesting shoreline for canoeists. Motors are permitted, but a 10 mile-per-hour limit prevails, and a rough dirt access road prevents crowds. Both Crescent Lake and Odell Lake have marinas with boat rentals.

26 Hardesty Mountain

Location: 25 miles southeast of Eugene
Size: 22 square miles
Status: Undesignated wilderness
Terrain: Densely forested valleys, ridges
Elevation: 940 feet–4616 feet
Management: Willamette NF, Umpqua NF
Topographic map: Mount June (USGS)

Soothing shades of green—moss, sword ferns, vanilla leaf—line the trails of Hardesty Mountain, where hiking is available year round, just 30 minutes from Eugene.

Climate

The ridges here are usually snow-free by mid-April, and lower trails are open year round. Rain accounts for the area's 55 inches of annual precipitation. Mount June's name commemorates a year when snow lingered there until that month.

Plants and Wildlife

In the area's lush old-growth forests of Douglas fir, western red cedar, and bigleaf maple, watch for rare Pacific giant salamanders. Shiny, 7 to 12 inches long, they are easily distinguished from the orange-bellied, rough-skinned newts common in western Oregon. Also look for delicate calypso orchids on the forest floor in May and showy Cascade lilies and bear grass on ridges in June. Spotted owls and goshawks nest throughout the area, while osprey and bald eagles prefer lower elevations nearer to Lookout Reservoir. Whenever eagles nest in a tree within a quarter mile of a trail, the Forest Service closes that trail January through September.

Geology
Though dense forest obscures most rocks, ridge-top outcroppings reveal volcanic andesite typical of the Old Cascades, 16 to 25 million years old.

History
The Civilian Conservation Corps built most of the area's trails between 1933 and 1938 to access lookout towers on Hardesty Mountain and Mount June. Foundations of the towers remain.

THINGS TO DO
Hiking
Three hikes begin at a well-marked parking area near milepost 21 of Highway 58. For a good kids' hike, walk up the Hardesty Trail 0.2 mile and turn right on the Goodman Creek Trail. This path contours 1.8 miles to a small waterfall and log footbridge, continues 2.2 miles through towering old-growth woods to a crossing of Road 5833, and continues as the 2.5-mile Eagles Rest Trail, climbing past the Ash Swale Shelter and crossing

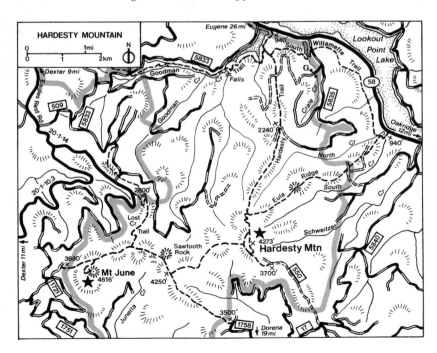

Fog on the trail to Mount June

paved Eagles Rest Road before reaching Eagles Rest's 3022-foot summit viewpoint.

For a low-elevation walk from the same trailhead, hike 0.3 mile up the Hardesty Trail and turn left 5 miles on the South Willamette Trail to its end at the Eula Ridge Trailhead on Highway 58.

The Hardesty Trail itself gains 3300 feet in 5 steep miles to a partly overgrown lookout site. For a loop, return on the even steeper, 3.7-mile Eula Ridge Trail and the 5-mile South Willamette Trail. An easier, 0.9-mile route to Hardesty Mountain's summit begins on Road 550, an unimproved spur of Patterson Mountain Road 5840.

Mount June, a loftier former lookout site than Hardesty Mountain, commands a much better view from Mount Jefferson to Mount Thielsen. A 1.2-mile trail switchbacks up to Mount June's cliff-edged summit opening. For a longer hike, continue eastward along meadow-topped Sawtooth Ridge on a trail lined with wildflowers, viewpoints, and rock spires. Hardesty Mountain is 3.6 miles past Mount June on this scenic route.

To reach Mount June, drive 11.4 miles east from Interstate 5 on Highway 58 to

Dexter Dam and turn right at a sign for Lost Creek. After 3.7 miles, turn left across a somewhat hidden bridge onto the signed Eagles Rest Road. Follow this paved, one-lane route 7.8 miles to a fork. Following a hiker-symbol pointer, keep left on Road 20-1-14 for a mile to a sign on the left identifying the Lost Creek Trail. This pleasant path does lead to the top of Mount June in 4 miles; however, those seeking the easier 1.2-mile trail to Mount June's summit should continue 5.1 miles farther on this road, which soon turns to gravel. At the far edge of a fenced tree plantation turn left on Road 1721 for 0.1 mile, then turn left on Road 941 for 0.4 mile to the Mount June Trailhead.

Boulder Creek

Location: 47 miles east of Roseburg
Size: 33 square miles
Status: 30 square miles designated wilderness (1984)
Terrain: Steep, forested valley
Elevation: 1600 feet–5600 feet
Management: Umpqua NF
Topographic maps: Boulder Creek Wilderness (USFS)

Boulder Creek's swimmable pools and small waterfalls are the center of a broad, steep valley of old-growth forests with ponderosa pines. Because this wilderness is not in the High Cascades, it is often overlooked, yet it is one of the few Oregon wilderness areas hikable in winter. If you are eager to start the summer's backpacking in April or May, try Boulder Creek.

Climate
Lower trails are generally snow-free all year. Winter and spring rains swell Boulder Creek, requiring knee-deep wading on trail fords. The area's annual precipitation is 60 inches.

Plants and Wildlife
Pine Bench features an old-growth ponderosa pine forest with grassy openings, unusual so far west of the Cascade summit. Elsewhere, the forest is an interesting mix of gigantic sugar pine, Douglas fir, western hemlock, droopy incense cedar, and gnarled yew. A 1996 fire swept through nearly half of this wilderness, clearing out underbrush and leaving a healthier patchwork of old-growth trees. The rugged valleys are home to an estimated 30 black bear and 100 Roosevelt elk, but both species are shy.

Geology
Eagle Rock and other spires of the Umpqua Rocks are eroded remnants of 30-million-year-old Old Cascades volcanoes. Pine Bench's basalt plateau, however, is only a few

thousand years old, part of a lava flow that originated 20 miles away in the High Cascades and poured down the North Umpqua River Valley, filling the canyon from wall to wall. Later erosion has left fragments of the old flow as pinnacles and benches along the river.

History
Several caves in the area preserve evidence of Indian camps. Arrowheads and other artifacts are federally protected.

THINGS TO DO
Hiking
The most popular introduction to this wilderness is the 2.3-mile trail to Pine Bench's cliff-edge viewpoint. To find the Soda Springs Trailhead, drive Highway 138 east of Roseburg 54.7 miles. Between mileposts 54 and 55, turn left at a sign for Slide Creek, and immediately turn left again onto gravel Soda Springs Road for 1.4 miles to the trailhead on the right. The path ducks under a 12-foot pipe that carries most of the North Umpqua River to a power station, and then climbs 1.3 miles amid 4-foot-thick Douglas firs and June-blooming rhododendrons to Pine Bench's plateau. Continue 0.6 mile across the mesa, turn right for 0.4 mile, and follow the sound of water left 100 yards to a gushing spring near several campsites. Climb out a rock promontory nearby for a breathtaking view of Boulder Creek's canyon.

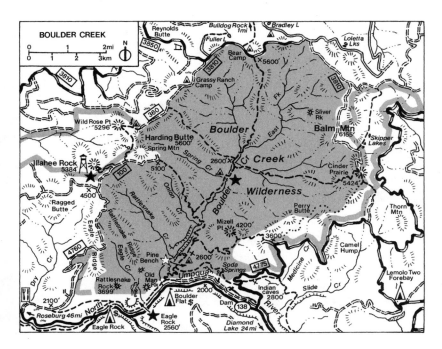

For a longer day hike, follow the trail north from Pine Bench 1.7 miles to a log crossing of pebbly, 20-foot Boulder Creek. Explore upstream 100 yards to a waterfall and cold, swimmable pool. Backpackers can continue on the trail upstream another 2.9 miles, past good campsites and three easy creek crossings, to the forks of Boulder Creek. From there the trail climbs a ridge 3.9 miles to Road 3810 near Bear Camp.

Two of the area's best viewpoints are Mizell Point and Illahee Rock. The 1.2-mile route to Mizell Point follows the faint Perry Butte Stub Trail from a spur of paved Road 4775 up and down to the viewpoint's 200-yard side trail along a rocky ridge.

The view from Illahee Rock is so good that two lookout towers remain there, a 1925 cupola-style building and a 1958 tower that is still in use. To find the 0.7-mile trail to Illahee Rock, drive Highway 138 to the Dry Creek Store, turn north on Road 4760 for 8 miles, go straight on Road 100 for 1.3 miles, and turn left on steep Road 104 for 0.2 mile to its end. The nearby Wild Rose Trail starts from Road 100 in a clearcut but leads 1.4 miles to Wild Rose Point, a bluff strewn with wildflowers.

The well-built, 79-mile North Umpqua River Trail follows the river from its source at Maidu Lake in the Mount Thielsen Wilderness (see Area 28) to Swiftwater Park, just 22 miles from Roseburg. To sample the trail at Boulder Creek, where it is open to equestrians and bicyclists, start at the Soda Springs Trailhead and walk or drive the bumpy Soda Springs Road west 1.2 miles to a small trailhead. Then hike onward on the North Umpqua Trail 2.9 miles, below Eagle Rock's crags, to the Highway 138 river bridge.

Lookout buildings from 1958 and 1925 on Illahee Rock

Climbing

Eagle Rock is the largest of a cluster of rarely visited andesite crags with challenging technical climbs. Eagle Rock was first climbed in 1958 via the northern Madrone Tree Route (level I-5.2-A2). The 400-foot South Face cliffs present a level II-5.6 challenge.

Old Man Rock, rated I-5.4-A1, remained unclimbed until 1963. The spire directly north of it, Old Woman, has I-5.2 and I-5.6 routes. Other crags in the area are easier, including prominent Rattlesnake Rock (I-3).

28 Mount Thielsen

Location: 72 miles east of Roseburg, 80 miles northeast of Medford
Size: 126 square miles
Status: 86 square miles designated wilderness (1984)
Terrain: Snowpeak, high forest
Elevation: 4260 feet–9182 feet
Management: Umpqua NF, Deschutes NF, Winema NF
Topographic maps: Mount Thielsen Wilderness, PCT Central Oregon Portion (USFS)

The "Lightning Rod of the Cascades," Mount Thielsen's spire towers above the lakes, meadows, and high forests to the north of Crater Lake.

Climate

Snowfall from mid-October to April accounts for most of the area's 60 inches of annual precipitation. Most trails are snow-free by mid-June, but the Pacific Crest Trail (PCT) may remain blocked until late July. Mosquitoes are plentiful for about four weeks following snow melt.

Plants and Wildlife

Nearly pure stands of lodgepole pine blanket the lower areas, where the pumice and ash soils dry to dust in summer. Nearly pure stands of mountain hemlock cover the higher elevations, where lingering snow provides summer moisture. Clark's nutcrackers, gray jays, and golden-mantled ground squirrels are abundant throughout. Look for elk and red-headed pileated woodpeckers. Diamond Lake originally had no fish but is now stocked to provide trout.

Geology

A 5-foot-thick ground cover of lighter-than-water pumice rock remains as evidence that this area lay directly downwind of the cataclysmic explosion that created Crater Lake's caldera 7700 years ago.

Mount Thielsen, extinct for at least 100,000 years, was stripped to its central plug by the same Ice Age glaciers that carved the basins for Diamond Lake and Miller Lake. In 1965, after centuries with no glaciers at all, the peak was found to shelter two small moving ice masses on its northern flank.

Lightning strikes the Mount Thielsen's spire so often that carrot-shaped "lightning tubes" and glassy, brownish-green fulgurites of recrystalized rock form at the summit.

THINGS TO DO
Hiking

The most popular of the area's many viewpoint hikes is the Howlock Mountain Trail to Timothy Meadows. Starting from the horse corrals at North Diamond Lake, the route ducks through a tunnel under Highway 138 and climbs through viewless forests for 3 miles before reaching the meadows along splashing Thielsen Creek. Here are good picnicking swales with wildflowers and glimpses of Thielsen's summit. However, it is worth climbing 2.7 miles farther along the creek for the astonishing view at Thielsen Creek Camp, where the peak looms like the Matterhorn.

Once at Thielsen Creek Camp, there are two tempting alternatives to simply returning the way you came. It is 4.3 miles farther to make a loop to the north, following the PCT past serrated Sawtooth Ridge to Howlock Meadows and turning left back to Timothy Meadows. On the other hand, you will add only 2.4 miles to your return trip if you make a loop to the south, following the PCT to far-ranging views on the flank of Mount Thielsen before descending to Diamond Lake via the Mount Thielsen and Spruce Ridge Trails.

Mount Thielsen from Thielsen Meadow

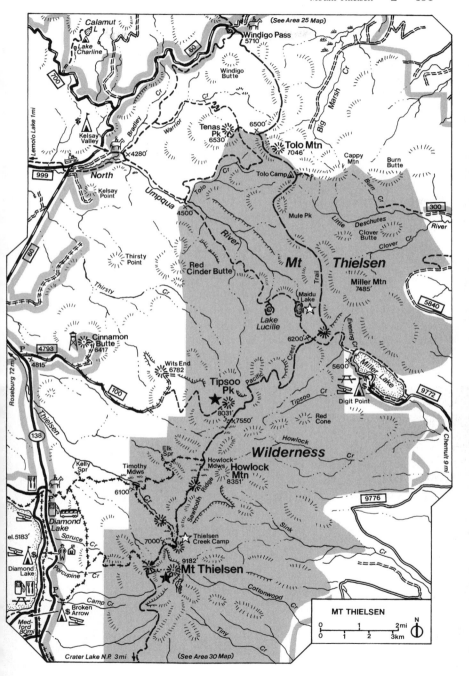

MT THIELSEN

Backpacking breaks these distances into shorter hikes. The only year-round water source on Mount Thielsen's flanks is Thielsen Creek. Be sure to camp in the forest well away from the fragile clearings at Timothy Meadows or Thielsen Creek Camp, and build no fire.

Tipsoo Peak is one of the few 8000-foot Cascade peaks with a well-graded trail to its summit. The view stretches from the Three Sisters to Mount Shasta, with Mount Thielsen front and center. The 3.1-mile trail up Tipsoo Peak gains 1780 feet of elevation from Wits End Road 100. From the top, it is an easy scramble down loose cinders to the alpine meadows along the PCT.

Those who have already climbed to Cowhorn Mountain on the PCT from Windigo Pass (see Area 25, Diamond Peak) might try three rarely visited viewpoint goals south of the pass. Tolo Mountain and Tenas Peak are both 5 miles; Windigo Butte's little cone is a 1.5 mile cross-country climb.

By far the most popular lakeside trail is the 11.5-mile paved bike path around Diamond Lake. It is easiest to start at the Diamond Lake Lodge, where you can rent bicycles. The path traverses 3 miles of campgrounds on the east shore, circumvents 2 miles of private cabins on the west shore, and delivers 2 miles of great mountain views on the north shore.

A much quieter, 5.1-mile lakeshore path circles Miller Lake from the Digit Point Campground. From the same trailhead, you can also climb 3.6 miles to a viewpoint on the PCT (where cliffs overlook Miller Lake), or cross the Cascade Divide to forest-rimmed Maidu Lake. Reach the trailhead via Road 9772, which leaves Highway 97 at a sign for the Chemult Recreation Site, between mileposts 202 and 203, 0.5 mile north of Chemult.

Backpackers and equestrians have several long-distance trip options. The PCT covers 29.4 miles from Windigo Pass to the North Crater Trailhead beside Highway 138, on the National Park boundary. Also, a popular 8-mile segment of the North Umpqua River Trail climbs to Maidu and Lucille Lakes from the Kelsay Valley Trailhead.

Throughout the area, water sources are scarce. For solitude, carry enough water for a dry camp and strike off cross-country through the open, easily traversed forests.

Thousands of hikers climb—or nearly climb—Mount Thielsen each summer. Those without technical climbing experience must settle for the excellent view at the base of the near-vertical, 80-foot summit spire. Even this goal is 5 miles away from Highway 138 and 3700 feet up. From the Mount Thielsen Trailhead on Highway 138 above Diamond Lake, follow the path 3.8 miles up to the PCT, and continue straight up a ridge crest on an unofficial trail 0.8 mile. When the path peters out above timberline, continue up dangerously slippery scree slopes 0.4 mile, spiraling slightly to the right, to a ledge at the eastern base of the summit pinnacle. The final 80 feet require the adept use of hands and feet to chimney up cracks in the rock.

Hikers who do not want to risk scaling Mount Thielsen might consider climbing Mount Bailey instead. This broad, 8368-foot summit rises from the opposite side of Diamond Lake. A 4.9-mile trail climbs 3100 feet from Road 300, a spur from the southwest part of the road around Diamond Lake.

Climbing

Mount Thielsen's summit pinnacle is a level I-3 climb from the southeast. A more difficult and extremely dangerous route to the summit, the III-5.7 McLoughlin Memorial, involves six rope lengths of technical work on rotten, east-facing cliffs, accessed via Thielsen Creek Camp.

Winter Sports

Resorts at North Diamond Lake and Lemolo Lake offer cross-country ski rentals and marked winter trails. All of the hiking trails between Diamond Lake and Mount Thielsen make good, if steep, cross-country routes. Perhaps the best level ski trail is the 11.5-mile bike path around Diamond Lake.

The fine view at Cinnamon Butte's lookout tower is 3 miles up from another Highway 138 sno-park. The reward for climbing 1600 feet on the lookout road's steady grade is a 2-mile downhill glide. For a backcountry adventure, ski 8 miles from Highway 138 to Tipsoo Peak and snow camp in the glorious, 7550-foot meadows along the PCT.

Boating

Diamond Lake and Miller Lake offer canoeing and sailing. Motors are permitted but with a 10-mile-per-hour limit.

29 Rogue-Umpqua Divide

Location: 75 miles east of Roseburg, 56 miles northeast of Medford
Size: 102 square miles
Status: 52 square miles designated wilderness (1984)
Terrain: High meadows, forested valleys, ridge-top rock outcroppings
Elevation: 2300 feet–6783 feet
Management: Umpqua NF, Rogue River NF
Topographic map: Rogue-Umpqua Divide Wilderness (USFS)

Atop a high divide west of Crater Lake, this relatively undiscovered area boasts alpine meadows, interesting rock formations, and small lakes.

Climate

Snow covers most trails from mid-November to mid-May. Annual precipitation is 50 inches; summers are dry.

Plants and Wildlife

The ridges feature showy Cascade lilies and red paintbrush in June and ripe huckleberries in August. The bright red snow plant, a rare saprophyte, brightens the Fish

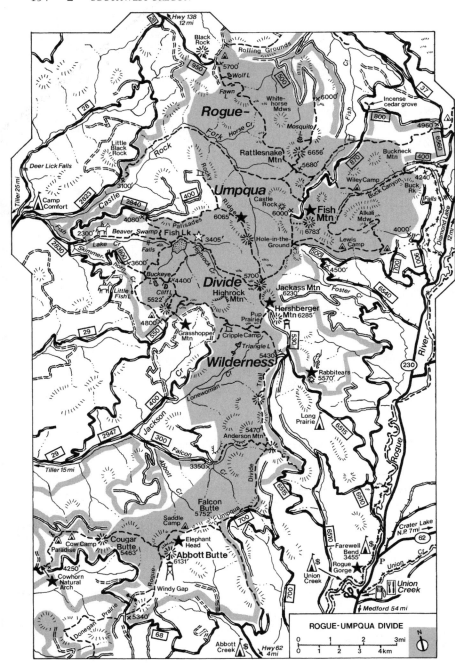

ROGUE-UMPQUA DIVIDE

0 1 2 3mi
0 1 2 3 4km

N

Lake area as snow melts. Forests include sugar p
eastern slopes, true firs on the ridges, and Dougla
like grove of old-growth incense cedars makes a
the area.

Geology
The area belongs to the heavily eroded, 16- to 25-mil
ciers broadened the valleys and left Buck Canyon, a m
slide from Grasshopper Mountain dammed Fish Lak
Falls about 6000 years ago. Buckeye and Cliff Lakes fil   uneven surface
of the old slide.

THINGS TO DO
Hiking
Two trails lead to popular Fish Lake from Road 2840. This 90-acre lake, rimmed with
forest and mountain views, was named by a group of 1889 explorers who caught 70
fish there in an hour, using venison for bait. A 3.8-mile route to the lake ascends Fish
Lake Creek through an old-growth forest and passes within earshot of an 80-foot
waterfall. The shorter Beaver Swamp Trail from Road 2840 loses 700 feet through a
regrowing burn area to reach Fish Lake in 1.5 miles. Once at Fish Lake, it is tempting
to add a 5.6-mile loop past Cliff and Buckeye Lakes, with their close-up views of Grasshopper Mountain's cliffs. Another side trip climbs to the excellent views (and avalanche
lilies) atop Grasshopper Mountain, 1.9 trail miles beyond Cliff Lake.

  For a spectacular 12.6-mile loop hike from the Beaver Swamp Trailhead, hike

At high elevations, phlox forms a cushion of white flowers

Buckeye Lake and Grasshopper Mountain

past Fish Lake on the trail up Highrock Creek (amid 10-foot-thick Douglas firs) and keep left at all junctions to return on the Rocky Ridge Trail, a path lined with wildflowers, viewpoints, and rock pinnacles.

To find the Beaver Swamp Trailhead from Interstate 5, turn off at Canyonville, follow signs for Crater Lake 23 miles to Tiller, turn left onto Road 46 (toward South Umpqua Falls) for 24 miles, veer right onto one-lane, paved Road 2823 for 2.4 miles, fork right on gravel Road 2830 for 3.9 miles, and fork left on Road 2840 for 5.1 miles.

If your goal is Buckeye Lake, a shorter, kid-friendly 1.4-mile trail begins at the Skimmerhorn Trailhead on nearby Road 600. This is also the place to start a lovely 10.4-mile loop around Grasshopper Mountain that visits Buckeye, Cliff, and Little Fish Lakes.

Elephanthead, a dramatic, elephant-shaped cliff on the shoulder of Abbott Butte, overlooks a lush wildflower meadow fringed with true firs and quaking aspen. It is a 4.3-mile hike along the Rogue-Umpqua Divide Trail from the summit of Road 68. Along the way you can detour 0.7 mile to the Cascade lilies, views, and abandoned lookout atop Abbott Butte. To find the trailhead from Medford, take the Crater Lake Highway north past Prospect 6 miles and turn left on Woodruff Meadows Road 68 for 4.9 miles of pavement and another 7.4 miles of one-lane gravel road to a trailhead pullout at a pass. To find the trailhead from Tiller, take Road 46 toward South Umpqua Falls for 5.3 miles, turn right on Jackson Creek Road 29 for 12.5 miles, and turn right at a "Huckleberry Gap" sign for 15 gravel miles.

Hershberger Mountain's restored 1925 fire lookout has a stunning view, accessed by a 100-foot trail from the end of Road 530. Just 0.5 mile down the road, a pullout at a switchback serves as the trailhead for several day hikes. A nearly level 3-mile trail north to Hole-in-the-Ground (a high meadow basin) provides a close look at Fish Mountain, the tallest point in Oregon's western Cascades. To the west of Hershberger Mountain, Grasshopper Mountain's viewpoint is 4.3 miles. The route passes Pup Prairie, the leaky Cripple Creek Shelter, groves of huge Douglas fir, and Grasshopper Meadow.

No trail scales the area's highest peak, Fish Mountain, but a cross-country scramble to the top yields views from Mount Shasta to the Three Sisters. From the end of Road 870, walk the trail 0.3 mile south to a crest, then turn left 0.5 mile up an open, trailless ridge to the summit.

To explore the high basins at the foot of Fish Mountain, try the 7.7-mile hike through Alkali Meadows and down Buck Canyon. June wildflowers in the beautiful area's unfortunately cow-trampled meadows include fawn lilies, marsh marigolds, and pink kalmia. If you can not arrange a car shuttle for this hike (between Road 700 and Road 400), park at the end of Road 400 and content yourself with a hike to the top of Buck Canyon's meadows.

Whitehorse Meadows, in a pass overlooking the forests of Castle Rock Fork's broad valley, makes a good day-hike goal. From the north, a 2.3-mile trail to the meadows from Road 950 offers a side trip to Wolf Lake. Reach Road 950 via Road 28, which joins the North Umpqua Highway 138 near Eagle Rock.

Another day-hike route to Whitehorse Meadows begins at Road 870 and traverses 4 miles along Rattlesnake Mountain. From this side, however, most hikers prefer instead to take a steep side trail up Rattlesnake Mountain (a fine viewpoint—with no rattlesnakes), making that summit's meadow their goal.

Several trips require backpacking gear. One of the best is the 13.4-mile loop trail from Fish Lake around the base of cliff-edged Highrock Mountain, traversing a series of high meadows and scenic passes.

The area's best-known backpacking route, the Rogue-Umpqua Divide Trail, follows a ridge crest the length of the wilderness—23.8 miles from Road 30 past Abbott Butte, Jackass Mountain, and Fish Mountain to Road 37—and even continues beyond toward Garwood Butte.

The 47.9-mile Upper Rogue River Trail parallels Highway 230 from Prospect to the northwest corner of Crater Lake National Park. Do not miss the dramatic section (not shown on map) that starts 1 mile south of Union Creek at the Natural Bridge Trailhead, where the river disappears into a lava tube. South of this point the path follows the river 3.5 miles to a crossing of Road 68 at Woodruff Bridge Campground, and then continues another 4.6 miles to River Bridge Campground, passing the churning slot of Takelma Gorge along the way.

Climbing

Hershberger Mountain Road 6515 passes within 300 yards of the base of Rabbitears, a pair of 400-foot pinnacles first scaled in 1921. Both spires require level I-4 climbing skills. Some summers the road to Rabbitears is gated closed until August 15 to protect endangered falcons nesting on the spires.

Winter Sports

When snow levels are low, nordic skiing is easy on segments of the Upper Rogue River Trail. Try the 3.5-mile trail section north from the snowed-under Union Creek Campground, along the narrow, 50-foot-deep Rogue River Gorge.

For deeper snow, try unplowed Road 6560, at the 4000-foot level. Ski past Muir Creek Falls to Buck Canyon, below towering Fish Mountain. Advanced skiers with compass and survival gear can continue west on the wilderness trail system. Beginners can prowl the level meadows between Road 900 and Highway 230.

30 Crater Lake

Location: 64 miles east of Medford, 49 miles northwest of Klamath Falls
Size: 286 square miles
Status: National park (1902)
Terrain: Cliff-edged lake, high forest, pumice desert
Elevation: 3977 feet–8929 feet
Management: Crater Lake National Park
Topographic maps: Crater Lake (USGS, 25 feet); PCT Central Oregon Portion (USFS)

Oregon's famous national park sees half a million visitors annually, yet away from the paved rim road the trails are only lightly used. On an average summer night, only a dozen backpackers camp in the area's 259 square miles of backcountry. In fact, the heaviest backcountry use comes in winter, when the snow is excellent for ski touring.

Climate

Average annual precipitation is 66 inches, largely measured by melting the area's 44 feet of snowfall. Snow closes most trails, and the rim road, from mid-October to mid-June. The eastern portion of the rim road past Mount Scott seldom opens before mid-July.

Plants and Wildlife

Virtually all life in the area was destroyed by Mount Mazama's eruption 7700 years ago. The 600 species of plants and many animals here are evidence of ongoing repopulation. Forests, largely of lodgepole pine, have spread nearly everywhere but the Pumice Desert, where volcanic debris fell 200 feet deep. The Pumice Desert's cinder soil holds so little moisture that only occasional bunchgrass and dwarf lupine can live there.

Most, but not all, Cascade wildflowers have reestablished themselves along the lake's alpine rim. Gnarled whitebark pines clinging to the rim withstand the cliff edge's fierce storm winds because their branches are so supple they can literally be tied in knots. The dominant animal species of the rim appear to be cute golden-mantled ground

Crater Lake and Wizard Island from the air in winter

squirrels and raucous, swooping Clark's nutcrackers, both of which aggressively encourage visitors to defy the park's ban on feeding wildlife.

Biologists theorize that the toads, garter snakes, and chipmunks living on Wizard Island migrated there overland when the lake was lower. The crayfish in Wizard Island's ponds were introduced by early visitors.

Visitors sometimes sight black bears, especially in or near the Mazama Campground. If you stay there, lock all food and cooler chests out of sight in your car at night. Though the bears generally avoid backcountry camps, backpackers should hang all food 10 feet off the ground and 5 feet from a tree trunk at night.

Geology

Crater Lake fills the caldera of Mount Mazama, a volcano that collapsed after a cataclysmic eruption about 5700 B.C.

Mount Mazama first began to form 500,000 years ago, when neighboring Union Peak and Mount Thielsen were already extinct. At its height, Mount Mazama was a broad, 12,000-foot mountain the size of Mount Adams. Ice Age glaciers gouged its flanks with valleys (still visible as Sun Notch and Kerr Notch). Smaller volcanoes sprouted on its sides (Timber Crater, Red Cone, and Hillman Peak). Its slopes oozed thick lava flows (visible in cross-section as The Watchman, Llao Rock, and Cloudcap).

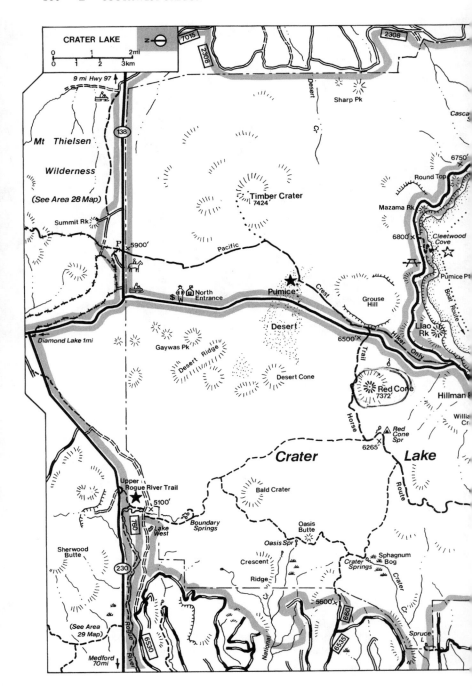

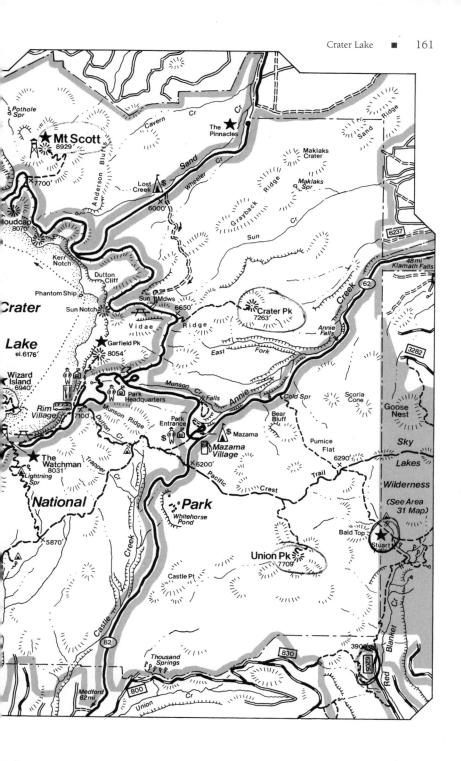

Pothole Spr

★ Mt Scott
8929

Cavern Cr

Cr

★ The Pinnacles

Sand Ridge

Maklaks Crater

✕ 7700

Anderson Bluffs

Lost Creek ⛺ $
6000'

Wheeler

Sand

Cr

Maklaks Spr

loudcap
8070

Grayback

Cr

Kerr Notch

Dutton Cliff

Sun

6237

Phantom Ship

Sun Notch

Sun Mdws
6650'

Crater Pk
7263'

Annie Falls

Creek

48 mi
Klamath Falls

62

Crater

Vidae Ridge

East Fork

3282

Lake
el. 6176'

★ Garfield Pk
8054'

Wizard Island
6940'

Rim Village

✕ 7100

★ The Watchman
8031

Lightning Spr

National

Munson Cr Falls

Park Headquarters

Munson Ridge

Park Entrance

Dutton Cr

Trapper Cr

Annie

Cold Spr

Scoria Cone

Goose Nest

$ Mazama

Bear Bluff

Sky

✕ 6200'

🏕 Mazama Village

Pacific

Pumice Flat
6290'
✕

Lakes

Wilderness

(See Area 31 Map)

Whitehorse Pond

Crest

Trail

Bald Top

★
Stuart Falls

✕ 5870'

Castle Pt

Union Pk
7709

Castle Creek

62

Red Blanket Cr

390
6205

Thousand Springs

830

800

Medford 62 mi

Cr

Union

Park

Then, in an eruption 150 times as massive as the 1980 Mount St. Helens blast, Mount Mazama suddenly exploded 14 cubic miles of pumice and ash into the sky, emptying its subterranean magma reservoir. Ash fell 10 feet deep at Klamath Marsh, and a half-inch deep as far away as Saskatchewan. As the hollowed mountain collapsed, a glowing avalanche of pumice and superheated gas raced down the slopes at freight-train speeds. Gas fumaroles in the fiery avalanche deposits welded pumice together around vertical vents. Later erosion exposed these as pinnacles along Annie and Sand Creeks.

Later, two cinder cones erupted on the caldera floor. Wizard Island's cone still rises 764 feet above the lake, but Merriam Cone was submerged as the caldera filled with rain and snowmelt.

The deepest lake in North America, Crater Lake has no outlet but maintains its level by evaporation and seepage. The lake's 1958-foot depth and remarkable purity account for its stunning blue color.

THINGS TO DO
Hiking
Popular day hikes lead to viewpoints on the lake rim and nearby peaks. The little-used backcountry trail system is largely dry and viewless, but it is the best bet for back-packing because camping is prohibited within a mile of the Rim Drive. Permits are required for backcountry camping. They are free and can be picked up at the Rim Village Visitor Center or at the Steel Center along the south entrance road.

Other park rules: Pets are prohibited on all trails. Saddle stock are limited strictly to the Pacific Crest Trail (PCT), and grazing is prohibited. Firearms and other hunting devices are forbidden. On the other hand, angling is permitted everywhere except Sun Creek, and no license is required to fish in the lake itself.

Only five hikes have views of the lake. Some of the best views are along the 1.7-mile trail switchbacking up 1000 feet from Rim Village to Garfield Peak, past alpine gardens of showy Davidson's penstemon, red paintbrush, and spreading phlox.

Hikers with less time can take the 0.8-mile path that climbs 400 feet from the Rim Drive to a lookout tower amidst twisted whitebark pines atop The Watchman. The PCT from Rim Village also leads to The Watchman—a 4-mile route that touches the highway four times.

Morning is the best time to scale Mount Scott for the farthest-ranging views in the park—from Mount Shasta to Mount Jefferson on a clear day. The 2.5-mile trail climbs steadily to the lookout on this geologically recent stratovolcano.

The park's most used trail (500 hikers a day) is a steep 1.1-mile path from the Rim Drive down to Cleetwood Cove, where 2-hour guided boat tours of the lake depart on the hour between 10 A.M. and 4:30 P.M. from early July until early September. The really fun hike here, however, is to take the boat tour as far as Wizard Island, where you can climb a 0.9-mile trail to the cinder cone's summit crater or follow the lava shore 0.7 mile to the cold green water of Fumarole Bay. Just do not miss the last boat back to Cleetwood Cove, because camping is banned on the island.

Craggy Union Peak lacks a lake view, but it commands a panorama of the rim peaks and of other Cascade summits. The 5.5-mile route there begins by following the PCT through a broad mountain hemlock forest south of Highway 62. Snow covers much of the route until mid-July.

Three other peaks make interesting hikes for those seeking respite from the rim's crowds. Plan a picnic to the wildflower meadow in the summit bowl of Crater Peak, a moderate 2.5-mile hike from the southernmost point of the Rim Drive. For views of Mount Mazama's other flank (and Cascade peaks as far north as the Three Sisters), try scaling Red Cone. It is an easy, obvious 1.5-mile cross-country hike from a turnout on the park's north rim access road, 1 mile north of the Rim Drive junction.

A third cinder cone, Timber Crater, is too well forested to offer views. Carry water on the 4-mile route from the Pumice Desert to the often snowy, flat summit—a crater filled to the brim by Mount Mazama's pumice. The final 2 miles are cross-country from the PCT.

Those staying at the popular Mazama Campground will not want to miss four short loop hikes nearby. The 1.7-mile Annie Creek loop trail from the campground passes abundant wildflowers and interesting gas-fumarole rock formations similar to those at The Pinnacles, in the

Wizard Island from the Pacific Crest Trail near Hillman Peak

park's distant southeast corner. Two miles farther up the south rim access road, the all-accessible 1-mile Godfrey Glen loop trail follows a cliff edge past more pinnacle formations. From the park headquarters, a 1-mile loop tours the headquarters' historic area, and the self-guiding 0.4-mile Castle Crest wildflower garden nature-trail loop shows off the park's alpine flora.

Massive Boundary Springs, the sudden source of the Rogue River, is a 2.4-mile hike through riverside woods from the Crater Rim Viewpoint, 5 miles west of the Diamond Lake junction on Highway 230. The hike starts at the beginning of the Upper Rogue River Trail, a path that continues 47.9 miles downstream to Prospect. No car is permitted within a quarter mile of Boundary Springs.

The ambitious hike to Sphagnum Bog, a floating moss field with four carnivorous plant species, will interest botanists with mosquito headnets and hip waders.

The national park portion of the PCT is a relatively uninspiring trudge—entirely viewless, with no water north of Red Cone Spring or south of Dutton Creek, and largely on abandoned roads. Equestrians still have to use that route, but hikers can now follow an alternative route that climbs Dutton Creek to the Rim Village and then traces the lake's scenic rim north past the Watchman and Hillman Peak.

Day hikers can sample this alternative PCT route on a 13.1-mile loop. From Rim Village, follow the trail north 2.5 miles along the lake rim, cross the highway, descend the Lightning Springs Trail 4 miles (passing the springs and a waterfall), turn left on the PCT equestrian bypass 4.2 miles to the wildflower meadow at Dutton Creek, and turn left for a 2.4-mile climb back to Rim Village.

The area's prettiest waterfall is not within the park at all. It is 40-foot Stuart Falls, at the head of Red Blanket Creek's scenic glacier-carved valley, in the Sky Lakes Wilderness. Crater Lake visitors can hike there from Highway 62's Cold Spring turnout on a dry, 5.4-mile route across forested Pumice Flat. But a shorter, more scenic trail reaches Stuart Falls from the west, passing 40-foot Red Blanket Falls on the way. The 4.3-mile trail from Road 6205 up Red Blanket Creek starts in a stately low-elevation forest and climbs 1500 feet. If you like huckleberries, add an extra 1.4 miles to the return trip by taking a fainter trail that loops past Lucky Meadow to Red Blanket Falls. To find the trailhead, turn off Highway 62 to the center of Prospect, take the Butte Falls Road 1 mile, turn left on Red Blanket Road for 0.4 mile, and fork left on gravel Road 6205 for 11.4 miles to its end.

Winter Sports

Within the park, Highway 62 and its short spur to Rim Village are plowed in winter, allowing nordic skiers access to excellent tours on the snowed-under Rim Drive and surrounding terrain. Snowmobiles are out of earshot, restricted to the Diamond Lake area and the park's north access road. The lake itself is an unforgettable spectacle in winter. Park rangers offer free, guided snowshoe walks from the Rim Village cafeteria building on winter weekends, and even provide the snowshoes.

The area's premier challenge, the 31-mile loop around the lake, is usually a three-day excursion, best attempted in March or April when winter's fiercest storms are over. The route is for experienced skiers and snow campers only. Because road cuts and slopes can calve avalanches, detours are marked around the two most dangerous areas. The Park Service recommends that ski parties carry avalanche beacons. Beware of approaching too closely to the rim, with its unseen cornice overhangs. By May, volcanic grit covers the snow, slowing progress and damaging skis. Permits are required for snow campers.

When choosing day trips and tours away from the Rim Drive, remember that scenic routes on steep slopes are prone to avalanches. Map, compass, and routefinding ability are essential in the flatter areas, where viewless forests hide landmarks.

31 Sky Lakes

Location: 36 miles northeast of Medford, 22 miles northwest of Klamath Falls
Size: 220 square miles
Status: 177 square miles designated wilderness (1984)
Terrain: Lake-dotted upland forests, peaks
Elevation: 3520 feet–9495 feet
Management: Rogue River NF, Winema NF
Topographic maps: Sky Lakes Wilderness, PCT Central Oregon Portion, PCT Southern Oregon Portion, Jackson Klamath Winter Trails (USFS)

Hundreds of lakes hide among the mountain hemlock forests on the Cascade crest between Crater Lake and Mount McLoughlin, highest point in southern Oregon.

Climate

The heavy winter snowpack blocks most trails until mid-June, and the Pacific Crest Trail (PCT) until mid-July. Mosquitoes are so numerous after the snowmelt that headnets and zippered tents are advisable throughout July. Summers are dry, with occasional thunderstorms. Snows return in mid-October. Average annual precipitation is 55 inches.

Plants and Wildlife

The wilderness is heavily influenced by adjacent Upper Klamath Lake, which may shelter a half million birds at once during the October–November migrations. Bald eagles and osprey nesting near Klamath Lake's swamps commonly visit the high wilderness lakes. Pelican Butte is named for Upper Klamath Lake's white pelicans, unmistakable with their 9-foot wingspans.

The best time to view the teeming bird life on Upper Klamath Lake's marshy fringe is during the July and August nesting season, when a canoe put-in at Rocky Point Resort (rentals available) enables birders to paddle 6 miles north up Crystal Creek, past red-necked grebes, white-headed woodpeckers, and possibly even sandhill cranes.

Sky Lakes' profusion of July mosquitoes coincides with a profusion of mosquito-pollinated wildflowers and a profusion of tiny, mosquito-eating boreal toads.

In August the omnipresent huckleberry underbrush of the mountain hemlock forest sags with ripe fruit—especially along the Wickiup Meadow Trail. By September the huckleberry leaves turn scarlet, filling the uplands with color.

Geology

Mount McLoughlin presents a smooth conical face toward Medford and Klamath Falls but conceals a craggy glacial cirque on its northern side. Strata exposed there show the mountain was once a tall cinder cone like nearby Pelican Butte, then erupted an armorlike covering of andesite, and finally lost its original summit when a glacier (since vanished) cut through its northern shell.

Other Ice Age glaciers scoured out most of the lake basins and gouged the deep, U-shaped valleys of the Rogue River's many forks. Narrow Alta Lake and Long Lake did not result from glaciers, however; they lie along a possibly active fault that extends through the Mountain Lakes Wilderness to California.

THINGS TO DO
Hiking

The area's most popular hike is also the most difficult: scaling 9495-foot Mount McLoughlin for a view of all southern Oregon. No technical equipment is required,

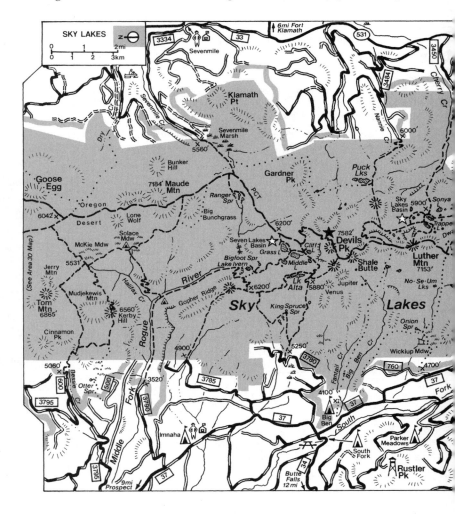

but you will need enough stamina to gain 3900 feet in 4.9 miles and return.

From Road 3650 hike 1.4 miles to the PCT, where there is a short spur to Freye Lake. If the lake doesn't have a nice mountain reflection, turn back and try the climb in better weather. Otherwise, follow the ridge-top trail to a frustrating false summit at timberline. The true top's abandoned lookout foundations are another steep, trailless mile up a rocky ridge. Remember the route well. Most search and rescue calls come for hikers who return by romping south from the summit, missing the trail.

Other popular hikes prowl three clusters of forest-rimmed lakes: the Seven Lakes Basin, the Sky Lakes Basin, and the Blue Canyon Basin. Overused portions of some lakeshores are closed for rehabilitation, particularly near trails.

Craggy Devils Peak towers above the Seven Lakes Basin—especially Cliff Lake,

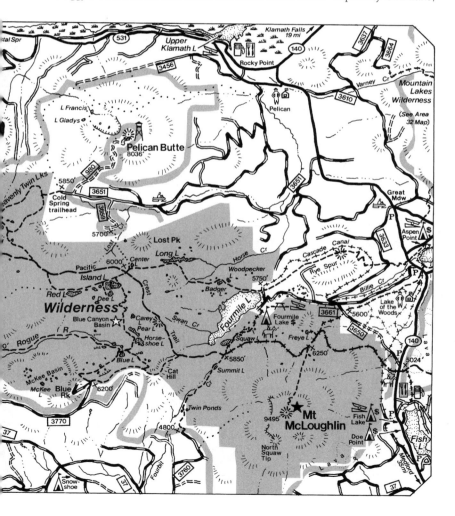

where swimmers can dive from cliffs into deep water. An easy 4.7-mile trail to shallow Grass Lake from the Sevenmile Marsh Trailhead on Road 3334 makes the entire lake basin accessible to day hikers, but the area deserves a two- or three-day trip.

Backpackers to the Seven Lakes Basin will not want to miss the 6-mile loop trail over Devils Peak. Follow the PCT to a 7300-foot saddle, where a short, rugged spur trail heads for the peak's former lookout site and sweeping view.

Have another day to spend? Try an 8-mile loop to rock-rimmed Lake Ivern and slender Lake Alta. The route requires an easy 0.5-mile cross-country traverse between the Lake Ivern Trail and the Middle Fork Trail; follow a compass bearing northwest from the Bigfoot Spring spur trail turnoff. At Lake Ivern, be sure to take an easy quarter-mile side trip due north to a 500-foot cliff overlooking the U-shaped canyon of the Middle Fork Rogue River.

To reach the trailhead at Sevenmile Marsh, take Nicholson Road 4.3 miles west from Highway 62 at Fort Klamath, then continue on gravel Road 3334 to its end.

Less heavily used trails access the basin from the west. The shortest, a 5-mile path from Road 3780 to Cliff Lake, climbs 1600 feet over a ridge on its way. The longest, the 9.7-mile Middle Fork Trail from Road 3790 to Alta Lake, follows a splashing fork

Devils Peak from Grass Lake in the Seven Lakes Basin

of the Rogue River through an old-growth forest with luxuriant, low-elevation greenery. The Sky Lakes Basin makes up for a shortage of mountain views with an abundance of forest-rimmed lakes. The aptly named Heavenly Twin Lakes are an easy 2.4-mile day hike (one way) from the Cold Spring Trailhead. It is worth the effort to continue on a 2.1-mile loop trail past deep Lake Notasha, swimmable Lake Elizabeth, and large Isherwood Lake. Another good extension to this day hike heads 1.9 miles north to scenic Trapper Lake, in a cluster of lakes with views of Luther Mountain's rocky ridge. Two quieter trails also make good routes into the Sky Lakes Basin. The Nannie Creek Trail from Road 3484 passes large, swimmable South Puck Lake after 2.4 miles (a good day-hike goal for kids), then descends another 4.1 miles to Trapper Lake. The Cherry Creek Trail from Road 3450 arrives at that lake in 5.2 miles, but climbs 1300 feet, making the route more popular with equestrians than hikers.

The popular lakes of the Blue Canyon Basin, nestled below Mount McLoughlin's snowy northern face, offer surprisingly few views of the nearby peak. Begin on the Blue Canyon Trail from Road 3770. It is 2.3 miles to deep, cold Blue Lake, with its cliff backdrop, and another 0.7 mile to Horseshoe Lake's peninsula. Trailside camps are closed here to allow the fragile flora to regrow. Best bets for solitude are off-trail Pear Lake and Carey Lake. Island Lake, largest of the group, is 5.5 miles from the Road 3770 trailhead. A rail fence at the lake protects the Judge Waldo Tree, inscribed in 1888 by the first pioneers to hike the length of southern Oregon's Cascades. For a good swim, try nearby Dee Lake.

Fourmile Lake is dammed for irrigation, but it is still scenic and serves as the starting point for several top day hikes. The 3.7-mile route to Long Lake tours a snag-filled bay of Fourmile Lake (with views of Mount McLoughlin) and passes wildflower meadows near beautiful Badger Lake. To the west of the trailhead at Fourmile Lake's campground, a level trail through the woods leads 1.8 miles to Squaw Lake and another 1.1 mile to little Summit Lake, crossing the PCT along the way. Turn right on the PCT to complete a 14-mile loop around Fourmile Lake, returning via Long Lake.

Little-used trails in the north of this wilderness lead to McKie Meadow and Solace Meadow's cabin, both popular with equestrians. The 5.3-mile Tom and Jerry Trail to McKie Meadow from Road 600 offers a good cross-country side trip to the view atop Tom Mountain. An alternate route to McKie Meadow crosses Kerby Hill; it is steep, but features a spectacular view of the Middle Fork Rogue canyon.

The shortest route to Solace Meadow—6.3 miles—follows the Middle Fork Trail from Road 3790, then switchbacks up the Halifax Trail through a rapid succession of botanical zones.

The nearly viewless 49.7-mile segment of the PCT between Highway 140 and Highway 62 in Crater Lake National Park manages to avoid all lakes and water sources, so savvy travelers detour off the PCT into the three major lake basins. Also be sure to take the 0.6-mile side trip to Ranger Spring, a welcome oasis. The Oregon Desert, on the northern part of the PCT route, is a lodgepole pine forest free of underbrush and notable for massive September mushrooms.

Cross-country hiking is easy and rewarding in all the upland lake basins, but particularly in the McKee Basin near Blue Rock and in the glacial cirque on Pelican Butte—areas lacking maintained trails.

Winter Sports

Marked nordic ski trails radiate from several sno-parks along plowed Highway 140. Snowmobiles dominate snowed-under roads and are permitted on most nonwilderness trails (except the PCT and the Cascade Canal).

A good beginner tour off-limits to snowmobiles follows the Lake of the Woods shoreline 1.9 miles from Highway 140 to snowed-under Aspen Point Campground. Another easy route, with good views of Mount McLoughlin, begins at the Fish Lake Resort and loops 3 miles on marked roads and trails south of that lake.

The PCT offers routes both south of Highway 140, to viewpoints in the vast lava fields around nearby Brown Mountain, and north of the highway, where it climbs steadily 3.5 miles to Freye Lake's mountain view. A 1.5-mile trail connects the PCT with Fish Lake Resort, but a closer access to the PCT is the sno-park at the junction of Highway 140 and Road 3650.

Road 3650 and the parallel Cascade Canal provide a scenic, well-graded 9.7-mile nordic route from Highway 140 to Fourmile Lake. A shortcut to that lake, along Road 3661, is shared with snowmobiles but allows snow campers quickest access to the wilderness trail system beyond.

The area's most challenging ski tour, to the summit of Mount McLoughlin, should only be undertaken in perfect weather by groups familiar with avalanche danger areas.

Boating

Canoes and sailboats do well on Fourmile Lake, Fish Lake, and the marshy bays and creeks of Upper Klamath Lake. Motorboats are limited to 10 miles per hour in all of these areas. Especially note the marked canoe trail from Rocky Point Resort, described under "Plants and Wildlife" earlier.

32 Mountain Lakes

Location: 38 miles east of Medford, 15 miles northwest of Klamath Falls
Size: 45 square miles
Status: 36 square miles designated wilderness (1964)
Terrain: Forested buttes, lake basins
Elevation: 4700 feet–8208 feet
Management: Winema NF
Topographic map: Mountain Lakes Wilderness (USFS)

This pocket wilderness is large enough that some of its alpine viewpoints and forest-rimmed lakes are best seen on backpacking trips.

Harriette Lake

Climate
Late summer brings occasional thunderstorms, but most of the area's 40 inches of annual precipitation comes as snow, which blocks trails from early November to late June. Mosquitoes are numerous in July.

Plants and Wildlife
Bald eagles, osprey, and a variety of ducks from nearby Upper Klamath Lake frequent the high lakes. The dense forests below 7000 feet are chiefly droopy-topped mountain hemlock and prim, Christmas-tree-shaped Shasta red fir. At higher elevations, only gnarled whitebark pines survive. Their seeds are a primary food source for the area's raucous Clark's nutcrackers.

Geology
This roughly circular upland was once thought to be the eroded remnant of a collapsed 12,000-foot volcano similar to Crater Lake's Mount Mazama. More recent research, however, has revealed the peaks here as a cluster of at least four overlapping volcanoes. Though glaciers have dissected them severely (Mount Carmine and Aspen Butte were once a single cone), they were probably never much taller than today. A feature of this volcanic hot spot is a swarm of faults running through the area—one of which aligned Seldom Creek's straight glacial valley.

THINGS TO DO
Hiking
Three trails climb to the 8.3-mile Mountain Lakes Loop, with its lakes and scenic passes. Because of the area's small size, groups are limited to ten—counting persons, saddle stock, and pack animals.

The most popular route into the wilderness is the Varney Creek Trail from Road 3664, which climbs among the creek's wildflowers (blooming in July) for 4.8 miles to Eb and Zeb Lakes. These heavily visited, scenic, but shallow lakes are often warm enough for swimming.

Here most day hikers must turn around. Backpackers have more choices. Eastward, the Mountain Lakes Loop Trail heads 1.9 miles to very deep and very beautiful 40-acre Harriette Lake, passing Como Lake and shallow Silent and Zephyr Lakes. Westward, the loop trail climbs 1 mile to a saddle, from which a 7708-foot summit with an excellent viewpoint is only a short cross-country hike away. Side trails from the 8.3-mile Mountain Lakes Loop lead to seldom-visited South Pass Lake, the Clover Lake basin, and the Hemlock Lake basin. Those ready for a grander cross-country viewpoint hike can head northeast from Eb Lake up a 2.5-mile ridge to Mount Harriman.

To find the Varney Creek Trailhead, drive Highway 140 west of Klamath Falls 21 miles. Between mileposts 46 and 47, turn south on Road 3637 for 1.8 miles, and turn left on Road 3664 for 1.9 miles to its end.

Another popular trailhead, on Road 3660 near Lake of the Woods, is the starting point of a 4.8-mile path up Seldom Creek's glacial valley to the Mountain Lakes Loop. After climbing 3 miles on this route, look for a spur trail to grassy Waban Lake, with its seasonal profusion of tree frogs.

A third path up to the Mountain Lakes Loop, the Clover Trail, is less used because it is shared with grazing cattle. It reaches small Clover Lake from Road 3852 in

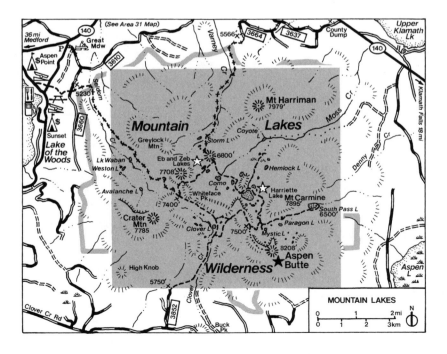

2.5 miles. Some hikers veer right at the 2.4-mile point, following an unmaintained shortcut to the Mountain Lakes Loop Trail, to reach a ridge top overlooking Harriette Lake. From here it is easy to strike off cross-country, following the alpine ridge up to the south past whitebark pines, dwarfed manzanita bushes, and showy Davidson's penstemons to Aspen Butte, whose summit view makes the strenuous 5.4-mile climb from Road 3852 worthwhile. Look for Crater Lake's rim peaks, Mount McLoughlin, and Mount Shasta.

Backpackers hiking the 8.3-mile Mountain Lakes Loop Trail may also want to explore the 1.7-mile spur trail eastward down a forested but increasingly arid glacial valley to large South Pass Lake.

Winter Sports

Nordic ski trips can begin from plowed Highway 140 either at the Great Meadow sno-park near Lake of the Woods or at the Varney Creek Trailhead turnoff between mileposts 46 and 47. Carry map, compass, and emergency gear, because wilderness trails are not marked for winter use.

Great Meadow is a snowmobile center, but skiers leave noise behind when they leave Road 3660 for the Mountain Lakes Trail up Seldom Creek. Lake Waban, 4.5 miles from the sno-park, is a good goal.

From the Varney Creek Trailhead turnoff, skiers follow unplowed roads 3.7 miles to the trailhead. Eb and Zeb Lakes are an additional 4.8 miles uphill.

33 Cascade-Siskiyou

Location: 13 miles southeast of Ashland
Size: 81 square miles
Status: National Monument (2000)
Terrain: Steep, mostly wooded slopes
Elevation: 2300 feet–6091 feet
Management: Medford District BLM
Topographic maps: PCT Southern Oregon Portion (USFS); Siskiyou Pass, Soda Mountain, Parker Mountain, Hornbrook [California], Iron Gate Reservoir [California] (USGS)

Soda Mountain stands at the center of the Cascade-Siskiyou National Monument, a biologically diverse area where the Cascade Range and the Siskiyou Mountains meet.

Climate

Moderate snowfall blocks the Pacific Crest Trail (PCT) from about December to March or April. Annual precipitation varies from 40 inches in the upland forests to less than 20 inches on the dry, southern slopes, where summer temperatures can soar.

Mount Shasta from the base of Pilot Rock

Plants and Wildlife

Soda Mountain stands at the intersection of three biologic zones: the Cascades, the Siskiyous, and the high desert. Dark fir forests on the high, north-facing slopes resemble woods in the High Cascades. Droopy, canyon-bottom cedars and stiff-limbed manzanita brush remind one of the Siskiyous. Pungent sagebrush and juniper on the dry southern ridges belong to the Great Basin steppe's bioregion.

The area is home to the showy Greene's mariposa lily (threatened in Oregon), though hikers are more likely to encounter trilliums and calypso orchids (in spring forests) or yellow-flowered rabbitbrush (among fall sagebrush).

A large herd of black-tailed deer from the Rogue Valley relies on the white oak grasslands of the lower southern slopes for winter browse. Other wildlife species include cougar, golden eagles, and quail. The area's unusual diversity allows desert species, such as kangaroo rats, to share habitat with forest species such as northern spotted owls and rough-skinned newts. The monument supports one of the highest diversities of butterfly species in the United States.

Geology

Soda Mountain is a block of 16- to 25-million-year-old Old Cascades, wedged between the much older Klamath Mountains to the west and the much younger High Cascades to the east. Pilot Rock is an eroded volcanic plug of columnar basalt.

History

Pilot Rock's landmark basalt monolith once guided gold miners and trappers toward a low Siskiyou Mountain pass on the Oregon/California Trail. Train tracks built across Siskiyou Pass in 1887 filled the final gap in a rail line around the United States' perimeter. The area remained remote enough, however, to harbor Oregon's last known grizzly bear, the legendary, 8-foot-tall Old Reelfoot, which was shot near Pilot Rock's base

174

in 1891. Later the D'Autremont brothers attempted a train robbery at Siskiyou Pass in 1923, murdering three men. They eluded a four-continent manhunt by camping under a deadfall tree beside Porcupine Creek.

THINGS TO DO
Hiking

Interstate 5 travelers can stretch their legs with a 0.5-mile walk on the PCT to the cliffs and views at the base of Pilot Rock. Take Interstate 5 to Mount Ashland exit 6, follow old Highway 99 south under the freeway 2 miles, and turn left on Pilot Rock Road 40-2E-33 for 1 mile to a PCT crossing. Do not park here. Instead drive another 1 mile to a quarry, keep right for 0.8 mile, and park at the road's crest. Walk left across the road, follow the PCT 300 yards, and fork to the right to Pilot Rock. Hikers should turn back at the rock's base, but cautious scramblers willing to use their hands can make their way straight up a steep chute to the top.

For a longer hike from the same trailhead, continue east on the PCT past Pilot Rock 6.5 miles to Soda Mountain's 1933 lookout tower, staffed each summer. For an easier route to the lookout, drive Highway 66 east of Ashland 14.5 miles. Just 200 feet before the Green Springs summit, turn right on Soda Mountain Road 39-3E-32.3 for 3.7 miles to a grassy pass with powerlines and small signs marking the PCT. Hike uphill to the right 1.1 mile, switchback to the left on a steep unmarked path 0.2 mile, and turn right on a road 0.8 mile to the lookout.

The best view of all is at Boccard Point's rocky promontory, an easy 0.2-mile walk from the end of Baldy Creek Road 40-3E-5. Take Interstate 5 to Ashland exit 14, follow Highway 66 east for 14.8 miles, turn right on Tyler Creek Road 1.5 miles, turn

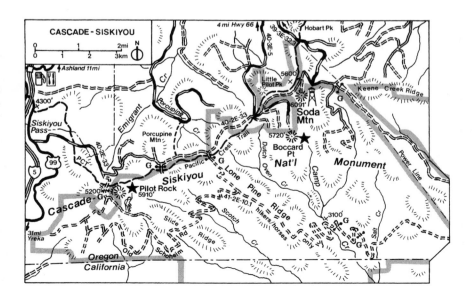

left on gravel Road 40-3E-5 for 7.5 miles to its end, and then hike south along the open, trailless ridge to the viewpoint.

Boccard Point also makes a good starting point for cross-country forays into the area's steep southern canyons. Trailless travel here is easiest through sagebrush and open grasslands along ridge tops, or along the creek's lush growth of moss and maples. Rock outcroppings and bands of nearly impenetrable scrub oak chaparral interrupt canyon slopes. Dutch Oven Creek's many small waterfalls make good goals.

The Old Schoheim Road, a rough track traversing the southern edge of the national monument, is becoming a more attractive hiking route now that it has been closed to unauthorized mechanized and motorized vehicles.

Climbing

Pilot Rock's columnar basalt tower offers seven mountaineering routes, including the scenic West Ridge (level I-5.3) and the South Face's broken basalt columns (rated II-5.6). The West Gully, a class 3 scramble route to the summit, is commonly used by technical climbers as a descent route. A pinnacle 200 yards southeast of Pilot Rock requires level I-5.7 skills.

34 Red Buttes

Location: 34 miles southwest of Medford
Size: 130 square miles total; 42 square miles in Oregon
Status: 31 square miles designated wilderness; 6 square miles in Oregon (1984)
Terrain: Rocky buttes, forested ridges, small lakes
Elevation: 1300 feet–7055 feet
Management: Rogue River NF, Siskiyou NF, Klamath NF, Oregon Caves National Monument
Topographic maps: Red Buttes Wilderness, PCT Southern Oregon Portion (USFS)

Straddling the rocky crest of the Siskiyou Mountains, this little-visited area's trail system extends along view-filled ridges and subalpine meadows from the Pacific Crest Trail (PCT) to the Oregon Caves National Monument.

Climate

Snowfall closes high trails from about mid-November to mid-May. Summers are very dry. Annual precipitation measures 60 inches.

Plants and Wildlife

Expect frequent signs of wildlife on the trails: deer tracks, coyote scat, and the palm-sized paw prints of cougar and bear. This is also a prime spot for Bigfoot fanciers. Alleged sightings of ape men date to 1895. The Forest Service issued a special-use permit

Lilypad Lake from the Pacific Crest Trail

for a Sasquatch trap on Collings Mountain (west of Applegate Lake) in 1973.

The area teems with the unusual flora of the Siskiyous. Knobcone pines, resembling bumpy flagpoles, dot Figurehead Mountain. Droopy weeping spruce are common. Massive incense cedars, hollowed by fire, could serve as extra camping accommodations in addition to Sucker Gap's shelter. A loop trail from the Oregon Caves leads to Big Tree, one of Oregon's largest Douglas firs. Some of the world's southernmost Alaska cedars grow on Mount Emily, while the world's northernmost Baker's cypresses grow on Steve Peak, a quarter mile east of Miller Lake.

June brings wildflowers familiar from the alpine Cascades as well as Siskiyou novelties, including two delicate, pink *Lewisia* species, best seen in Cameron Meadows or along the Fir Glade Trail to Azalea Lake.

Geology

Colorful rock cairns marking high trails here showcase these mountains' diversity. The rocks are up to 425 million years old (almost 20 times the age of the Old Cascades). Look for flat slate, shiny schist, green serpentinite, white marble, and speckled granite.

The Siskiyou or Klamath Mountains began as an island archipelago in the Pacific Ocean, but crustal movement "rafted" them to the edge of the North American plate about 200 million years ago, along with jumbled masses of sea-floor rock—including the red peridotite forming Red Buttes' twin peaks. The pressure of that collision also cooked limestone to marble, allowing later water seepage to create the white caverns of the Oregon Caves. Dripstone stalactites now grow in those caves at the swift rate of an inch per decade. Finally, hot granite intrusions melted out veins of mineral-rich quartz. Gold attracted swarms of prospectors in the 1850s. Mine tailings and washed-out, "hydraulicked" river bottoms remain.

THINGS TO DO
Hiking

Start with a 4.1-mile hike along the PCT from Cook and Green Pass to aptly named Lilypad Lake, at the foot of Red Buttes' double peak. Along the way take a 0.5-mile side trail down to Echo Lake, in a cliff-rimmed basin with blue gentians. Have energy for a longer hike? From Lilypad Lake, it is a nearly level 2.6 miles to Upper Devils Peak and a look at the Klamath River 4700 feet below. For a view toward Oregon, turn off the PCT at Kangaroo Mountain and head west 2.5 trail miles to the cliff-edged pass atop craggy Rattlesnake Mountain.

In much of this wilderness, dry, south-facing slopes confound cross-country hikers with impenetrable chaparral tangles of manzanita, snowbrush, and stunted chinkapin. Open forests on northern slopes, however, invite trailless exploration. A top cross-country trip from Cook and Green Pass takes off from Echo Lake and circles Red Buttes' ruddy double peak, passing wildflower meadows, springs, and five scenic cirque lakes on a sometimes rocky 5-mile traverse, returning via the PCT.

To reach Cook and Green Pass from Medford, take Highway 238 to Jacksonville and 8 miles beyond to Ruch. Turn left at an "Upper Applegate" pointer for 18.8 miles to a T junction at the end of Applegate Lake, turn left on Applegate Road 1.2 miles to a big gravel intersection, go straight on Road 1050 for 0.9 mile, and fork right on one-lane Road 1055 for 10 miles.

Visit the wildflowers at Frog Pond and Cameron Meadows with a 5.8-mile loop hike from Road 1040. From the meadows, scramble up a ridge to the south for a good viewpoint. If you plan a short car shuttle between the two trailheads, you will save a final 2.1-mile walk along Road 1040 back to your car.

Sucker Creek Gap, at the junction of the east–west Siskiyou Mountains and the north–south Grayback Range, is a cool, grassy dale surrounded by giant old-growth incense cedars. Hike there from the end of Road 1030 on a 3.3-mile trail through Steve Creek Valley's deep forest. A shorter, less scenic 1.4-mile route to the Sucker Creek Gap shelter takes off from the end of Road 098. From Cave Junction, head toward Oregon Caves for 14.5 miles, turn south on gravel Road 4612 for 9 miles, and then turn left onto Road 098.

At the Oregon Caves National Monument it costs about $6 to tour the famous caves, but there is no charge to hike the 3.8-mile loop trail to Big Tree, a Douglas fir 13 feet in diameter. Midway along the loop, a side trail heads up a ridge 2.1 miles to a viewpoint atop Mount Elijah. An easier, 1.3-mile path to that goal begins on Road 070.

At Grayback Mountain, a steep 1.3-mile path from Road 1005 climbs to a wild-flower meadow with Krause Cabin, a log shelter. Bushwhack uphill from the cabin through steep fields 1.1 mile to the mountain's summit for views from the ocean to Mount Shasta.

The swimmable Tannen Lakes, nestled in forest against a backdrop of Tannen

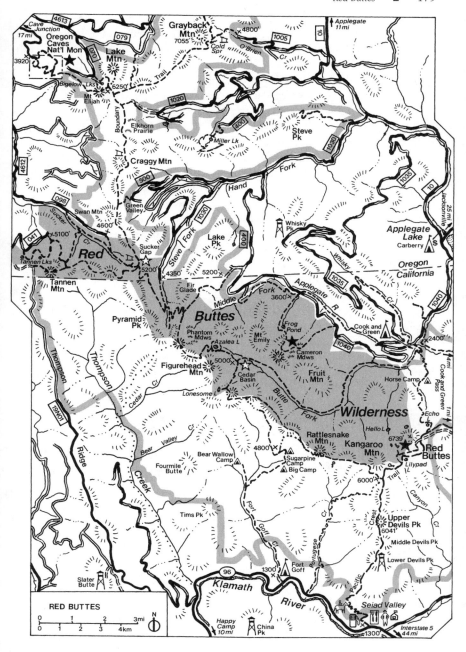

Mountain's rockslides, are a popular day-hike goal. A 0.4-mile trail leads to the larger Tannen Lake from Road 041. East Tannen Lake is another 0.9 mile along a well-graded route that tempts hikers to continue 4.9 miles to Sucker Gap. From Cave Junction drive south 7 miles on Highway 199, turn left on Waldo Road 5 miles, and go straight on Happy Camp Road 12.5 miles to a pass. Turn left at a "Tannen Lakes" sign, fork to the right after 0.8 mile, left after 1.4 miles, right after 1.8 miles, right after 4.2 miles, and left after 7.5 miles to the trailhead at mile 8.9.

Backpackers who make the 6.5-mile trek to Azalea Lake from the Fir Glade Trailhead are rewarded with June wildflowers and views of rocky Figurehead Mountain. A 0.5-mile shoreline trail loops around the popular little lake, with separate camp areas for hikers and equestrians. Continue to Cedar Basin and hike up to the rocky pass just south of Lonesome Lake for a look into the Klamath River country, or bushwhack up Figurehead Mountain for wider ranging views.

To reach the Fir Glade Trailhead from Grants Pass, follow signs south 6.5 miles to Murphy, continue straight on Highway 238 another 11.5 miles to a green steel bridge at Applegate, and turn right on Thompson Creek Road. After 14.7 miles turn right across a bridge and immediately fork left on Road 1030 for 5.2 miles. Then turn left on Road 400 (which becomes Road 1040) for 4.7 miles, and fork right on Road 800 for 0.6 mile to road's end.

Several long-distance backpacking routes surpass the PCT here, with its grueling, 4700-foot ascent out of Seiad Valley. The 20-mile Boundary Trail from Grayback Mountain to Tannen Mountain is a good choice. For a more thorough sampler of this wilderness, take a 33.5-mile loop backpack trip from Cook and Green Campground past Cook and Green Pass, Red Buttes, Rattlesnake Mountain, and Cedar Basin, returning via the Butte Fork Trail.

35 Kalmiopsis

Location: 33 miles southwest of Grants Pass
Size: 672 square miles
Status: 281 square miles designated wilderness (1964, 1978); Illinois federal wild and scenic river
Terrain: Steep, rugged canyons; sparsely forested ridges; river rapids
Elevation: 240 feet-5098 feet
Management: Siskiyou NF
Topographic map: Kalmiopsis Wilderness (USFS)

Cut by the green-pooled Illinois River's rugged gorge, the Kalmiopsis is Oregon's largest but perhaps least visited forest wilderness. Seen from one of the dry ridge-top trails, jagged canyonlands spread like a vast sheet of crumpled paper. This is a land of torrential winter rains and blazing summer heat, of rare wildflowers and shy black bears.

Hikers should expect challenge as well as beauty on the steep trails. Boaters on the wild Illinois must prepare for ten churning class 4 rapids and the monstrous, class 5 Green Wall.

Climate

Heavy rains from October to May (100 to 150 inches) swell the rivers, making crossings difficult in spring. There are no bridges. Snow usually covers trails above 4000 feet from December through March. Afternoon temperatures often exceed 90° F in virtually rainless July and August.

Plants and Wildlife

Unusual species have developed in the relatively isolated Klamath Mountains, and many have survived because Ice Age glaciers left most of the area untouched. Plant collecting is prohibited.

Carnivorous pitcher plants resemble green baseball bats sprouting from boggy land at springs. These plants make up for the area's poor soil by catching their own nutrients. A honey aroma lures insects into the plant's hollow stem, where tiny hairs prevent the insects from escaping and enzymes reduce the catch to liquid. Also at springs, look for brilliant blue gentian and white death camas.

Rare *Kalmiopsis leachiana* fills forests with pink blooms in June. This azalealike shrub, found only in and near the Kalmiopsis, is best seen at Bailey Mountain, Dry Butte, Gold Basin, and Taggarts Bar.

Forests are often Douglas fir and canyon live oak but include an odd mix of other species. Look for madrone, with peeling red bark, and chinkapin, with spiny fruit ("porcupine eggs"). Port Orford cedar and Brewer's weeping spruce, elsewhere rare, are common here.

Tail-twitching, orange Douglas squirrels scold hikers from trees. On rocky slopes, watch for western fence lizards, blue-tailed skinks, and the area's unaggressive rattlesnakes. Quiet hikers frequently surprise black bears foraging for sugar pine seeds, yellow jacket ground nests, or manzanita berries. The bears dislike dogs but do all they can to avoid humans, typically climbing trees or fleeing on sight. Encourage this by wrapping smelly food tightly and hanging all food at night.

Geology

The Klamath Mountains began as a Pacific island archipelago with coral reefs and volcanoes, but the entire island chain crumpled against the advancing shore of North America about 200 million years ago when the continent began drifting westward at the speedy rate of an inch a year. The collision buckled up masses of sub-seafloor rock and folded Klamath strata like taffy.

Today, outcroppings of sub-seafloor rock (red peridotite and shiny green serpentinite) are so infertile they visibly stunt vegetation. They also provide the traces of rare, heavy metals that account for the area's many gold-mining cabins and abandoned chrome mines.

Though new mining claims are prohibited in designated wilderness, recreational gold panning is allowed. To try, wash out heavy black sands gleaned from bedrock cracks in creekbeds. Be sure to avoid private claims, particularly in the Little Chetco River area. Rockhounds can also look for jasper along the Illinois River below Florence Creek.

THINGS TO DO
Hiking

The 27-mile Illinois River Trail over Bald Mountain is well graded and maintained. Nearly all other paths in the area, however, are steep, rocky miners' pack trails or bulldozed mining roads. Hikers may meet four-wheel-drive vehicles even inside the designated wilderness, because miners with valid pre-1984 claims have keys to the road gates.

A few other cautions: Beware of the shiny, autumn-red, three-leaved poison oak prolific at lower elevations. Vast brushfields of tough, red-limbed manzanita stymie most cross-country travelers. The danger of stumbling onto illegal marijuana plantations has declined from the 1970s and 1980s, when off-trail hikers sometimes encountered guarded marijuana patches, especially near creeks or springs within a mile or two of trailheads.

The two most popular short hikes lead to cirque lakes high in the mountain forests: Babyfoot Lake in the east of the wilderness and Vulcan Lake in the west.

An easy, 1.2-mile trail through a designated botanical area reaches Babyfoot Lake from Road 140. For a 5.3-mile loop, continue past the surprisingly green lake 0.5 mile, turn left on a mining road 1.8 miles to a cairn, and climb up to the left on a view-filled ridge-top trail. For even better views of the area's rugged canyonlands—and a glimpse of the distant ocean—head for Eagle Mountain or the abandoned lookout site atop Canyon Peak, both less than 4 trail miles from Babyfoot Lake. Reach the trailhead via Eight Dollar Mountain Road 4201, which branches off Highway 199 north of Cave Junction 5 miles.

Vulcan Lake is the same size as Babyfoot Lake (4 acres), but instead of being set in a lush forest, it fills a dramatic rock basin of stunted pines below broad Vulcan Peak. The red peridotite rock shores not only exhibit glacial scratch marks of interest to geologists; they also make ideal sunbathing spots for swimmers. A well-maintained 1.4-mile trail from the end of Road 1909 crosses a scenic ridge on its way to Vulcan Lake.

Other trails near Vulcan Lake make good day trips. The old lookout site atop Vulcan Peak, with views of the Kalmiopsis and the Pacific Coast, is up a 1-mile trail (gaining 1000 feet). A mostly level 4-mile ridge-top route passes Red Mountain on its way to austere Chetco Lake. Another trail with views from an open ridge-top heads north 3 miles to Dry Butte's fields of *Kalmiopsis leachiana*. Trailhead access is from Brookings; turn off Highway 101 at the north end of the Chetco River bridge, follow the road along the Chetco River 16.5 miles, and then turn right on Road 1909 to its end.

Where trails exist at all along the Chetco River's rugged inner gorge, they generally traverse canyon slopes several hundred feet above the green-pooled stream. A day

Vulcan Peak from Vulcan Lake

hike from the western edge of the wilderness samples one such trail, a 3-mile route from a spur of Road 360 to a ford and chilly swimming hole at Boulder Creek Camp. From there, hikers can climb an extra mile to a view of the Big Craggies from Lately Prairie, or else continue 3 miles along the Chetco River for a look up Tincup Creek's gorge. To reach the trailhead, drive 23 miles up the Chetco River from Brookings, turn off Road 1376 onto dirt Road 360 for a mile, then switchback onto spur Road 365.

Several hikes begin near the McCaleb Ranch Boy Scout camp, on the Grants Pass side of the wilderness. The prettiest part of the Fall Creek Trail is its first 0.8 mile. The path begins with a dramatic suspension footbridge over the Illinois River, passes near Illinois River Falls, and follows rushing Fall Creek. The other hikes in this area begin at Chetco Pass—a problem because the rutted, bouldery 5.1-mile road there from McCaleb Ranch is impassable to nearly all vehicles and is sometimes gated closed altogether. It is simplest to cross the Illinois River suspension footbridge and walk the awful road up to the pass. Then you can either trek onward 4.2 miles on the closed road to the Chetco River ford or turn right on a 5.9-mile loop to the restored 1954 Pearsoll Peak fire lookout (open for free public use), the highest point in the region.

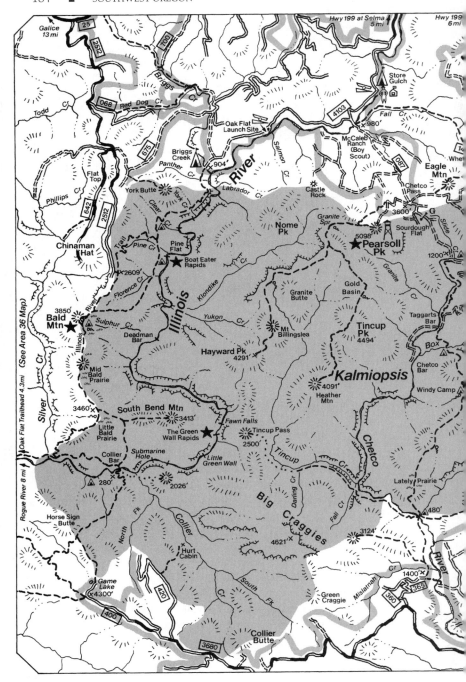

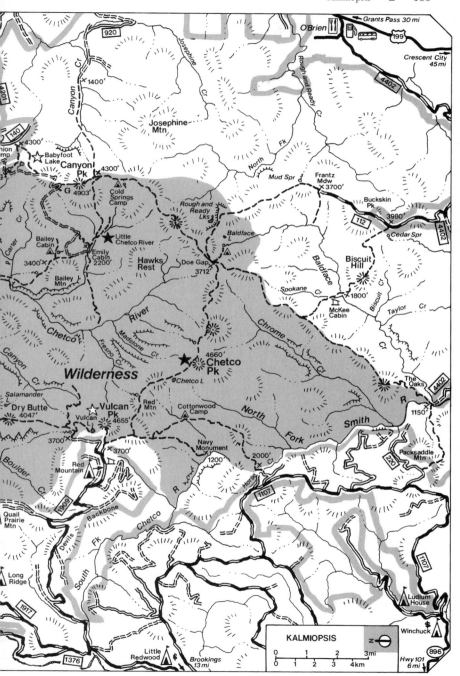

The insectivorous pitcher plant,
Darlingtonia

To find the Illinois River suspension footbridge, drive Highway 199 south of Grants Pass 20 miles to Selma and turn right at a flashing yellow light onto Illinois River Road for 11 miles. At an "End Maintenance" sign look for a tiny "Camp McCaleb" pointer and turn left on steep Road 087 for 0.5 mile.

The popular 27-mile Illinois River Trail traverses wildflower-filled meadows on Bald Mountain's long crest, then descends through the wild Illinois River's remote inner gorge. Side trips to viewpoints at South Bend Mountain or to Collier Bar (a river ford passable from mid-June to November) can make the trip even more spectacular. Start at Briggs Creek, at the bumpy end of dirt Road 4103, and finish at a paved road 3 miles from Agness (see the Wild Rogue map, Area 36). Those who can not arrange the long car shuttle can catch a Rogue River jet mail boat (available May 1 to November 1) from Agness to bus connections in Gold Beach.

Backpackers with a yen for solitude and rugged beauty will find both in the vast interior of the Kalmiopsis. The premier trip is a 42-mile trail loop from Vulcan Lake past Dry Butte, Taggarts Bar, Emily Cabin, Doe Gap, and Chetco Peak. Beware of dehydration, because trails follow dry ridges and canyon slopes. Carry plenty of water and study maps carefully for trailside springs and perennial streams.

Boating

Oregon's most difficult white-water run, the Illinois River from Oak Flat to Agness packs 156 rated rapids into 35 miles. The setting is a breathtakingly stark, trailless, 4000-foot-deep canyon. The brilliant green river is so clear that mossy boulders 30 feet underwater seem within reach.

Only very experienced river runners in kayaks, narrow inflatables, or portageable hard boats should attempt the Illinois, and then only in April or May when water levels range between 600 and 1400 cubic feet per second (gauged at the Kerby station). The lower water of early summer turns the run to a gamut of rock dodging and boat bashing. Higher water after heavy spring rains converts Boat Eater and the Green Wall to deadly maelstroms.

Start the three-day trip at the unmarked Oak Flat launch site 13 miles west of Selma where Road 4103 dips close to the river. A box here contains free, unlimited, self-issuing permits. Drift an easy 3 miles before coming to Panther Creek and the first of many rapids that must be scouted. The next 2 miles wallop boaters with seven increasingly powerful class 3 and 4 rapids, culminating with York Creek Rapids, a 4+ churner with an underwater shelf and tall standing waves in the preferred left channel.

Boat Eater Rapids, 3 miles downriver at the mouth of Pine Creek, funnels the river past a cabin-sized boulder into a roaring suckhole with a record of trapping every third or fourth craft it meets. Boaters usually camp immediately after this class 4+ trial.

Ten miles of swift but manageable water the second day out lead to the big stuff. It starts with class 4 Fawn Falls, down a 10-foot chute into a boulder obstacle course. Hardly a half mile beyond, an ominous wall covered with green moss looms above the river, signaling all but the most athletic daredevils to portage around the coming class 5 water.

The Green Wall Rapids drops boaters 50 feet in less than 300 yards. First comes a fast stretch of rocks and holes, then a drop through a barricade of truck-sized boulders, then another 12-foot cascade, and finally a possible crush against the wall itself.

Three-quarters of a mile farther, Little Green Wall's class 4 rocks hang up their share of boats. White water is then nonstop for 2 miles to Submarine Hole's treacherous midstream boulder, which must be run on the left side (though this positioning requires strong rowing). Exhausted river runners will find no campsite for yet another 1.7 miles.

The third day is an easy drift to the Agness pullout on the Rogue River. The car shuttle between ends of the run totals 120 miles over several poor roads (Oak Flat, Grants Pass, Galice, Agness). If this route is closed by lingering snow, plan on 150 miles via Crescent City and Gold Beach. Arrangements may be made by calling Whitewater Cowboys at (541) 479-0132.

36 Wild Rogue

Location: 27 miles northwest of Grants Pass
Size: 224 square miles
Status: 56 square miles designated wilderness (1978); federal wild and scenic river
Terrain: Steep, rocky, forested river canyon
Elevation: 140 feet–5316 feet
Management: Siskiyou NF, Medford District BLM
Topographic maps: Wild Rogue Wilderness (USFS)

The irascible Rogue River, cutting through the mountains to the sea, is at times a string of sunny, green pools, lazily drifting past playful otter and circling osprey. But the river can also be misty mayhem—raging over Blossom Bar's boulders like a giant pinball game, swirling boats helplessly in The Coffeepot, and standing on edge in Mule Creek Canyon, a chasm so narrow boats sometimes bridge from wall to wall.

The Coffeepot in Mule Creek Canyon

More than 20,000 visitors a year run the Rogue's famous white water. But the beautiful 40-mile Rogue River Trail is seldom crowded, and the rest of this river's rugged, 4000-foot-deep canyon remains virtually untrodden.

Climate

Toward the end of the reliably rainless, hot summers, river temperatures rise to 70° F, making the water attractive for swimmers but driving fish into cooler tributaries. Intermittent rains from September to May total 90 inches in the damp western end of the canyon but only 50 inches in the east.

Plants and Wildlife

It is easy to spot wildlife attracted to the river: deer, merganser ducks, otters, mink, black bears (catching salmon), osprey (and their nests atop tall snags), great blue herons, kingfishers, swooping cliff swallows (with mud nests on overhangs), and water ouzels. Try identifying the many tracks on the riverbanks each morning.

The river itself teems with salamanders, newts, and more than twenty species of fish, including chinook salmon, steelhead, rainbow trout, sturgeon, shad, carp, lamprey, sculpin, stickleback, and dace. Among Oregon rivers, only the Columbia provides a higher annual fish catch.

Hikers encounter scurrying lizards, blue-tailed skinks, and occasionally rattle-snakes on the dry slopes. This is the northernmost habitat for the nocturnal ringtail, a tiny, big-eared relative of the raccoon once employed by miners to catch mice in mines. The Douglas fir forests include lush red cedar and rhododendron in the west but yield to canyon live oak and red-barked madrone in the more arid east. Brushfields of manzanita and chinkapin limit cross-country travel. May brings trailside blue iris and white bear grass blooms; expect blue lupine and California poppies in June.

Geology

Tough, 150-million-year-old lava restricts the Rogue River through much of its lower gorge. A massive landslide visible just west of Whisky Creek briefly dammed 15 miles of the Rogue in the 1880s. Unusual kettle-shaped potholes in the riverbank rock, best seen near Clay Hill Rapids, form when floodwaters swirl pebbles in depressions, drill-ing them deeper.

History

The river's name comes from the Tututni and Takelma Indians, whom the early French trappers called *coquins* or "rogues." After white miners attacked a peaceful Indian vil-lage on a reservation near Medford in 1855, killing twenty-three, the Indians responded by killing Rogue Valley settlers and retreating to this remote part of the river canyon for winter.

The next April, soldiers tracked the Indians to Battle Bar and traded fire across the river before turning back. A month later, a Takelma band under Tyee John besieged an Army unit on a knoll at Illahe's Big Bend, killing eleven. Relief troops from the east fled when Indians rolled rocks on them from a hillside near Brushy Bar, but a column of soldiers from Gold Beach broke the siege. More than 1400 Tututni and Takelma tribespeople were transported north to the coastal Siletz Reservation.

In 1926, author Zane Grey bought a miner's cabin at Winkle Bar, where he fished and wrote his popular Wild West books. Few unguided parties ran the river until the 1930s, when boatmen dynamited boulders in the most difficult rapids. Slim Pickens Rapids and Blossom Bar dropped to class 3 and class 4 white water, respectively.

Until 1963, mules packed mail on the Rogue River Trail from Marial to Agness, where mail boats left for Gold Beach. Although pavement now extends up the canyon to Agness, jet-powered mail boats still make the run, carrying tourists.

THINGS TO DO
Hiking

The prime trip here is the 40-mile Rogue River Trail backpack trip from Illahe to Grave Creek. Day hikers can sample scenic parts of the route. Because the sometimes rocky trail traverses steep slopes several hundred feet above the river, it is closed to horse use.

A 4.3-mile walk from Illahe to Flora Dell Creek's shady glen reaches a trailside

WILD ROGUE

0 1 2 3mi
0 1 2 3 4km
N

Powers 11 mi

Pioneer

Buck Creek

3348

Eden Valley

$

Diamond Pk

43193'

Mt Bolivar

Coquille

235

Lockhart

5520

Buck Pt

×2800'

Daphne Grove

$

140

Hanging Rock

Mul Fork

Rogue River Ranch Museum

Grave Cr 29 mi

Peacock

Island

Squaw Lake

5520

Rogue

3954'

Tu ker Flat

Mule Cr

G

Rock Creek

Panther Ridge

Marial

Quall Cr

Azalea

3630'

020

Devils Stairs Rapids

Mule Creek

Zane Grey's Cabin

Paradise Cr

Mule Cr Canyon

33

Devils Backbone

390'

Bald Knob

026

3200'

Brushy Bar

Blossom Bar

The Coffeepot

Stair Creek Falls

Flora Dell Cr

Tate Cr

3730

Clay Hill Rapids

Wild River

East Fork

Stair Cr

Illahe

33

×207'

Rogue

Fall Cr

Watson Cr

Bobs Garden Mtn
4325'

Foster Bar

Illahe

$

Green Knob

23

Costa Cr

Shasta

Whitten Prairie

High Ridge

Brandy Pk
5316'

Bear Camp Pasture

Galice 17 mi

Agness

Gold Beach 26 mi

Lucas Lodge

Raspberry Mtn

2308

Squirrel Pk

Lazy Cr

33

150

070

West Fork

055

450

North Fork

Sugarloaf Mtn

510

Oak Flat

×234'

Indigo Prairie

161

Fish Hook Pk
5030'

×2950'

Illinois

Nancy Cr

3600'

East Fork

Buzzards Roost

1146'

Lawson Cr

Indigo

Cr

Lawson Butte

Horse Sign Cr

R

Silver Pk

N Fk

Silver Cr

Silver Prairie

4126'

Little Silver Cr

(See Area 35 Map)

waterfall. Those who drive the gravel road to Marial, at the Rogue River Trail's mid-point, can hike 2.1 miles downriver, past inspiring viewpoints of The Coffeepot and Slide Creek Falls to Blossom Bar, a good spot to photograph frantic boaters. East of the trailhead at Marial's Rogue River Ranch Museum, a 4.8-mile hike up the river trail leads to Winkle Bar, where Zane Grey's log cabin is on private land. At the east end of the Rogue River Trail, from the Grave Creek Trailhead, a 3.5-mile walk passes 15-foot Rainie Falls on the way to Whisky Creek, where an 1880 mining cabin is open as a museum.

Hikers should be alert for yellow jackets, wood ticks, rattlesnakes, and prolific growths of head-high poison oak. Campers can expect nocturnal visits by the area's

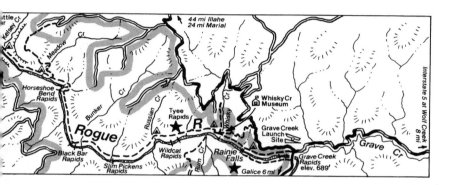

numerous black bears, particularly in the Brushy Bar–Clay Hill area. Here, bears have grown bold from finding easy meals in boaters' cooler chests and hikers' backpacks. Hang all food at least 10 feet above ground and 5 feet from a tree trunk.

Lodges at Illahe, Clay Hill Rapids, Paradise Creek, and Marial offer meals and lodging by reservation. Scheduled daily jet boats take hikers from Gold Beach to the Clay Hill and Paradise Lodges between May 15 and October 15 and to Lucas Lodge in Agness between May 1 and November 1. Expect to pay about $80 for the boat trip and $190 for a double room with meals. For reservations, call (800) 525-2161.

Surprisingly few day hikers have discovered the first-rate viewpoints on a ridge crest high above the Rogue River's north shore. Two short hikes are tops here: a 1.4-mile path gaining 1160 feet up scenic Mount Bolivar, and a rhododendron-lined 2-mile trail from Buck Point to Hanging Rock (bring binoculars to spot rafters on Blossom Bar, 3600 feet below). For a longer trip, hike 10.5 miles along Panther Ridge from Buck Point to Bald Knob's lookout tower. Backpackers can tackle a 38-mile loop: hike from Illahe on the Rogue River Trail to Marial, climb to Buck Point on a trail up the West Fork of Mule Creek, and return along Panther Ridge and Road 026.

The Illinois River Trail, south of Agness, offers an excellent 2.5-mile day hike (one way) to the craggy promontory of Buzzards Roost, with views in both directions along this green-pooled river's canyon. Backpackers will want to hike the entirety of the 27-mile Illinois River Trail (see Area 35, Kalmiopsis, for a description). Those who can not arrange the required car shuttle can make a base camp at Indigo Creek for forays to the meadows and old-growth ponderosa pines in the rarely visited Silver Peak and Indigo Prairie areas, swept by fire in 1987.

One of the area's best-kept secrets is a 1-mile trail to 60-foot Silver Falls, in the narrow, fern-draped gorge of Silver Creek. This hike is not shown on the map and is difficult to locate because of missing signs and confusing, muddy roads. From Galice, drive 0.3 mile toward Merlin, turn west on paved Galice Access Road for 9.5 miles to a 5-way junction, turn left on Road 35-9-1 for 4.2 miles, and fork left on rough Road 050 for 6 miles to its end.

Boating

The 40-mile, wild stretch of Rogue River between Grave Creek and Illahe is Oregon's most famous and popular three-day white-water trip.

Rafts, kayaks, and drift boats have hardly left the launch before they hit the spray of class 3 Grave Creek Rapids. Half an hour later the increasing roar of 15-foot-tall Rainie Falls warns boaters to portage by lining craft down the shallow fish ladder on the right. Large, well-constructed rafts of inner tubes sometimes succeed in running massive Rainie Falls, but such vehicles later often wedge side-to-side in Mule Creek Canyon or hang up on Blossom Bar's boulders.

Beyond the falls, pull in at Whisky Creek for a quarter-mile side trip to a well-preserved mining cabin. Downstream 1.2 miles, pull out again to scout class 4 Tyee Rapids. Keep to the far right to avoid a suckhole and then a house-sized rock. Promptly thereafter come class 3 Wildcat Rapids, with a submerged, spiny-backed rock known as The Alligator.

After passing the historic Rogue River Ranch Museum at Marial on the second day (or third, for slower drifters), boats accelerate toward class 4 Mule Creek Canyon, a chasm so narrow and turbulent that it is easy to lose an oar just when the need is greatest. After spring floods, scout from shore for logs jammed sideways. Past the canyon's final, dizzying Coffeepot comes Stair Creek's lovely side waterfall—a good swimming area.

Blossom Bar, 1.3 miles beyond, requires scouting from the right. Following this treacherous, class 4 boulder field are the Devils Stairs, where the river drops 30 feet in a 300-yard series of chutes.

On the trip's final day, hike up to Tate Creek's shady waterfall pool, with a 25-foot natural slide of rock so smooth swimmers can zip down its chute *sans* suit.

Campers on the heavily used riverbars and creek benches must use stoves or bring their own firewood and metal fire pans. In summer, seek out solitude by camping away from side creeks on gravel bars or dry benches. Bring an approved pump to filter river water.

Perhaps the greatest challenge of the Rogue River is getting a permit to launch at all. During the restricted season from May 15 to October 15, only 120 permits are issued for each day, chosen by lottery from ten times that many applications. To join the lottery, contact Tioga Resources Inc. at (541) 672-4168 or *www.umpcoos.com/rogue*

and submit your application between December 1 and January 30. More than one person from each group can apply. Expect a $4 application fee and an additional $12 per person fee if you actually win a permit. If you do not win in the lottery, you can either sign up on a waiting list for cancellations, pay $500 or more to go on a commercially guided trip, or plan a trip in the off-season's iffy weather. By October, skies turn a misty gray and the river grows chilly. During winter rainstorms, high water can make the river too dangerous to run. When snow closes the 55-mile car shuttle route's twisty mountain roads (usually from November to May), the only alternative is to drive a 180-mile detour on highways via Crescent City.

37 Grassy Knob

Location: 51 miles south of Coos Bay, 9 miles east of Port Orford
Size: 39 square miles
Status: 27 square miles designated wilderness (1984)
Terrain: Rain forest–covered canyons and ridges
Elevation: 100 feet–2924 feet
Management: Siskiyou NF
Topographic maps: Father Mountain, Mount Butler, Sixes, Port Orford (USGS)

Fog drips from the tangled forest of this virtually trailless wilderness, where ridge tops provide surprising glimpses out to Cape Blanco's fringe of ocean islands.

Climate
Heavy winter rains push the average annual precipitation to more than 130 inches. Summers are mostly sunny, because the area lies just inland of the coastal fog belt.

Plants and Wildlife
The rain forests here provide something precious in the heavily roaded southern Coast Range: pure, cold water. Close to 90 percent of the Sixes River's salmon spawn in Dry Creek and the South Fork Sixes River. Upriver clearcutting has pushed the Elk River's summer water temperatures to levels nearly fatal for fish, but Grassy Knob's small, shady creeks offer a cool retreat.

Rare, old-growth Port Orford cedar grow as large as 6 feet in diameter here, with snaky limbs and characteristic white Xs on the underside of green leaf scales. Popular worldwide as a landscaping shrub, this fragrant cedar's small native range (five coastal counties) is shrinking rapidly. Japanese buyers pay as much as $10,000 for a single tree, because its wood is a close substitute for Japan's highly prized, and nearly extinct, hinoki cypress.

The *Phytophthora* root-rot fungus, accidentally introduced here from a Portland nursery in 1944, travels easily through groundwater, killing every Port Orford cedar in an infected drainage. Because the fungus can be carried in dirt on tire treads, the roadless side of Grassy Knob may be the wild Port Orford cedar's last stand.

Geology

Though largely hidden by forest, Grassy Knob's rocks consist of heavily folded and compacted sea-floor sediment scraped up the Klamath Mountains in the past 200 million years while that range slowly moved westward, overriding the Pacific plate.

History

A reconnaissance plane for a Japanese submarine dropped a 170-pound incendiary bomb into the forest between Grassy Knob and Dry Creek in 1942 in an attempt to start a fire. Alarmed rangers at the mountain's lookout tower radioed the Army Air Force. Because of confusion about the lookout's location—south of the city of North Bend—U.S. fighters streaked to the central Oregon town of Bend, where there were no submarines. Japanese pilot Nubuo Fujita landed his plane on pontoons, unbolted the wings, mounted the craft to his submarine's deck, and dived to safety.

However, the Japanese bomb failed to explode. Despite many searches, it has never been found.

THINGS TO DO
Hiking

The area's only official footpath, the Grassy Knob Trail, was converted to a 30-foot-wide gravel road in the waning months of the 1984 wilderness designation battle. A local

View from the summit of Grassy Knob

Forest Service supervisor with an antiwilderness bias had ordered the road-building project to disqualify the area for wilderness status. Congress was so angry at this "legislation by bulldozer," however, that they declared Grassy Knob a wilderness nonetheless. Today the old roadbed, closed to vehicles by a barricade and stripped of its culverts, has regrown with trees and wildflowers to serve once again as a surprisingly pleasant trail.

Hike 0.4 mile up the trail and detour 100 yards up to the right to the viewpoint on Grassy Knob's summit, once a fire lookout site. Then continue 0.7 mile up the trail to its end at a 2-acre gravel turnaround. Once intended as a base for logging the wilderness' forests, the plain of young trees and flowers now serves as an unofficial monument to the difficult task of wilderness preservation. A very roughly brushed-out trail route continues a mile to Anvil Mountain.

To drive to the Grassy Knob Trail from Port Orford, drive 4 miles north on Highway 101 and turn right on the Grassy Knob Road for 7 miles to the barricade.

Photographers looking for emerald green glens of waterfalls, autumn-red vine maple, and droopy Port Orford cedar will want to hike the passable cross-country route up misnamed Dry Creek. Another option is to ford the shallow Elk River and explore the mossy canyons of Sunshine Creek or Red Cedar Creek. For views of the area's forested ridges, try the abandoned trail to Mount Butler from Road 390, or follow an abandoned road along Moon Mountain's ridge-top crest to a regenerating, square-mile clearcut within the designated wilderness.

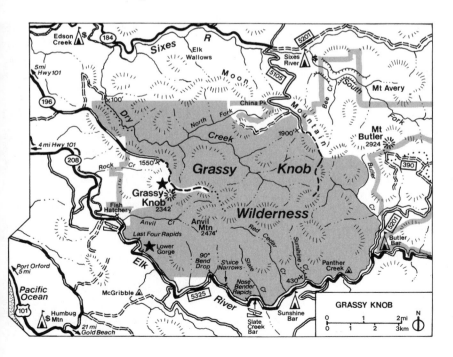

Boating

The Elk River winds between narrow rock walls, alternating emerald green pools with lots of class 4 white water. Launch at unmarked Slate Creek Bar, 6.3 miles by road from the take-out point at the Elk River fish hatchery. Just 0.2 mile from the launch, beware of Nose Bender Rapids, especially in low water, when this 6-foot drop's rating increases from 3 to 4. Other class 4 rapids include Sluice Narrows, 90° Bend Drop, the scenic Lower Gorge, and Last Four Rapids.

To drive to the river, turn off Highway 101, 3 miles north of Port Orford. While driving to the launch site, scout the river for sweepers, the area's chief hazard.

38   Oregon Dunes

Location: Coos Bay to Florence
Size: 50 square miles
Status: National recreation area (1972)
Terrain: Sand dunes, ocean beach, lakes, forest
Elevation: 0 feet–1000 feet
Management: Siuslaw NF
Topographic map: Oregon Dunes NRA (USFS)

Sea and sand lovers take note: Here you can backpack through an oceanfront Sahara, hang glide off the top of 400-foot dunes, or gallop on 45 miles of beach. Bird watchers can count 247 species where meandering creeks cross the sand. Hikers can explore the wind-rippled sand hills that inspired Oregon author Frank Herbert to write the science fiction classic *Dune*.

Climate

The marine climate brings cool summers and wet, mild winters. Summer fogs occasionally burn off by afternoon. Spring and fall see the most sunshine. Average annual precipitation hits 75 inches.

Plants and Wildlife

On the beach itself, watch the waves for harbor seals and the spouts of gray whales (December to May).

At creek mouths, bald eagles swoop for fish. Snowy egrets and great blue herons stand stilt-legged in the shallows. Canada geese migrating on the Pacific Flyway stop to forage wild grains in the estuaries. Hundreds of elegant tundra swans winter in the south Siuslaw spit's sandy marshes. In all, it is possible to tally 118 species of aquatic birds, 108 species of songbirds, and 21 species of birds of prey.

Rarest of the coastal birds is the small, chubby, western snowy plover, distinguished from sanderlings by its white shoulder yoke—and by its refusal to run piping along

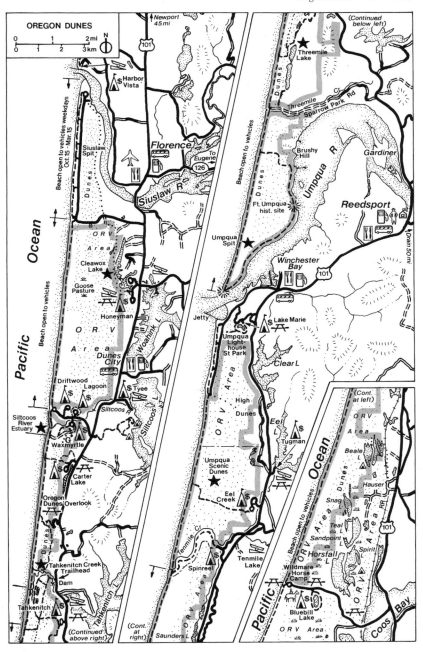

OREGON DUNES

the beach's wet sand in search of food. Instead the plover finds sand fleas among drift-wood and beachgrass near creek mouths, where it also scoops out its shallow sand nest in plain sight. Off-road vehicles (ORVs) and nest-robbing crows have cut coastal plover populations to less than 100, although about 900 birds of the same species eke out a living beside desert lake playas in southeast Oregon, where ORVs are also becoming a threat to their survival.

Plants and sand battle each other here on two fronts. To the east, winds shift the steep face of the high dunes 6 to 10 feet farther inland each year, burying forests alive. To the west, European beach grass (originally introduced to stabilize sand near developments) has spread along the entire beachfront, creating a 30-foot-tall foredune that blocks sand from blowing inland. Behind the foredune, winds have stripped a broad "deflation plain" of sand, allowing a succession of brush and trees to gain a foothold.

In the deflation plain, watch for the insect-eating sundew plant, which traps prey in sticky drops of imitation dew. Among the alder and coast willow of the forest drainageways, look for yellow skunk cabbage and eight of Oregon's fifteen salamander species. In the spruce and hemlock forests, admire white trilliums in March, 20-foot-tall pink rhododendrons in April, and chanterelle mushrooms in October.

Geology

Most of Oregon's coastline is too steep and rocky to collect much sand, but here winds have repeatedly pushed waves of dunes inland across a coastal plain. Each fresh on-slaught of sand buries forests, peters out, then sprouts with brush and trees of its own.

However, European beach grass stabilized a wall-like oceanfront foredune in the 1950s, blocking off the area's sand supply. The present high dunes are expected to run out of sand and stop their eastward march within ninety to 200 years. Because the stubborn European beach grass regrows when burnt or plowed, the Forest Service has experimented with breaching the foredune with bulldozers to set the dune-formation cycle in motion again.

The broad mudflats at the mouths of Oregon's coastal rivers are indirect products of the Ice Age. When enlarged polar ice caps converted much of the earth's water to ice, oceans dropped 300 feet and rivers cut their valleys deeper to match. When the ice melted 6000 years ago, the ocean rose into the widened river mouths. Sand and river silt have since converted these fjords to shallow estuaries.

History

The U.S. Army established Fort Umpqua on the Umpqua River spit in 1856 to watch over Indians of the Siletz Reservation to the north. After a visiting paymaster in 1862 found every officer, commissioned and noncommissioned, away on a hunting trip, the fort was permanently closed.

Before completion of a coast highway in the 1930s, stagecoaches traveled the hard sand beaches of low tide between Florence, Reedsport, and Coos Bay. This led to public ownership of all Oregon beaches under the Department of Transportation. Beaches are now park land.

Tracks in the Oregon Dunes

THINGS TO DO
Hiking

Short forest trails lead to the open sand, where hikers can explore dunes, tree islands, and lakes without need of marked routes. Remember that walking in dry sand takes twice the time and energy of a hike on solid ground.

Off-road vehicles (ORVs) are allowed in about half of the area. The noise, tracks, and danger of speeding dune buggies in these areas reduce their appeal to hikers. Beaches are subject to varying vehicle closure rules (see map) but warrant hiking regardless. The following hikes, listed from north to south, are outside ORV areas unless otherwise noted.

Swimmers at Cleawox Lake slide down a 100-foot sand dune into the clear water. This extremely popular lake borders both Girl Scout Camp Cleawox and Honeyman Park, a 382-unit state campground. While ORVs are banned near the south end of the lake, expect motor traffic when prowling over the dramatic dunes toward the area's interesting tree islands, Goose Pasture (a brushy bird-watching site), or the beach.

The short Siltcoos River meanders through campgrounds and dunes. A 0.7-mile, self-guided nature trail loops around Lagoon Campground, touring an oxbow slough of the river. From Waxmyrtle Campground, a trail leads 1 mile along the river past open dunes to the beach. To make a pleasant 2.6-mile loop, wade the warm, calf-deep river at its mouth and return on a trail past Driftwood Campground.

Want a break from sun and sand? Hike inland from Highway 101 on a 4.3-mile loop through a cool, lush forest of ferns and Douglas firs to several primitive campsites on the shore of Siltcoos Lake.

Marked by posts in the sand, a fun 4.8-mile loop trail through the dunes and along the beach to Tahkenitch Creek begins at the Oregon Dunes Overlook picnic area.

Some of the quietest and most spectacular sand landscapes lie between Tahkenitch Creek and remote Threemile Lake. From the Tahkenitch Creek Trailhead (between mileposts 202 and 203 of Highway 101), a network of trails explores the creek's estuary. Possible loop trips are 1.6, 2.6, and 4.2 miles long. From Tahkenitch Campground, a 6.5-mile loop trail climbs 2.7 miles along a forested ridge to backpacking campsites at the edge of the dunes overlooking Threemile Lake. The loop path then follows posts to the beach and north 1.3 miles before returning through the dunes.

Clams, huckleberries, dunes, and views lure hikers to the 6.5-mile-long Umpqua River Spit. For a scenic route to this vast sand peninsula, cross by boat from nearby Winchester Bay. Otherwise, park at the end of gravel on the Threemile Creek Road (100 yards short of the beach), hike south a mile on the beach, and follow a dune-buggy road inland to the dunes. Look for late August huckleberries on Brushy Hill; very low tides expose clamming mudflats along the Umpqua River below the hill. The long, rock jetty at spit's end is a good spot to watch pounding waves and ocean-going ships.

An easy warm-up hike near Winchester Bay loops 0.5 mile around forest-lined Lake Marie at Umpqua Lighthouse State Park. Top the walk with a visit to the adjacent lighthouse.

ORVs dominate Oregon's tallest dunes, south of Lake Marie. Hikers bent on exploring these 400-foot sand mountains should watch for the red flags ORVs display atop 9-foot antennas, because dune buggies often zip blindly over dune crests.

The 280-foot-tall Umpqua Scenic Dunes provide a 4-square-mile sand playground off limits to ORVs. A 2.4-mile trail from Eel Creek Campground leads through woods to the open sand and continues to the beach.

Beale Lake's scenic dunes, meadows, and isthmus make another good goal. Park at Hauser and hike along the railroad tracks 1 mile north to the lake.

Long-distance hikers can tramp the beach 23.7 miles from the tip of the Siuslaw Spit to the tip of the Umpqua Spit, but more interesting routes alternate beach hiking with dune exploration.

Throughout the Oregon Dunes, hikers should heed a few tips: Carry plenty of water. When hiking cross-country to the beach, mark the return route through the foredune with a stick in the sand. The open dunes have few landmarks, especially in the frequent fogs. When lost, simply listen—the sound of surf or traffic will point the way to the ocean or Highway 101. Camp well above the beach's driftwood line (night has its high tide too), and bring a sleeping pad (sand is rock hard). Fires on the beach are discouraged, and fires in piles of driftwood are banned.

Equestrians often begin beach rides at Wildmare Horse Camp near Bluebill Lake Campground, though many other beach access points are also feasible.

Boating

The coastal dunes have dammed dozens of large, many-armed freshwater lakes. Sinuous shorelines make for interesting canoe paddling. Steady west winds provide first-rate sailing conditions but can create large waves on summer afternoons. Warm water makes windsurfing practical.

Cleawox Lake, with its steep sand dune shore and long, narrow arms is the most popular nonmotorized boating site. Launch at crowded Honeyman Park.

Launch at Tyee Campground to canoe up the Siltcoos River to 5-square-mile Siltcoos Lake. For an overnight trip, paddle to the lakeshore campsites on the Siltcoos Trail loop.

Tahkenitch Lake covers 3 square miles but has nearly 100 miles of shoreline worth exploring by canoe. Launch at a boat ramp on Highway 101. Carry a canoe 160 yards down the Tahkenitch Creek Trail to launch there and paddle the lazy creek 2 miles to its mouth. Both Tahkenitch Lake and Siltcoos Lake are heavily used by fishermen for warmwater bass and easily caught yellow perch.

Hang Gliding

Reliable west winds and unobstructed landing sites make the 400-foot-tall High Dunes an excellent practice area. Hike 1 mile east from the last parking lot south of Winchester Bay on the jetty road. Watch for ORVs.

39 Wassen Creek

Location: 13 miles east of Reedsport
Size: 24 square miles
Status: Undesignated wilderness
Terrain: Steep, densely forested creek valley
Elevation: 20 feet–1760 feet
Management: Siuslaw NF, Coos Bay District BLM
Topographic maps: Scottsburg, Smith River Falls, Deer Head Point, North Fork (USGS)

In this forgotten Coast Range valley, Wassen Creek splashes over stairstep falls and eddies against dark cliffs. Side streams tumble from steep slopes of sword fern and salmonberry. Rain drips from the great, drooping branches of age-old red cedar, Douglas fir, and western hemlock.

Trillium

Adventurers exploring the creek's 14 miles of trailless, twisting canyon must follow paths blazed by elk and bear—or else hike the route of the canyon's cheery water ouzels, the creekbed itself.

Climate

Torrential winter rains boost annual precipitation to 90 inches. The dry summers are free of the coastal fog that socks in Highway 101 just a few miles west.

Plants and Wildlife

In the deep forest look for white trillium and yellow Oregon grape in early spring. Rhododendrons put out pink blooms in April. By early fall both blue and red huckleberry are ripe for picking.

Expect great blue herons and Pacific giant salamanders at Wassen Lake. In old-growth woods, watch for the red top-feathers of pileated woodpeckers and the dark eyes of silent spotted owls. Bald eagles soar above the creek canyon. Sea-run fish cannot leap the falls at the Devils Staircase, leaving the upper creek to small trout and bright red crawdads.

Geology

This part of the Coast Range began as mud-covered sea floor 50 million years ago. It lay directly in the path of the North American continent, which was crunching westward over the Pacific sea floor at the geologically speedy rate of an inch a year. However, a fracture in the Pacific floor lifted the Coast Range above the waves, where it became the western edge of the advancing continent.

As a result, Wassen Creek now flows over layers of weak sandstone and nutrient-poor, washed-out red clays that originated on the bottom of the sea. The area is roadless in part because roadcuts in such soils send entire hillsides sliding toward the creek. Wassen Lake itself formed when a slump dammed the creek's headwaters about 150 years ago. Snags of drowned trees still stand in the 5-acre lake.

THINGS TO DO
Hiking

Trails are in short supply, but the valley's solitude and beauty inspire cross-country exploration. Canyon slopes are so steep and rugged that it is easiest to wear tennis shoes and wool socks and wade along the creekbed itself. Wading is most pleasant in the warm weather of summer and early fall. Because the sandy creek bottom has some slippery mudstone, a walking stick is essential, and hikers with packs will want two. Occasional parklike openings invite camping.

The area's only trail begins at Wassen Lake. Rimmed with alder and old-growth conifers, the shallow lake teems with rough-skinned newts. A very rough 2-mile path follows 10-foot-wide Wassen Creek upstream and climbs to a road landing near the National Forest boundary. Bushwhackers can also circle Wassen Lake or prowl downstream along Wassen Creek.

Road access to Wassen Lake is entirely paved. Drive Highway 38 (between Reedsport and Drain); a quarter mile west of milepost 19 turn north on Wells Creek

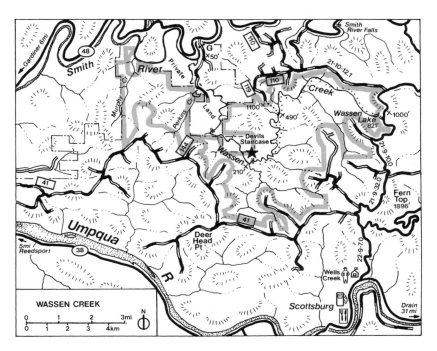

Road (BLM 22-9-7.0) for 2.3 miles. Then fork left onto paved Fern Top Road (BLM 21-9-32.0) for 3.3 miles, veer right on Wassen Lake Road (BLM 21-9-10.0) for 3.7 miles, and park at an unmarked pullout. Walk 100 yards down an old road to the left to the lake.

Only a handful of mortals have penetrated Wassen Creek's central canyon to visit the Devils Staircase, a series of five stair-stepped falls totaling 40 feet, with circular, greenish potholes large enough for swimming. For a bushwhacking route to Wassen Creek's central canyon, drive a mile north past Wassen Lake on the paved Wassen Lake Road, turn left on gravel Road 21-20-12.1 for 4 miles to Road 110, continue straight 1.7 miles, and then turn left on Road 119 to its end, avoiding smaller spur tracks. From here, walk out the ridge to find a trail paralleling the clearcut's edge. This rough path continues into the forest down to the creek. Hang a bright marker by the creek to help locate the route back to the car. Four trailless miles downstream is the Devils Staircase, but the trek is too rugged for a one-day trip.

 Oregon Islands

Location: Along Oregon coast
Size: 1477 islands/groups (1.2 square miles)
Status: 56 islands/groups (0.8 square miles) designated wilderness and national wildlife refuge (1970, 1978)
Terrain: Small, wave-swept, rock islands
Elevation: 0 feet–327 feet
Management: Coos Bay District BLM, U.S. Fish and Wildlife Service
Topographic maps: Tillamook Head, Newport North, Cape Blanco, Cape Sebastian, and others (USGS)

Nesting seabirds and lolling sea lions crowd the nation's smallest and least accessible designated wilderness—the surf-pounded islands scattered along the length of Oregon's Pacific shore.

Climate

Wet, frost-free winters and cool, fog-shrouded summers push annual precipitation from 60 to 100 inches. In summer, north winds generally bring fair skies, while south winds presage storms. In winter, storms come from all angles, battering the islands with 40-foot waves and high winds. Six- to twelve-foot tides submerge many rocks twice daily.

Plants and Wildlife

The islands' fascinating bird and sea mammal colonies are best observed from mainland viewpoints, particularly with the aid of binoculars or a spotting scope. Access to wilderness islands is generally impossible, but it is banned nonetheless, and boats are

Tufted puffin

allowed no closer than 200 yards to islands included in the federal wildlife refuge. In many areas, island wildlife has already been severely hurt by people who venture within 200 yards by boat, sailboard, kayak, jet ski, scuba gear, or airplane. The approach of humans startles seabirds, allowing their eggs to fall from nests and break. Similarly, human contact can cause sea lions and seals to abandon their pups.

From April to August, thousands of murres crowd the rocks to nest—the only time these black-and-white, loonlike birds visit land. Also in summer look for tufted puffins (with unmistakable, red-and-orange-striped bills) and their close relatives, the virtually neckless little auklets and murrelets.

When these birds leave for winter, other species arrive: long-necked loons, scoters (small sea ducks), and grebes (resembling clumsy, dark-backed swans). Year-round residents include five species of gulls and two kinds of black, crook-necked cormorants.

The brown dots seen on these islands from a distance are often 600- to 2200-pound Steller sea lions. Smaller harbor seals among the waves often watch humans with a curiosity rivaling our own. Also look for the spouts of gray whales, which pass here from December to February as they migrate toward Mexico, and from March to May as they return to Alaska. Sea otters, whose fur first brought regular European trade to these shores, were driven to extinction in Oregon by 1911. An attempt to reintroduce sea otters near Cape Blanco in 1970 failed.

Most islands support few plants beyond sea palms and bobbing kelp seaweed.

Others are topped with brushy salal, twinberry, and stunted spruce. Seacliff stonecrop, a thick-leaved flower threatened in Oregon, is known only from these islands.

The best wildlife viewing sites are at the Yaquina Head lighthouse 3 miles north of Newport, on the Cape Meares Loop Road west of Tillamook, at Cape Kiwanda near Pacific City, at the state park on Cape Blanco, at Boardman State Park north of Brookings, and from the shore at Brookings itself.

Geology

Wave erosion separated these islands' resistant rock from the softer rock of the mainland, much as tides reduce a sand castle to the pebbles that once topped its towers. All islands along the northern half of the Oregon Coast, from Astoria to Seal Rock, consist of tough, black Columbia River basalt. This lava welled up near Idaho about 15 million years ago and poured west 300 miles through the Columbia Gorge to the ocean in a series of long lava flows.

The islands south of Bandon are 20 times older, belonging to the ancient Klamath Mountains. Many of these islands consist of heavy, resistant blueschist, a rock prized for use in jetties.

History

Two of Oregon's offshore islands have been inhabited. Sea lion bones and clamshells remain from an Indian camp on Zwagg Island beside Brookings. Dutch hermit Folker Von Der Zwaag, who moved to the island in 1889 with his dog Sniff, is remembered for the trolley he devised to retrieve fresh water from the mainland automatically.

A lighthouse built with great difficulty on Tillamook Rock in 1879 was abandoned in 1934 and sold as surplus government property in 1957. After shifting ownership several times, the island ended up with Eternity at Sea, a funeral business that helicopters out urns with the ashes of people who want to be buried in the lighthouse when they die.

Though an estimated 2 million birds used Oregon's offshore rocks in 1940, their numbers have declined to fewer than 500,000 because of development along the coast.

Opposite: *The Pine Lakes in the Eagle Cap Wilderness*

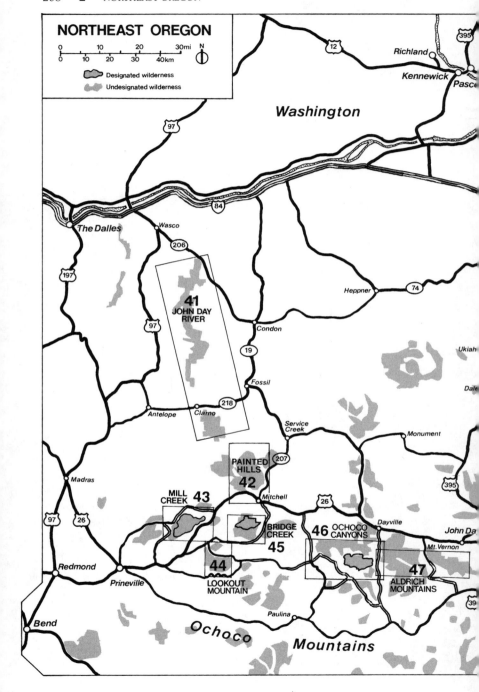

NORTHEAST OREGON

| 0 | 10 | 20 | 30mi | N |
| 0 | 10 | 20 | 30 | 40km |

Designated wilderness

Undesignated wilderness

Washington

Richland

Kennewick   Pasc

The Dalles   Wasco

Heppner

41
JOHN DAY
RIVER

Condon

Ukiah

Dale

Fossil

Antelope   Clarno

Service
Creek

Monument

PAINTED
HILLS
42

MILL
CREEK 43   Mitchell

BRIDGE
CREEK
45

46 OCHOCO
CANYONS

Dayville

John Da

Mt. Vernon

Madras

44
LOOKOUT
MOUNTAIN

47
ALDRICH
MOUNTAINS

Redmond

Prineville

Paulina

Bend   Ochoco   Mountains

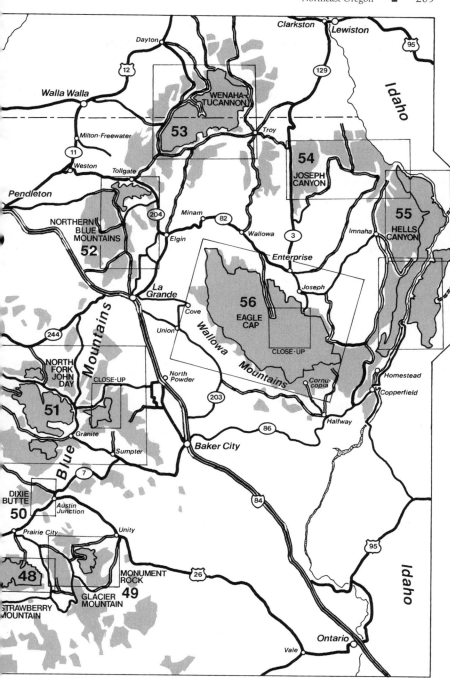

41 John Day River

Location: 41 miles southeast of The Dalles
Size: 93 square miles
Status: Federal wild and scenic river
Terrain: Sagebrush canyonlands, river rapids
Elevation: 540 feet–3600 feet
Management: Prineville District BLM
Topographic maps: Muddy Ranch, Clarno, Chimney Springs, Bath Canyon, Shoestring Ridge, Horseshoe Bend, Indian Cove, Harmony, Esau Canyon (USGS)

Boaters on the uncrowded John Day River often float for days through the winding, cliff-lined canyons without seeing more than a dozen people. Pictographs, fossils, and abandoned ranch houses make good goals for day hikes near the river.

Climate

The hot summers are virtually rainless. The freezing winters accumulate no snowpack. With just 10 inches of annual rainfall, this portion of the John Day flows as a river only because of precipitation in the distant Ochocos and Blue Mountains.

Plants and Wildlife

The sagebrush steppe here features hedgehog cactus (blooms red in April) and matlike prickly pear cactus. Look for rare yellow hairy paintbrush in May. Occasional junipers dot slopes, while creeks harbor wild rose, red osier dogwood, and snowberry.

Golden eagles and prairie falcons patrol the canyon skies. Canada geese, mergansers, goldeneyes, and green-winged teals paddle ahead of boaters. The river's salmon runs died in 1889 with construction of a since-demolished grist mill dam. Steelhead trout, bullhead, and suckers remain. Smallmouth bass, introduced in 1971, thrive.

Hikers should be alert for scorpions and rattlesnakes, though chances are greater of meeting cattle, wild horses, mule deer, coyotes, and startled, partridgelike chukars.

Geology

Fossils from the Clarno Unit of the John Day Fossil Beds National Monument indicate this area was a coastal rain forest 34 million years ago. Primitive rhinoceroses and tapirs flourished alongside ferns and avocado trees.

The creation of the Cascade Range 16 to 33 million years ago not only dried up this area by blocking moisture from the sea but it also buried the landscape repeatedly with volcanic ashfalls, preserving countless fossils, including the skeletons of saber-toothed tigers and small, three-toed horses. The many layers of red, buff, and green volcanic ash form the Painted Hills visible on the west riverbank 4 miles north of Clarno. Vast floods of Columbia River basalt 13 to 16 million years ago capped the area with a rimrock of black lava. Cliffs exhibit basalt's characteristic hexagonal pillars.

History

Numerous Indian house-pit sites and pictographs (painted rock carvings) testify to more than 4500 years of human habitation along the river. From 1866 to 1930 white settlers built the remote riverside ranches whose abandoned buildings remain. Be sure to leave all homesteading memorabilia in place.

THINGS TO DO
Hiking

The area's only marked trails are interpretive nature paths at the John Day Fossil Beds National Monument's picnic area on Highway 218, east of the Clarno Bridge 3 miles. A 0.3-mile connector path leads from the picnic area west to an unmarked parking pullout where two trails begin. The Trail of the Fossils is a 0.2-mile loop on a slope with boulders containing leaf and branch fossils. The Clarno Arch Trail climbs 0.2 mile to a viewpoint by a massive cliff with a dainty, 10-foot natural rock arch.

Spring Basin is a good spot to try cross-country hiking in the high desert. Wear sturdy shoes and carry water. From the basin's sagebrush plateau, climb to Horse Mountain's pinnacled viewpoint or explore the winding side canyons leading toward the John Day River (though the river's bank is private here). To reach Spring Basin from Clarno, drive 1.5 miles east on Highway 218, turn right onto a dirt road for 3 miles, park, and hike 2 miles up a Bureau of Land Management (BLM) track to the east.

Walk up sandy-bottomed Rattlesnake Canyon between narrow rock

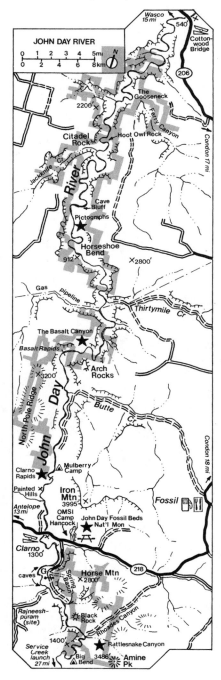

walls, and then scramble cross-country up Amine Peak for one of the area's highest viewpoints. To reach the mouth of Rattlesnake Canyon, park in the same spot as for the Spring Basin hike, but then walk south along the riverside dirt road 5 miles.

Some of the area's finest cross-country hikes prowl the river's side canyons and bluffs in the BLM-owned land between Clarno and Cottonwood Bridge. Because the only public access to these remote lands is by boat, hikes must be planned in conjunction with float trips.

Climbing

The John Day Fossil Beds National Monument near Clarno offers several small blocks and towers, ranging from the level I-4 Steigomonster to the II-5.2-A3 Hancock Tower.

Boating

Plan for four lazy days by raft or three thrilling days by open canoe to drift the 70 scenic miles between Clarno and Cottonwood Bridge. Timing is critical, because this undammed river varies from an unnavigable maelstrom in winter to an unfloatable

Trail at the Clarno Unit of the John Day Fossil Beds National Monument

dribble in September. The river is technically runnable between 800 and 23,000 cubic feet per second (measured at the Service Creek gauging station), but expect the easiest levels (3000-7000 cfs) from April to July and again in November.

The river's wildest water, Clarno Rapids, begins 4.4 miles downstream from the Clarno Bridge launch site. This class 3, canoe-swamping rapid becomes a class 4 canoe-wrecker at water levels above 4000 cfs. Scout or portage on the left, remembering that Lower Clarno Rapids (class 2) lies just downstream. Beyond, however, the only serious white water is class 2+ Basalt Rapids, 15.9 miles from Clarno Bridge.

Expect good camping spots in the Basalt Canyon, a 4-mile-long gorge below Basalt Rapids. Then look back upriver to spot Arch Rocks' twin hoops atop a cliff. Just before Horseshoe Bend, watch the right bank for two wagons used in a movie filmed here in 1928. Then, a mile past Horseshoe Bend, stop at Potlatch Canyon on the right to observe (but not touch) the cliff's Indian pictographs. Cave Bluff's river-level cavern makes a fun stop 3.5 miles further downstream. Another 10 miles along are Hoot Owl Rock, an owl-shaped cliff-top pillar, and Citadel Rock, a fortress-shaped palisade. Cottonwood Bridge is the last public take-out site before a falls and the tamed Columbia's backwaters.

Many who float the John Day launch 44 miles upriver from Clarno at Service Creek, where the BLM maintains a recreation area with campsites. The two- to three-day run to Clarno includes class 2 rapids located 6, 15, and 23 miles downriver from Service Creek.

42 Painted Hills

Location: 40 miles northeast of Prineville
Size: 77 square miles
Status: 4 square miles national monument
Terrain: Colorful badlands, sagebrush rimrock
Elevation: 1750 feet–4694 feet
Management: Prineville District BLM, John Day Fossil Beds National Monument
Topographic maps: Sutton Mountain, Painted Hills, Mitchell, Toney Butte (USGS)

Oregon calendars often feature photographs of the John Day Fossil Beds' colorfully striped ash hills, so many people are familiar with this small national monument's short nature trails. But few have explored Sutton Mountain, in the vast roadless country surrounding the monument.

Climate

With just 12 inches of annual rainfall, these arid hills feature blue skies that are rarely troubled by thunderclouds during the hot summers or snowstorms in the cold winters.

Plants and Wildlife

No plants grow on the soft, fast-eroding clays of the Painted Hills, but the surrounding rimrock plateaus host cheatgrass, bitterbrush, bunchgrass, and sagebrush. A sparse juniper forest clings to Sutton Mountain's slopes, with surprising patches of ponderosa pine and even Douglas fir in the draws.

Geology

The rounded, colorfully striped Painted Hills began as ash that erupted from the ancestral High Cascades volcanoes 33 million years ago and settled in a vast lake here. The resulting yellow claystone was colored by trace minerals—red from oxidized iron and black from manganese. The soil is so soft that footprints last for years, so please stay on designated paths.

Vast floods of Columbia River basalt 13 to 16 million years ago capped the area with a rimrock of black lava. Erosion has uncovered the colorful ash in the Painted Hills' valley, but half a dozen layers of rimrock remain as Sutton Mountain's tilted plateau.

View across the Painted Hills Unit of the John Day Fossil Beds to the west cliff of Sutton Mountain

History

When gold was discovered near John Day in 1862, entrepreneurs built a military road, stagecoach line, and supply route from The Dalles to Canyon City. The road followed Bridge Creek past the Painted Hills. The U.S. government granted the builders a checkerboard of land along the route as payment for their work. Not until the 1990s did the Bureau of Land Management (BLM) reacquire the alternate square miles of private land on Sutton Mountain, opening the area for public use and for study as a designatable wilderness. Cattle grazing is still permitted on the northern two-thirds of Sutton Mountain.

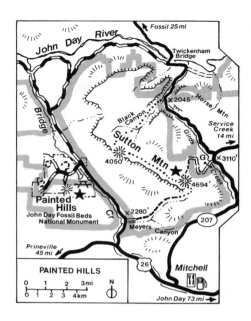

Shortly after the stagecoach road opened in the 1860s, frontier minister Thomas Condon recognized the Painted Hills as a remarkable source of fossils. Condon later became the University of Oregon's first paleontologist and organized excavations here that drew international attention. At Leaf Hill in the 1920s, excavators unearthed more than 20,000 leaf fossils in less than 100 cubic feet of shale.

THINGS TO DO

Hiking

A grassy picnic area and four short hiking trails are the top attractions of the Painted Hills Unit, one of three widely separated parts of the John Day Fossil Beds National Monument. Start by following signs to the Painted Hills Overlook parking area. From there, a 0.3-mile path strolls south along a broad ridge to panoramic views of the colorfully striped clay slopes. For an even better look around, hike the 0.8-mile Carroll Rim Trail, which starts opposite the parking area's entrance road and climbs 400 feet to a viewpoint atop a lava rimrock cliff. Then drive west to visit two short (0.2-mile) interpretive nature loops, the very scenic Painted Cove Trail and the interesting Leaf Hill Loop.

Sutton Mountain presents a nearly unscalable rimrock cliff to the west, but the eastern side of this tilted plateau is much gentler. Several routes climb to the summit rim, where hikers can amble cross-country along the cliff edge for views of the colorful Painted Hills valley. The easiest route, a 3.4-mile abandoned roadbed that gains 1580 feet to the top, begins at a driveway near milepost 15 of Highway 207. Park along the highway and cross Girds Creek on the driveway to a "Road Closed" sign marking the public roadbed.

A different route to the summit begins at the paved road along Bridge Creek and follows an abandoned roadbed up Meyers Canyon. Keep left for 3.6 miles to the track's end at a spring and then bushwhack up a forested ridge 1.5 miles to the top. A third route to the summit plateau follows cattle trails up narrow, cliff-lined Black Canyon from the paved road to Twickenham.

Mill Creek

Location: 20 miles northeast of Prineville
Size: 27 square miles
Status: Designated wilderness (1984)
Terrain: Forested upland valley
Elevation: 3725 feet–6240 feet
Management: Ochoco NF
Topographic maps: Mill Creek Wilderness (USFS); Steins Pillar, Whistler Point (USGS)

Mill Creek is a wholly preserved Ochoco Mountain valley with excellent forest trails, good rock climbing sites, and sweeping viewpoints. Considering that this valley lies just one hour's drive east of Bend, it is surprising Mill Creek is a little-known wilderness in a generally overlooked mountain range.

Climate
The area receives only 25 inches of precipitation annually, primarily as winter snow. Summers are dry and fairly hot. Late spring and fall are pleasant.

Plants and Wildlife
Mill Creek preserves one of the Ochocos' few remaining climax forests of ponderosa pine and bunchgrass. Wildfires traditionally cleared such forests of underbrush. However, decades of overzealous fire suppression have allowed an understory of Douglas fir to grow, enabling fires to reach above the large ponderosa pines' fire-resistant trunks to their flammable crowns, as happened in 1995 when a fire burned 2 square miles at the headwaters of Belknap Creek.

Livestock grazing in some areas limits native flora. Fauna include Rocky Mountain elk, mule deer, bobcat, cougar, and an occasional black bear.

Geology
The Ochoco Mountains formed as a string of coastal volcanoes 40 to 50 million years ago, before the Cascade Range existed. Twin Pillars remain as the plug of an eroded

volcano. When the Ochoco volcanoes subsided and the Old Cascades roared to life 25 million years ago, massive ash deposits covered Eastern Oregon, collecting in lakes and rivers. Rhyolite ash deposits subsequently welded together to form the resistant tuff outcropping at Whistler Point and the 350-foot tower of Steins Pillar. At Whistler Point, in the Ochoco Agate Beds off Road 27, look for baseball-sized thundereggs. The thunderegg, Oregon's state rock, forms when small cavities in the tuff fill with quartz and agate.

THINGS TO DO
Hiking

For a good introduction to this wilderness, take the Twin Pillars Trail from Wildcat Campground through an old-growth ponderosa pine forest along East Fork Mill Creek. To reach Wildcat Campground from Prineville, follow Highway 26 east 10 miles to the far end of Ochoco Reservoir, then turn left for 10.7 miles on Mill Creek Road 33.

The first 2.9 miles of the creekside path are nearly level but include several bridgeless crossings. By summer the crossings can usually be accomplished dry-footed, and even in spring's high water it is possible to avoid wading by staying entirely on the creek's south bank, using short scramble trails between crossings. After 2.9 miles, there is a nice campsite in a grassy glen at the junction of the faint Belknap Trail.

For a longer hike, continue straight on the Twin Pillars Trail, gaining 1400 feet in 2.6 miles, to a viewpoint at the base of Twin Pillars' 200-foot rock towers. A shorter

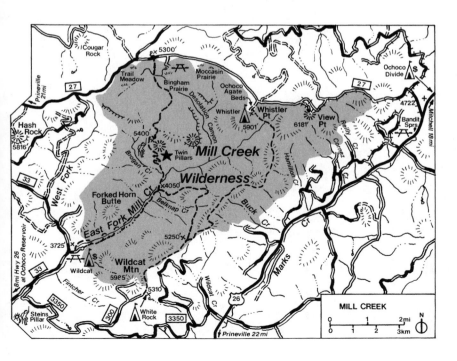

but less scenic 2.6-mile route to Twin Pillars begins at a different trailhead, on the northern edge of the wilderness on Road 27.

For other hikes, Wildcat Campground is nearly always the end point, because its elevation is 2000 feet lower than that of the wilderness's other trailheads. One 8.6-mile route starts at the White Rock Campground, on the shoulder of Wildcat Mountain. Another route to Wildcat Campground, from Whistler Point on Forest Road 27, is 13.1

Twin Pillars

miles. Potential backpacking campsites are plentiful throughout. Only creeks named on the map are year-round water sources.

An easy 2-mile trail to 350-foot Steins Pillar (shown in the lower left of the map) features views, flowers, and ponderosa pines. From Highway 26 at the east end of Ochoco Reservoir, drive Mill Creek Road 33 for 6.7 miles and turn right on Road 500 for 2 miles to a gravel turnaround on the left, 0.2 mile before road's end.

Climbing

Twin Pillars are a pair of vertical-sided, 200-foot andesite plugs at 5400 feet. Though quite scenic and challenging (rated II-5.7), they are rarely climbed because of the proximity of the more challenging Steins Pillar. This 350-foot, overhanging spire of welded tuff, unscaled until 1950, offers routes from difficulty III-5.6-A3 to IV-5.7-A4.

Winter Sports

Ochoco Divide on U.S. Highway 22 offers good cross-country skiing and snowshoeing from January through March. The highway is plowed in winter, allowing access to unplowed roads along the eastern edge of the wilderness. View Point makes a scenic goal, 5 miles up Road 27.

 Lookout Mountain

Location: 25 miles east of Prineville
Size: 26 square miles
Status: Undesignated wilderness
Terrain: Forested ridges, sagebrush plateau
Elevation: 3793 feet–6926 feet
Management: Ochoco NF
Topographic maps: Lookout Mountain, Gerow Butte (USGS)

From the wildflower-spangled sagebrush meadows of Lookout Mountain's plateau, views stretch beyond the forested Ochoco Mountains to a string of High Cascades snowpeaks.

Climate

Winter snow accounts for most of the area's 30 inches of annual precipitation. Summers are dry and warm.

Plants and Wildlife

An amazing variety of wildflowers bloom on the vast summit plateau in June, including desert parsley, mountain bluebells, balsamroot, wild peony, paintbrush, and yellowbell.

This is prime elk, wild horse, and mule deer range. Watch for herds in the high meadows during summer and in the cover of low-elevation forests during winter. Open, parklike forests of ponderosa pine invite cross-country travel, while wetter northern slopes host Douglas fir and grand fir. Storm-stunted subalpine fir struggle in the summit meadows.

Geology

A lava flow forms the flat top of Lookout Mountain. This basalt oozed from vents north of the John Day River about 25 million years ago, smothering most of the Ochoco Mountains. Outcroppings of older Ochoco rock in the valleys prompted an 1873 gold rush. The abandoned Independent Mine's buildings and mineshafts are off-limits because the cinnabar once mined there has contaminated the area with poisonous mercury.

THINGS TO DO
Hiking

Half a dozen trails climb to the vistas atop Lookout Mountain. Three of the best paths fan out from the Independent Mine Trailhead on Road 4205, making possible nice 4.6- to 7-mile loop hikes to the summit. The original lookout is gone, but the building's stone corral remains atop a panoramic rimrock lip. Just 400 yards east is a three-sided shelter (GPS location N44°19.637' W120°22.234'), built in 1989 primarily as a winter retreat for skiers and snowmobilers.

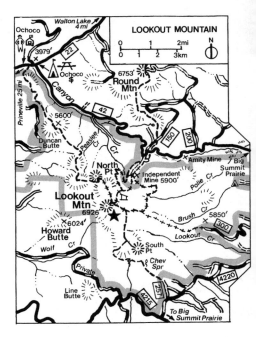

From Prineville, drive Highway 26 east for 17 miles. Near milepost 35, fork to the right at an "Ochoco Creek" sign for 8.2 miles to the Ochoco Ranger Station. Continue 0.3 mile, veer right on paved Road 42 for 6.8 miles to a pass, and turn right on Road 4205. If you are driving a delicate passenger car, park at the Round Mountain Trailhead near the start of this bumpy road and hike a trail 0.9 mile up to the Independent Mine Trailhead; otherwise, drive on up.

The more difficult, 7.3-mile Lookout Mountain Trail begins at a roadside pullout 200 yards east of the Ochoco Ranger Station and climbs nearly 3000 feet along a forested ridge to the summit, passing viewpoints at Duncan Butte and North Point along the way.

Lookout Mountain

The Line Butte Trail, a backdoor route to Lookout Mountain's plateau, gains 1000 feet in 3.9 miles from Road 257 to South Point's rimrock viewpoint. Drive as to the Independent Mine but continue straight on Road 42 an extra 7 miles to Big Summit Prairie, turn right on Road 4215 for 9 miles, turn right on Road 4220 for 1 mile, and turn left on Road 257 for 1 mile to the Fawn Creek Trailhead.

From Road 42, the well-marked Round Mountain Trail climbs 4.1 miles through open woods and wildflowers to a crest. From there, either take a side road 0.3 mile to Round Mountain's summit or continue straight 4.6 miles down the north side of the mountain to popular Walton Lake Campground.

Winter Sports

Cross-country skiers can drive up Road 42 to snow level and ski up the marked loop trail (shared with occasional snowmobiles) past the Independent Mine. The reward is great, for Lookout Mountain's high, 2.5-mile-long summit meadows have the Ochocos' best snow and superlative views.

45 Bridge Creek

Location: 39 miles east of Prineville
Size: 8 square miles
Status: Designated wilderness (1984)
Terrain: Forested plateau, cliffs, slopes
Elevation: 4320 feet–6816 feet
Management: Ochoco NF
Topographic map: Mount Pisgah (USGS)

At the edge of the Ochoco Mountains' summit plateau, North Point's 600-foot cliff overlooks Central Oregon and Cascade peaks from Mount Adams to the Three Sisters.

Climate

The area receives 30 inches of precipitation annually, primarily as winter snow. Summers are dry and hot.

North Point

Plants and Wildlife

Mixed conifer thickets of Douglas fir, grand fir, and larch dominate the area, with bands of lodgepole pine and ponderosa pine. Openings of sagebrush, bunchgrass, and sparse, gnarled mountain mahogany break up the plateau forests.

Mule deer and elk find good cover and browse here year round, but especially when hunting season drives them from roaded areas. Watch for prairie falcons, goshawks, and the large, red-headed pileated woodpeckers that, because of their reliance on forest snags, are an indicator species for old-growth Ochoco forests.

Geology

North Point's cliff of pillar-shaped basalt columns is the edge of a lava flow capping most of the Ochoco crest. Vents north of the John Day River produced this lava about 25 million years ago.

THINGS TO DO
Hiking

The breathtaking view at North Point is an easy 1.2-mile walk up an old, closed jeep track from the Bridge Creek crossing of Road 2630 near Pisgah Spring. To reach the starting point from Prineville, follow Highway 26 east 16 miles, at a sign for Ochoco Creek turn right for 8 paved miles to Ochoco Ranger Station, continue straight on paved Road 22 for 8.5 miles, turn left on Road 150 for 0.5 mile, and turn right on Road 2630 for 7 miles (the last 2 miles are rough and rutted).

Conifer thickets stymie most off-trail hikers in this wilderness, but frequent winds at North Point have stunted vegetation there, allowing easy and interesting cross-country hiking along the cliff edge for a mile on either side of the point. Bushwhacking becomes increasingly difficult—but possible with map and compass—for hikers intent on making a loop trip by continuing west to Thompson Spring, or along the cliff rim southeast to Bridge Creek.

East Point's rounded knoll offers lesser views; it is 1.5 miles along an arrow-straight jeep track from Road 2630.

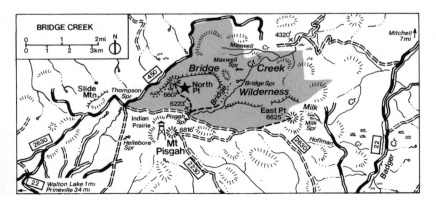

The trail to Bridge Spring has been abandoned to the cattle that graze this sparse wilderness range each summer. Although the watershed is the domestic water supply for the town of Mitchell, Bridge Spring and Bridge Creek usually are churned to mud by hooves.

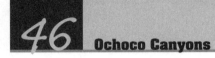

46 Ochoco Canyons

Location: 77 miles east of Prineville, 40 miles west of John Day
Size: 54 square miles
Status: 21 square miles designated wilderness (1984)
Terrain: Steep, forested canyons; sagebrush slopes; rocky creeks
Elevation: 2840 feet–6871 feet
Management: Ochoco NF
Topographic maps: Central Oregon (BLM); Aldrich Gulch, Wolf Mountain, Six Corners, Antone, Day Basin, Dayville (USGS)

Three major canyons—each with its own trail system and splashing creek—provide scenic examples of the Ochoco Mountains' remarkable transition from dense forests to sagebrush lowlands.

Climate

Summers are hot and dry. Snowfall from November to April brings the annual precipitation to a sparse 20 to 30 inches.

Plants and Wildlife

Water determines where there will be forest and where sagebrush dominates in these steep mountains. Exposed ridge tops and sunny south slopes are brown and bald. Green swaths of forest cling to shady north slopes and fill the steep canyons—like biological glaciers winding downhill to the arid lowlands, where all melts to brown again.

A hike through the forest reveals bands of lodgepole pine, ponderosa pine parklands, and dense thickets of Douglas fir and grand fir. At creek's edge, expect an oasis of false Solomon's seal, coneflower, snowberry, wild gooseberries, and delicate twinflower.

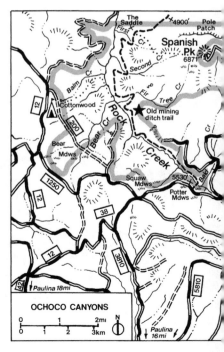

Bear, coyote, mountain lions, deer, and elk are common year round. Watch for migratory cranes and geese passing overhead on their way to the Malheur Refuge to the southeast.

Geology

Black Canyon's winding, cliff-lined lower gorge, and the similar canyon of the adjacent South Fork John Day, resulted when these streams cut through the basalt lava that once flooded much of central Oregon. In Picture Gorge, 12 miles to the north, the John Day River has cut through no fewer than 17 layers of this basalt. The lava, now characterized by rusty specks of weathered olivine, erupted from vents north of Dayville 16 million years ago. Nonetheless, this outpouring was dwarfed a few million years later by Oregon's next round of basalt floods, which filled much of the Columbia River Basin.

History

When miners found gold flakes in the dry hills north of Spanish Peak in the late 1800s, E.O. Waterman built a water flume from Rock Creek to help miners wash out the gold. The ditch was converted to a hiking trail in the 1970s.

In the early 1920s, rangers built a "crow's nest" fire lookout platform in the top of a tall tree on Wolf Mountain. No longer climbable, the lookout tree offers good views

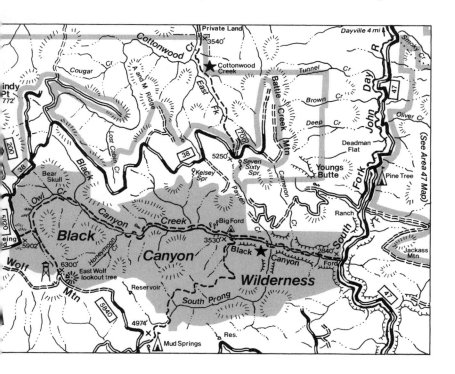

Black Canyon

of Black Canyon from ground level. The nearby replacement lookout, a 107-foot tower built in the 1940s, is still staffed in summer.

Boeing Field's name recalls a B-18 bomber that crashed nearby on Wolf Mountain during a World War II transit flight.

THINGS TO DO
Hiking
The area's prettiest trail is not in the relatively popular Black Canyon Wilderness but rather in the roadless valley of Rock Creek next door. This 8-mile path ambles from Potter Meadows down scenic Rock Creek for 2.4 miles, and then follows the course of an abandoned, historic mining flume, contouring past viewpoints. Good goals are the flume builders' cabin ruins at Fir Tree Creek (3.8 miles from Potter Meadows) and The Saddle (7 miles), a ponderosa pine knoll with good campsites. Adventurers can leave the trail here to explore the Pole Patch (a ponderosa pine grove at the foot of Spanish Peak's north cliff), or to climb open ridges to the summit of Spanish Peak.

To find the Rock Creek Trailhead from Prineville, drive Highway 26 east 1 mile, turn right at a sign for Paulina, and follow the Paulina Highway 59.5 miles. Beyond the village of Paulina 3.7 miles, turn left on South Beaver Creek Road toward the Rager Ranger Station 7.7 miles, fork left onto paved Road 42 for 1.5 miles, go straight on gravel Road 3810 for 3.2 miles, fork right to stay on Road 3810 another 3.9 miles, turn right on paved Road 38 for 1.5 miles to a junction, and keep straight on gravel Road 38 for 1.7 miles.

The 11.9-mile Black Canyon Trail descends along a rushing stream from the forests on Wolf Mountain to a narrow, cliff-walled gorge at a ford of the South Fork John Day River. Along the way, the trail crosses Black Canyon Creek seventeen times without bridges. Generally, only the ten crossings in the final 1.8 miles require wading. Most people access the upper end of the trail on a shortcut from gravel Road 5820 at Boeing Field, a broad meadow of June wildflowers: mules ears, desert parsley, larkspur, and owls clover.

To find the Boeing Field trailhead, follow directions to the Rock Creek Trailhead (above), but after driving 7.7 miles on South Beaver Creek Road, keep right for 1.3 miles to the Sugar Creek Day Use Area, and turn left onto gravel Road 5810 for 11.1 miles. If you would rather start your hike on Wolf Mountain, drive only 9.8 miles on Road 5810 and turn east on Road 5840 for 2.4 very rough miles.

The lower end of the Black Canyon Trail is separated from Road 47 by a ford across the South Fork John Day River (GPS location N44°20.023' W119°33.909'). The river is uncrossable in high water from January to March but idles along only calf-deep in summer.

The South Prong Trail also accesses Black Canyon, dropping 5.6 miles from Mud Springs Campground to Big Ford.

Cottonwood Creek meanders through the most isolated canyon of all. A lovely forest trail drops 1500 feet in 3 miles to the forks of the creek. Downstream, the trail ends in 0.8 mile at an off-limits, private dirt road leading to the Mascall Ranch at Picture

Mariposa lilies vary in shape and color throughout eastern Oregon.

Gorge; upstream, 8 miles of creek await exploration by hardy bushwhackers. The trailhead is at the junction of Road 38 and spur Road 700.

Winter Sports

Snowed-under ridge-top roads provide quiet routes for ski tours. Spanish Peak makes the most challenging and spectacular goal. Expect sufficient snow for skiing from mid-December to late March. Skiers must drive to snow level and park, because roads are rarely plowed.

Aldrich Mountains

Location: 11 miles west of John Day
Size: 91 square miles
Status: Undesignated wilderness
Terrain: Broad mountains, sagebrush slopes, forest
Elevation: 2649 feet–7363 feet
Management: Malheur NF, Prineville District BLM, Oregon Department of Fish and Wildlife
Topographic maps: McClellan Mountain, Big Weasel Springs, Aldrich Mountain south, Aldrich Gulch, Aldrich Mountain north, Dayville (USGS)

This little-known range between the Ochoco and the Strawberry Mountains preserves two wild areas. In the west, the Aldrich Mountain lookout rises above the forests and sagebrush gulches of the Murderers Creek Wildlife Area. In the east, a dozen peaks with bare, 2000-foot-tall shoulders cluster along the 13.9-mile McClellan Mountain Trail.

Climate

Most of the area's scant 20 annual inches of precipitation fall as snow from November to April. Hot summer afternoons may bring thunderstorms.

Plants and Wildlife

Bighorn sheep are a highlight of the Murderers Creek Wildlife Area, between the South Fork John Day River and the Aldrich Mountain summit. Once hunted to extinction here, the wild sheep were reintroduced in 1978. They prefer Smoky Gulch and Oliver Creek's upper canyon. Sleek pronghorn antelope summer along Murderers Creek and winter in the north of the area. Elk rely on the timbered areas for winter cover, and mule deer come from as far as Strawberry Mountain for winter forage. Mountain lions, coyotes, rattlesnakes, meadowlarks, and mountain cottontails are also in the area. Bald eagles winter near Dayville.

Sagebrush, bunchgrass, juniper, and yellow-bloomed rabbitbrush dominate the lower elevations and south-facing slopes. Douglas fir and grand fir forests cling to north

McClellan Mountain from the summit of Fields Peak

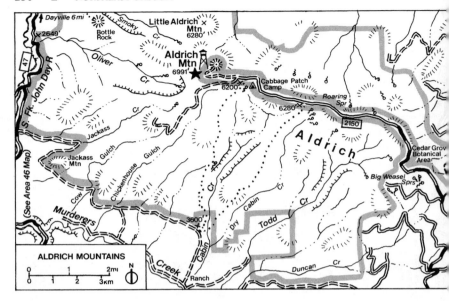

slopes and cap Aldrich Mountain. Near McClellan Mountain, canyon bottoms are forested with stately ponderosa pine and larch. Bitterroot and phlox bloom on bare ridges in June.

The Cedar Grove Botanical Area preserves a biological oddity—60 acres of Alaska cedar, isolated 130 miles from other Alaska cedar stands. An easy 1-mile trail from Road 2150 leads to the grove.

Geology

The Aldrich Mountains began as the mud, sand, and reefs of a Pacific island chain 190 to 230 million years ago. The Earth's crustal movements "rafted" this island rock to Oregon's coast 150 million years ago. The later eruption of the Ochoco volcanoes, and then the Cascade volcanoes, left the Aldrich Mountains progressively farther inland.

THINGS TO DO
Hiking

A steady 2.3-mile climb reaches the area's highest point, Fields Peak, a former lookout site with panoramic views of the John Day Valley and beyond. Although all-terrain vehicles (ATVs) are allowed on this route, they are rare, and they are banned from other parts of the McClellan Mountain Trail. Find the trailhead by turning south from Highway 26 on Fields Creek Road 21 (the junction is 13 miles east of Dayville or 18 miles west of John Day). Follow this one-lane paved road 8.6 miles, turn left on gravel Road 115 for 0.4 mile, turn right on Road 2160 for 200 yards, and fork left on rough Road 041 for 1.2 miles to its end.

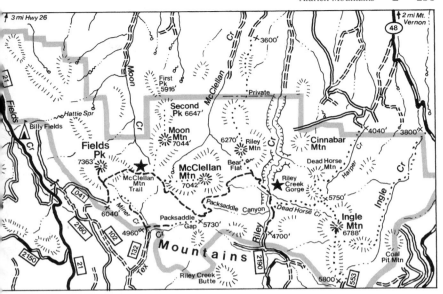

For a longer hike without risk of ATV noise, start out toward Fields Peak for 1.5 miles, but then keep right on the McClellan Mountain Trail. For the next 7.6 miles the path threads through high, scenic passes, traversing the crest of the range to Bear Flat. Along this route, bare side ridges invite cross-country detours to the scenic summits of Moon Mountain and McClellan Mountain. Beyond Bear Flat the trail angles down into Riley Creek's gorge and then follows the stream up through ponderosa pine woods to a more remote trailhead. To find the Riley Creek Trailhead from Highway 26, drive Fields Creek Road 21 for 13.7 miles to Murderers Creek, turn left to continue on Road 21 for 6.4 miles, turn left on Road 2190 for 5.6 miles (keeping right at unmarked junctions) to the road's end.

Pika or "rock rabbit"

A topographic map, compass, and water are essential for cross-country hiking on the steep, western flanks of Aldrich Mountain where wildlife observation is best. To spot bighorn sheep in winter, park on the South Fork John Day Road 47 between Smoky and Oliver Creeks and hike up the ridge to an excellent viewpoint at Bottle Rock. In summer, start at Aldrich Mountain and hike down.

48 Strawberry Mountain

Location: 4 miles southeast of John Day
Size: 123 square miles
Status: 107 square miles designated wilderness (1964, 1984)
Terrain: Snowpeak, forest valleys, high meadows, lakes
Elevation: 3570 feet–9038 feet
Management: Malheur NF, Prineville District BLM
Topographic map: Strawberry Mountain Wilderness (USFS)

For a lesson in eastern Oregon's diversity, visit the Strawberry Range. Above the John Day River's alfalfa fields, and above an arid band of sagebrush and juniper, dense conifer forests rise past blue lakes, waterfalls, and alpine wildflowers to palisades of snow-draped crags.

Climate

Because most of the wilderness is above 6000 feet in elevation, snow closes trails from November to June and snow patches linger in high passes until August. Summers are fair and warm, with some thunderstorms and freezing nights. Snow flurries may interrupt October's typically cool, clear Indian summer. Annual precipitation measures 40 inches.

Plants and Wildlife

Five of the United States' seven major biological zones are packed into this relatively small mountain range. Larch, the only native conifer to lose its needles in winter, spangles the high forests with autumn gold. Other trees include Engelmann spruce, white pine, Douglas fir, grand fir, lodgepole pine, and ponderosa pine. The area's name derives from the wild strawberries rampant in mid-elevation forests. Watch for their fruit in July and their bright red leaves in October.

Bighorn sheep, reintroduced here after local extinction, now thrive on Canyon Mountain. Look for them up Sheep Gulch from Highway 395. Rocky mountain elk and mule deer summer here in profusion, and seek shelter during autumn hunting season. Other wildlife include black bears, coyotes, mountain lions, bobcats, ground squirrels, and golden eagles.

Geology

The western half of the Strawberry Range is a chunk of sea floor and island debris buckled up from the Pacific by the westward drift of North America 200 to 250 million years ago, before the creation of the Cascades and Coast Range made this an inland area. Canyon Mountain consists of reddish peridotite, greenish serpentinite, and crumbly brown basalt—all indicative of oceanic crust.

Strawberry Lake

The eastern half of the Strawberry Range, beginning at Indian Creek Butte, consists of much younger volcanic rock. About 15 million years ago, volcanoes here spewed out immense amounts of ash and lava, burying the southern Blue Mountains. Rabbit Ears is the eroded plug of one vent. Above Wildcat Basin, colored ash deposits have weathered into a scenic badlands.

Ice Age glaciers carved the many broad, U-shaped mountain valleys. They also left sandy moraines (visible in Indian Creek Canyon) and cirque lakes. Strawberry Lake formed when glacial ice retreated and the remaining, steep valley wall collapsed, blocking Strawberry Creek with a landslide.

History

Traces of gold in Canyon Mountain's peridotite launched a decade of intense placer mining in 1862, when Canyon City began as a tent town of 10,000 men. Pioneer Oregon poet Joaquin Miller lived and wrote in the boomtown during 1863–69.

THINGS TO DO
Hiking

This compact mountain range features rugged alpine scenery and a thorough trail system with room for week-long backpacking treks. Mountain lakes are rare in eastern

Oregon, so the seven in this area are popular. To limit overuse, do not camp beside these small lakes, but do try the many scenic trails to less-trodden meadows, ridges, and creek valleys.

From Strawberry Camp, a 1.3-mile uphill walk reaches Strawberry Lake with its photogenic backdrop of snowy crags. But save some film; another 1.2 miles up the valley Strawberry Falls cascades 40 feet onto boulders glowing with moss. Once at the falls, day hikers have at least three options: head back, ramble on another 0.6 level miles to a good lunch stop at Little Strawberry Lake, or tackle the climb to Strawberry Mountain's panoramic viewpoint. The climb makes for a demanding 6.3-mile hike from trailhead to summit and gains 3300 feet in elevation, but the trail grade is good and after all, this is one of Oregon's tallest peaks. Get to the trailhead via Prairie City on Highway 26; turn south on Main Street 0.4 mile to a T-shaped junction, turn left for two blocks, and turn right onto Bridge Street (Road 60) for 10.7 miles to Strawberry Campground.

Slide Lake is another popular destination from the Strawberry Camp trailhead. It is 3.9 miles, with Little Slide Lake just a short distance beyond.

For a shortcut to the top of Strawberry Mountain, start at a trailhead on the southern side of the wilderness, 0.4 mile from the end of Road 1640 above Indian Springs

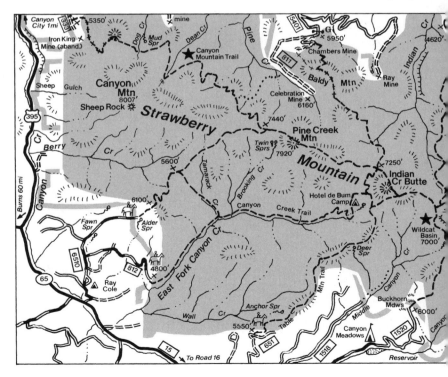

Campground. From there, a 3.6-mile trail climbs just 1100 feet to the top. From a trailhead at the end of Road 1640, a good beginners' day hike ambles 1.3 miles down into High Lake's scenic basin. Those who continue 1.6 miles past High Lake up to a pass are rewarded with a view of Slide Lake's glacier-carved valley. For an even broader view, hike cross-country from this pass up a cliff-edged ridge past Rabbit Ears' rock pillars to Indian Springs Butte. To reach this trailhead, take Highway 395 south of John Day 9.7 miles, turn left on paved county Road 65 (which becomes Road 15) for 13.6 miles to a stop sign, turn left on Road 16 for 2.5 miles, and turn left on gravel Road 1640 for 10 miles.

Wildcat Basin's ash badlands and July wildflowers make a good goal. Take the 2.4-mile trail up from Buckhorn Meadows, at the end of Road 1520. Follow Road 65 from Highway 395 for 8.9 miles, turn left on Road 1520 for 4 miles to Canyon Meadow Campground, and continue 3 rough miles to road's end.

Baldy Mountain's broad ridge of wildflowers and views is one of the Strawberry Mountains' least discovered scenic destinations. From John Day, drive Highway 26 east 6 miles, turn right on Pine Creek Road 54 (later 5401) for 8 miles to a gated trailhead parking area, walk up the closed road 0.3 mile, turn left up the abandoned Chambers Mine road 0.5 mile to the second switchback, and strike off on a genuine trail through

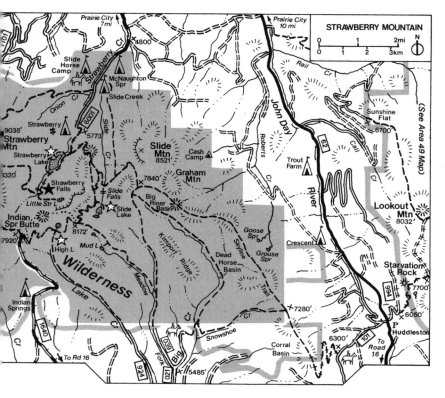

meadows 1.1 miles to the ridge's crest. The path continues 3.9 scenic miles, traversing to the Canyon Mountain Trail junction at a pass beside Indian Creek Butte.

Two uncrowded day hike trails on the south side of the wilderness follow creeks to mountain lakes. One trail heads up Lake Creek 3.7 miles to High Lake, and the other follows Meadow Fork 3.2 miles, past a waterfall, to Mud Lake. With a car shuttle, hikers can either combine the two hikes or else start out at the high-elevation Road 1640 trailhead and make the trip into an easy downhill romp. From Highway 395, take Road 65 for 13.6 miles, turn left on Road 16 for 6.5 miles to Logan Valley, then turn left on Road 924 to Murray Campground. From there the Lake Creek Trail begins 1.5 miles ahead at the end of Road 924. For the Meadow Fork Trailhead to Mud Lake, turn right from Murray Campground for 0.5 mile on Road 1648, turn left on Road 021 for 1.4 miles, and turn left on rough Road 039 for 1.6 miles.

The East Fork of Canyon Creek splashes through a stately forest in a deep canyon. Backpackers and equestrians often use the trail along this stream when trekking into the range's high country, especially to the small meadow and spring at Hotel de Bum Camp, 7.3 miles from the Road 812 trailhead. Day hikers will find the creekside path soothing but may have trouble deciding when to turn back.

The Canyon Mountain Trail offers a different challenge. Blasted into the rugged upper slopes of the Strawberry Range, this route offers lots of scenery but very few campsites. For 15 miles between Dog Creek and Hotel de Bum there is only one reliable creek, and the flattest tent sites are in possibly windy passes. Still, the route's start makes a first-rate day hike, and it is the closest trail to Canyon City, although the access road is confusing. At the Grant County Museum in downtown Canyon City, turn uphill on Main Street 1.9 miles, turn right on paved Road 77 for 0.3 mile, curve right onto an oiled road for 0.3 mile to a fork, go straight on a dirt road 0.4 mile, fork left onto a rutted dirt track (which becomes undrivably muddy in wet weather) for 0.4 mile, switchback up to the right, and keep on the straightest, uphill route for 1.2 miles to a three-way junction in a saddle. Keep straight on the middle fork 200 feet to a blazed pine tree, and turn left for 300 yards to road's end (GPS location N44°21.75' W118°55.565').

A complete circuit of the area's high lakes makes a fun two- or three-day backpacking trip. The 13.3-mile loop from the Road 1640 trailhead passes Strawberry Mountain, Strawberry Lake, Slide Lake, and High Lake. Add 2.3 miles if starting from Strawberry Campground. Allow time for side trips.

To really experience the Strawberries, try backpacking the entire length of the mountain range's crest. It is 42 miles, starting with the Canyon Mountain Trail's rugged slopes in the west to the Skyline Trail's forested ridge in the east, where trails are faint.

Winter Sports

There is plenty of winter snow in these mountains. The challenge is to get to it when most access roads are unplowed. From January to March, when snow covers low-elevation roads, one solution is to drive 15 miles south of John Day on plowed Highway 395 to the Starr Bowl winter sports area, with its network of snowmobile and ski trails among nonwilderness hills.

Paved county Road 62 south of Prairie City is also plowed as far as the Huddleston sno-park at the road's summit (elevation 5899 feet). From there, snowmobiles roar onward along the snowed-under road to Logan Valley and Road 16, along the southern edge of the Strawberry Range. Cross-country skiers and snowshoers, however, can trek from the Huddleston sno-park west on Road 101 and the woodsy Skyline Trail into the Strawberry Mountain Wilderness. A steeper tour heads east up Road 994 and the trail to Lookout Mountain.

Another midwinter option is to park 1.9 miles up Canyon City's Main Street and travel backroads for 2.8 miles to the Canyon Mountain Trail. The first 2.4 miles of this trail are not too rugged, yet offer excellent viewpoints.

Strawberry Lake in winter is worth a journey. Expect snow to block the unplowed access road 2 to 4 miles short of the trailhead. A spectacular goal is to climb past frozen Strawberry Falls to Little Strawberry Lake.

Some of the best snow, and best views, are atop Baldy Mountain. Access is via Pine Creek Road 54 (alias Road 5401). Although this road is not plowed, it is seldom blocked by snow more than 2 or 3 miles before the Chambers Mine, where a spur climbs left to treeless upper slopes. The Pine Creek Road joins Highway 26 east of John Day 6 miles.

 Glacier Mountain and Monument Rock

Location: 26 miles east of John Day, 52 miles southwest of Baker City
Size: 91 square miles, including Wildcat Creek area
Status: 31 square miles designated wilderness (1984)
Terrain: Steep, forested canyons, open ridges
Elevation: 4300 feet–8033 feet
Management: Malheur NF, Wallowa-Whitman NF
Topographic maps: Monument Rock Wilderness (USFS); Bullrun Rock, Little Baldy Mountain, Deardorff Mountain (USGS)

At the southernmost edge of the Blue Mountains, this area's subalpine, once-glaciated ridges offer views across much of eastern Oregon. The canyon forests are dense enough to shelter the reclusive, bearlike wolverine.

Climate

The John Day Valley funnels winter storms and summer thundershowers eastward to the mountain ridges here. As a result the area receives 40 inches annual precipitation, twice as much as the surrounding arid lowlands. Expect snow to block trails above 6000 feet from November to late June. Summer brings hot days and chilly nights.

Plants and Wildlife

A wolverine sighted west of Table Rock in 1980 provides rare evidence that this unusual animal still exists in Oregon. Named "skunk bear" for its habit of scenting uneaten food, and *Gulo gulo* (Latin, "glutton glutton") for its diverse appetite, the wolverine resembles a small, bushy-tailed, gray-headed bear. Though only 18 to 42 pounds, its ferocity successfully drives coyotes, bears, and even mountain lions away from contested carrion.

Wolverines and mountain lions are among the few predators that dare to eat porcupines, a locally abundant species. Watch for porcupines during the day on low tree limbs (where they gnaw on bark and sleep) and at night in human campsites (where they eat sweaty backpack straps and fishing rod handles for the salt).

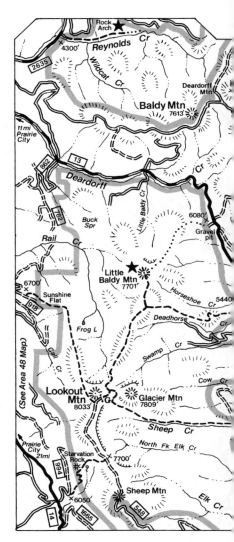

The unstocked Little Malheur River preserves a population of rare, red-banded trout. The area's seventy bird species include the creek-loving water ouzel and the red-headed pileated woodpecker.

Ponderosa pine and juniper sparsely forest the lowlands and dry south-facing slopes. Subalpine meadows, June wildflowers, and spire-shaped subalpine fir top the high ridges. Thickets of mixed conifers crowd other areas.

Geology

Glacier Mountain, Lookout Mountain, and Little Baldy Mountain are glacial horns, their sides steeply scalloped by the U-shaped valleys of vanished Ice Age glaciers. That the equally high Monument Rock area shows so little of this scenic glacial topography remains a puzzle.

The rocks are mostly 15-million-year-old lava and ash from vents near Strawberry Mountain, but an outcropping of much older, more mineralized rock on Bullrun Mountain and Mine Ridge has spawned several small mines.

History

The lichen-covered 8-foot cylindrical stone monument atop Monument Rock may have been erected by pioneer sheepherders in the early 1900s. The Snake Indians who once roamed here are not known to have built such megaliths. The tribe has no tradition of rock paintings, either, so the ancient pictographs on a natural rock arch at Reynolds Creek evidently belong to a mysterious, earlier culture.

THINGS TO DO
Hiking

The area's high ridges feature easy trails to dramatic viewpoints. Even the road to the Lookout Mountain Trailhead, dirt Road 548, provides thrilling views as it traces

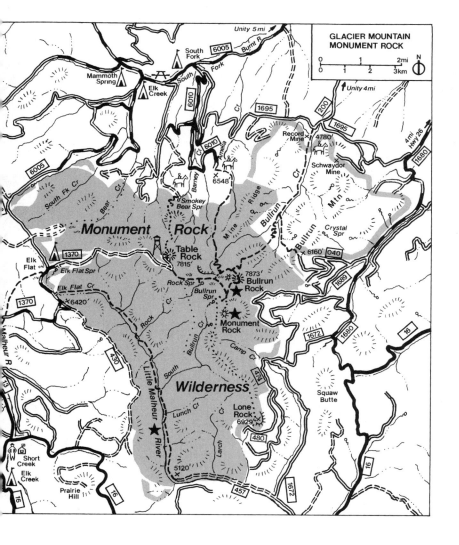

Monument Rock

a narrow ridgeline from Sheep Mountain. From Road 548's gate, the tops of Lookout Mountain and Glacier Mountain are a half hour's hike away, but require some cross-country scrambling. A popular day hike continues past the gate on the abandoned road (now maintained as a trail) along the nearly level ridgeline 3.6 miles to Little Baldy Mountain's summit meadow, and the best view of the John Day Valley. All-terrain vehicles are uncommon but allowed on the closed road.

Reach Road 548 from Prairie City by turning south on Main Street. At a stop sign after 0.4 mile, turn left onto what becomes Road 62 for a total of 20 paved miles, turn left on gravel Road 1665 for 4 miles, turn left on very rough Road 548 past Sheep Mountain for a total of 6 miles to the gate at Lookout Mountain.

The fire lookout tower on Table Rock is a good place to begin a visit to the Monument Rock area. After taking in the view, backtrack 0.5 mile down the lookout road and take a level, 2-mile stroll along an ancient dirt road to Bullrun Rock's 150-foot cliffs. Scramble to the top for a good view. A faint fork of the abandoned road winds close to Monument Rock. About 0.4 mile of easy bushwhacking through open sagebrush is required to climb to the monument itself. Adventurers can continue 3.5 miles to Lone Rock.

To reach the Table Rock lookout from Highway 26 in downtown Prairie City, turn south on Main Street 0.4 mile, turn left at a stop sign, and then keep straight on what becomes Road 62. After 8 miles, turn left on paved Road 13 for 11.7 miles, turn left on gravel Road 1370 for 4.4 miles, fork left to stay on Road 1370 for another 1.5 miles, and turn right at a "Table Rock" sign to continue on Road 1370 (now much rougher) for 4.8 miles. If you are coming from Unity, drive west of downtown up the South Fork Burnt River 16 miles following Road 6005, turn left on Road 2652 for 2 miles, and then take Road 1370 to the left.

Several streamside trails in deep forest offer cool retreats during summer's heat. The 1.4-mile path up Reynolds Creek traces this moss-banked, splashing stream well into its shady canyon. The final 0.2 mile follows a rough path through the canyon's narrows. At that point, just after a major gulch appears on the left, adventurers can scramble steeply 0.2 mile up a ridge to the left to a large basalt outcrop with a natural rock arch, some pictographs, and a nice view of the valley (GPS location N44°25.449' W118°29.082'). Do not camp near the arch, and touch nothing. The pictographs can be damaged even by the oil of a fingerprint. To find the trailhead from Highway 26, turn south on Prairie City's Main Street 0.4 mile, turn left at a stop sign, and then keep straight on what becomes Road 62. After 7.5 miles, turn left on gravel Road 2635 for 4.3 miles.

A 7.4-mile trail descends the Little Malheur River from the river's source at Elk Flat. Day hikers can aim for a lunch stop where South Bullrun Creek joins the river.

The Little Malheur River

Although the trail crosses the creek seven times, logs and rocks allow hikers to avoid wading. To find the Elk Flat Trailhead from Highway 26 in Prairie City, turn south on Main Street 0.4 mile to a stop sign, turn left on what becomes Road 62 for 8 miles, turn left on Road 13 for 11.7 miles, and turn left on Road 1370 for 5 miles. The lower trailhead, on rough Road 457, can be accessed by high-clearance vehicles via Roads 16 and 1672.

Sheep Creek's trail is most often used by equestrians, but day hikers who arrange a car shuttle can easily make the trip one-way downhill. It is 5.2 miles from the Road 548 gate at Lookout Mountain to Road 13 at the bottom. In October the creek's broad glacial valley glows with bright orange quaking aspen and larch.

Conveniently accessed via Unity, the Bullrun Creek Trail gains 1300 feet in 4.3 miles to Bullrun Rock. From Highway 26 in downtown Unity, head west on Road 6000 for 7.2 miles and turn left on Road 6010 for 5.2 miles.

50 Dixie Butte

Location: 26 miles northeast of John Day, 50 miles west of Baker City
Size: 19 square miles
Status: Undesignated wilderness
Terrain: Forested butte and bench cut by creek valleys
Elevation: 4000 feet–7592 feet
Management: Malheur NF
Topographic maps: Bates, Dixie Meadow (USGS)

This prominent, cone-shaped butte overlooks a broad slope of pristine forestland— an island in an otherwise heavily roaded and logged portion of the Blue Mountains.

Climate

Snow blocks the Davis Creek Trail from about Thanksgiving to late April, the same period during which the Dixie Mountain ski area operates. The 30 inches of annual precipitation are chiefly snow. Summers are dry.

Plants and Wildlife

Mule deer and elk rely on the area for browse and for cover during fall hunting season. Larch trees and creekside golden currant bushes provide orange foliage in October. The virtually unbroken forests are mostly Douglas fir and grand fir, with some ponderosa and lodgepole pine.

Geology

Though shaped like a volcano, Dixie Butte was born of water. The peak's rocks are sea-floor sediments and Pacific island debris buckled up by the westward-moving seacoast

Dixie Butte in April

of the North American continent 200 to 250 million years ago. Lava flows from the Strawberry Mountains 15 million years ago cover the plateau below the Davis Creek Trail.

History

During the Civil War, Southern gold prospectors christened Dixie Butte and (Jefferson) Davis Creek to spite the Union men who named the area's new county for Ulysses S. Grant. In 1910, the narrow-gauge Sumpter Valley Railroad opened a line past Dixie Butte, linking Prairie City with Baker City. Known as the "Stump Dodger" because it was used to log the area's forests, the railroad closed this line in 1947.

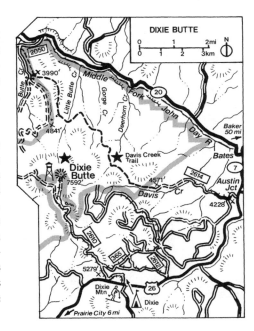

THINGS TO DO
Hiking
For a quick break while driving Highway 26, stop at milepost 184 at Dixie Summit (opposite Dixie Campground) to hike a 0.2-mile interpretive trail that explores the abandoned track of the historic Sumpter Valley Railroad. The paved loop trail is accessible even for wheelchairs.

The Davis Creek Trail contours 7.8 miles through Dixie Butte's forests. Small log bridges cross three creeks. Elk often show themselves along the way. After the hike, plan to drive to the Dixie Butte lookout tower for an overview of the trail's route, as well as a bird's-eye view of the snowy Strawberry Mountains across the John Day Valley.

Winter Sports
The snowed-under roads looping through the foothills of Dixie Butte make ideal cross-country ski trails. Start at the Dixie Mountain Ski Area, where there is a warming hut and rope tow. In midwinter, park at Austin Junction for a nearly level, 3.2-mile jaunt along Road 2614 to icy Davis Creek.

The area's premier challenge is the 5.5-mile climb up Road 2610 to the summit's unmatched winter view. Beware of avalanche danger on steep roadsides.

 North Fork John Day

Location: 61 miles south of Pendleton, 13 miles west of Baker City
Size: 617 square miles
Status: 190 square miles designated wilderness (1984)
Terrain: Snowy mountain ranges, rugged river canyons, forested benchlands, cirque lakes
Elevation: 3356 feet–9106 feet
Management: Umatilla NF, Wallowa-Whitman NF, Malheur NF, Prineville District BLM
Topographic maps: North Fork John Day Wilderness (USFS); Anthony Lakes, Crawfish Lake, Bourne, Elkhorn Peak (USGS)

The largest wild area in the Blue Mountains, this sprawling complex of wilderness lands encompasses two entire mountain ranges—the craggy Elkhorns and the Greenhorns—as well as a major river, the North Fork John Day. Here roam a good share of the Blue Mountains' 52,000 elk and 150,000 mule deer.

Though separated by paved or well-graveled roads, each of the three units of this wilderness has plenty of room for day hikes or long backpacking trips. Not to be missed are the Elkhorn Crest Trail's 22.8 miles of alpine scenery and the North Fork John Day River Trail's 24.6 miles of winding gorge. In addition, Anthony Lake offers a nordic skiing center with access to the wilderness in winter.

Gunsight Mountain from Anthony Lake

Climate

Snowfall is heaviest in the Elkhorn Mountains, where the Anthony Lake Ski Area usually operates from Thanksgiving to April 15. Snow blocks hiking trails above 7000 feet until early July, but the lower part of the North Fork John Day River Trail clears of snow as early as April.

Annual precipitation hits 45 inches in the Elkhorns but drops to 20 inches in the western canyons. Summers are dry. October, though generally pleasant, may bring sudden snowstorms. Night temperatures can dip below freezing even in summer.

Plants and Wildlife

This is elk country, where 800-pound bulls with 5-foot-wide antlers bugle challenges to rival males each fall. More than twice as large as mule deer, elk bulls assemble harems

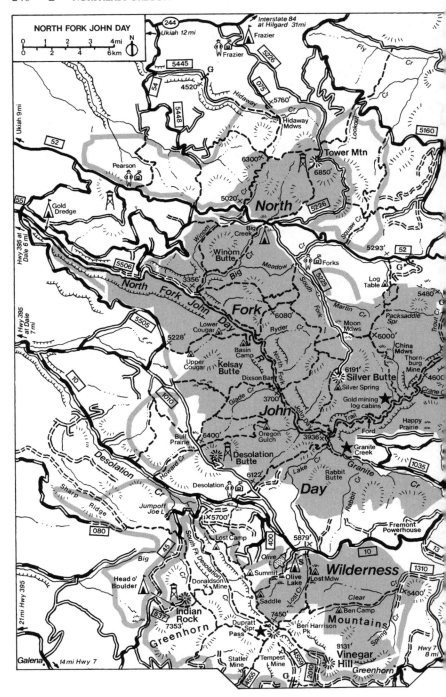

NORTH FORK JOHN DAY

0 1 2 3 4mi
0 2 4 6km

Ukiah 12 mi
244
Interstate 84 at Hilgard 31mi
Frazier
Frazier
5445
5226
G
54
4520'
075
Hidaway
5760'
Hidaway Mdws
5160
Ukiah 9 mi
52
Pearson
W
Tower Mtn
6300'
6850'
North
5020'
5226
55
Gold Dredge
Big Creek
Squaw Cr
5293'
52
Hwy 395 at Dale 6 mi
5506
Winom
Winom Butte
Big
Meadow
Forks
Log Table
3356'
Fork
South
Martin
5480
North Fork John Day
6080'
Ryder
Moon Mdws
6000'
Packsaddle Spr
Hwy 395 at Dale 7 mi
5505
Lower Cougar
Cr
China Mdws
Thornburg Mine
10
5228'
Upper Cougar
Basin Camp
Kelsay Butte
Dixson Bar
6191'
Silver Butte
Silver Spring
4600'
1010
Glade
3700'
John
Gold mining log cabins
Happy Prairie
Bull Prairie
6400'
Oregon Gulch
3936'
Ford
Trail
Granite Creek
Desolation
Howard Cr
Desolation Butte
6122'
Lake
Rabbit Butte
Granite
1035
Sharp Ridge
Jumpoff Joe L
Day
Rabbit
Cr
Fremont Powerhouse
080
5700'
400
5879'
10
T3
Lost Camp
Big
45
South Fk Desolation
Olive L
Olive Lake
Wilderness
1310
21 mi Hwy 395
Head o' Boulder
Donaldson Mine
Summit
Lost Mdw
5400'
Saddle
Clear
Indian Rock
7353'
Ben Camp
Ben Harrison Pk
Mountains
8131'
Greenhorn
Dupratt Spr
7450'
Pass
Vinegar Hill
Hwy 395 8 mi
Galena
14 mi Hwy 7
Statler Mine
Tempest Mine
Greenhorn

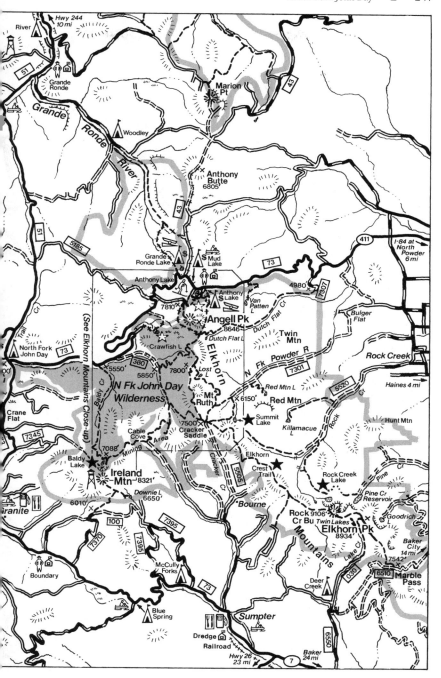

of up to sixty cows during the August to November rut. In this season, listen at dawn or dusk for the bulls' bugles: snorts that rise to a clarinetlike whistle and end with several low grunts. Also look for saplings stripped of bark to mark territory and elk wallows—small bogs dug by hooves and laced with urine as a bull's private orgy site.

Many of the area's deer and elk winter in the Bridge Creek Wildlife Area south of Ukiah, but others remain, able to survive in this high country's heavy snows by shifting daily between north- and south-facing slopes. The north-facing canyon slopes' dense conifer forests provide shelter from snow and wind. South-facing slopes are sparsely forested, allowing winds to expose the dried grass important to elk for food.

Summer hikers in the lower canyonlands find bright green moss, shiny-leaved twinflower, and pink-bloomed prince's pine on the shady north slopes of canyons, while sunny south slopes feature wild strawberry and huckleberry on a dry floor of pungent ponderosa pine needles.

The highest of the alpine Elkhorn Mountains' rock-lined glacial lakes appear to have just been released from a glacier's grip, while others have filled in to become marshy wildflower meadows. Lower basins have grown over with subalpine fir and Engelmann spruce. Reintroduced mountain goats have become so common near the range's highest point, Rock Creek Butte, that they sometimes nibble on backpackers' gear for salt.

Recovering from occasional dredging of stream gravels for gold from 1920 to 1954, the North Fork John Day River now provides spawning grounds for 70 percent of the John Day River's steelhead and 90 percent of its chinook salmon. The fish runs, which peak in late August, help feed a population of bald eagles.

Geology

The granite and scrambled sedimentary rock here reflect the Blue Mountains' history as a volcanic island archipelago in the Pacific Ocean 210 to 270 million years ago. The Earth's crustal movement "rafted" this oceanic debris onto the advancing North American continent about 200 million years ago. Later bubbles of relatively light granitic rock known as batholiths rose through the sediment to form the granite cores of the

Bull elk

Elkhorn and Greenhorn Ranges. When magma cools slowly to form large-crystaled granitic rock, gold and silver collect along the rock's quartz veins—hence this area's colorful mining history.

Columbia River basalt flows buried the area about 15 million years ago. Basalt rimrock remains on the western benchlands, but erosion has stripped this lava from the rising Elkhorn and Greenhorn Mountains. Finally, relatively recent Ice Age glaciers scalloped the ranges with scores of U-shaped glacial valleys.

History

Sumpter, Bourne, Granite, and Greenhorn are picturesque mining boomtowns from 1860s gold strikes. Ancient prospects, tailings, and a few small active mines dot hills near the towns, though the easy placer diggings are gone. A floating gold dredge (now restored as a state heritage site in Sumpter) once churned many valleys in these mountains to gravel wastelands. Part of the North Fork John Day River Trail follows an abandoned mining ditch once used to bring water to gold sluices.

THINGS TO DO
Hiking

The most popular day hikes explore the Elkhorn Mountains' alpine scenery. Anthony Lake, ringed with rugged peaks, is easily accessible from Interstate 84, making it the only destination in the entire area likely to be crowded.

For starters, take the 1-mile trail around Anthony Lake. A worthwhile 0.9-mile side trail skirts rugged Gunsight Mountain to Black Lake. Another easy side trail loops 2.3 miles from the south end of Anthony Lake, ascending Parker Creek to the Hoffer Lakes and returning down a ski area service road. From the Hoffer Lakes loop, however, the area's best view is just another 1.3 miles away and 900 feet up; hike up the service road to a pass and keep left on a path up a craggy ridge to The Lakes Observation Point.

For an excellent sample of the high Elkhorns' scenery, take the 8.2-mile loop trail from Anthony Lake entirely around Angell Peak and Gunsight Mountain. The well-built path gains only 1300 feet along the way, passing views of Crawfish Meadow's basin and Dutch Flat Lake.

Other lakes make good goals. Pretty Crawfish Lake is 1.3 or 1.4 miles from Road 73, depending on the trailhead. From Crawfish Lake, it is easy to bushwhack 1 mile due east along the inlet creek up to Crawfish Meadows' wildflowers. Van Patten Lake, in an alpine cirque, is a steep 1.5-mile hike from the defunct Little Alps Ski Area 2.6 miles east of Anthony Lake on Road 73; the hike begins up an old service road. Nearby, the 7-mile trail to Dutch Flat Lake ascends a cattle-grazed, U-shaped glacial valley from Road 7307.

The spectacular Elkhorn Crest Trail contours from pass to pass for 22.8 miles along the granite backbone of the Elkhorn Range from Anthony Lake to Marble Pass. By sticking to the crest, the trail narrowly misses a number of pretty alpine lakes, so plan on taking a few short detours. Day hikers starting from the Elkhorn Crest Trailhead on paved Road 73 near Anthony Lake can aim for Black Lake (0.9 mile), Dutch Flat Lake (4.3 miles), Lost Lake (6.4 miles), or even Summit Lake (10 miles).

The Marble Pass Trailhead at the southern end of the Elkhorn Crest Trail is accessible only by rugged, high-clearance vehicles. From Baker City, drive 10th Street north a mile, turn left on Pocahontas Road for 7.6 zigzagging miles, and go straight on gravel Marble Creek Road 6510 for 7.8 increasingly awful miles to the pass. From there, a lovely 4.8-mile hike leads to Twin Lakes, in a gorgeous alpine bowl below Rock Creek Butte. Continue an extra mile along the Elkhorn Crest Trail and scramble cross-country up 0.8 mile to reach Rock Creek Butte's summit. Expect mountain goats and views across Baker City's valley to the distant Wallowas.

If you do not want to risk your vehicle on the rugged road to Marble Pass, access the southern end of the Elkhorn Crest Trail via the Twin Lakes Trailhead on Road 030. To find it, drive Highway 7 east of Phillips Lake. Between mileposts 28 and 29, turn north on Deer Creek Road for 4.2 miles, and go straight on Road 030 for 3.8 miles to its end. From there, a 3.1-mile trail gains 2270 feet to Twin Lakes.

Repeated forest fires have left snags along the faint trails that begin at the 1934 Peavy Cabin on Road 380. Still, it is fun to rent the historic cabin ($40 a night; call 541-523-4476 for reservations). To tackle an adventurous 10.8-mile loop, follow the faint Peavy Trail from the end of Road 380 up 1700 feet in 3.6 miles to Cracker Saddle, turn left on the Elkhorn Crest Trail for 4.4 scenic miles, and return to Peavy Cabin on the steep, 2.8-mile Cunningham Trail.

Rock Creek Lake fills a breathtakingly stark, treeless cirque, backed by the cliffs of the Blue Mountains' highest peak, 9106-foot Rock Creek Butte. The 3.5-mile trail to this beautiful lake would be more popular, but the trailhead access up Rock Creek Road is miserably rough. Likewise, the nice hiking routes to scenic Pine Creek Reservoir, Killamacue Lake, and Red Mountain Lake all require horrific drives on steep, rocky roads. Drive only as far as you feel comfortable; then park and walk.

On the west side of the Elkhorns, a quiet 6.3-mile trail up Baldy Creek from Road 73 leads to Baldy Lake, overtowered by Ireland Mountain. A 1.2-mile short-cut path to the lake begins off Road 7345, but requires some routefinding skills.

For a hike to Ireland Mountain's staffed lookout tower, drive 12.2 miles west of Sumpter on Road 73, turn right on Road 7370 for 3 miles (keeping left

Mountain goat

at unmarked forks after 0.6 and 2.4 miles), and turn right on Road 100 for 0.3 mile to a trailhead sign. Hike up abandoned Road 130 for 240 yards to a confusing junction and continue straight up a ridge-crest path 2 miles to a signpost. The lookout is 1.1 miles up to the left, while Downie Lake is 1.3 miles down to the right.

The Greenhorn Mountains, dotted with small, active mines, offer trails and old mining tracks among broad, subalpine summits. Start with the lovely 4.8-mile trail from the Olive Lake Campground past Upper Reservoir's marshy meadow and Saddle Camp to Dupratt Spring's pass, on a rocky ridge between deep, glacier-carved valleys. For a 360-degree view, scramble 0.5 mile east to Ben Harrison Peak. For a loop, follow an old road-trail 2.3 miles northeast and fork left on a 2.9-mile path through Lost Meadow to a Road 10 trailhead. From there you can either walk the road 1.4 miles back to the Olive Lake Campground or return on a 1.7-mile connector trail that follows a portion of a historic redwood pipeline.

To explore more of the Greenhorn Mountains, park where Road 45 bridges South Fork Desolation Creek and hike a creekside path 7 miles to the head of that glacial valley. Or start at primitive Head O' Boulder Campground, just below Indian Rock's staffed lookout tower, and either follow the level Princess Trail 6 miles east to Dupratt Spring's pass or take the Squaw Rock Trail 3.1 miles north, descending Big Creek to Road 45.

The winding, 24.6-mile North Fork John Day River Trail traces a rimrock canyon with new vistas at every bend. Forests plunge down 1000-foot slopes into the brawling stream. The dilapidated log cabins of gold mining claims that remain along the trail have mostly returned to public ownership.

Day hikers can easily sample this impressive canyon trail at several points. The most popular route follows Granite Creek 3.3 miles from Road 1035 to a footbridge across the North Fork John Day and a meadow with a log cabin ruin. At the canyon's eastern end, hikers starting from the North Fork John Day Campground can follow the river 2.6 miles to a bridge across rushing Trout Creek near a small, public log cabin known as the Bigfoot Hilton. For a 13.5-mile loop, continue 4 miles downriver to a cold, deep ford, turn left on the Crane Creek Trail to a trailhead on Road 73, and follow the 2.6-mile North Crane connector trail back to your car. At the canyon's western end, Road 5506 provides another river-level access to the North Fork John Day River Trail, but this remote road is far rougher than the other access routes.

Those unable to arrange a car shuttle for end-to-end backpacking trips along the Elkhorn Crest or North Fork John Day River Trails should consider several loop hike alternatives. A 19.8-mile, figure-eight-shaped loop from Anthony Lake follows the Elkhorn Crest Trail south to Cracker Saddle and returns via Lost Lake. A 31-mile loop from the Granite Creek Trailhead climbs from Dixson Bar to Moon Meadows before returning via China Meadows and the upper portion of the North Fork John Day River Trail.

Climbing

The Elkhorn Mountains feature granite cliffs (rare in Oregon) up to 300 feet tall. Though scenic, the area lacks named routes and does not attract crowds of climbers because of its remoteness and because all peaks have walk-up sides.

Winter Sports

The Anthony Lakes Mountain Resort charges a fee to use their 10 kilometers of groomed nordic trails, including the 1-mile loop around Anthony Lake and the scenic side trip to the Hoffer Lakes' basin. However, nordic skiers and snowshoers have many other options. Start with a 1.5-mile jaunt past the east edge of Anthony Lake to Black Lake.

Van Patten Lake, set in a narrow basin below Van Patten Ridge's cliffs, is a steep 1.7-mile climb from plowed Road 73. Iced-over Crawfish Lake and broad, snowy Crawfish Meadow are also good destinations. Ski to these goals cross-country from the top of the Anthony Lakes ski lift, or else ski 4.3 miles along Road 73 (unplowed west of Anthony Lake) to spur Road 216 and follow a 1.6-mile trail to the lake. The two routes can be connected to make a loop.

Take the Anthony Lake chairlift to start the dramatic, 7-mile loop around Angell Peak. Pass up this challenging trip, however, if bad weather or avalanche danger threatens— or if you find a cornice blocking the pass on the Elkhorn Crest Trail east of Angell Peak.

Boating

The North Fork John Day is not generally considered navigable through its wilderness portion due to boulders and low water levels. Raft and kayak trips on the North Fork commence at Dale and follow 40 miles of class 2+ white water to Monument.

Motorless boats are allowed on small, scenic Anthony Lake.

52 Northern Blue Mountains

Location: 26 miles east of Pendleton, 9 miles northwest of La Grande
Size: 233 square miles
Status: 32 square miles designated wilderness (1984)
Terrain: Plateaus cut by steep, partly forested canyons
Elevation: 2000 feet–6064 feet
Management: Umatilla NF, Wallowa-Whitman NF
Topographic maps: North Fork Umatilla Wilderness (USFS); Bingham Springs, Andies Prairie, Tollgate, Thimbleberry Mountain, Drumhill Ridge (USGS)

One of the roughest barriers confronting Oregon Trail pioneers in the 1840s and 1850s, the northern Blue Mountains still harbor enough wilderness to challenge hikers and hide elk.

Climate

Autumns are renowned both for delightful Indian summer weather and surprise blizzards. Shade is at a premium during summer's heat, especially on the unforested, south-facing slopes. Annual precipitation—mostly winter snow—ranges from 30 inches in the canyons to 45 inches on the tablelands. The ski season at Spout Springs runs from mid-November to mid-April.

Plants and Wildlife

Road building and logging have largely been confined to the area's plateaus, leaving wilderness in the steeply dissected canyonlands. There, only the relatively wet and shady north-facing slopes support forests (chiefly grand fir and Douglas fir). As a result, nearly every ridge offers a view to the south of forest and a view to the north of seemingly uninterrupted, dry grasslands, giving the illusion that you are always on the edge of a steppe.

The low-elevation creekbanks sprout lush foliage, with sword fern, wild ginger, Oregon grape, yew, alder, wild cherry, stinging nettle, and snowberry. Look for beaver ponds and gnawed trees along the North Fork Umatilla. Expect to find boggy wallows made by bull elk along the North Fork Meacham and Five Points Creek.

Geology

The northern Blue Mountains do not resemble the southern part of the same range. Forty miles to the south the Blue Mountains are craggy, granite peaks. Here the range consists of dissected basalt tablelands. The difference is that when the Columbia River lava flows spread out from the Grande Ronde area 17 million years ago, the lava floods mostly spared the southern Blue Mountains. Here, flow upon flow of lava buried the

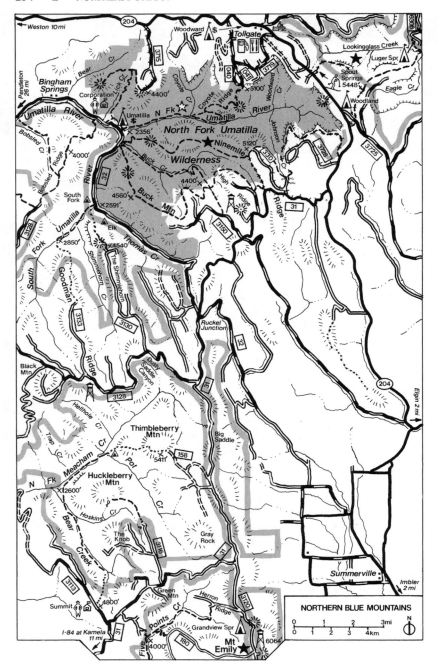

NORTHERN BLUE MOUNTAINS

landscape 4000 feet deep. Even where subsequent uplifting has allowed creeks to cut the leveled terrain into a jagged canyonland, the older rock presumably below has still not been exposed.

History

This mountain range once divided the Cayuse and Nez Percé Indian tribes. Lookingglass Creek commemorates Nez Percé leader Apash-wa-hay-ikt, dubbed Chief Lookingglass because he often carried a hand mirror.

The first white men here were crossing the continent to establish a fur-trading post at Astoria in 1812. In 1827 botanist David Douglas hiked to the Blue Mountain crest and found 4-foot-tall yellow lupine blooming—possibly the rare Sabine lupine, found only in these uplands.

In 1836, missionaries Marcus and Narcissa Whitman rode on horseback across the range on a primitive route now interpreted by the Forest Service as the Whitman Route (south of Mount Emily, across Five Points Creek and Meacham Creek, then down Horseshoe Ridge toward Walla Walla). Marcus Whitman returned in 1843 leading a wagon train. Within five years, 9000 settlers had followed on what became the Oregon Trail, winching their wagons onto the tablelands west of La Grande to avoid the narrow, brushy canyon bottoms.

THINGS TO DO
Hiking

A cluster of campgrounds near the forks of the Umatilla River form the hub of eight radiating hiking trails. All of these paths gain some 2000 feet in elevation on their way to progressively higher and more compelling canyon viewpoints. The trails that follow creeks climb gently at first, while the ridge trails start out briskly. Only three of the eight trails connect, so up-and-back day hikes are customary. Those who wish to hike the trails only downhill must arrange car shuttles to the remote upper trailheads.

The most heavily trafficked trail follows the North Fork Umatilla River 2.7 nearly level miles from a trailhead near Umatilla Campground to a good picnic spot in an old-growth fir forest at the mouth of Coyote Creek. Here crowds thin out, because the trail then climbs another 1.6 miles along the river and switchbacks 4.8 miles up grassy Coyote Ridge to Road 041 on Tollgate's plateau.

Several less crowded trails nearby also feature rushing streams. One traces the South Fork Umatilla River 1.8 miles before petering out in brush. Another, the Lick Creek Trail, charges up Lick Creek's ravine 2.3 miles and then follows a ridge 1 mile to an upper trailhead on Road 3715; an alternate spur follows a ridge crest to end at Grouse Mountain's viewpoint.

Three paths begin at the Buck Creek Trailhead. If you go straight on the well-built Buck Creek Trail, you will amble upstream 3 miles to a ford and climb a ridge 3 miles to a four-way junction with the Umatilla Rim Trail, a connector route for loop hikes. If you start at the Buck Creek Trailhead but keep right on the faint, rough Buck Mountain Trail, you will zoom up 2100 feet in 2.2 miles. At the top, the path contours

Ninemile Ridge

along the canyon rim 5.7 miles (crossing clearcuts and logging roads) to the four-way junction mentioned above, making a 13.9-mile loop possible.

The third, and perhaps prettiest, trail from the Buck Creek Trailhead veers left and switchbacks up Ninemile Ridge at a good grade. The route extends 6.5 miles to the Umatilla Rim Trail, but most people turn back at a summit after 3.6 miles. As with all of the local ridgeline hikes, the first mile has most of the elevation gain while the remaining miles follow an open, view-filled crest with wildflowers (cat's ears, paint-brush, balsamroot).

The 4.9-mile trail up Bobsled Ridge starts out with a tricky ford of the deep Umatilla River, then rockets uphill.

For canyon solitude, try the Lookingglass Creek area, east of Highway 204. After floods obliterated the original creekside trail in the 1990s, the Forest Service built a new trail system along the canyon's rim and ridges. These trails are open to mountain bikes. The Lookingglass Rim Trail starts at the Spout Springs ski area's parking lot and contours along the rimrock's edge for 3.9 miles, largely on abandoned roads. The Eagle Ridge Trail starts at the Woodland Campground entrance, crosses Road 3725, and follows a ridge 4.9 miles down to a footbridge across Lookingglass Creek at the mouth of Eagle Creek—a good turnaround point. On the far shore, the path climbs 1.2 miles to the primitive Luger Spring Campground on a spur of Road 6306. The area's largest roadless tract has been named Hellhole by the Forest Service— a name that misrepresents the area's lovely canyon scenery. For proof of this, search out the long-abandoned trail down Bear Creek from the Summit Guard Station. The route gradually descends 6 miles through a cool, old-growth forest, then follows the clear North Fork Meacham Creek 2.5 miles to a grassy campsite at Pot Creek before climbing 3.5 miles to flat-topped Thimbleberry Mountain.

Winter Sports

Highway 204, plowed in winter, provides nordic skiers and snowshoers with access to snowed-under roads on the tablelands fringing the North Fork Umatilla Wilderness. Expect competition from snowmobiles on routes near Tollgate. A good strategy is to find quieter routes along the rims of wilderness canyons. Top bets are the Lookkingglass Rim Trail from Spout Springs, the Eagle Ridge Trail from the sno-park opposite Woodland Campground, and the Umatilla Rim Trail from Andies Prairie sno-park at the junction of Road 3728 and Highway 204.

Warm up at Spout Springs, a major winter center with three lifts, two day lodges, and a restaurant.

 Wenaha-Tucannon

Location: 50 miles north of Enterprise, 28 miles east of Walla Walla
Size: 363 square miles total; 122 square miles in Oregon
Status: 277 square miles designated wilderness; 104 square miles in Oregon (1978); Grande Ronde and Wenaha federal wild and scenic rivers
Terrain: Steep, partly forested river canyons; dissected plateaus
Elevation: 1700 feet–6401 feet
Management: Umatilla NF
Topographic map: Wenaha-Tucannon Wilderness (USFS)

This huge canyonland on the Oregon-Washington border supports the nation's highest elk population density. The excellent trail network, popular with equestrians, has room for week-long backpacking trips.

Climate

Snowfall from late November to April averages 8 to 12 feet at Oregon Butte and 1 to 2 feet along the Wenaha River. Trails to 4000 feet elevation clear of snow by early May, but higher routes may be blocked until June. August afternoon temperatures often exceed 100° F, while fierce winters bring weather as cold as –40° F and occasionally freeze the Grande Ronde River. Sudden snowstorms may interrupt autumn's cool, clear weather.

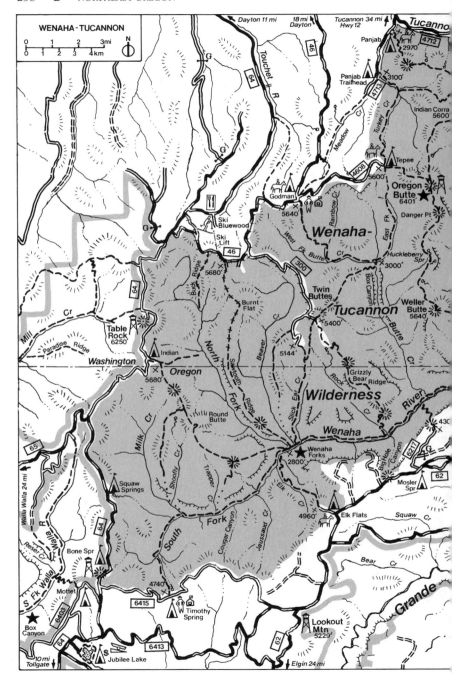

WENAHA - TUCANNON

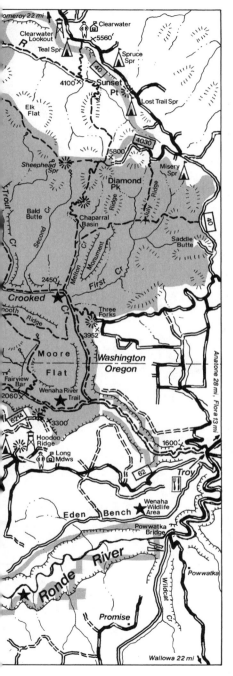

Plants and Wildlife

Elk dominate the area, but white-tailed deer and big-eared mule deer are also plentiful. The herds move down from the mountains in winter to the Wenaha Wildlife Area, where the state supplies them with supplemental feed. These feeding stations are probably the best spot in Oregon to observe elk and deer. For a look at the herds, drive the road from Troy along Eden Bench from mid-January to late May.

Other mammals include the whistling marmot, Columbia ground squirrel, snowshoe hare, black bear, mountain lion, coyote, bobcat, and marten. Bald eagles winter along the Grande Ronde River. Chukar and grouse startle hikers by bursting out of trailside brush.

The trailside brush with elegant white berries is snowberry. When Lewis and Clark passed north of here they collected snowberry seeds and brought them to Thomas Jefferson, who delighted in the "very handsome little shrub" and presented a bush to Lafayette's aunt in Paris as a gift from America. Snowberry is now considered an invasive alien weed in some European gardens.

Old-growth cottonwood, fir, and ponderosa pine line the Wenaha River. Sparse bunchgrass covers the steep canyons' dry, south-facing slopes. Dense mixed conifer forests cover other slopes and tablelands. Expect wildflowers in June and the beautiful red foliage of non-poisonous sumac bushes in October.

Geology

This area was the main source of the Columbia River lava flows that buried the landscape from Idaho to Astoria 15 million years ago with up to 5000 feet of

The town of Troy, from the Wenaha River Trailhead

basalt. For proof of this look in the canyons, where stream erosion has cut deep into the old lava plain. Running vertically through the basalt layers are occasional, wall-like outcroppings of jointed rock, looking almost like stacked cordwood. These are dikes, formed when the lava oozed up from the earth and squeezed into cracks on the way.

The distinctive red layers between rimrock levels are old soil horizons, indicating that thousands of years of forests had time to grow between lava eruptions.

History

The Nez Percé name *Wenaha* signifies that this area was once the *ha* ("domain") of Wenak, a Nez Percé chief. Similarly, the Imnaha River to the east must once have been a chief's *ha,* or domain.

THINGS TO DO
Hiking

Part of the wonder of this area is its enormity. Even day trips open vistas of seemingly endless canyonlands, wild rivers, and rugged ridges.

Troy (population 58) offers the only river-level trailhead on the Oregon side. Start here for a 6.4-mile walk up the Wenaha's arid, winding canyon to a footbridge and campsites near the mouth of Crooked Creek. Troy can be reached year round by paved road from Boggan's Oasis, Washington, which is 32 miles south of Lewiston on Highway 129. To reach Troy from the Oregon side, take Highway 3 north from Enterprise for 35 miles, turn left at a sign for Flora, and follow a steep gravel road (icy in winter) for 15 miles to Troy. The trail begins at a switchback of the Bartlett Road toward Pomeroy, 0.4 mile from downtown.

A good way to sample the area's rugged scenery is to hike from a canyon rim down to one of the rivers. Of the many possible routes, here are three that are neither too steep nor too long: The Hoodoo Trail switchbacks 3 miles from Road 6214 to a river ford in a narrow part of the Wenaha River's chasm near Fairview Bar, losing just 1400 feet. A 3.5-mile route from the Three Forks trailhead loses 1600 feet on its way to Crooked Creek. And finally, those who prefer a longer, gentler trail through forest might try the 4.6-mile path from the Elk Flats Campground down 2100 feet to a knee-deep ford at Wenaha Forks. The canyon-bottom flat at Wenaha Forks features big cotton-woods, snowberry, and gravel bars.

Other day trips follow ridgelines to high viewpoints. Start at Indian Campground on Road 64 for a 3.4-mile walk to Round Butte and a view down the length of the Wenaha River; the final quarter mile to the summit is cross-country. A different day trip climbs to the fire lookout on Oregon Butte, the wilderness's highest point. The view is well worth the 2.2-mile hike from Tepee Campground.

Trailheads on the southwest side of the wilderness are best reached via Walla Walla or Tollgate. From Walla Walla, take Highway 12 east 3 miles and turn right onto paved Mill Creek Road, which becomes Road 65. From Tollgate—located on Oregon Highway

204 halfway between Weston and Elgin—take gravel Road 64 for 11.5 miles to the popular Jubilee Lake Campground, shown on the map.

Much of the vast backcountry can only be reached by overnight trips. Do not miss the 31.4-mile Wenaha River Trail from Timothy Spring Campground to Troy. This well-maintained route fords small, calf-deep streams at the 2.3-mile and 4.5-mile marks but requires no fords of the tricky Wenaha River itself.

Of the many possible loop trips, here are three suggestions for exploring the wilderness' interior: An 18.2-mile route begins at the Twin Buttes trailhead on Road 300, follows Grizzly Bear Ridge's mesa to the Wenaha River, then returns to Twin Buttes via Wenaha Forks and Slick Ear Creek. For a 29.2-mile loop, start at Diamond Peak, follow the ridge to Indian Corral, descend Trout Creek and Crooked Creek, then return via the trail up Melton Creek. A spectacular 41-mile loop visits Oregon Butte, Moore Flat, Crooked Creek, and Indian Corral. Access this loop from any of the eastern trailheads.

Just west of the Wenaha-Tucannon area, the South Fork Walla Walla River rushes through Box Canyon, a rocky gorge where stream-loving water ouzels dip and sing. Day hikers can reach Box Canyon by switchbacking down 1900 feet in 3.3 miles from a trailhead near Mottet Campground. This scenic path crosses the river on a footbridge by a small campsite. Keep left and amble downstream a mile or two into the canyon. Backpackers can start at the head of the South Fork Walla Walla Trail at Road 65 and follow the river 18.4 miles downstream to Road 600, although the lower portion of this route shows evidence of all-terrain vehicle use.

The Wenaha River near Crooked Creek

Winter Sports

The best access to winter snow is via Dayton, Washington. Take Fourth Street to plowed Road 64 and the Ski Bluewood ski area. From there, ride the lift to the canyon rim and set out on snowshoes or cross-country skis. Snowed-under Roads 46 and 300 provide well-defined, nearly level ridge-top routes with views into the North Fork Wenaha River canyon. The trail along narrow Buck Ridge stays level for 2 miles and then descends dangerously. Another tour from Road 46 climbs slightly for 2.5 miles to Burnt Flat's plateau.

Boating

The Grande Ronde River winds through a 2400-foot-deep canyon of steep forests and interesting basalt formations. Canoeists can navigate the river except in high water, from April to June, which kayakers often prefer. Low water grounds most craft in September.

The run begins at Minam on Highway 84, follows the Wallowa River 8.5 miles to Rondowa, then continues down the Grande Ronde River 28.5 miles to Powwatka Bridge, 8 miles south of Troy. All rapids in this section can be scouted by boat. The most serious of these is the Minam Roller (class 3), 1.5 miles below the Minam put-in.

From Powwatka Bridge, boaters can continue 26 miles to Boggan's Oasis (on the Enterprise-Lewiston highway), and then another 26 miles to Heller's Bar on the Snake River. In low water The Narrows, below Boggan's Oasis, poses a class 4 hazard.

54 Joseph Canyon

Location: 20 miles north of Enterprise
Size: 39 square miles
Status: Undesignated wilderness
Terrain: Steep, sparsely forested canyon
Elevation: 2400 feet–4920 feet
Management: Wallowa-Whitman NF
Topographic maps: Table Mountain, Roberts Butte, Sled Springs (USGS)

Birthplace of the Nez Percé tribe's famous Chief Joseph, this stark canyon features the same kind of awe-inspiring scenery as the larger Hells Canyon nearby.

Climate

The canyon's wildflowers bloom and the bunchgrass greens April to June. In summer, temperatures top 100° F. Fall is dry, infrequently interrupted by brief snowstorms. Winter temperatures remain below freezing for weeks at a stretch. Highway 3, though plowed of snow, is often icy and treacherous from December to March. Annual precipitation is an arid 15 inches.

Plants and Wildlife

The canyon's sides are corrugated with steep gulches. Forest grows only on north-facing gulch slopes, while bunchgrass grows on dry south-facing slopes. The result is the distinctly stripy vegetative cover popular with elk, who need to shift between shelter and grazing areas, especially in winter.

Every decade or so a wildfire sweeps through the canyon, performing the maintenance work traditionally reserved for fire here: clearing out deadfall, brush, and mixed conifer thickets, while leaving the old-growth ponderosa pine intact.

Bring binoculars to distinguish raptors in flight: golden and bald eagles, goshawks, Cooper's hawks, and sharp-shinned hawks. All of these nest here, as do blue grouse, ruffed grouse, and chukars. Joseph Creek and its tributaries provide spawning grounds for salmon and steelhead.

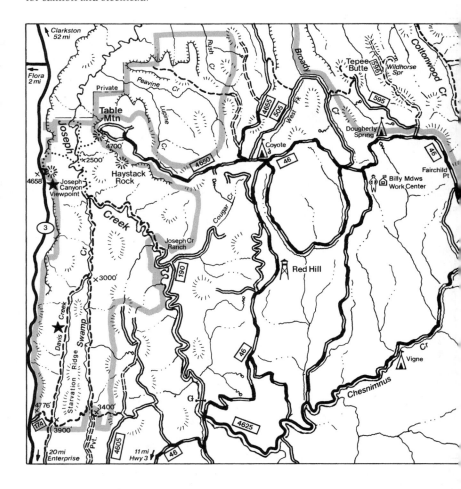

Geology

This canyon exposes some of the state's most interesting basalt formations. The area was a major source of the colossal Columbia River basalt flows 15 million years ago. Not only are dozens of horizontal basalt flows visible in cross-section, but basalt dikes show as vertical stripes, formed when the upwelling lava squeezed into cracks. The basalt has eroded into cliffs, caves, and crags, including domed Haystack Rock.

When the land here began to rise about 13 million years ago, creeks swiftly cut canyons into the lava plain, following the areas' north–south fault lines.

History

Chief Joseph, leader of the Wallowa band of the Nez Percé, was born in a cave along this portion of Joseph Creek. The original 6.5-million-acre Nez Percé Reservation of

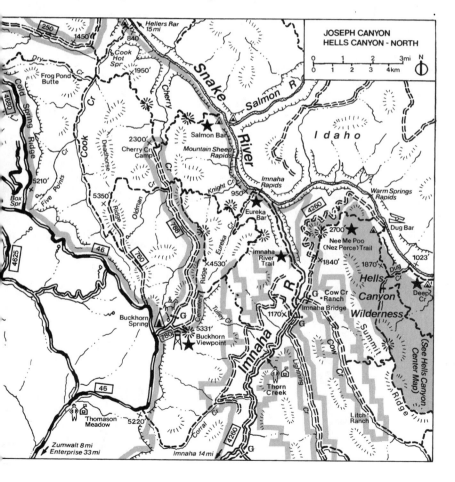

Joseph Creek

1855 included Joseph Canyon. A divisive 1863 treaty left the tribe with only a small tract of land in Idaho. The Wallowa band refused to sign the treaty or to recognize it. President Grant upheld their right to the Wallowa Valley and Joseph Canyon in 1873, but under mounting pressure from settlers, the Army in 1877 ordered the Indians to leave, setting in motion the Nez Percé's famous, ill-fated march toward freedom in Canada. After his capture, Chief Joseph was never allowed to return to his Oregon homeland.

In 1997, the Bonneville Power Administration admitted that its dams had decimated fish runs pledged to the Nez Percé by treaty and offered the tribe financial compensation. The Nez Percé used the money to buy the canyon's 10,300-acre Joseph Creek Ranch, to be managed for wildlife and cultural values.

THINGS TO DO
Hiking
Begin with a visit to the Joseph Canyon Viewpoint on Highway 3. West of the highway stretches an unassuming plain of forest and wheatfields, while to the east the land suddenly falls away into a gaping, 2100-foot-deep chasm.

The Davis Creek Trail offers the gentlest route into this canyonland. Drive 9 miles south of the Joseph Canyon Viewpoint (or 21 miles north of Enterprise). Between mileposts 23 and 22, turn east on Road 174 and keep left for 0.3 mile to the Chico Trailhead. The trail angles down through parklike stands of old-growth ponderosa pine, losing 900 feet in 1 mile to Davis Creek. Intensive cattle grazing has hammered the canyon bottom here. The official trail then crosses Starvation Ridge 2.3 miles to Swamp Creek (gaining 700 feet and losing 1250 feet), but it is also possible to follow cattle

Joseph Canyon

trails 9 miles down Davis and Swamp Creeks downstream to Joseph Creek.

Adventurers with good shoes and sound knees can hike to the bottom of Joseph Canyon in just 2 miles by following the steep, abandoned Wilder Trail down from the Joseph Canyon Viewpoint on Highway 3. To avoid the cliffs below the viewpoint, first hike north along the canyon rim 0.2 miles, then descend a rounded ridge past the remains of a log cabin. The faint trail heads southwest halfway down but is easy to lose.

At the bottom, another unmaintained route follows the winding creek through its cliff-edged gorge—a narrow oasis of green shaded by noble ponderosa pines. Bring creek-wading sneakers, for the cold, calf-deep creek crosses the narrow canyon often. Private land blocks creek bushwhackers 2.3 miles downstream from the Wilder Trail terminus and 6.8 miles upstream at the Joseph Creek Ranch.

The grassy edge of Table Mountain's forested plateau affords a sweeping view of the entire canyon and the distant Wallowa Mountains. Haystack Rock provides an easy cross-country goal across the grassy slopes from Road 4650.

55 Hells Canyon

Location: 80 miles east of Baker City, 36 miles east of Enterprise
Size: 761 square miles
Status: 336 square miles designated wilderness (1975, 1984), Snake and Imnaha federal wild and scenic rivers, national recreation area
Terrain: Immense unforested chasm, white-water river, forested tablelands, snowpeaks, lakes
Elevation: 840 feet–9393 feet
Management: Hells Canyon National Recreation Area, Wallowa-Whitman National Forest
Topographic maps: Hells Canyon NRA, Wild and Scenic Snake River (USFS)

The deepest river gorge in the United States, Hells Canyon inspires awe for its sheer size. From the gentle wildflower meadows on its rim, this chasm gapes like the ragged edge of a broken planet. Basalt rimrock and stark, treeless terraces alternate downward toward a tiny curve at the bottom: the brawling whitewater of the mighty Snake River, more than a vertical mile below. And stacked 9000 feet high on the Idaho rim loom the crags of the snowy Seven Devils Mountains.

Climate

Two different climates prevail here at once. Heavy snows drape the subalpine rim from November to May or June, while the relatively balmy, arid canyon bottom receives less than 10 inches of precipitation in an entire year. Summer temperatures often hit a sweltering 100° F along the river but remain in the 60s on the rim, where nights can freeze in any season. Spring and fall are pleasant in the canyon.

The Snake River at Saddle Creek

Plants and Wildlife

Bring binoculars to spot big-eared mule deer and herds of up to 100 elk from miles away in this open canyonland. Also watch for mountain goats, with shaggy coats and spike horns, and bighorn sheep, with curling horns. The black bears in Hells Canyon are a distinctive cinnamon brown. Wolves had long been extinct in the Pacific Northwest, but they were reintroduced in Idaho in the 1990s and have since begun crossing Hells Canyon into Oregon on their own.

Birds include great blue herons and nonmigrating geese, enticed to year-round residency by the river's mild climate.

The Snake River itself provides rare habitat for giant white sturgeon up to 12 feet long. Sea runs of salmon and steelhead died forever from the entire upper Snake River system when the Idaho Power Company built the Hells Canyon, Oxbow, and Brownlee dams in 1958–64 with inadequate fish-passing facilities. The company has since built a hatchery on the Rapid River in an attempt to perpetuate Snake River strains of fish in the free-flowing Salmon River system.

In April and May the canyon slopes glow green with bunchgrass. Flowers include tiny pink phlox and prickly pear cactus. In June, red paintbrush and yellow desert

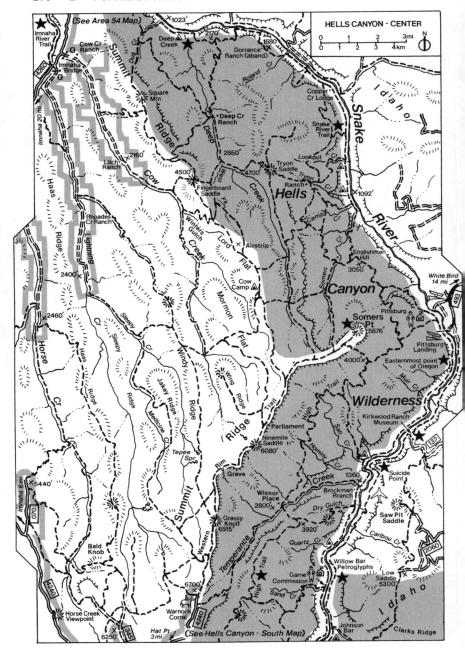

HELLS CANYON - CENTER

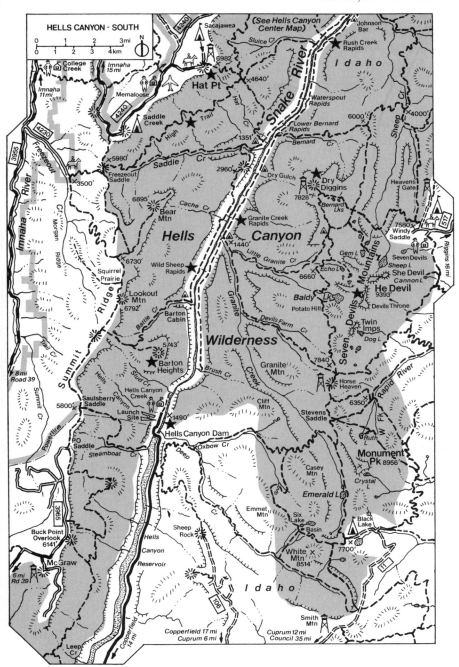

HELLS CANYON - SOUTH

0 1 2 3mi
0 1 2 3 4km

N

parsley carpet the alpine meadows interspersed with forest along the rim. The canyon turns brown in summer, but balsamroot brightens river benches with miles of little sunflowers. Summer is the only likely time to spot rattlesnakes. By October most gulches flame with the beautiful scarlet leaves of (nonpoisonous) sumac bushes. Sumac's relative, poison oak, grows in low-elevation creek bottoms.

Geology

This enormous chasm did not exist as recently as 16 million years ago, because Columbia River basalt flows of that age are continuous across the Oregon and Idaho rims.

Surprisingly, Hells Canyon was not carved by the Snake River. The ancestral Snake flowed across southern Oregon to the sea. When Great Basin faulting lifted large chunks of eastern Oregon about 13 million years ago, the Snake backed up, creating a lake over most of southern Idaho. Meanwhile, north–south fractures from the Great Basin faults allowed Columbia tributaries to cut deeply into the new northern Oregon uplands, carving the parallel canyons of the Imnaha, Salmon, and an unnamed creek that dead-ended in Hells Canyon. When this unnamed creek cut its canyon to the edge of the huge lake in Idaho, the waters suddenly poured northward to the Columbia, and the Snake River raged into Hells Canyon.

The canyon cuts through 4000 feet of Columbia River basalt to expose the older surface below. This light gray rock, forming the Snake's rugged Inner Gorge, consists of jumbled sedimentary and volcanic strata that began as a Pacific Ocean island chain 280 to 220 million years ago and was scraped up as an ancient coastal range by the westward-moving North American continent.

At first it seems puzzling that the tablelands bordering Hells Canyon slope upward to the canyon's edge. However, the earth's crust floats on a molten mantle. When Hells Canyon's erosion removed some 500 cubic miles of rock here, the crust floated upward like an emptied gravel barge. This in turn caused the river to cut the canyon still deeper. The Seven Devils Mountains, between the vast, empty canyons of the Salmon and Snake, have bobbed highest of all.

Ice Age glaciers ground out the many lake basins in the Seven Devils Mountains and rounded the valleys of the Imnaha River, Rapid River, and upper Granite Creek.

History

Pit house depressions along Tryon Creek testify to ancient habitation, as do pictographs at Willow Bar and elsewhere. Vandalism by pottery- and basket-seekers threatens study of the estimated 160 to 200 archaeological sites in the canyon. All artifacts are federally protected, including arrowheads and old bottles.

Nez Percé Indians under Chief Toohoolhoolzote established domination of the canyon by obliterating a Shoshone village at Battle Creek. In 1877, U.S. Army negotiators took Toohoolhoolzote hostage in an attempt to convince the Nez Percé to move to a small Idaho reservation. The Wallowa band's Chief Joseph led 400 Indians and several thousand head of Appaloosa horses and cattle toward the reservation. The tribe marched down the Imnaha River and managed to cross the Snake in flood stage. A

4.1-mile portion of the amazingly rugged route they followed is preserved as the Nee-Me-Poo (Nez Percé for "the real people") Trail. A shoot-out near the reservation, however, sent the tribe on a four-month tactical retreat, ending with defeat just 30 miles short of permanent sanctuary in Canada.

Hells Canyon frustrated an 1811–12 overland expedition to Astoria and other explorers seeking a navigable river route west. Once, in 1870, a full-size steamboat built on the upper Snake River ran the canyon downriver but lost 8 feet of its bow in the process.

A copper and gold strike at Eureka Bar in 1900 brought regular steamboat service from Lewiston to the mouth of the Imnaha River. A 125-foot ship winched herself up the river with the aid of giant iron rings still visible in the cliffs above Wild Goose and Mountain Sheep Rapids. The ship lost power on a 1903 run, drifted backward into Mountain Sheep Rapids, bridged the 62-foot-wide canyon there, and broke in half. Visible at Eureka Bar are remains of the steamboat landing and a huge, never-completed ore mill.

In 1887, a group of seven Idaho cowhands robbed and murdered 32 Chinese gold miners panning river gravel at Deep Creek. The robbers buried their loot at the scene. One vial of gold dust turned up there in 1902.

Homesteaders built hardscrabble ranches in the canyon bottom during 1910–30. The Forest Service later acquired the abandoned ranches and has restored the Kirkwood Ranch's clapboard ranch house and log bunkhouse as a museum of that era.

THINGS TO DO
Hiking

Nearly all of the trails crisscrossing this huge, open canyonland provide shake-your-head-in-wonder viewpoints. The area is so remote, however, that trailheads require long drives on poor roads. Many of the rugged trails involve wearying elevation gains of up to 6000 feet. Expect that rarely used paths (not described here) will be faint and hard to follow.

Several lookout towers reachable by car provide good starting points. Most popular is Hat Point, near the middle of the Oregon rim. Day hikers can savor views of the Seven Devils from wildflower meadows along the start of the trail switchbacking down from Hat Point. Drive Highway 82 to Joseph, then continue 30 miles to pavement's end at Imnaha (general store, no gas). Hat Point is an hour beyond Imnaha on a 23-mile, one-lane gravel road.

Buckhorn Viewpoint, on the northern part of the Oregon rim, overlooks the jumbled canyonlands at the mouths of the Imnaha and Salmon Rivers (see the map for Area 54). To drive to Buckhorn Point, take Highway 82 east of Enterprise 3.5 miles, turn left on Crow Creek Road for 1.2 miles to a fork, veer right to stay on Crow Creek Road another 4.2 miles, fork right onto Zumwalt Road for 32 gravel miles, and turn right on Road 780 for 1 mile to the Buckhorn Lookout's short spur road on the right. For the best view, however, hike or drive an extra 1.2 miles out Road 780 to a gate and walk on out Cemetery Ridge.

The most popular viewpoint on the Idaho side is the Heavens Gate lookout, close to the Seven Devils' crags. From Highway 95 at Riggins (Idaho) take gravel Road 517 for 17 miles to the trailhead at Windy Saddle, then drive north 1.5 miles to the lookout.

Only a few hikes in the area are short enough and level enough to qualify as day trips. Perhaps the most accessible begins at the south end of the canyon near the Hells Canyon Dam. A 1.2-mile river trail from the Hells Canyon Creek boat launch site (just past the dam) reaches Stud Creek before the path is stopped by cliffs. Farther south, a 2.6-mile path follows the Oregon shore of Hells Canyon Reservoir from Copper Creek (not shown on map) to Spring Creek. To find these trailheads from Baker City, take exit 302 off Interstate 84, and drive 65 miles east on Highway 86 to the bridge at Oxbow (Copperfield). The boat launch trailhead is 24 paved miles north on the Idaho side of the river, while the Copper Creek trailhead is 9.2 gravel miles north on the Oregon side.

Other three-day-hike trails are in the north end of Hells Canyon. All of these begin with a grueling 21-mile drive north of Imnaha on the horribly rough, dirt Lower Imnaha Road 4260 (see the map for Area 54). Park at the Cow Creek Bridge on the Imnaha River to hike a delightful, nearly level, 4.2-mile trail down the raging Imnaha River through a cliff-edged defile to the Snake River at Eureka Bar's mile-long gravel beach. Here, prowl the ruins of Eureka's gold mill and watch boats run Eureka Rapids.

The Nee-Me-Poo Trail, tracing Chief Joseph's route, begins 2.8 miles past the Cow Creek Bridge on Road 4260. This faint 4.1-mile path climbs 900 feet to the excellent view at Lone Pine Saddle before descending to the road near Dug Bar.

Road 4260 ends at Dug Bar, but the last 11.4 miles of road (past Imnaha Bridge) are too rough for trailers and most cars. From the primitive camping area and boat launch at Dug Bar, a 4.3-mile portion of Oregon's Snake River Trail climbs over a ridge to Deep Creek's bar, where an old Chinese miners' camp overlooks the Snake River and cliffs.

Pittsburg Landing, the only road access to the middle of Hells Canyon, is the start of the Idaho shore's Snake River Trail. An up-and-back day hike along the trail's first 6 miles penetrates the narrows opposite Oregon's easternmost point and reaches the museum at Kirkwood Ranch. To drive to the trailhead from Highway 95 at White Bird, Idaho, take gravel Road 493 for 16 miles to Upper Pittsburg Landing.

Backpacking or horseback trips are needed to reach most of the trails in this enormous wilderness. Maximum group size is eight people and sixteen head of stock. Keep in mind that open fires are banned within a quarter mile of the Snake River. Fragile streambank and lakeshore areas see such heavy use that visitors are advised to keep campsites and stock 200 feet away from water.

The commercial jet boats roaring up and down the river detract from the wilderness atmosphere but provide backpackers with an alternative to dusty trailheads. For about $100 per person, any of several jet boat outfitters will take backpackers from Lewiston to the Idaho shore at Pittsburg Landing or Johnson Bar and back. Prices from Pittsburg Landing to Johnson Bar are about $30. The short run from Hells Canyon Dam to Wild Sheep Rapids (where hikers can join either the Idaho or Oregon Snake

Wilderness boundary sign near Dug Bar

River Trails) costs about $30. Most outfitters require reservations. Some operate only from Memorial Day to September 15. For names and schedules, contact the Clarkston office of the Hells Canyon National Recreation Area, P.O. Box 699, Clarkston, WA 99403; (509) 758-0616.

The Idaho Snake River Trail is not only spectacularly scenic, it is nearly level for 35 miles from its start at Pittsburg Landing to its end at Brush Creek, 3 miles short of the Hells Canyon Dam. Still, the path is too faint and rugged for a family trip with small children. At Suicide Point, the trail has been blasted from sheer cliffs nearly 500 feet above the river. Four major side trails climb 6000 feet into the Seven Devils Mountains, increasing the options for longer treks.

The Oregon shore's Snake River Trail is equally scenic, but longer (56 miles from Dug Bar to Battle Creek), and climbs sharply away from the river on five occasions. Side trail options abound. Most notable are the route up Dry Gulch to the High Trail, trails from Sluice Creek and Saddle Creek to Hat Point, the Saddle Creek Trail to Freezeout Saddle, and the Battle Creek Trail to Saulsberry Saddle.

The Western Rim Trail hugs the plateau edge. Somers Point's remote view is 14.7 miles (mostly on an old road) from the Warnock Corral Trailhead north of Hat Point. South of Hat Point, the Summit Ridge Trail continues another 15 miles from Road 4240 to PO Saddle. Side trails lead to photogenic Snake River vistas atop Bear Mountain and Barton Heights. To reach the PO Saddle Trailhead from Joseph, drive toward Imnaha

8 miles, turn right onto Road 39 for 31 paved miles, then turn left onto Road 3965 for 16 miles to its end, passing the Hells Canyon Overlook, the McGraw lookout tower, and several other viewpoints along the way.

The High Trail zigzags through the canyon halfway up, passing grassy slopes, big ponderosa pines, and tumbling creeks. Try a portion of this route for variety on a longer trek, or hike along this rugged bench the length of the canyon, 63 miles from the Freezeout Creek Trailhead to Dug Bar, via Freezeout Saddle, Englishman Hill, Tryon Saddle, and Deep Creek.

There are those who swear the best canyon view is at Dry Diggins in Idaho and that the most scenic loop hike circles the Seven Devils Mountains. A 25-mile trip combines the two. From Road 517 at Windy Saddle, a 7-mile trail to the lookout building at Dry Diggins dips 1000 feet crossing Sheep Creek's glacial valley. Continue south to the spectacular Horse Heaven lookout. Return to Windy Saddle along the range's east face. The trail passes only the Bernard Lakes, but worthwhile side trails climb to Sheep, Echo, Baldy, and Cannon Lakes.

Boating

Huge canyon scenery and several huge rapids make the Snake River a popular float trip. Plan on two to eight days from the boat ramp below Hells Canyon Dam, depending on whether the goal is Pittsburg Landing (32 miles), Hellers Bar at the mouth of the Grande Ronde River (79 miles), or Asotin, Washington (104 miles). Be forewarned that all the big white-water thrills jam into the first 17 miles below the dam. For this stretch, ranger-issued permits are required from the Friday before Memorial Day through September 10. Self-issuing permits suffice for the slower water below. For permit reservation information, call (509) 758-1957.

Wild Sheep Rapids, 6 miles below Hells Canyon Dam, can easily flip 18-foot rafts. This class 4 white water, the longest on the river, concludes with big diagonal waves that must be run head-on. Two miles beyond lie Granite Creek Rapids, where a large submerged rock in the river's center creates a variety of unpredictable class 4 turbulence (class 5 at high flow levels).

Lower Bernard Creek Rapids, at river mile 12 below the dam, is a 6-foot, class 4 drop that washes out in high flows. Beyond it 1.3 miles, Waterspout Rapids develops a class 4 suckhole, especially at low levels; better scout it. The final rapid requiring scouting is Rush Creek, at river mile 16, with a boat-hungry, class 4 hole on the Idaho side.

This is no river for open canoes or rafts under 12 feet, although jet boats and rafts with up to 30 passengers are allowed. Camping is not allowed at the Hells Canyon Dam. Each year landing beaches grow smaller as upriver dams silt in, blocking the supply of fresh sand. Open campfires are banned within a quarter mile of the river. Bring camp stoves or use firepans that contain all fire and ashes. There is no firewood along the river.

The Snake is runnable year round, with 70° F water and low flows in summer, chilly water and some squalls in fall, cold weather in winter, and very challenging high water in spring.

56 Eagle Cap

Location: 7 miles south of Enterprise, 21 miles east of La Grande
Size: 715 square miles
Status: 560 square miles designated wilderness (1964, 1972, 1984)
Terrain: Snowpeaks, high lakes, alpine meadows, valley forests
Elevation: 2700 feet–9845 feet
Management: Wallowa-Whitman NF
Topographic maps: Wallowa Mountains (Imus Geographics), Eagle Cap Wilderness (USFS)

This wilderness in the Wallowa Mountains encompasses Oregon's largest single alpine area. Here are wildflower meadows and ice-bound lakes. Of the 29 mountains in Oregon more than 9000 feet tall, seventeen are here. Presiding at the hub of eight radiating valleys rises 9595-foot Eagle Cap.

Climate

The wettest area east of the Cascades, the Wallowas collect up to 100 inches of precipitation each year. Heavy winter snows close most trails from about the end of October to the start of July. Snowdrifts cling to high passes into August, but the lower Minam River Trail clears of snow as early as April. High water from snowmelt can make river fords difficult in May and June.

Mosquitoes can be thick in lake basins throughout July, when wildflowers are at their peak. Come prepared for brief afternoon thundershowers in July and August. September often brings clear Indian summer weather with freezing nights.

Plants and Wildlife

Rocky Mountain bighorn sheep were reintroduced here in 1971 after local extinction. In winter, bring binoculars to spot them on the slopes above the Lostine River near Pole Bridge Picnic Area. In spring they lamb on high ledges, where the young's only predators are golden eagles. In summer these curly-horned sheep range into the high country, where males butt heads during the November rut. Also watch for the area's spike-horned mountain goats that winter on Sacajawea Peak. Easier to find, however, are mule deer, especially in winter when they browse the moraines of Wallowa Lake.

The little, round-eared "rock rabbits" whistling warnings to each other from the Wallowas' alpine rockslides are pikas. These cute, industrious animals clip and sundry large piles of grass and wildflowers, then store them in tunnels under rockslides, where the pikas winter without hibernating. One of their few predators here is the weasel-like marten, which likewise does not hibernate. The marten may travel 15 miles a night through treetops in pursuit of squirrels.

Chipmunks and cinnamon-colored black bears are numerous enough that food

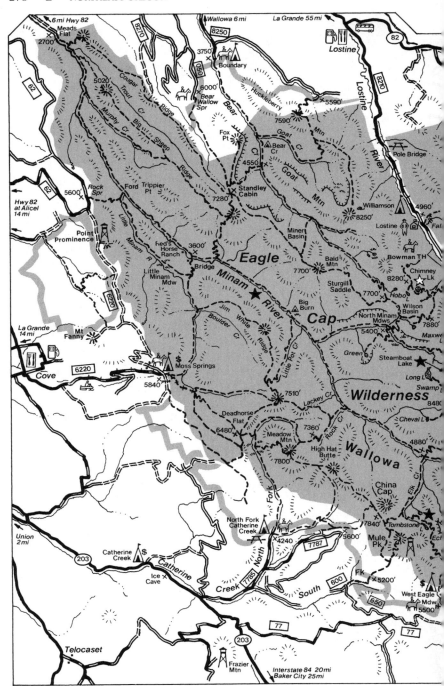

Eagle Cap from Glacier Lake

must be hung at night for safe-keeping. Campers also report nighttime visits from porcupines that chew fishing rod handles and sweaty backpack straps for their salt.

Wallowa Lake attracts geese, ducks, and occasional tundra swans in winter. Summer bird-watchers can watch for the rare Wallowa gray-crowned rosy finch. Known chiefly from just three locations—Glacier Lake, Petes Point, and a tarn near Tenderfoot Pass—this finch feeds on numbed insects that have fallen onto high snowfields. Its winter home remains a mystery.

July brings an impressive show of wildflowers to the area's many alpine meadows—notably at the Bonny Lakes south of Aneroid Mountain. Blue gentian, yellow monkeyflower, and purple elephanthead brighten wet areas, while drier fields host blue lupine, aster, scarlet gilia, and heather.

Douglas fir and lodgepole pine dominate the forests. The twisted trees at timberline are whitebark pine and limber pine—both sporting five-needle clusters and limbs so flexible they can literally be tied in knots. Limber pine, identified by its longer cones, grows nowhere else in Oregon but the Wallowas.

Geology

The predominantly granite Wallowas have been called America's Little Switzerland, and in fact resemble the Alps geologically.

Many of the Wallowas' jumbled strata began as sediment from a string of volcanic islands in the Pacific Ocean. Greenstones forming the peaks directly south of Wallowa Lake are 250-million-year-old metamorphosed basalt. The stunning white marble and contorted limestone of the Matterhorn and Marble Mountain began 200 million years ago as compacted coral reefs. Dark outcroppings are usually slate and shale: sea-floor mud.

All this island debris was buckled up from the Pacific by the advancing North American continent and then cooked by magma bubbling up from below 100 million years ago. The magma cooled slowly to form granite. Next, erosion must have nearly leveled the mountain range, because Columbia River basalt flows 15 million years ago successfully blanketed the entire area with lava. Shortly afterwards, Great Basin faulting lifted the Wallowas as much as 5000 feet above the surrounding plain, allowing stream erosion and glaciers to strip the basalt from most of the range. Basalt rimrock still tops ridges along the lower Minam River.

Ice Age glaciers ground out U-shaped valleys and basins for the area's fifty-eight

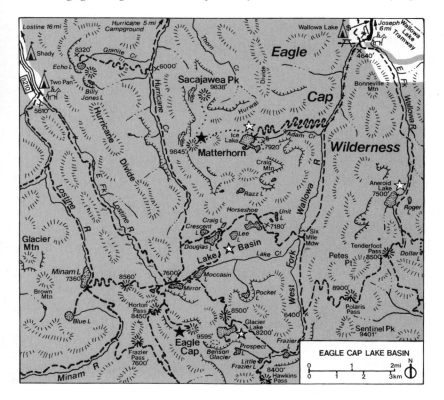

named lakes. The last major glacial advance left the smooth moraines that dam Wallowa Lake on three sides. Global warming in the late 1900s eliminated eastern Oregon's last glacier, the Benson Glacier above Glacier Lake.

History

The Wallowa band of the Nez Percé occupied a summer village on the site of the present Wallowa Lake State Park until their flight in 1877 under Chief Joseph. The names of Joseph and his U.S. Army adversary, General Howard, now grace opposing mountains across Wallowa Lake. A lakeside monument contains the remains of Joseph's father, the elder Chief Joseph.

The 1885 boomtown of Cornucopia produced $15 million in gold before its mines closed in 1941.

THINGS TO DO
Hiking

Ninety percent of all visits by horseback riders and hikers begin at just three adjacent trailheads: Wallowa Lake State Park, Hurricane Creek Campground, and Two Pan Campground. As a result, trails in this central area are crowded, camping space is tight, and some lakeshores are roped off altogether as restoration sites. For solitude, skip the Lake Basin. The Wallowas have four other lake clusters and 400 miles of quieter trails.

Scenic Wallowa Lake offers only a few paths short enough for day hikers. For an easy panoramic view, ride the gondola of the Wallowa Lake Tramway to the top of Mount Howard ($14 for adults, $8.50 for children). From the top, a 1.9-mile loop circles the summit, but adventurers can bushwhack south along an open ridge 2 miles to 9380-foot East Peak. To avoid the gondola fare, climb the nearby trail to Chief Joseph Mountain instead. It is 7.5 miles to the base of the peak's summit cliffs, with vistas of Wallowa Lake along the way.

Perhaps the most popular day hike from the heavily used Wallowa Lake area, however, is the dusty, 6-mile climb to the rustic log cabins at beautiful Aneroid Lake. Other trail destinations from the Wallowa Lake Trailhead are a little too far for day hikers and so are mostly left to backpackers and equestrians: spectacular Ice Lake (7.5 miles away and 3300 feet) and Horseshoe Lake at the start of the Lake Basin (9.2 miles away and 2500 feet up).

To appreciate the enormity of the Matterhorn's 1800-foot, west-facing marble cliff, park at the end of Hurricane Creek Road 8205. Hike up Hurricane Creek 4.9 miles to a ford with a view of the mountain's base—or, better yet, climb an additional 3 very steep miles to Echo Lake for a bird's-eye view across the valley.

Chimney Lake is one of several good day-hike goals from the dirt Lostine River Road 8210 south of Lostine. The 5.1-mile route from the Bowman Trailhead to Chimney Lake climbs 2400 feet, but it is worth continuing another mile to Hobo Lake in order to scramble to the view atop 8831-foot Lookout Mountain.

Frances Lake fills an alpine valley in the midst of bighorn sheep country, where open slopes tempt hikers to scramble up nearby 9000-foot peaks. The 9-mile trail from

Road 8210 (near the Bowman Trailhead) gains 3300 feet before dropping 900 feet to the lake.

The switchbacking, 3.8-mile trail from Shady Campground up to Maxwell Lake is much shorter and also quiet.

Popular trails from Two Pan Campground, at the end of Road 8210, lead to large Minam Lake in 5.8 miles and to a view of Eagle Cap across the East Lostine River's

The view south from Mount Nebo, above the Big Sheep Creek ski camp, in April

beautiful meadows in just 2.8 miles. Longer trail trips extend to the Lake Basin at Mirror Lake (7.4 miles) and the summit of Eagle Cap (9.8 miles). Eagle Cap is not the area's tallest peak, but its summit view is unsurpassed, and a register box at the top immortalizes those who make the trip.

For a look at the vast canyonlands in the northwest of the wilderness, climb the steep, 1.9-mile trail from a spur of Road 8250 to Huckleberry Mountain's former fire lookout site. Below Huckleberry Mountain, river-sized Bear Creek drains the northwest corner of the wilderness. A 5-mile day hike follows the stream from the Boundary Campground to a historic log cabin that served as a guard station in the early 1900s.

Or, farther west, take a relatively level 5.1-mile trail from Bear Wallow Spring through a 1990s forest fire zone to Standley Guard Station's 1932 cabin. Do not expect canyon views until you have gone a mile south past the cabin. Drive to Bear Wallow Spring via Big Canyon Road 8270, which leaves Highway 82 at milepost 35.

Day hikers can sample the lower Minam River's rugged, V-shaped canyon by hiking down the canyon's side 3.4 miles from Rock Spring on Road 62 to a derelict, long-abandoned lodge at a riverside meadow. A second, once popular trailhead to the lower Minam River was at Meads Flat. A locked gate now blocks the private road there, but equestrians can still reach the trailhead by riding up the river itself 7 miles from the Highway 82 bridge at Minam.

The Wallowas' most popular equestrian trailhead, Moss Springs Campground, accesses a network of dusty canyon trails on the southwest side of the wilderness—notably, a 7.6-mile path down the Little Minam River to Red's Horse Ranch, a closed lodge and huge meadow with the only bridge across the Minam River for miles. Although the ranch buildings are not open for public lodgers, the Forest Service caretaker often gives tours. For a less heavily used trailhead nearby, start at North Catherine Creek and climb a curving glacial valley 4 miles to Catherine Creek Meadows.

On the south side of the Wallowas, the Mule Peak lookout offers a view extending to the Blue Mountains. A steep, faint 11.4-mile loop trail from Road 600 includes the 3700-foot climb to the abandoned lookout.

The headwaters of Eagle Creek fan out in U-shaped valleys to a dozen granite-rimmed lakes in different high mountain bowls. From West Eagle Meadow on Road 77, hike 5.3 miles to cliff-backed Echo Lake, gaining 1800 feet on countless, gentle switchbacks. Even more spectacular Traverse Lake is 1.6 miles beyond and another 500 feet up.

Eagle Lake, in a bare granite bowl rimmed by 9000-foot peaks, is 7.3 trail miles from the main Eagle Trailhead and Boulder Park Campground at the end of Road 7755—almost too far for a day trip. Closer goals from the same trailhead include Lookingglass Lake (7.1 miles), Bear Lake (6.4 miles), Culver Lake (5.8 miles), and Arrow Lake (5.3 miles). Elevation gains to these timberline pools average 2300 feet. Unfortunately, small irrigation dams have converted Eagle Lake and Lookingglass Lake to reservoirs, giving these two largest lakes "bathtub ring" shorelines.

The eastern edge of the Wallowa Mountains remains relatively uncrowded. A nearly level path follows the rushing Imnaha River from Indian Crossing Campground on Road 3960 for 2 miles to Blue Hole's 50-foot-deep river slot. Continue 3.7 miles and listen for the roar of white water to find churning, 10-foot Imnaha Falls, 100 yards off the trail. To reach the trailhead from Joseph, drive 8.3 miles toward Imnaha, turn right on paved Road 39 for 32 miles, and turn right on Road 3960 for 9 miles.

Most hikers headed for the wildflower fields above Aneroid Lake trudge up the long trail from Wallowa Lake. But an easier route to the same alpine area begins at the little-used Tenderfoot Trailhead on Big Sheep Creek at the end of Road 100. From there, you can hike either 3.9 miles to the Bonny Lakes or 5.6 miles to the pass above Aneroid Lake. Looking for an even less visited wildflower patch? Try McCully Basin, 5.6 miles up from Tucker Down Road 3920.

Backpackers and equestrians in the wilderness should note camping is banned within 200 feet of any lake. Stock cannot be grazed or confined within 200 feet of lakes. Group size is limited to six in the Lake Basin and twelve elsewhere in the wilderness. Campers are not allowed to cut firewood from standing trees, alive or dead. Downed firewood is scarce; bring a camp stove.

The most popular goals for overnight trips are the fragile lakes overtowered by the Matterhorn and Eagle Cap. At Ice Lake (7.5 miles) and Horseshoe Lake (9.2 miles) most level, wooded ground is closed for restoration. Expect to search away from trails or lakes for a low-impact campsite.

Ice Lake is a scenic timberline base for hikers scaling Oregon's sixth- and seventh-tallest mountains, the Matterhorn and Sacajawea Peak. Though high enough to warrant caution, the route from the lake gains only 1900 feet and requires no special gear or use of hands. A ridge between peaks allows ambitious hikers to reach both summit viewpoints on the same trip.

Stark, island-dotted Glacier Lake climaxes a 12.1-mile trail ascending the West Fork Wallowa River past Six Mile Meadow, through a rocky gorge, and past Frazier Lake. For a scenic 27.3-mile loop trip, continue north from Glacier Lake across a pass (with a sweeping view) and return through the Lake Basin.

Steamboat Lake and North Minam Meadows highlight a less-crowded region of peaks, lakes, and winding glacial valleys. For a 29.3-mile loop from Two Pan Campground, climb 2900 feet along Copper Creek and descend past gorgeous (but misnamed) Swamp Lake to Steamboat Lake, with its ship-shaped rock formation. Continue 5.3 miles down to North Minam Meadows, and turn right through the Wilson Basin to the Bowman Trailhead. If you have not left a shuttle vehicle here, you will have to walk 3.2 miles up Lostine River Road 8210 to your car.

Want to track a river to its source? Take the Minam River Trail 46 miles to Blue Lake's alpine cirque. The rugged lower canyon is V-shaped, while the valley's forested upper canyon has been cut to a U shape by vanished glaciers. Start at the Rock Springs or Moss Springs Trailheads, head for the Minam River bridge at Red's Horse Ranch, and continue upriver.

Part of the appeal of scenic Tombstone Lake is the difficulty of getting there. It is roughly 9 miles from any of the three closest trailheads, and all routes cross high passes. The trail up East Fork Eagle Creek's valley is just long enough to call for an overnight trip. Head for the alpine meadows, tarns, and campsites near Hidden Lake, 8.3 miles upstream.

Start near Cornucopia, a semiabandoned mining boomtown, for the 7.4-mile hike to Pine Lakes. From the Cornucopia Wilderness Pack Station, walk through the horse ranch on a road that soon becomes the Pine Lakes Trail. In a vast granite bowl, the green lakes shimmer amid rock gardens of heather, gentian, paintbrush, and monkeyflower. For an 18.2-mile loop trip, circle Cornucopia Mountain by continuing over Nip and Tuck Pass and keeping left through Little Eagle Meadows back to a different Cornucopia trailhead, a mile from your car. From Baker City, take exit 302 off Interstate 84, head east 52 miles to Halfway's Business Loop, keep straight on Main Street (Cornucopia Road 4190) for 12.3 miles, and turn right 0.5 mile to the pack station.

Climbing

Although all peaks have walk-up sides, granite cliffs provide technical challenges in Yosemite-like rock. The Matterhorn's 1800-foot marble west face is toughest of all. Winter ascents of the Matterhorn and Sacajawea can be undertaken with snowshoes or even skis from Ice Lake.

Winter Sports

A good warm-up jaunt for nordic skiers traverses the snowed-under park and shore of Wallowa Lake at the end of plowed Highway 82. Nearby, the trail up the West Fork Wallowa River is gradual enough for skiers, but the Chief Joseph Mountain Trail has more viewpoints. For the best view of all, ride the Mount Howard gondola to the 8256-foot summit and ski 2.5 miles up to East Peak. The small Ferguson Ridge ski area, 6 miles east of Joseph, opens lifts for a fee when snow levels permit.

Avalanche danger makes backcountry tours into the Wallowas' U-shaped valleys risky; Hurricane Creek won its name from the swaths of broken trees left not by windstorms but by snowslides. Snow shovels, avalanche beacons, and training are essential. Wing Ridge Ski Tours offers trips to rental cabins at Aneroid Lake and floored tents at the Bonny Lakes, Big Sheep Creek, and Wing Ridge in the mountains' northeast corner. A 20-mile ski route connects the snow camps. For information, call (800) 646-9050 or check *www.wingski.com*. Road 39 is plowed as far as the Salt Creek Summit sno-park, the starting point for many of the Wing Ridge tours. Even if you have not booked a cabin, try the 10.2-mile loop over Wing Ridge, returning along a level canal from Big Sheep Creek.

Opposite: *Steens Mountain from the Alvord Desert*

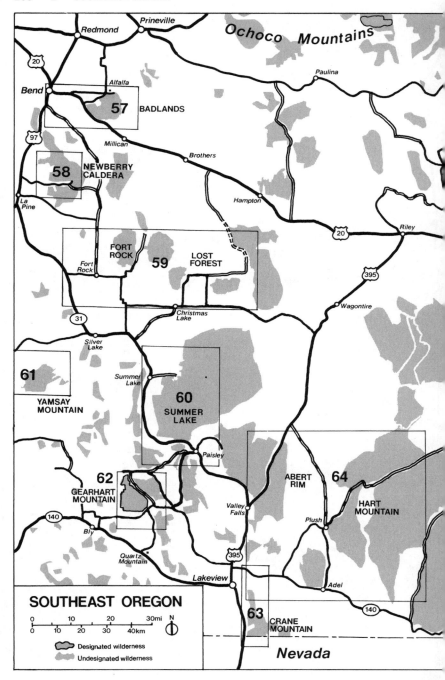

Redmond   Prineville
Ochoco Mountains
20
Bend   Alfalfa   Paulina
97   **57** BADLANDS
Millican   Brothers
58 NEWBERRY CALDERA
La Pine   Hampton   Riley
20   395
FORT ROCK   LOST FOREST
Fort Rock   **59**   Wagontire
31   Christmas Lake
Silver Lake
61   Summer Lake   **60** SUMMER LAKE
YAMSAY MOUNTAIN
Paisley
62   ABERT RIM   **64**
GEARHART MOUNTAIN   Valley Falls   HART MOUNTAIN
140   Plush
Bly
Quartz Mountain   395
Lakeview   Adel
140

SOUTHEAST OREGON

0   10   20   30mi   N
0   10   20   30   40km

Designated wilderness
Undesignated wilderness

63 CRANE MOUNTAIN

Nevada

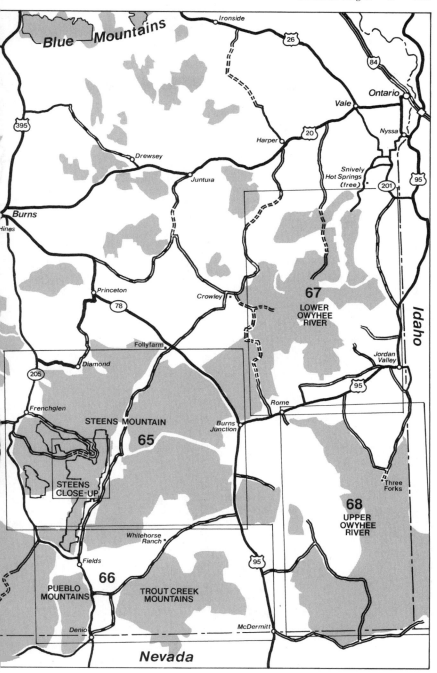

57 Badlands

Location: 10 miles east of Bend
Size: 50 square miles
Status: Undesignated wilderness
Terrain: Juniper-forested lava plain, sandy basins, dry river gorge
Elevation: 3400 feet–3865 feet
Management: Prineville District BLM
Topographic maps: Alfalfa, Horse Ridge, Millican, Horse Butte (USGS)

Just 10 miles from sprawling Bend, but a world apart, this maze of lava formations, ancient juniper trees, and hidden sandy basins is a little-known wilderness retreat.

Climate
Cold, windy winters give way to pleasant spring weather as early as March. Summers are hot and dry, but fall arrives cool and clear. Annual precipitation is just 12 inches.

Plants and Wildlife
An old-growth forest of scenic, gnarled juniper dots these rugged lava lands, increasing the feeling of isolation by blocking most long-range views. Sagebrush adds its pungent desert smell. Bright yellow and orange lichens encrust many rocks. Watch for mule deer, lizards, and sign of bobcats. Evening brings bats from lava tube caves.

Geology
This basalt lava flow's rugged ridges and caves formed when molten rock continued to move beneath the flow's hardened crust. During the wetter climate of the Ice Age, a since-vanished lake in Millican's broad valley spilled northwest across the lava here to the Crooked River, leaving the colossal dry gorge of the Dry River. Pumice and ash

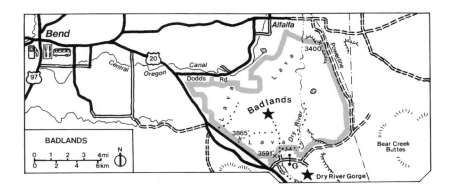

Cave along the Dry River

dusted the lava repeatedly from eruptions at distant Mount Mazama (Crater Lake) and Newberry Crater. This ash, plus windblown sand, created the area's sandy openings.

THINGS TO DO
Hiking

Start by following a sandy wash into the Dry River's canyon of colorful 300-foot cliffs. Drive east of Bend on Highway 20 for 17.6 miles to a junction just before milepost 18, at the lowest point of the highway. Turn left on a gravel road, cross a cattle guard, immediately turn right past highway department gravel piles, and continue on a rough track across the desert 0.8 mile to a fork. Park to the right, but hike up the undrivable left-hand track 0.2 mile. Then continue on deer trails or the sandy streambed itself for 2 miles. Turn back when brush and rockslides block your way.

For other cross-country explorations, turn off Highway 20 at the same junction, but keep to the left on the main gravel road that ends at a private gravel quarry gate. Park along the road and explore left on tracks into the desert. Explorers here can find and follow other sections of the long-extinct Dry River, where pictographs in "riverside" caves remain from wetter ages. Hikers can also climb up craggy basalt ridges for views, photograph 200-year-old junipers, hunt for lava caves, or head for the interior of the area in search of secluded, sandy openings—excellent campsites for high desert study.

Bring good boots for the rough rock and plenty of water (there is none here at any time of year). Also pack a compass or GPS device, because the lack of landmarks in this level, forested lava land can be disorienting. The occasional, overgrown ruts of old, meandering roads offer little guidance.

58 Newberry Caldera

Location: 23 miles south of Bend
Size: 51 square miles
Status: National monument
Terrain: Forested peaks, high lakes, lava flows, cinder cones
Elevation: 4750 feet–7984 feet
Management: Newberry National Volcanic Monument
Topographic maps: Paulina Peak, East Lake, Lava Cast Forest, Fuzztail Butte (USGS)

Oregon's only national volcanic monument features the remnants of an ancient volcano, Mount Newberry, which collapsed in Crater Lake fashion to form Newberry Caldera (a 6-mile-wide pit) and the Paulina Mountains (the caldera's ragged rim).

Climate
Patches of snow remain in the campgrounds and ice still fringes the lakes when crowds arrive for the opening of fishing season here in late May. Snow blocks the higher Rim Trail until July. By August all streams are dry except Paulina Creek. Winter snows, commencing again in November, account for most of the area's 15 to 30 inches annual precipitation.

Plants and Wildlife
A lodgepole pine forest covers almost the entire area. Big ponderosa pines grow at lower elevations. The woods harbor wildlife typical of both the Cascades and the high desert, though raucous gray jays and inquisitive golden-mantled ground squirrels seem prevalent. The state stocks East Lake and Paulina Lake with 300,000 trout annually.

Geology
This volcanic hot spot marks the western end of the Brothers Fault Zone, a line of recent eruptive centers running from here to Idaho. This major fault, and the jumble of Great Basin faults south of it, resulted from the North American continent's shearing collision with the Pacific seafloor's plate. Oregon is being stretched diagonally, and lava is leaking through the resulting cracks.

The remains of the Newberry volcano form one of Oregon's most massive and least noticed mountains. Countless thin basalt lava flows stack here into an enormous shield shape 25 miles in diameter and 4000 feet above the surrounding plain. From the highways at the mountain's perimeter, however, the overall silhouette seems low. People mostly notice the mountain's 100 parasitic cinder cones, which dot the slopes like giant molehills.

After the Newberry volcano had been built of basalt, the magma became richer in silica, causing more violent eruptions of pumice. Hollowed by explosions and massive lava outpourings, the volcano collapsed inward. Eruptions continued inside the caldera. Two obsidian flows and the 1900-year-old Central Pumice Cone have separated Paulina and East Lakes.

At the Lava Cast Forest, a fluid basalt flow surged through a stand of large trees, then ebbed, leaving the trees encased with lava up to the flow's highest level. The trees burned, but their lava shells retain even the checked pattern of the wood.

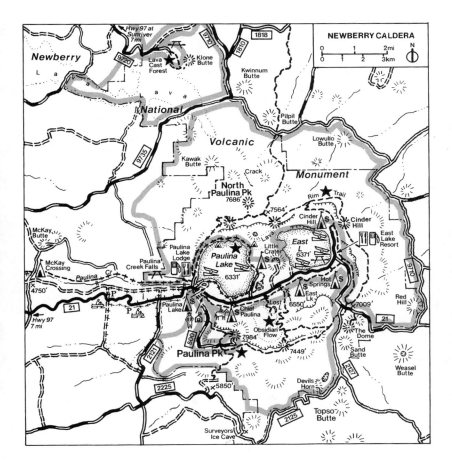

THINGS TO DO
Hiking

A paved, 1-mile interpretive trail loops through the Lava Cast Forest. The road there joins Highway 97 just opposite the turnoff to Sunriver.

For most other hikes you will have to pass the entrance fee booth at Paulina Lake and buy a Northwest Forest Pass for your car, if you do not have one already. Beyond the booth 1.5 miles, turn left through Little Crater Campground, park, and hike 7.5 miles around Paulina Lake. The circuit passes two campgrounds on the north shore accessible only by boat or trail, a beach with underwater warm springs, and an obsidian lava flow on the northeast shore.

Drive Road 21 beyond the fee booth 1.8 miles to find the Big Obsidian Trailhead, where a partly paved, 0.8-mile path climbs a staircase and loops across an even larger flow of glassy obsidian. Views range to the distant Three Sisters.

Two fun, short hikes climb to views atop the rims of little cinder cones: a 1.5-mile loop path from Little Crater Campground at Paulina Lake, and a 0.7-mile trail from Road 21 to the horseshoe-shaped rim of The Dome.

A lovely 8.5-mile trail follows Paulina Creek from Paulina Lake's outlet down to

Paulina Lake from Paulina Peak in winter

the Ogden Group Horse Camp (not shown on map), located on Road 21, 2.8 miles from Highway 97. Both ends of this trail make for easy day hikes. You can either walk the lower 2.8 miles (open year round) up to a 15-foot waterfall at McKay Crossing Campground, or you can hike the trail's topmost section to 100-foot Paulina Creek Falls. Although Paulina Creek Falls is just a few hundred yards from a signed parking area on Road 21, hikers can continue upstream 0.3 mile, cross the lake outlet, and hike back downstream to a quieter viewpoint on the opposite shore.

Gravel Road 500 climbs to the area's most popular view and highest point, Paulina Peak. Here the vista extends from the peaks of the Cascades to Fort Rock in the high desert. A dusty 2-mile path from the top drops 1500 feet to a lower trailhead on Road 500.

The 21-mile Rim Trail passes several other viewpoints—all less crowded than Paulina Peak. Take the trail north from the bridge by Paulina Lake Lodge for increasingly fine views of Paulina Lake. At the 4-mile mark, make an easy cross-country side trip to the summit of North Paulina Peak for a view of Bend and possibly even Mount Adams.

Those who prefer to climb less for their views can join the Rim Trail at the 7009-foot-level, where it meets Road 21 above East Lake. From this pass, head north along the broad, nearly level rim top, or cross Road 2127 and hike the narrow, up-and-down rim west toward Paulina Peak, 5.9 miles away.

Hikers here must carry water, and backpackers must plan on dry camps. Cross-country travelers will find solitude and unobstructed hiking outside the caldera area. The most interesting goals on the mountains' flanks are the dozens of small cinder cones, many with summit craters.

Winter Sports

Clear weather, dry snow, and plowed access make these mountains attractive to snowshoers and nordic skiers despite the presence of snowmobiles. Two methods work to avoid the noisy snow machines: visit on a weekday, or steer clear of their favored haunts—the snow-covered humps of the Big Obsidian Flow, the road up Paulina Peak, and the lakeshores.

From the uppermost sno-park on Road 21, follow the snowed-under road 2.5 miles to the Paulina Lake Lodge, open year round. Explore the lakeshore or head north up the Rim Trail for viewpoints. Do not miss icy Paulina Creek Falls, 0.5 mile below the lake.

If Road 21 is heavily trafficked, two much quieter, parallel routes also lead to the lake. Just north of Road 21, a snowed-under dirt road follows powerlines to the lodge. Still farther north, confident trackers can cross Paulina Creek and search for the Paulina Creek Trail.

Boating

Paulina Lake and East Lake are both large enough for sailing and scenic enough for rowing or canoeing. Sail over the hot springs near the southeast shore of East Lake. Squalls and choppy water can appear quickly. Motors are allowed.

59 Fort Rock and Lost Forest

Location: 64 miles south of Bend
Size: 263 square miles
Status: Undesignated wilderness
Terrain: High desert plain, lava beds, sand dunes
Elevation: 4290 feet–5585 feet
Management: Lakeview District BLM
Topographic maps: Cougar Mountain, Sixteen Butte, Fox Butte, Hogback Butte, Crack In The Ground, Fossil Lake, Sand Rock, Moonlight Butte, Mean Rock Well (USGS)

The high desert here is full of curiosities: Oregon's largest inland sand dunes, Fort Rock's imposing citadel, Hole in the Ground's enormous crater, Crack in the Ground's fissure, a "lost" forest of ponderosa pine, a lava cave with "skylights," and three large lava beds.

Climate

Studies of tree rings in the Lost Forest show that the current, bleak 9 inches of annual precipitation has been the average here for more than 600 years. Up to a foot of snow may fall in very cold December and January. In July and August, afternoon heat can be withering. Clear skies are the rule.

Plants and Wildlife

The Lost Forest's puzzle is how a 5-square-mile stand of ponderosa pine thrives in a sagebrush steppe with barely half the rainfall usually required for such stately trees. There are no other ponderosas for 40 miles. The answer is that during the wetter climate of the Ice Age, pines grew throughout southeast Oregon. This relict grove survives where rainfall collects in windblown sands underlain by the impermeable hardpan of an ancient lakebed. Oregon's largest juniper, with a trunk 18 feet around, is also in the Lost Forest.

More than a century of intense cattle

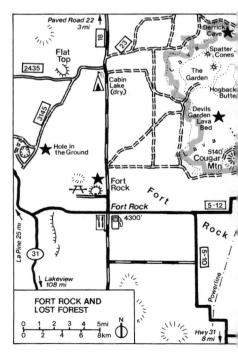

grazing cleared the high desert savanna of its original grassy cover, allowing sagebrush and juniper to spread. Ungrazed "islands" within lava flows here provide a rare glimpse of ungrazed bluebunch wheatgrass and other hard-pressed native species.

Bald eagles winter here, relying for carrion on mule deer that die during harsh weather. Many local and migratory birds gather at Cabin Lake Campground's spring; a public blind there provides first-rate bird-watching. Throughout the area, bobcats and coyotes hunt jackrabbits, cottontails, and kangaroo rats.

Geology

The fresh-looking volcanism here is a by-product of an east–west fault zone extending from Newberry Caldera to Jordan Craters near Idaho. When the Ice Age brought heavier rains, a 170-foot-deep lake collected in the Fort Rock and Christmas Lake valleys. Eruptions during that time met surface water and exploded in blasts of steam and rock, leaving rimmed craters, or **maars**. Mile-wide Hole in the Ground looks like a meteorite crater but is actually a maar. Fort Rock, another explosion crater, lay in water deep enough that waves eroded its once-sloping rim to sheer, 320-foot-tall walls. Maars at Flat Top and Table Mountain later filled to the brim with basalt.

Bones preserved at Fossil Lake reveal that this enormous Ice Age lake attracted camels, elephants, horses, and a profuse bird population of flamingos, gulls, and

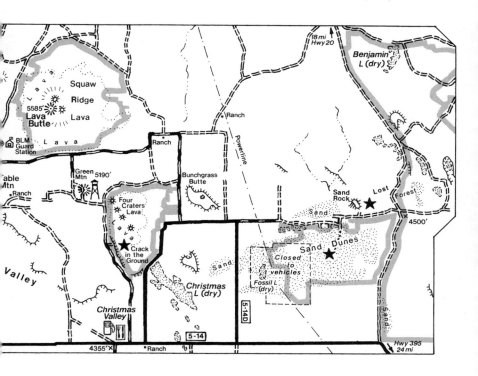

cormorants. Winds have collected the vanished lake's sands into miles of dunes as tall as 60 feet near Fossil Lake.

Most of the Devils Garden Lava erupted from a low, U-shaped vent in the extreme northeast of the flow. When the basalt's crust hardened, lava flowed on underneath, leaving lava tubes like Derrick Cave. South of Derrick Cave, a line of small vents formed circular spatter cones 5 to 30 feet across and two larger cones, the 400-foot-wide Blowouts. The soupy, pahoehoe lava of this flow left a relatively smooth surface with ropy wrinkles. In the south of the flow, collapsed lava tubes left sinuous depressions and circular dips that filled with pumice from the eruption of Newberry Caldera 1900 years ago.

Both the Squaw Ridge Lava Bed and the Four Craters Lava Bed consist of much more rugged, blocky, aa lava. Crack in the Ground, at the edge of the latter flow, is a 2-mile-long tension fissure that formed along the edge of a broad valley. The valley was created when the Four Craters' eruptions emptied an underground magma chamber and the ground sank.

History

Archaeologists here rocked the scientific world in 1938 with the discovery of more than seventy sandals more than 9000 years old, pushing back estimates of man's arrival in North America. The sandals, woven from sagebrush bark, were found in a cave a mile west of Fort Rock. Flourishing wildlife at the area's once-huge Ice Age lake apparently attracted early hunters. Artifacts found in caves on nearby Cougar Mountain date back 11,900 years.

The federal government opened this region to homesteading in 1906, and settlers staked out hundreds of dry-land farms. Nearly all were abandoned after the drought of 1913. In the village of Fort Rock, an outdoor museum (open 10 A.M.-4 P.M., Friday through Sunday in summer) has collected some of the homesteaders' buildings.

THINGS TO DO
Hiking

From the Fort Rock State Park picnic area, climb 0.1 mile to a viewpoint below the rock's east cliff to see the wave-cut terrace there. Cliff swallows swoop from nests in the rock, watched by prairie falcons. Then continue on abandoned road beds for a 1-mile loop around the inside of the "fort's" open center for June wildflowers and views across the valley. In the evenings watch for owls leaving perches on the eastern rim.

The Lost Forest and nearby sand dunes offer easy and rewarding cross-country hiking. In the Lost Forest, climb a small basalt outcropping near the forest's center for a view. Then trek southwest into the dunes' vast Saharan landscape to explore the sand—but watch out for the noisy, dangerous dune buggies that plague this area on summer weekends.

To reach the area, drive east 8 miles on paved Road 5-14 from the village of Christmas Valley, turn left on paved Road 5-14D for 8 miles to a T intersection, take gravel Road 5-14E right 3.3 miles to a corner, and go straight on a dirt track past a "Rough

Road Ahead" sign for 4.4 miles. This sandy road can be impassable in wet weather. Park at a wood rail fence at a T junction. The dunes are 0.4 mile to the right. For the Lost Forest, drive left 0.3 mile to another T junction and turn right for 2.2 miles of rough, sandy road to Sand Rock, an orange bluff with the area's best view.

Crack in the Ground is a 2-mile-long basalt slot 10 to 70 feet deep and often so narrow that it is bridged by boulders. From the far east end of the village of Christmas Valley, drive 7.2 miles north on gravel to a parking lot. A trail leads 0.2 mile to the crack's northern end and traces the slot 0.3 mile south before petering out. North of the crack, adventurers can cross a rugged lava flow to four prominent cinder cones.

The Devils Garden Lava Bed attracts both hikers and volcanologists. Drive 5.8 miles east of the village of Fort Rock, turn left on paved Road 5-12 for 9.1 miles to a guard station entrance, and continue straight on gravel 6.1 miles. Stop here to explore

Crack in the Ground

a row of giant spatter cones on the left. Then drive another 0.7 mile to Derrick Cave's signed parking area. Bring lanterns and warm clothes to explore this 0.2-mile lava tube. Above ground again, hike a mile southwest of Derrick Cave over rough lava to reach Little Garden, an old lava dome island in the fresher basalt flow.

For an overview of the smoother, southern part of the Devils Garden flow, make the short climb up Cougar Mountain. Then head north from that summit across the lava to find small sandy openings and desert solitude.

The highest point and best view in the area is atop Lava Butte, 3 miles from a road over the extremely rugged Squaw Ridge Lava.

Hikers should carry plenty of water. Fort Rock and Cabin Lake Campground have the only public sources of drinking water. All lakes and streambeds are dry. Wear sturdy boots when hiking on the area's sharp, rugged lava flows. Expect dirt roads to be badly rutted, slow, and unsigned. Side roads can be confusing, and after a rain, mud can stop even four-wheel-drive vehicles.

 Summer Lake

Location: 73 miles south of Bend, 49 miles north of Lakeview
Size: 757 square miles
Status: 29 square miles wildlife refuge; undesignated wilderness
Terrain: Marshes, high desert rimrock, brush-covered sand, alkali flats
Elevation: 4130 feet–6145 feet
Management: Lakeview District BLM, Oregon Department of Fish and Wildlife
Topographic maps: Diablo Peak, Ana River, South of Ana River, Loco Lake, Sharp Top, Bull Lake, St. Patrick Mountain (USGS)

Birdlife thrives at the marshes of Summer Lake's refuge. To the east, Diablo Mountain's 1800-foot cliff overlooks the high desert hills and salt lakebeds of a vast roadless area.

Climate

July and August afternoons top 100° F. Intensely cold, December and January bring light snows. Spring and fall are pleasant. Annual precipitation is a scant 9 inches.

Plants and Wildlife

Marshes north of Summer Lake attract bald eagles and tundra swans in winter, migratory species in spring and fall, and white pelicans, Canada geese, and sandhill cranes in summer. The most commonly sighted birds are ducks (seven species), song sparrows, marsh wrens, blackbirds, herons, egrets, terns, American avocets, black-necked stilts, curlews, and gulls. The best bird-watching is in March and April.

Unusually salt-tolerant plants survive in Summer Lake's vast alkali flats, including three spiny shrubs: greasewood, shadscale, and hopsage (blooms brilliant orange in July). Sagebrush dominates Diablo Mountain, but May brings wildflower shows of yellow, orange, and red paintbrush.

Bobcats are common in uplands, but they are shy. Bighorn sheep were reintroduced in 1990. Watch for sage grouse and flocks of western bluebirds. Raptors nest in rimrock.

Geology

Great Basin faults left the impressive, east-facing scarps of Winter Rim and Diablo Mountain. Summer Lake, with no outlet, is the salty remnant of a 40-mile-long Ice Age lake.

THINGS TO DO
Hiking

Start with a level 2.3-mile walk along a wildlife refuge dike through the bird-rich marshlands to a culvert where the Ana River enters Summer Lake. Drive Highway 31 to the refuge headquarters near milepost 70, follow

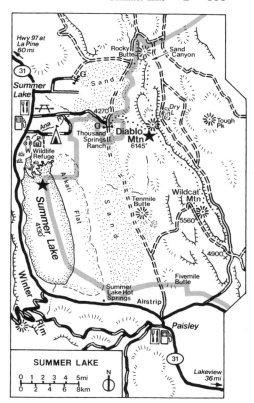

Summer Lake and Winter Rim

"Wildlife Viewing Area" pointers 1.6 miles to a T junction, turn right for 0.9 mile to a bleak camping area, and walk out Windbreak Dike.

Diablo Mountain's breathtaking, 1800-foot cliff deserves an overnight trip, but a 5.5-mile (one way) day hike also reaches the summit. Drive east from the Summer Lake Store 7 miles to a fenceline. Hike east and north around the fenceline to the peak.

Wildcat Mountain is the best viewpoint in the south, a 1-mile cross-country hike from either of two dirt roads. In the north of the area, drive past the area's only brushless dunes to the base of Rocky Butte, then explore cliff-rimmed Sand Canyon.

Boating

Canoes are perfectly suited for exploring the sinuous meanders of the Ana River and the mazelike marshlands north of Summer Lake. Bring binoculars for bird-watching. Motors are prohibited.

 Yamsay Mountain

Location: 87 miles south of Bend, 75 miles northeast of Klamath Falls
Size: 40 square miles
Status: Undesignated wilderness
Terrain: Forested mountain, canyons, streams
Elevation: 5840 feet–8196 feet
Management: Fremont NF, Winema NF
Topographic maps: Yamsay Mountain, Gordon Lake (USGS)

Like a misplaced High Cascades peak, this solitary 8196-foot cone rises from the ponderosa pine forests 40 miles due east of Crater Lake.

Climate

Snow caps Yamsay Mountain from November to early July. Summer and fall are pleasant, with the hottest days cooled by afternoon thundershowers. Annual precipitation tops 40 inches.

Plants and Wildlife

Lodgepole pine thickets cloak the lower slopes of the mountain, with meadows and parklike ponderosa pine groves in creek canyons. Above 7000 feet the forests shift to mountain hemlock, white fir, and weather-gnarled whitebark pine.

Geology

Like Newberry Caldera to the north, Yamsay Mountain is a shield volcano, but its cliff-rimmed crater was formed by ice, not fire. An Ice Age glacier on the shady north face gouged the craterlike cirque and Jackson Creek's canyon.

Ponderosa pines along the Fremont Trail on Silver Creek

History

Klamath Indians called this mountain *Yamsi,* "the north wind," and believed it to be the home of *Kmukamtch,* a supreme deity who sometimes took the weasel-like form of Marten. The area is still sacred to the tribe.

THINGS TO DO
Hiking

The Fremont Trail climbs 16.6 miles from Silver Creek Marsh Campground to a top-of-the-world view on Yamsay Mountain. The path's lower 4.8 miles (to Road 3038) make a nice day hike, following a fork of Silver Creek through a canyon full of old-growth ponderosa pine. For a backpack trip, take the path's upper 8.6 miles from the Antler Trailhead on Road 038 up a broad ridge to the summit. Antler Springs, 0.2 mile off the trail along abandoned Road 024, offers a logical camp stop. Cross-country explorers can strike off from the springs to find the idyllic meadows in Buck Creek's basin.

For these hikes, drive Highway 31 a mile west of the town of Silver Lake. Between mileposts 46 and 47, turn south onto paved Road 27, and follow signs for Silver Creek Marsh Campground or the Antler Trailhead.

On the west side, a road once led to a lookout tower on Yamsay Mountain's summit. With the tower gone, the abandoned road has become an alternate trail to the top, climbing 3.4 miles from the end of Road 4973.

Though trailless, Jackson Creek's open forests and creekside meadows invite

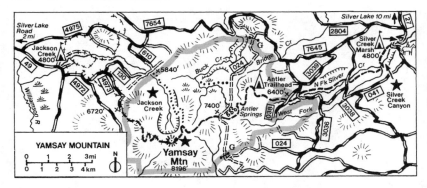

bushwhacking—especially along the 4-mile section from Road 130's crossing to the creek's forks in a bowl-shaped cirque below the summit cliffs.

To find westside hiking routes, drive Highway 97 to the Klamath Forest Wildlife Refuge sign near milepost 228, turn east on the Silver Lake Road for 21 paved miles, and turn right on Road 49 for 5 miles to Jackson Creek Campground.

Winter Sports

Jackson Creek Campground, accessed by plowed Road 49, is a winter nordic ski center with 25 miles of marked trails. For starters, ski 1.4 miles up Jackson Creek on a snowed-under road, cross the creek, and climb east 0.8 mile to a viewpoint of Yamsay Mountain. Loop routes return either along the north rim of Jackson Creek's canyon or south through ponderosa pine woods. The area's toughest goal is Yamsay Mountain's summit, 8.7 miles from the Jackson Creek Campground and 3400 feet up.

62 Gearhart Mountain

Location: 36 miles northwest of Lakeview, 66 miles east of Klamath Falls

Size: 72 square miles

Status: 35 square miles designated wilderness (1964, 1984)

Terrain: Forested ridges, cliffs, valleys

Elevation: 5700 feet–8364 feet

Management: Fremont NF

Topographic maps: Gearhart Mountain Wilderness, Fremont National Forest Visitors Map (USFS); Coleman Point, Coffeepot Creek, Lee Thomas Crossing, Cougar Peak (USGS)

Picturesque cliffs, rock domes, and pinnacles top this long mountain. Nearby, trails climb from Campbell and Dead Horse Lakes to cliff-top viewpoints above a vast lodgepole pine forest.

Climate

Summer days shine clear and are seldom hot in this forested upland. Be prepared for possible afternoon thunderstorms and frosty nights. Snow blocks the upper portions of trails at Gearhart Mountain and Dead Horse Rim from November to mid-June. Roads and lower trails are usually clear by May. Winters can be extremely cold. Annual precipitation ranges from 35 inches at Gearhart Mountain to 20 inches in the lowlands.

Plants and Wildlife

The rare, parklike stands of ponderosa pine here survive wildfire well. Because old-growth ponderosas lack low branches, fires burn brush and grass without reaching the trees' crowns. Ponderosa bark, which turns orange after a century or more in the sun and develops a pleasant vanilla smell, features a jigsaw-puzzle surface that flakes off during fires to remove heat from the trunk.

The smaller, denser lodgepole pines burn easily in forest fires but reseed profusely because their cones open after a fire's heat. Lodgepoles have two needles to a cluster, while ponderosas have three and other local pines five.

Mammals here include mule deer, black bear, coyotes, and porcupine. Listen for little, round-eared pikas whistling from their rockslide homes.

Geology

Both Gearhart Mountain and Dead Horse Rim began as shield-shaped volcanoes built of many thin basalt layers. The older of the two, Gearhart Mountain may once have stood 10,000 feet high. Erosion uncovered the resistant lava that forms its summit cliffs, The Dome, and The Palisades—an area of weirdly shaped, 30-foot pinnacles. Ice Age glaciers scooped out the impressive U-shaped valleys of Gearhart Creek, Dairy Creek, and Dead Horse Creek.

Coleman Rim's cliff is the scarp of a fault block, like most cliff-edged mountains in the Great Basin.

THINGS TO DO
Hiking

From the north end of the popular, well-graded Gearhart Mountain Trail an easy 2.4-mile hike reaches Blue Lake and a view of the long, low mountain. Either circle the lake on a 0.8-mile path or continue 4.4 miles up the trail to its highest point at The Notch, a spectacular 8120-foot pass directly below Gearhart Mountain's summit cliff.

From the south end of the Gearhart Mountain Trail, hikers start near Lookout Rock's tower, pass through The Palisades at the 1-mile mark, and climb another 3.7 miles to a viewpoint in a 7930-foot saddle. This makes a possible turnaround point, but it is worth continuing 1.3 easy miles through alpine meadow openings to the better view at The Notch.

On a clear day, hikers atop Gearhart Mountain's summit can spot Steens Mountain, the Three Sisters, and even Mount Lassen. Take the trail from Lookout Rock 3.7 miles to the 7930-foot pass, then scramble left up to a ridge top, and follow it for an easy, nearly level mile to the summit. No special gear or use of hands is required.

To drive to these trailheads from Paisley (on Highway 31 between Lakeview and Summer Lake), take Mill Street (Road 34) west from town for 19 paved miles, turn right on paved Road 28 for 2.5 miles, and turn left on paved Road 34 for 6 miles to Dairy Creek. To find the northern trailhead from this junction, turn right on gravel Road 3372 for 8 miles, and turn left on Road 015 to its end at the North Fork Trailhead. To find the southern trailhead from the Dairy Creek junction, continue straight on paved Road 34 another 4.5 miles and turn right on gravel Road 012 for 1.5 miles to its end, passing the pleasant Corral Creek Campground along the way.

The Boulder Spring Trail offers a backdoor route to Gearhart Mountain's high country. This 6-mile route gains 2600 feet from a ponderosa pine forest at Road 018

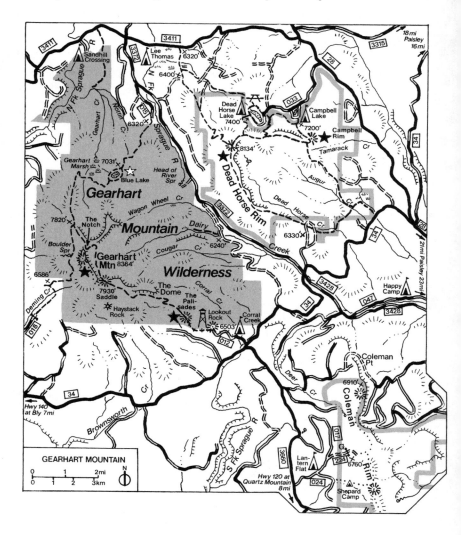

Campbell Lake from Campbell Rim

to a trail junction on the peak's shoulder, passing the meadows at Boulder Spring on the way. The first 3 miles of the trail follow an old road that was closed to improve fish habitat in Deming Creek. To reach the trailhead from Bly (between Klamath Falls and Lakeview), take Highway 140 east of town 1.4 miles, turn left on Campbell Road for 0.6 mile, turn right on paved Road 34 for 4 miles, turn left on gravel Road 335 for 1.5 miles, and turn right on Road 018 for 3 miles.

Dead Horse Rim, though nearly as tall as Gearhart Mountain, is much less craggy and more accessible. For a 4.9-mile loop in this area, start at a trailhead pullout in the midst of Campbell Lake's campground, climb 1.5 miles to a viewpoint on Campbell Rim's lip, and then keep right at junctions to return to Campbell Lake. For a slightly longer loop (7.4 miles), continue from Campbell Rim to Dead Horse Rim, and then return via Dead Horse Lake.

A larger network of faint trails, particularly popular with equestrians, extends for miles through the open, but largely viewless lodgepole pine forests beyond Dead Horse Rim. Two different routes lead southeast from Dead Horse Lake about 8 miles to the ponderosa pine woods of Augur Creek at Road 34. Another two trails head northwest from Dead Horse Lake (for 3.9 miles and 6 miles) to the Lee Thomas Trailhead on Road 3411.

Cross-country hiking is easy in the area's open forests; bring a compass and to-pographic map. At Gearhart Mountain and Dead Horse Rim, strike off from established trails to follow ridges or find meadows in high creek basins. Old trails at Dairy Creek and to Gearhart Creek from Road 3411 provide good starts. Likewise, cross-country hikes are the way to explore Coleman Rim's interesting ridge crests, ponderosa pine forests, and meadows. Two routes lead to Coleman Rim from the primitive Lantern Flat campsite on Road 024. Either drive 0.7 mile past Lantern Flat on Road 024 and hike east through aspen-filled meadows (known as Shepard Camp), or drive north from Lantern Flat 0.7 mile on Road 017 and hike abandoned Road 224 east to meadows along the rim.

Backpackers can hike the entire 12.1-mile Gearhart Mountain Trail or simply spend a few days in the high country exploring from a base camp. Firewood is scarce and fire danger often high, so bring a camp stove. Saddle stock are only allowed within 200 feet of open water in the designated wilderness for watering, loading, or travel on trails.

Winter Sports

Though none of the roads in the area is plowed in winter, cars can usually drive from Lakeview or Bly to the Corral Creek Campground (elevation 5960 feet) by early April. From there, ski or snowshoe 2 miles up to the Lookout Rock tower and another nearly level mile to The Palisades.

Boating

Small craft do well on 0.5-mile-long Dead Horse Lake and smaller Campbell Lake. No motors are allowed.

63   Crane Mountain

Location: 5 miles east of Lakeview
Size: 60 square miles
Status: Undesignated wilderness
Terrain: Forested fault block mountain, high meadows
Elevation: 5200 feet–8454 feet
Management: Fremont NF
Topographic maps: Crane Mountain, Crane Creek (USGS)

The highest point in south-central Oregon, Crane Mountain lifts its sudden scarp above the sagebrush flatlands and shore marshes of vast Goose Lake.

Climate

Very cold winters whiten the mountain's crest by late November. The snow lingers to mid-June. Summer temperatures are pleasantly mild. Despite 40 to 60 inches of average annual precipitation, blue skies predominate.

Plants and Wildlife

May and June bring wildflower displays to the high meadows covering much of this long mountain. Expect paintbrush, aster, balsamroot, clarkia, penstemon, phacelia, yarrow, and spreading phlox. In fall, white-barked quaking aspen brighten the gulches with brilliant orange leaves. Evergreen trees range from spire-shaped subalpine fir at the highest elevations to mountain mahogany on dry slopes and tall ponderosa pine in lower forests.

Hikers may spot mule deer, jackrabbits, porcupines, and coyotes. Goose Lake's tremendously varied bird population, which peaks during spring and fall migrations, includes pelicans, herons, tundra swans, geese, and many ducks. Bald and golden eagles soar above the mountain and lake in winter.

Quaking aspen in winter

Geology

Great Basin faulting has chopped much of southeast Oregon into broad valleys and blocky mountains. The huge fault scarp forming Crane Mountain's abrupt western cliffs continues north 40 miles to Abert Rim. Basalt lava flows that once covered this area as a level sheet have been hoisted 3700 feet to the top of Crane Mountain, exposing underlying John Day rhyolite tuff on the mountain's western flank. Rockhounds find agate nodules and thundereggs in this rhyolite layer east of Highway 395.

The optimistically named Highgrade Mining District uncovered small amounts of gold-bearing quartz in the basalt flows capping the southern end of Crane Mountain. The find still puzzles geologists, because basalt is usually a hopeless place to look for gold.

Older residents in the area recall when Goose Lake drained via the Pit River to the Sacramento. Irrigation has since lowered the lake, leaving it landlocked and increasingly saline.

THINGS TO DO
Hiking

Start with an overview of the area from a fire lookout on Crane Mountain's crest. Dirt Road 015 leads there but is far too rough and steep for passenger cars, so park at the junction with gravel Road 4011 and walk the final 2.7 miles, gaining 1400 feet. Just

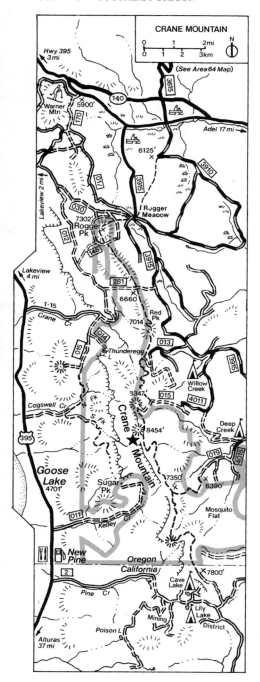

before Road 015's end, the Crane Mountain Trail branches south. This scenic, 8.7-mile route, with views from Mount Shasta to Steens Mountain, parallels the rim's edge into California. Motorcycles are allowed, but rare. The highest point on Crane Mountain is a mile south along this trail and a short scramble west.

A newer section of the Crane Mountain Trail heads north from Road 015. It begins 0.8 mile below the end of Road 015 and switchbacks down the ridge crest past Red Peak for 10.5 miles to cross Road 3915 at Rogger Meadow's quaking aspen groves. For an easily accessible sample of this route, park at Road 3915 and follow the trail south a few miles to ridge-top viewpoints. Equestrians can also follow the trail north of 3915 for 3 miles and continue along backroads 6 miles north to the Walker Trailhead on Road 3615. From there, the Crane Mountain Trail continues north (mostly along abandoned roads) 7.9 miles to the Fremont Trail at Crooked Creek (see Area 64).

The high meadows and open forests lend themselves to cross-country exploration. One rugged route follows a bench on the western face of Crane Mountain from Kelley Creek to Cogswell Creek.

Winter Sports

The Warner Mountain ski area operates a lift and day lodge from mid-December to mid-March, depending on snow conditions. The area serves as a base for cross-country ski trips south on snowed-under roads toward Crane Mountain.

64   Abert Rim and Hart Mountain

Location: 25 miles northeast of Lakeview, 93 miles southwest of Burns
Size: 718 square miles (including Drake Peak and Fish Creek Rim)
Status: Undesignated wilderness; 430 square miles national wildlife refuge
Terrain: High desert block mountains, ephemeral lakes
Elevation: 4237 feet–8405 feet
Management: US Fish and Wildlife Service, Lakeview District BLM, Fremont NF
Topographic maps: Lake Abert South, Little Honey Creek, Crook Peak, Drake Peak, Hart Lake, Warner Peak, Campbell Lake, Flagstaff Lake, Priday Reservoir, Adel, Guano Lake, Alger Lake, and 14 other maps (USGS)

Pronghorn antelope and bighorn sheep here roam the edges of the nation's tallest fault-scarp cliffs. Marshes at the Warner Lakes attract pelicans, cranes, and swans. In the uplands, sagebrush plains stretch to the horizon.

Climate
As upland snow melts from March to late May, dry lakes fill and mud may close some dirt roads. Wildflowers bloom in late May and June. July and August afternoons can top 100° F, although nights are cool. Fall brings mild days and frosty nights. Sub-zero snowstorms close the Plush–Frenchglen road and Highway 140 east of Adel periodically between December and March. Blue sky presides 300 days a year in this region of only 9- to 20-inch annual precipitation.

Pictograph at Petroglyph Lake atop Poker Jim Ridge

Plants and Wildlife

Graceful pronghorn antelope browse sagebrush throughout the area. North America's swiftest animals at up to 65 mph, they flash their white rumps and release a musk when alarmed to flight. Nearly 2000 live on the Hart Mountain National Antelope Refuge, although they retreat during severe winters to Nevada.

Overhunting and domestic sheep diseases drove bighorn sheep to extinction in Oregon by 1915. Twenty of the curly-horned sheep reintroduced at Hart Mountain from British Columbia in 1954 multiplied with such success that animals have since been trapped here and released at many southeast Oregon locations. About 250 now live on rimrock ledges from Hart Mountain to Poker Jim Ridge, with smaller herds on the cliffs of Fish Creek Rim and Abert Rim.

Warner Lakes' marshes sustain elegant egrets, awkward white pelicans, eared grebes, ruddy ducks, geese, and many other birds. Visit in March or April for the spectacular spring migrations.

Bald eagles, golden eagles, and prairie falcons nest in rimrock ledges. Fish Creek Rim averages four aeries built of sticks per mile. Ask refuge employees for the best spots to watch sage grouses perform their peculiar strutting, puffing, gurgling courtship displays at the crack of dawn from mid-March to mid-May.

Twelve species of sagebrush grow here. Silver sage graces alkali playas. In rich soils, big sagebrush reaches 15 feet tall with 8-inch-diameter trunks. Near big sage expect profuse displays of paintbrush, larkspur, buckwheat, and sage buttercups in spring. The low sagebrush of rocky, high elevations protects different spring flowers: bitterroot, crag aster, and

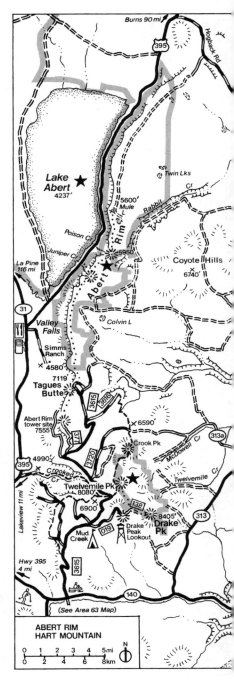

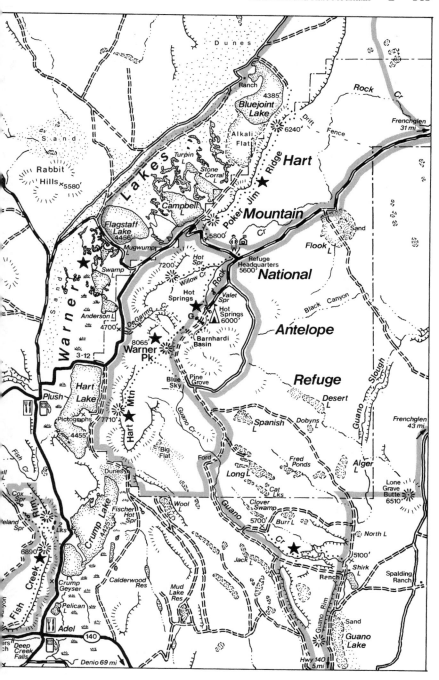

goldenweed. Rarest plants in the area are salty Lake Abert's endangered Columbia watercress, South Abert Rim's delicate blue-leaved penstemon, and Guano Creek's threatened Crosby's buckwheat.

In fall, quaking aspens in rim gulches turn stunning yellow and orange. Small groves of ponderosa pine—remnants of a vast Ice Age forest—survive near Hart Mountain's Blue Sky area and at Abert Rim between Colvin Lake and Juniper Creek. The snowier Warner Mountains about Drake Peak support fir forests.

Geology

Although history records no major earthquakes here, the rocks do. Very fresh-looking fault scarps at Abert Rim, Poker Jim Ridge, Hart Mountain, and Fish Creek Rim show that blocks of earth have shifted 2400 feet vertically, leaving plateaus and gaping lake valleys. The landscape here must have been mostly flat 10 million years ago, because Steens Mountain basalt flows of that age cover all these disjointed rims. Hot springs and the Crump Geyser also suggest ongoing crustal activity.

The Ice Age brought rain instead of ice to this warm region. Lake levels rose about 200 feet, unifying the Warner Lakes and connecting Lake Abert with Summer Lake (see Area 60). Beaches of these once-huge lakes remain as gravel terraces on valley edges near Plush and along Poker Jim Ridge. Now even Lake Abert and Hart Lake run dry in lean years.

Jasper, agate, and opal have been found on Hart Mountain's western face. The wildlife refuge allows collection of 7 pounds of rocks per person. Ask in the Plush general store for directions to a designated sunstone collecting area north of that village.

History

Northern Paiute Indians sailed these lakes on rafts of bundled bulrushes to hunt ducks and gather eggs in disposable cattail baskets. Hundreds of pictographs, evidently from a culture predating the Paiutes, remain at Hart Lake, Colvin Lake, Petroglyph Lake, and the southern tip of Fish Creek Rim. This ancient rock art can be damaged even by fingerprint oils, so touch nothing. Caves in the rimrock overlooking Guano Lake may have been occupied in the Ice Age. All other artifacts are federally protected.

The Hart Mountain National Antelope Refuge was created in 1936, but cattle grazing was not banned until the late 1990s. The ranchers' barbed wire fences limited the antelope, a species that does not leap well, and are still being removed.

THINGS TO DO
Hiking

The area has few marked trails, but rim edges, creeks, and ridges offer abundant natural pathways in this open landscape.

Drive slowly along the gravel road from Plush toward the Hart Mountain refuge, watching with binoculars for birdlife in the Warner Lakes and for bighorn sheep on the eastern cliffs. A pullout at Hart Lake has a short, overgrown nature trail and a wildlife viewing blind. A more interesting roadside stop is halfway up Poker Jim Ridge, where a 0.3-mile trail loops to a viewpoint across the lakes far below. For a better view, park where the road crests Poker Jim Ridge and follow the rim north 2.2 miles to a cliff-edged knoll (GPS location N42°35.479' W119°40.999'). Rocks and matted sagebrush make for slow walking. To return on a loop, set off east across the desert a mile to Petroglyph Lake's ancient rock art (GPS location N42°34.538' W119°40.446'), and then angle southwest 1.5 miles back to your car.

At the refuge's Hot Springs Campground, relax in the hot springs' 104° F natural pool. Bring your own drinking water to this free campground (containers may be filled at the refuge headquarters), or use a filtration pump to purify water from Rock Creek.

For a nice 5.3-mile loop from the campground, follow animal trails up Rock Creek 2.8 miles to a dilapidated cabin at Barnhardi Basin's broad meadow (GPS location N42°28.790' W119°43.200). Return along Barnhardi Road, a dirt track that is gated closed to vehicles December 1 to August 1. For a longer hike or a backpacking trip, climb from Barnhardi Cabin to DeGarmo Notch's pass (GPS location N42°29.094' W119°43.917'). From there, you can either follow a broad ridge south 2 miles to the panoramic view atop Warner Peak, the refuge's highest point (GPS location N42°27.579' W119°44.474'), or you can hike down DeGarmo Canyon 4.7 miles to the paved road to Plush.

One of the refuge's nicest hikes follows a trail up the scenic lower portion of DeGarmo Canyon to a 35-foot waterfall. Drive paved Road 3-12 from Plush 10 miles to a "DeGarmo" Canyon pointer, back up 100 yards, and take a rough dirt road uphill 0.3 mile to a parking area at road's end (GPS location N42°29.005' W119°47.327'). Follow the trail into the canyon's mouth for 0.7 mile to the falls. The path ends here, but if you scramble up the canyon's left slope you will find an abandoned cattle path that leads upstream 3 miles to the canyon's upper end.

Other cross-country routes follow Rock Creek 5 miles downstream to the Refuge Headquarters, passing beaver ponds along the way. Or hike 4 miles northwest onto the plateau at the head of Willow Creek to visit a bighorn sheep corral and get an impressive rim-edge view of Flagstaff Lake.

Permits are required to camp anywhere in the refuge except Hot Springs Camp-ground. The headquarters at the refuge is often unstaffed, but a visitor information room is left unlocked, and self-issuing permits can be filled out there. The refuge bans off-road-vehicle travel, hang gliders, excessive noise, and destruction of live plants. Firearms are restricted. Mountain bikes are permitted only on established roads.

Abert Rim's stark face may look unhikable, but a little-known 2-mile scramble route from Highway 395 takes hikers right to the top. Park at the watchable wildlife parking area at the southern end of Abert Lake and climb beside Juniper Creek to a breathtaking overlook of alkali-fringed Lake Abert, 1700 feet below. From the top, it is easy to follow the rim 3 miles north to a spring and ancient, rock-walled Paiute hunt-ing blind on the rimrock above Poison Creek. For an 11-mile backpack trip, trek Abert Rim south from Juniper Creek to the hang-gliding launch site atop Tagues Butte, a good place to leave a shuttle car.

For a break from sagebrush bushwhacking, try the trail system through fir forests

The Warner Lakes and Poker Jim Ridge

and quaking aspen groves of the Drake Peak area. Three trail routes converge at the South Fork Crooked Creek Trailhead on paved Road 3615. To the west, a 6.9-mile portion of the Fremont Trail descends Crooked Creek's canyon, dropping 2100 feet to the Mill Trailhead, on a dirt spur road that joins Highway 395 near milepost 132. To the north, a fainter portion of the Fremont Trail skirts rounded Twelvemile Peak and Crook Peak through alpine sagebrush fields with far-ranging views. The trail crosses Road 3720 at the Swale Trailhead after 6.7 miles, and continues faintly 4 more miles to Vee Lake at the end of Road 3616. To the southwest of the South Fork Crooked Creek Trailhead, a third trail follows a roaded, logged rim toward Crane Mountain (see Area 63).

For the best overview of the half dozen peaks surrounding the once-glaciated basins of Twelvemile and McDowell Creeks, drive to the Drake Lookout (which is not on Drake Peak). To rent the historic lookout building for overnight use, call (541) 947-3334. For a hike, take spur Road 138 a mile east of the lookout, and walk cross-country along an open ridge another mile to Drake Peak's real summit.

The cliffs of little-known Fish Creek Rim rise 2400 feet above the Warner Lakes, providing a view across 5 miles of thin air to Hart Mountain. Best routes for cross-country exploration follow the rim's edge or else descend through a break in the rimrock 3.5 miles from Cleland Spring to the Plush–Adel Highway at Crump Lake. Drive to the upper rim by taking paved Road 313 north from Highway 140 for 12 miles; turn right on a rough dirt road for 8 miles, then park and hike east.

Guano Creek is a misnamed oasis. Park at the creek crossing north of Shirk Lake and hike up this green-banked stream as it meanders between low rimrock walls. From Adel, drive 21 miles east on Highway 140, and then take a dirt road 13 miles north.

On all hikes, carry plenty of water. By summer all lakes and streams are dry or undrinkable due to salinity or cattle pollution. Dirt roads shown by dashed lines on the map may be impassable for passenger cars; inquire locally.

Boating

In wet years, the Warner Lakes feature 300 miles of canoe routes. Of particular interest are the sinuous waterways linking Campbell Lake with a primitive campsite at Turpin Lake, as well as routes linking Mugwump, Swamp, and Anderson Lakes.

Hang Gliding

Abert Rim's 2000-foot west scarp faces the west wind, and thermals off Lake Abert make 20-mile flights along the length of the rim possible. To find the launch site at Tagues Butte from Highway 140, drive 21 miles north on Road 3615, turn left at the second entrance to loop Road 032, and after 0.8 mile take a 0.5-mile spur through a gate.

Land on the west side of the road to Simms Ranch, avoiding guarded private land along adjacent Highway 395.

65 Steens Mountain

Location: 63 miles south of Burns
Size: 1293 square miles (including Alvord Desert and Sheepshead Mountains)
Status: 273 square miles designated wilderness (2000)
Terrain: Snow-capped fault-block mountain, glaciated canyons, desert playas, sagebrush hills
Elevation: 4025 feet–9733 feet
Management: Burns District BLM, Vale District BLM
Topographic maps: Alvord Desert, Steens Mountain to Alvord, Steens Mountain to Page Springs, Page Springs to Diamond (Desert Trail Association); Fish Lake, Wildhorse Lake, Alvord Hot Springs, and 33 other maps (USGS); Steens Mountain (nontopographic, BLM)

Landmark for all of southeast Oregon, 50-mile-long Steens Mountain looms snowy and sudden a vertical mile above the Alvord Desert's stark alkali flats.

Huge, U-shaped gorges dissect the western flank of Steens Mountain's 9733-foot-tall plateau. Rushing western streams lead to the Donner und Blitzen River, which winds through a rimrock-lined canyon on its way to the bird-rich marshes of the Malheur National Wildlife Refuge. The vast, treeless Sheepshead Mountains stretch to the northeast, a jumble of sagebrush ridges and dry lakebeds.

Cross-country hiking routes and a 77-mile segment of the Desert Trail lead to the popular uplands of Steens Mountain and dozens of lesser-known attractions.

Climate

A sign at the foot of the Steens Mountain Loop Road notes, "Weather Advisory: The Steens Mountain area experiences frequent and sudden storms. Be prepared for sudden and extreme lightning, snow, rain and high winds." Winter snow and gates block access to the Steens' uplands from about mid-November to the first of July. However, summer on the mountain is generally cool and clear with freezing nights. Prepare for thundershowers and July mosquitoes or gnats. Avoid trees and high places during lightning storms. To check Steens weather conditions before a visit, call the BLM's Burns office at (541) 573-4400.

April, May, and June are pleasant below 6000 feet elevation, with abundant wildflowers and water. In these months, the Alvord Desert and other playas may become lakes. July and August are pleasant above 6000 feet, but these same months bring blazing heat to lower elevations, with little or no shade. Fall is cool but bone dry. December to February, fiercely cold winds rake the region.

Annual precipitation drops from 40 inches on Steens Mountain to just 7 inches in the Alvord Desert—Oregon's driest spot.

Plants and Wildlife

Five life zones band the mountain. Above 8000 feet, expect bunchgrass, colorful rock-encrusting lichens, and a blaze of August wildflowers. Steens paintbrush, moss gentian, a dwarf blue lupine, and showy Cusick's buckwheat grow atop Steens Mountain and nowhere else in the world. In high cirques, look for bleeding heart, shooting star, bitterroot, buttercup, and wild onion. A herd of bighorn sheep also likes these cirques; watch for them from the East Rim overlook.

Quaking aspen groves dot the 6500- to 8000-foot zone, with flashing leaves in summer and orange foliage in fall. Look for (but do not deface) the bawdy graffiti Basque shepherds carved in the aspen's white bark near old camps in Little Blitzen Gorge and Whorehouse Meadows. Beldings ground squirrels and marmots thrive here, as do July flowers: clarkia, monkeyflower, and prairie star.

Juniper and low sagebrush dominate between 5500 and 6500 feet elevation. Listen at dawn for sage grouse strutting and puffing in courtship displays March to mid-May. Wild horses and antelope run here, especially on the benchlands west of Blitzen Crossing. Jackrabbits, coyotes, and rattlesnakes are common. May brings blooms of penstemon, buckwheat, and (in the Stonehouse Creek area) rare Biddle's lupine.

Below 5500 feet, tall sagebrush rules. Watch for young burrowing owls standing about their ground holes in June. At small, multientranced burrows, listen for the

Steens Mountain's East Rim viewpoint in April

thumping of long-tailed kangaroo rats scolding within. The kit fox, once thought extinct in Oregon, still hunts the southern Sheepshead Mountains by night. Lizards abound.

Alkaline playas such as the Alvord Desert are virtually devoid of life, but salt-tolerant species cling to their sandy fringes: bright green greasewood bushes, leafless orange iodine bush, salt grass, and spiny shadscale. Silver sage covers other dry lakebeds, such as Follyfarm Flat. Spadefoot toads emerge en masse from the ground after rains. Antelope ground squirrels scamper even in summer heat, shaded by their curled white tails.

Huge flocks of migrating birds begin arriving at the Malheur National Wildlife Refuge in late February: snow geese, lesser sandhill cranes, tundra swans, and pintails. The spectacle peaks from mid-March to mid-April. Greater sandhill cranes nest in April, when migrant curlews, avocets, and stilts arrive. Songbirds pass through in April and May. By June grass is so tall at the refuge that birds are more often heard than seen. Watch for muskrats in the refuge's canals and porcupines and great horned owls in streamside willow thickets.

Because the creeks here have had no outlet to the sea for millennia, unusual fish species have evolved, including redband trout and the Catlow tui chub. Wildhorse Lake, Mann Lake, and Juniper Lake have been stocked with rare Lahontan trout.

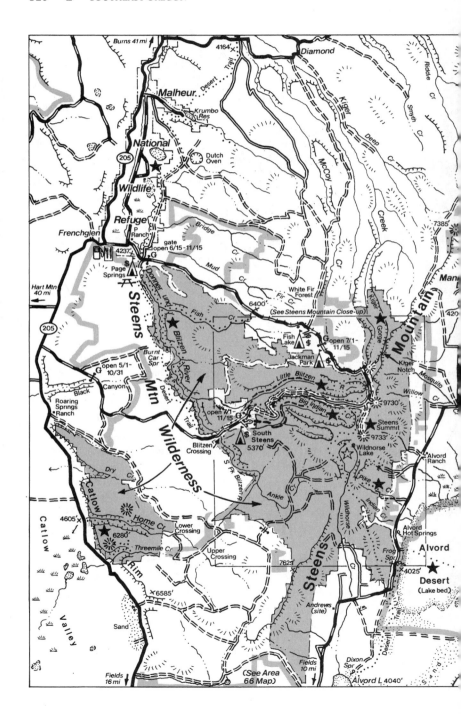

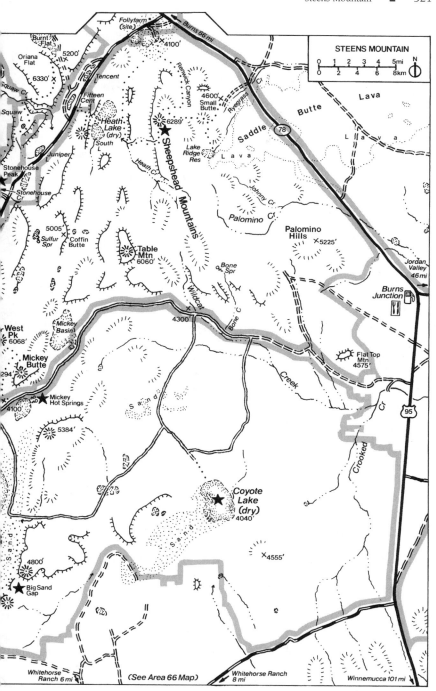

STEENS MOUNTAIN

0 1 2 3 4 5mi
0   2   4   6   8km
N

Follyfarm (site)
Burnt Flat
5200'
Oriana Flat
6330' X
Squaw Cr
Squaw
Tencent
Fifteen Cent
X4100'
Renwick Canyon
4600' Small Butte
Ryegrass Cr
78
Saddle   Butte
Lava
L a v a
Jordan Valley 46 mi

Heath Lake (dry)
South
6289
Sheepshead Mountains
Heath Cr
Lake Ridge Res
L a v a
Johnny Cr
Palomino Cr
Palomino
Palomino Hills
X5225'

Juniper
Stonehouse Peak
Stonehouse Cr

5005'
Sulfur Spr
Coffin Butte
Table Mtn 6060'
Bone Spr
Bone Cr
Wildcat

Burns Junction

West Pk 6068'
Mickey Basin
4300
Creek
Flat Top Mtn 4575'

Mickey Butte
294'
X
4100'
Mickey Hot Springs
5384'
S a n d
Crooked Cr
95

Coyote Lake (dry) 4040'
X4555'

4800'
S a n d

Big Sand Gap

S a n d

Geology

All rocks here are volcanic: layers of dark basalt lava and light rhyolite ash. When this rock erupted about 15 to 20 million years ago, it covered most of southeast Oregon 4000 feet deep, leveling the landscape. Nonetheless, the eruptions here were smaller than the massive Columbia River basalt floods in northeast Oregon. The Steens basalt is different—full of big feldspar crystals.

Then North America's shearing collision with the Pacific crustal plate stretched Oregon diagonally, shattering southeast Oregon into north–south-aligned basins and ranges. Steens Mountain rose entirely in the past 5 to 7 million years, while the Catlow Valley and Alvord Desert fell. The Sheepshead Mountains consist of smaller rims and basins. Hot springs indicate continuing fault movement.

The Ice Age brought increased rain as well as snow. A lake filled the Alvord Basin 200 feet deep all the way to Coyote Lake but found no outlet. Glaciers formed on Steens Mountain, gouging seven U-shaped canyons 2000 feet deep. The canyons left only narrow fingers of the original Steens plateau intact, and even these were breached by glaciers at Rooster Comb and Kiger Notch.

As the Ice Age drew to a close about 10,000 years ago, eruptions along the Brothers Fault Zone produced rugged, fresh-looking basalt flows at Diamond Craters (north of Diamond) and the Saddle Butte Lava Field.

Today, look for smooth bedrock polished by glaciers at the head of Big Indian Gorge. Along Pike Creek and Little Alvord Creek, exposed ash formations contain thundereggs, agates, and petrified wood. In desert basins, note where wind has stripped the ground to "desert pavement," fields of pebbles stained brown by "desert varnish," a crust of oxides.

History

Seminomadic Northern Paiute Indians lived in brush lean-tos and caves in this area, relying chiefly on jackrabbits for meat and fur. Peter Skene Ogden led beaver trappers to the area's creeks in 1825–29. Army Major Enoch Steen battled the Paiutes and named the mountain in the late 1860s, exiling Indians to reservations at Yakima and later Burns.

Pete French built a cattle empire here during 1872–97; his P Ranch near Frenchglen is now owned and maintained by the Malheur Wildlife Refuge. By 1901, Basque and Irish shepherds were grazing more than 140,000 head of sheep on Steens Mountain, obliterating once-lush grasslands. Domestic sheep were banned from public land on the mountain in 1972. Cattle were excluded from the mountain's fragile summit and canyons in 1982, and were banned from other wilderness upland areas in 2001, but, ironically, still dominate the wildlife refuge.

THINGS TO DO
Hiking

The area's most spectacular views are just a short walk from the Steens Mountain Loop Road. Start by driving the well-maintained northern portion of this gravel road east from Frenchglen. After 2.9 miles, turn right for 0.6 mile to the far end of the Page

Springs Campground. Two trails begin here: a 0.7-mile path that follows the Donner und Blitzen River into a rimrock canyon, and a 1.4-mile interpretive nature loop that climbs to a rimrock viewpoint.

Then return to the Page Springs Campground entrance, turn right on Steens Mountain Loop Road, follow it 18.9 miles uphill, and follow a pointer left 0.4 mile to the Kiger Gorge Viewpoint. A 100-yard trail leads to a cliff overlooking the colossal canyon. Adventurers can bushwhack 0.5 mile left along the rim to find a very steep scramble trail that descends 1400 feet to the valley floor.

Next, drive 2.7 miles farther along the Loop Road to a four-way junction. First drive the left-hand fork 0.3 mile to the East Rim's breathtaking vista of the Alvord Desert. Then, drive the middle fork 2 miles to a parking lot at road's end, where two trails

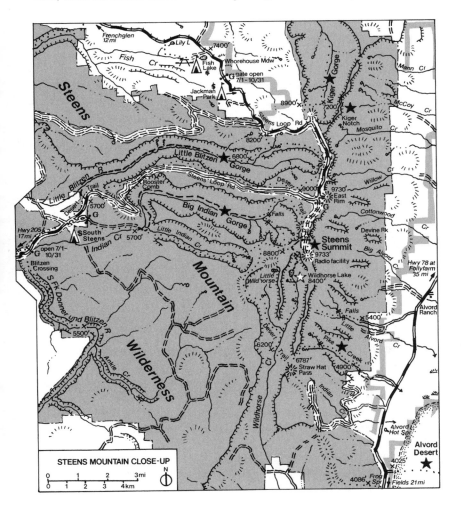

begin. For an easy 0.3-mile walk, follow a closed road up to five small radio buildings on the mountain's panoramic 9733-foot summit. For a longer hike from the parking area, take a downhill path 1.2 miles into a gaping canyon to Wildhorse Lake's spectacular alpine wildflower meadows.

Passenger cars and motor homes should return to Frenchglen as they came, but tougher vehicles can return on a longer loop. From the summit parking area, drive back to the four-way junction and turn left—but be warned that this portion of the Steens Loop Road includes 6 miles of steep, rocky road descending the Rooster Comb's narrow ridge.

Trails follow both Big Indian Creek and the Little Blitzen River up long, glacially carved canyons from South Steens Campground. Expect wildflowers, plenty of springs, scenic quaking aspen, and waterfalls. From a gate in the group camp area at the far left end of the campground, hike a closed, shadeless dirt road 1.9 miles to its end at a ford of Big Indian Creek. Usually it is possible to cross dry-footed on a log downstream. A genuine trail continues up the scenic canyon (with two other creek crossings) for 4.6 miles before petering out at a creekside cottonwood grove. Bushwhackers can continue through sagebrush meadows another 2 or 3 miles, but serious scrambling is required to scale the canyon's steep, 2000-foot headwall to the road on the rim.

To find the Little Blitzen Canyon Trail, drive the Steens Loop Road 0.3 mile east of the South Steens Campground, park at a message board, walk up the road another 0.2 mile, and take a signed trail left along a fenceline 0.9 mile to the Little Blitzen River. Expect fords as you hike upstream 3 miles, gaining 750 feet. Adventurers can continue 5.8 miles to the canyon's end, gaining 3000 feet and climbing a steep headwall to the loop road.

For most of the Desert Trail's route across Steens Mountain, it is not a specific footpath but rather a general corridor marked by cairns. Hikers must pick their own route through the open, generally treeless terrain. A topographic map and compass are essential. To see the most, plan to backpack. There is no firewood, so bring a camp stove.

A 15-mile section of the Desert Trail traverses impressive Wildhorse Canyon on the way from Frog Spring (on the Fields–Follyfarm Road) up to the Steens Loop Road. Day hikers can climb just 2 miles to a viewpoint knoll. Farther up the route, side trips explore the alpine basins of Wildhorse and Little Wildhorse Lakes.

The Donner und Blitzen River cuts a 400-foot-deep, rimrock-lined canyon through the sagebrush tablelands south of Page Springs Campground. The Desert Trail route parallels this canyon across the tableland 14 miles to the Steens Mountain Loop Road at Blitzen Crossing. Adventurers can also follow the river itself, but expect thick brush and many deep fords. Fish Creek's brushy side canyon is also worth exploring.

North of Page Springs, the Desert Trail follows Malheur Wildlife Refuge backroads. Camping is banned on refuge lands, as are horses, open fires, swimming, and rock collecting.

The east side of Steens Mountain also offers interesting day hikes and overnight trips. Check the gas gauge before driving the Fields–Follyfarm Road to the Alvord

Desert. If the desert lakebed is dry, hike out onto the cracked, alkali surface a few miles to experience this remarkably empty playa and to admire the view of snowy Steens Mountain. Better yet, camp in the desert, continue to the greasewood-covered sand hummocks of the far shore (7 miles distant), prowl Big Sand Gap's canyon, and climb to the rimrock viewpoints nearby.

For this and other desert hikes, do not travel in midsummer heat, carry a gallon of water for each day, and bring a hat or cloth for shade. Expect roads shown by dashed lines to be passable only by four-wheel-drive vehicles.

Conclude a visit to the Alvord Desert with a relaxing soak in Alvord Hot Springs at an easily visible tin shed 100 yards from the Fields–Follyfarm Road. The Alvord Ranch owns the springs but allows the public to use the site. Reward this courtesy by keeping the area free of litter.

Driving north from the Alvord Desert, choose one of Steens Mountains' steep eastern canyons to explore on a day hike. To find the trail up Pike Creek, turn off the Fields–Follyfarm Road 3.7 miles south of the Alvord Ranch at a yellow cattle guard (GPS location N42°34.275' W118°31.26'), drive up a very rough road 0.6 mile to a campsite by a house-sized boulder, and hike across the creek. An old mining track leads 1.4 miles up the canyon through a rugged rock narrows with wildflowers and views of the desert playa below. Bushwhackers can continue along the canyon's right-hand slope 1.3 miles to the creek's forks.

Mickey Hot Springs features steam vents, boiling mud pots, and the 30-foot-deep, turquoise Morning Glory Pool, a dangerously scalding cauldron that has claimed more than one life. The only pool that may be cool enough for humans is a bathtub-sized basin carved into the ground by frustrated bathers. Drive the Fields–Follyfarm Road 5.8 miles north of the Alvord Ranch to the second 90-degree corner. At a green cattle guard, turn east on a gravel road for 6.5 zigzagging miles. After cautiously exploring the hot springs area, hike to the nearby playa, or climb treeless Mickey Butte for a bird's-eye view of Steens Mountain.

The Sheepshead Mountains are the most barren and forbidding-looking hills in Oregon. And therein lies their secret charm. For even when spring fills the creeks and fires the sagebrush slopes with wildflowers, there are no crowds in this huge world of hidden canyons, cliffs, and valleys. To sample this range, hike 2 miles east from Fifteen Cent Lake (on the Fields–Follyfarm Road) through a canyon to hidden Heath Lake's playa, and scale an unnamed rim nearby for a view. To see more, backpack south from Follyfarm Flat at Highway 78, hike up Renwick Canyon, follow the high rim of the Sheepshead scarp, descend North Heath Creek's canyon, and return to Follyfarm—23 miles in all.

Try these other utterly uncrowded scenic areas for hiking:

The far northern end of Steens Mountain. Hike north from Stonehouse Peak's castle-shaped rock along a 7000-foot rim or explore the lakes and aspen groves near perennial Squaw Creek.

Catlow Rim. Walk up the canyons of Threemile Creek or Home Creek between sheer, 1300-foot walls and hike to a rim-edge overlook of Catlow Valley and distant Hart Mountain.

Coyote Lake. Devotees of pure desert delight that this desolate playa is even more remote than its Alvord Desert twin.

Runners compete each August on Oregon's highest 10-kilometer course, the Steens Rim Run from Fish Lake to the 9730-foot East Rim. Record time is 47 minutes.

Winter Sports

Powder snow and far-ranging winter vistas are plentiful on Steens Mountain's crest, but difficult access and treacherous weather stop all but the most accomplished snow campers from skiing or snowshoeing there. Sudden whiteouts and freezing winds can occur in any month. Arrange with the Burns District BLM office (541-573-4400) to pick up a permit and gate key. Skiers and snowmobilers are issued permits for different times to avoid conflicts. In April, expect snow to block the road about 3 miles before Fish Lake.

66 Pueblo Mountains and Trout Creek Mountains

Location: 105 miles south of Burns, 100 miles north of Winnemucca
Size: 641 square miles
Status: Undesignated wilderness
Terrain: Fault-block mountains, creek canyons, desert flats
Elevation: 4040 feet–8634 feet
Management: Burns District BLM, Vale District BLM
Topographic maps: Pueblo Mountains, Alvord Desert (Desert Trail Association); Chicken Spring, Little Whitehorse Creek, Doolittle Creek, Oregon Canyon Ranch, Van Horn Basin, Ladycomb Peak, and 16 other maps (USGS)

South of the desolate Alvord Desert, the treeless Pueblo Mountains surprise hikers with high meadow basins nestled against snowy crags. In the Trout Creek Mountains, a dozen creeks have cut scenic, rimrock-lined canyons into a high tableland.

Climate

In the Pueblos, snow blocks the Desert Trail from November to late May. Wildflowers peak in June. July and August are hot only in the lowlands. Sudden storms bring lightning and occasionally even snow in summer.

In the Trout Creek Mountains, the snowpack melts in early May, and wildflowers appear in May and June. Cattle grazing July 1 to September 15 diminishes midsummer appeal. Fall is cool and dry.

Annual precipitation, just 7 inches in the lowlands, creeps to 25 inches in the Trout Creek Mountains and 15 in the Pueblos.

Borax Hot Springs, with Steens Mountain on the horizon

Plants and Wildlife

Unusual fish have evolved here, cut off from the sea for millennia. The 90° F alkaline hot springs at Borax Lake support their own species: the 2-inch-long Borax chub. Trout Creek is named for its redband trout, while Willow and Whitehorse Creeks contain Lahontan cutthroat trout, a federally listed threatened species. Many of the streams are closed to fishing; obey signs.

Sagebrush and bunchgrass dominate, but willow and quaking aspen turn streams into linear oases. On open slopes, stubby mountain mahogany trees develop elongated crowns—a result of browsing below and shearing winds above.

Wildflowers in meadows include blue lupine, sunflowerlike balsamroot, phlox, and the showy Bruneau mariposa lily. In dry areas, look for delicate penstemon and pink bitterroot. Along creeks expect tall larkspur, mint, and 3-foot-tall bluebells.

At the eastern edge of the Trout Creeks, Oregon Canyon is a veritable museum of rare and endangered wildflowers: red buttercup, Lemmon's onion, two-stemmed onion, and bristle-flowered collomia. The Pueblos' Cottonwood Creek harbors one of the northernmost populations of Mormon tea, a green, leafless bush used to brew a mild stimulant. Oregon's only long-flowered snowberry bushes grow along Fifteenmile Creek.

Beavers work virtually every stream in the Trout Creek Mountains. Bighorn sheep live in the Pueblos, but mule deer are more often sighted. Partridgelike chukars by the hundreds cluck in lower canyons of the Pueblos. Listen for the California quails' three-syllable call, the western meadowlarks' territorial songs, and the omnipresent Brewers sparrows. Watch for sage grouse and prairie falcons.

Geology

Steens basalt lava and ash buried all of southeast Oregon 15 to 20 million years ago. Great Basin faulting then hacked the flattened landscape into block-shaped, tilted plateaus, including these two ranges. Fault scarps here have exposed the older rock beneath the basalt. Granite, greenstone, and schists along the eastern base of the Pueblos and in canyons of the western Trout Creek Mountains contain traces of gold, copper, and mercury.

Two enormous, violent volcanoes in the Trout Creek Mountains collapsed about

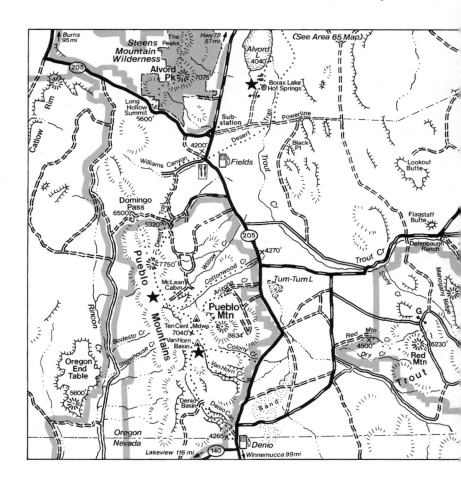

14 million years ago, leaving 15-mile-wide, Crater Lake–style calderas. The lakes filled with sediment and breached their rims. Willow Creek and McDermitt Creek now drain the two basins. A long arc of cliffs between Disaster Peak and the head of Oregon Canyon marks the McDermitt Caldera rim.

History

The 1860s Pueblo Mining District gave the range its name. Look for stone cabin ruins in Denio Canyon and along the Pueblos' Willow Creek. Mining continues in Denio Basin.

The Rose Valley Borax Company once shipped 400 tons of borax a year from Borax Lake to Winnemucca via 16-mule-team wagons. The Nature Conservancy bought the lake and surrounding hot springs in the late 1990s to protect the unusual ecosystem.

Whitehorse Ranch, headquarters for John Devine's cattle empire during 1869–89, remains a showplace of the old West.

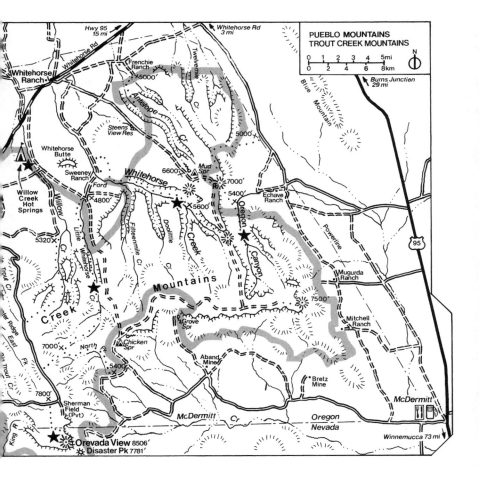

THINGS TO DO
Hiking

The Desert Trail route parallels the Pueblo Mountains' crest for 22 miles from Denio to Fields. The trail's cross-country route is marked by 48 cairns, and although each rockpile is supposed to be within sight of the last, it is still easy to miss them. A topographic map and compass are essential.

Day hikers can sample the route at Denio Canyon and from a very rough side road near Fields. To find this northern access, drive the paved road south of Fields 3.1 miles, turn right at a "Domingo Pass" pointer for 3.8 miles, fork right for 0.5 mile, veer left 0.2 mile to a yellow cattle guard, turn left and then keep straight on the largest road 2.1 miles to park at a cairn (GPS location N42°10.67' W118°43.25'). Hike southwest for 2 steep miles to the range's crest, and follow the ridge south 1.6 miles to a viewpoint knoll at cairn #14 (GPS location N42°8.275' W118°44.20').

Other cross-country routes that climb to the Desert Trail in the Pueblos ascend Cottonwood Creek, Colony Creek's canyon meadows, and Van Horn Creek's narrow, rugged gorge.

Perhaps the best view of all is at the 8634-foot summit of Pueblo Mountain, southeast Oregon's second-highest point. Hikers climb there by following an old road up along Arizona Creek 5.7 miles to Stergen Meadow, and then bushwhacking southeast 2 miles up a sagebrush slope.

Even named creeks are often dry in the Pueblos and Trout Creek Mountains. Always carry a gallon of water per day. Sagebrush is the only firewood.

Borax Lake's hot springs make a fascinating day-hike goal. From Fields, drive the paved road 1.3 miles north, go straight on the gravel Fields–Follyfarm Road 0.4 mile to a power substation, turn right on a dirt road along a powerline 2.1 miles to a fork, veer left for 1.8 miles, and park at a wire gate with a hot springs warning sign. Hike the road 0.9 mile to a rusting borax vat beside Borax Lake, and then follow a spur road north toward Steens Mountain 0.6 mile along a string of small, algae-colored hot spring pools and steam vents. Be careful near these scalding, deep pools. To protect visitors and the springs' ecosystem, the Nature Conservancy bans any attempt to bathe here. If you continue 1.4 miles north, you will reach the sandy shore of alkaline Alvord Lake.

For a desert challenge, hike the Desert Trail 25 miles across sagebrush flats from Fields to the Alvord Desert (see Area 65 map). The Steens, Pueblos, and Trout Creek Mountains look deceptively near all the way. Avoid midsummer's blazing heat. The only water source is Dixon Spring, 14 miles from Fields.

In the Trout Creek Mountains, hikers often begin excursions from base camps at Willow Creek Hot Springs, Mud Spring, or Chicken Spring.

To find Willow Creek Hot Springs, drive the paved road 8.1 miles south of Fields, and turn left on a broad gravel road for 26.2 miles to the Whitehorse Ranch entrance, where the road narrows to a single lane. Now turn around, backtrack 2.3 miles, and turn left on an unmarked dirt road 2.5 miles to a primitive campground at the swimmable, natural hot springs pool. Park here and explore upstream along Willow Creek or neighboring Little Whitehorse Creek.

If you are starting at Mud Spring instead, hike east 2 miles to an overlook of 1600-foot-deep Oregon Canyon. Many possible routes lead to the bottom. Backpackers can prowl Oregon Canyon Creek's forks and botanize. Less difficult access to this canyon requires permission to cross the Echave Ranch downstream.

Whitehorse Creek's many-branched canyon lies 1 mile west of Mud Spring. Pick one of many routes down through breaks in the rimrock and explore side canyons for beaver dams, waterfalls, and colonnades of spire-shaped rock formations.

From Chicken Spring, drive south 5 miles to McDermitt Creek and hike up the North or South Fork to high meadows amid extensive stands of quaking aspen. From there, backpackers can continue 15 miles down Little Whitehorse Creek's winding, rimrock-lined canyon.

Orevada View, this range's highest area, is a 8506-foot plateau overlooking cone-shaped Disaster Peak and four states. The 4-mile cross-country route across the plateau skirts private land at Sherman Field.

Winter Sports

Fierce winter weather limits skiing or snowshoeing in the Pueblo Mountains to experts. By late March snow level is typically at 5600 feet, but winds have sorted things into icy slopes and awkward drifts.

Lower Owyhee River

Location: 40 miles south of Ontario, 104 miles east of Burns
Size: 606 square miles (including Jordan Craters)
Status: Federal wild and scenic river, undesignated wilderness
Terrain: Cliff-lined desert river, colored rock formations, lava
Elevation: 2670 feet–6000 feet
Management: Vale District BLM
Topographic maps: Pelican Point, Rooster Comb, Diamond Butte, Jordan Craters north and south, The Hole In The Ground, Rinehart Canyon, Lambert Rocks, Owyhee Butte, and 25 other maps (USGS)

Whitewater boaters on this desert river drift into a remote world of towering stone canyons, wild rapids, cliffside caves, and rock pinnacles. Hikers can follow the river canyon too, or investigate the colorfully honeycombed crags of Leslie Gulch's many side canyons. Nearby, the Jordan Craters Lava Bed includes spatter cones and Coffeepot Crater.

Climate

Blue sky and frosty nights predominate from April to June, but even in this popular season the desert climate can bring surprise snow flurries or 100° F heat. July and

August are too hot for travel, but autumn's coolness again allows hiking. The very cold winter brings only light snows to this region of just 11 inches annual precipitation.

Plants and Wildlife

Wild horses and bighorn sheep roam the rock gulches east of Owyhee Reservoir. In the winter they are joined by an average of 850 mule deer. Commonly sighted smaller wildlife include lizards, rattlesnakes, and white-tailed antelope ground squirrels.

The river and reservoir attract 150 species of songbirds and numerous waterfowl. Bald eagles come to hunt these birds and usually stay until the reservoir is drained for winter. Another good birding spot is Batch Lake, a cluster of marshy potholes amid the Jordan Craters lava. Look for white pelicans, sandhill cranes, and egrets.

Sagebrush dominates here, although juniper survive atop the tallest peaks and gnarled hackberry trees hug some river benches. The only pine trees, at last count, were 49 ponderosas on a ridge south of Leslie Gulch. The ashy soils of this area have produced a wealth of rare wildflowers. Ertter's groundsel, Packard's blazing star, MacKenzie's phacelia, Owyhee clover, two species of milk vetch, and grimy ivesia are known chiefly from Leslie Gulch. A new penstemon was identified in the early 1980s north of Dry Creek Buttes.

The Honeycombs near Leslie Gulch

Geology

Erosion carved the colored badlands and rock pinnacles here from compacted volcanic ash deposits as much as 2000 feet thick. Sandwiched throughout this immense ash layer are resistant basalt lava flows also 15 to 20 million years old. This volcanic activity may have dammed the ancestral Snake River, for the ash's stripy strata indicate lakebed deposition.

The old basalt now forms a rimrock cap at Table Mountain, Red Butte, and many other places. The partially welded ash of the Honeycombs contains weak spots that have eroded into caves, ledges, and honeycomblike indentations. Paleontologists unearthed horse, bear, camel, and antelope fossils from ash near Red Butte. Succor Creek State Recreation Area allows amateur collecting of thundereggs, agates, and petrified wood from ash deposits there.

Coffeepot Crater and Lava Butte vented the Jordan Craters Lava Beds within the past 9000 years. Look for lava tubes and spatter cones near these two source vents. The relatively smooth, ropy surface of these pahoehoe-style lava flows has been jumbled by pressure ridges, cracks, domes, and collapsed caves. Jordan Craters sits atop the Brothers Fault Zone, source of a string of recent eruptions across southeast Oregon.

History

Cave campsites, pictographs, and arrowheads indicate humans have lived along the Owyhee River for 12,000 years. Defacing pictographs or removing cultural artifacts is a federal crime. The name Owyhee—a nineteenth-century spelling for Hawaii—commemorates two Hawaiians hired by the Hudson's Bay Company as beaver trappers and killed here by Indians in 1819. Fish runs on the Owyhee died when the Owyhee Dam was built in the 1930s. The reservoir now teems with black crappies, while the river supports sparse catfish, suckers, and carp.

THINGS TO DO
Hiking

Start by visiting Leslie Gulch's narrow canyon of colorful rock crags. From Interstate 84 at Ontario, follow signs south 14 miles to Nyssa. In Nyssa, turn right at a pointer for Adrian onto Highway 201 for 20.6 miles. Then turn right on gravel Succor Creek Road for 25 miles to a sign for Leslie Gulch, and turn right down this canyon 14.5 miles to its end at the Owyhee Reservoir boat ramp. If you are driving here from Jordan Valley, take Highway 95 north 27 miles, turn left at a sign for Succor Creek for 8.4 gravel miles to a T junction, turn left another 1.8 miles, and turn left on Leslie Gulch's road. Camping in Leslie Gulch is permitted only at Slocum Campground, a barren gravel flat 0.2 mile up from the boat ramp. Horses are not allowed in the canyon at all.

Take the time to explore a few of the five hikable side canyons of Leslie Gulch. The only official trail starts at the marked Juniper Gulch Trailhead (3.6 miles up the road from Slocum Campground) and heads 0.8 mile up through a narrow wash with overhanging cliffs. An even prettier 0.6-mile route up Timber Gulch's "honeycombed" rock slot is not signed, but begins 2.35 miles up the road from the campground. The

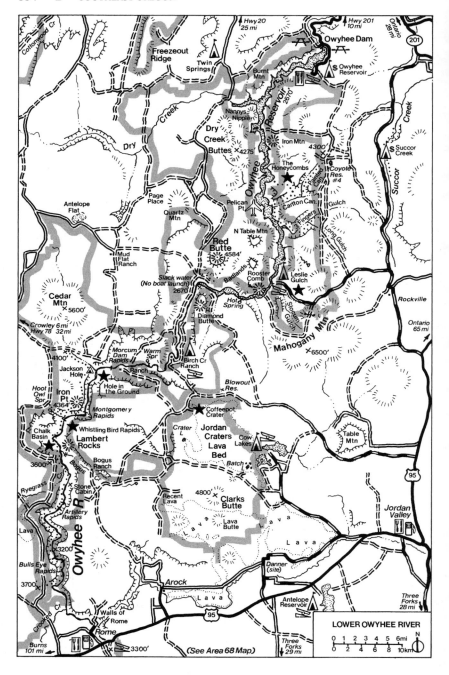

LOWER OWYHEE RIVER

old road up scenic Dago Gulch (4.6 miles from the campground) is blocked by a gate and private land after 0.8 mile. Faint paths up Slocum Gulch (at the campground) and Upper Leslie Gulch (4.8 miles from the campground) peter out within 0.5 mile, but adventurers can continue an extra mile or more.

Boats provide a good way to reach many hiking areas. While drifting the Owyhee north of Rome, stop at Chalk Basin to spend a day exploring the colored rock formations and delicately fluted cliffs there. Not far downstream, stop at a huge, river-level cave near Whistling Bird Rapids and hike up a sandy-bottomed gulch past rock narrows and dry waterfalls to Hoot Owl Spring. From the same base camp, another good cross-country hike climbs up 1300 feet in elevation to the canyon rim and Iron Point, practically overhanging the river.

From the shore of Owyhee Reservoir, hikable sandy washes lead to The Honeycombs, an area of gulches lined with sculpted pinnacles. The formations are most concentrated north of Carlton Canyon but extend to Three Fingers Gulch and Leslie Gulch. Rugged passes provide routes between canyons.

Those who boat to the south end of Owyhee Reservoir can climb to viewpoints at Rooster Comb and Red Butte. Between these lies a colorful badlands of rounded hills.

Motorboats to access areas along the reservoir can be rented at the marina by the Lake Owyhee State Park Campground.

Overland access to The Honeycombs is difficult, but possible by hiking from unmarked, nearly undrivable backroads off of Succor Creek Road.

Three dirt roads access the inner part of the Owyhee Canyon, but they are accessible only in dry weather by high-clearance vehicles. One road heads north from Rome, coming within a 2-mile walk of scenic Chalk Basin, and within 4 miles of Iron Point. A different, very steep road descends from the Jordan Craters Lava Bed area to the riverside Birch Creek Ranch, maintained as a living museum by the BLM. A third, unmarked route leads to within a 4-mile hike of Jackson Hole, where Lower Owyhee Canyon is deepest and grandest. Turn off Highway 78 at Follyfarm Junction, 66 miles east of Burns. Take the gravel Crowley Road 25 miles and turn right, through a gate, onto an unmarked dirt road. After 8 very rough miles the track becomes impassable for vehicles. Continue 1 mile on foot, then hike a cattle trail down a gulch to the river.

Wear sturdy boots to explore Jordan Craters' lavaland. Coffeepot Crater is the most popular day-hike goal, though Batch Lake's wildlife and Lava Butte's lava tubes are also of interest. To find Coffeepot Crater, drive Highway 95 north of Jordan Valley 8.3 miles, turn left on a gravel road 11.4 miles, fork right onto a dirt road 6.7 miles, veer left onto a rough road 5.9 miles, fork left 1.5 miles, and fork left again 1.4 miles to road's end (GPS location N43°8.77' W117°27.54').

Backpacking? Spend a few days exploring The Honeycombs, or else prowl the Owyhee's rim from Jackson Hole to Chalk Basin. From Chalk Basin it is possible to hike 24 miles south along the trailless riverbank toward Rome; hike up to the road before hitting private land at Crooked Creek.

On all hikes, bring plenty of water. Pure water sources are limited to infrequent

The Owyhee River at The Hole in the Ground

springs along the Owyhee River. A U-shaped tent peg helps tap these dribbles, but by late summer many are dry.

Boating

First floated in 1953, the 55-mile stretch of Owyhee River between Rome and the reservoir has become a popular four- to six-day trip. Intermediate-level rafters and kayakers generally portage or line through the class 4 rapids (Whistling Bird, Montgomery, and Morcum Dam). Caution is important, because losing a boat on this very remote desert river means trouble. Boaters must register at the launch site or the BLM office in Vale. Commercial boaters need special permits.

Upstream snowmelt makes the river runnable only from March to early June (kayaks sometimes run until mid-June). Bring gear for cold weather. Also carry a day's supply of drinking water; springs are few. Motors are banned on the river.

The first serious white water comes 11.5 miles down from the Rome launch site: class 3 Bulls Eye Rapids. Nineteen miles beyond, stop on the left to scout or portage Whistling Bird Rapids. A slab of canyon wall has tumbled into the river here on the right, forcing boaters to a hard left. Two miles downstream, Montgomery Rapids provides a class 4 drop at a sharp-right riverbend. The last major hurdle is 7 miles farther along, where an abandoned rock dam partially blocks the river. In low water, line boats on the left. In high water, experts can also run Morcum Dam's middle.

Owyhee Reservoir's slack water at mile 55 leaves boaters 11 miles to paddle (4 hours for rafts) to the Leslie Gulch ramp. An alternative is to take boats out at the staffed campground at the historic Birch Creek Ranch, although driving there requires a high-clearance four-wheel-drive vehicle.

Canoes and sailboats can do well on the reservoir despite competing powerboats and strong winds. Shoreside campsites abound.

68 Upper Owyhee River

Location: 105 miles southeast of Burns
Size: 750 square miles
Status: Federal wild and scenic river, undesignated wilderness
Terrain: Sheer-walled river canyons, white water, sagebrush tablelands
Elevation: 3300 feet–6500 feet
Management: Vale District BLM
Topographic maps: Three Forks, Whitehorse Butte, Skull Creek, Indian Fort, Dry Creek, Scott Reservoir, Drummond Basin, No Crossing, and 23 other maps (USGS)

Oregon's wildest white-water river cuts a dramatic, 1000-foot-deep slot through the sagebrush tablelands where Oregon, Idaho, and Nevada meet. Drift boaters here pass cliffside caves and hot springs on their way to raging Widowmaker Rapids. Hikers either follow the branching canyon's arid rims or trace the canyon bottoms, wading when streams careen between sheer cliffs.

Climate

From March to June, when the river is high enough to be run, prepare for unpredictable weather: balmy blue sky, freezing nights, searing heat, or even snow. After a rain, dirt roads may be impassably muddy—especially the final mile to Three Forks. May and June are best for hiking in the uplands. Plan canyon bottom hikes for September or October when streams are low and fordable. Avoid the freezing winds of winter or the scorching heat of July and August. Annual precipitation is just 11 inches.

Plants and Wildlife

Watch for kingfishers and water ouzels along the water's edge, fat chukars in the side gulches, and raptors nesting in the rimrock: golden eagles, buteos, and prairie falcons. Sage grouse, jackrabbits, and rattlesnakes are more numerous here than anywhere else in Oregon. Pronghorn antelope and mule deer are common.

Sagebrush and bunchgrass dominate this treeless terrain. Plant life in the canyons remains pristine, because cliffs restrict most cattle grazing to the uplands. Phlox and evening primrose provide delicate flowers in spring. Rabbitbrush and sunflowerlike balsamroot bloom yellow in fall.

Geology

During immense volcanic eruptions 15 to 20 million years ago, rhyolite ash exploded from vents and basalt lava spread across this entire area. Later, as the land gradually rose, the Owyhee River cut downward, exposing the orange welded ash layers and black basalt flows in canyon walls.

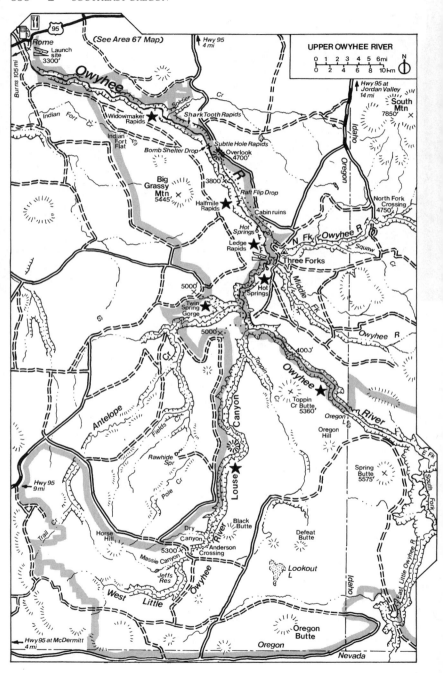

The Owyhee River at Three Forks

THINGS TO DO
Hiking

Three Forks, a remote ford near the confluence of three major Owyhee River branches, serves as a base for cross-country exploration of this trailless canyonland. Before setting out, put on boots that can get wet.

Start by hiking up the main Owyhee River, wading across a tributary and following part of an old military wagon road. A swimmable hot springs with a waterfall, on the north bank 2.1 miles upriver, is on unmarked private land.

Next, put the wet boots back on and try walking up the North Fork's streambed a few miles into that river's inner gorge, where calm, wall-to-wall water reflects the towering canyon above. For a more rugged day hike, explore the Middle Fork's slotlike canyon 3 or 4 miles up from its mouth. The Middle Fork may stop flowing altogether by fall but leaves deep, wall-to-wall pools that require chest-deep wades.

Streamside cliffs and swift water prevent hikers from following the main Owyhee riverbank downriver from Three Forks. It is possible to bushwhack atop the canyon rim for 40 miles to Rome, but a more realistic hiking goal along this rim would be the Owyhee Overlook pullout, 12 miles away.

Drive to Three Forks either via dirt Three Forks Road (which joins Highway 95 near milepost 36, 16 miles west of Jordan Valley) or on the partly paved State Line Road from Jordan Valley. Both routes are marked as the Soldier Creek Watchable Wildlife Loop. The final 1.4 miles of the spur road descending the canyon to Three Forks is so steep and rough that hikers with passenger cars should park and walk.

Antelope Creek and the West Little Owyhee River both have long, deep, scenic, and very remote canyons. Cross-country hikers following these canyon bottoms must wade (or swim!) some pools and must boulder-hop across a few rockslides, but they can discover towers, caves, columns, chutes, and colored rock walls. By midsummer, both streams are dry in places. To access the lower ends of these canyons from Three Forks, hike up the Owyhee River 8.4 miles (to Antelope Creek) or 10.5 miles (to the West Little Owyhee).

A fairly good road accesses Anderson Crossing, at the upper end of the West Little Owyhee River canyon (also known as Louse Canyon). Drive Highway 95 south of Burns Junction 40 miles, turn left on gravel Antelope Flats Road 15 miles, and then turn right for 20 additional miles to Anderson Crossing. From here the canyon extends 35 miles downstream to the main Owyhee River. Plan on a full week for the 45.5-mile trek to Three Forks.

Boating

The 39 miles of Owyhee River between Three Forks and Rome provide one of the most challenging and scenic runs in the state. Boaters must register at the put-in or at the BLM office in Vale. Commercial boaters need special permits. The run can only be made from March to early June (kayaks sometimes run until mid-June), and only if water levels are neither too high nor too low. Possible cold weather and cold water in these months make hypothermia a danger; wet suits or dry suits are advisable.

Just 1.5 miles below the deceptively calm waters of the Three Forks launch site, the rushing, narrow chutes of Ledge Rapids leave many a boater swimming through a rugged, quarter-mile-long rock garden. Scout this class 4+ white water carefully (from the left side); there is no easy way out of this remote desert canyon for those who lose their boat.

Nine miles beyond Ledge Rapids stop at a sharp right bend to scout Halfmile Rapids ahead. This class 4+ rapids begins with rocks jutting into the current on the right and continues with a full 0.5 mile of rough water. After only a 100-yard lull, boaters face Raft Flip Drop's big wave (class 3-4).

Subtle Hole (class 3+), at river mile 15 below Three Forks, is longer than Raft Flip Drop. Bomb Shelter Drop (class 3) follows immediately; pull left in order to stop at the interesting cave below it. Three miles beyond, two rocks in midstream mark the start of Shark Tooth Rapids (class 3).

Class 5+ Widowmaker Rapids, at river mile 21.5, must be portaged by all but daring experts in medium-length rafts. Part of this fall's treachery is that it is preceded by 0.5 mile of class 3 rapids. Begin a difficult portage on the right before the river ahead disappears between huge boulders. This chute, sometimes briefly mistaken for the Widowmaker itself, is actually a class 3 drop that fills boats with water, making them unmanageable at the brink of Widowmaker's 10-foot waterfall immediately ahead.

Another, less frequented Owyhee River white-water run begins near the town of Owyhee, Nevada, and follows the South Fork Owyhee to Three Forks.

APPENDIX A: STATE TRAIL PLAN

A network of existing and proposed long-distance trails links many of Oregon's wild areas. Four trail routes entirely cross the state. Other routes follow rivers or serve as connectors between Oregon's population centers and the longer trail routes.

The Pacific Crest Trail and routes east of the Cascades are open to both hikers and equestrians. However, all long-distance trails west of the Cascade summit (except the North Umpqua River Trail) are for hikers only.

The Pacific Crest Trail (PCT) follows the Sierra Nevada and Cascade Range on a 2638-mile route from Mexico to Canada. The PCT's last gap (in California) was completed in 1993. The 424-mile Oregon section began in the 1920s as the Oregon Skyline Trail and was finished in 1987. The PCT was one of two trails authorized by Congress in the 1968 National Trail Systems Act. Today the well-marked route, built with a wide tread and gentle grade, has become so popular that sections near highway trailheads may be dusty by late summer. Snow closes much of this high-elevation trail from mid-October to early July.

The Oregon Coast Trail (OCT) uses the open sands of Oregon's publicly owned beaches for much of its 360-mile route between Washington and California. Only about 70 miles of the route consists of actual trail, while 200 miles of the route follows public beaches, and about 90 miles still follows the shoulder of Highway 101 and other roads. Forested trail segments often lead hikers over headlands between beaches. Gray cedar posts mark completed sections of this all-season route, notably the northernmost 64 miles from Fort Stevens (on the Columbia River) to Garibaldi (near Tillamook).

The Desert Trail (DT), crossing Oregon's southeast corner, explores high-desert mountain ranges, rimrock canyons, and wide-open landscapes where sagebrush dominates. Rock cairns mark the trail's general route, allowing travelers to pick their own way through the open terrain. Trail markers and published trail guides define the completed 150-mile section between Denio on the Nevada border and Highway 20 east of Burns.

The Desert Trail Association, cooperating with the Bureau of Land Management, proposes continuing the trail as far as Mexico and Canada. The planned route south traverses Nevada to connect with an existing southern Californian portion of the Desert Trail. The route north briefly joins the New Oregon Trail in the Blue Mountains and then crosses Hells Canyon and Idaho to follow the Continental Divide National Scenic Trail to Canada.

The New Oregon Trail (NORT), 57 percent complete, follows the crests of four mountain ranges on its 1300-mile route from Oregon's westernmost point at Cape Blanco to the state's easternmost point in Hells Canyon. The NORT connects the trans-state Oregon Coast Trail and Desert Trail and follows a portion of the PCT. The route, first hiked end-to-end by William L. Sullivan in 1985, also incorporates two earlier long-distance trail proposals: the Ochoco Trail and the Blue Mountain Trail.

Nearly all of the existing trail segments of the NORT traverse wild areas and are thus included in this book. Hikers can fill trailless gaps by following logging roads and highway shoulders, although the route is still unmarked. Snow blocks high portions of the mountain ranges in winter.

The Columbia Gorge Trail leads from the Portland area through the Columbia Gorge, where it crosses the PCT. Hikers can currently follow the route 25 miles from Sheppards Dell State Park (near Bridal Veil Falls) to Starvation Creek (near Viento State Park). Weather rarely closes this low-elevation route, even in winter. Plans would

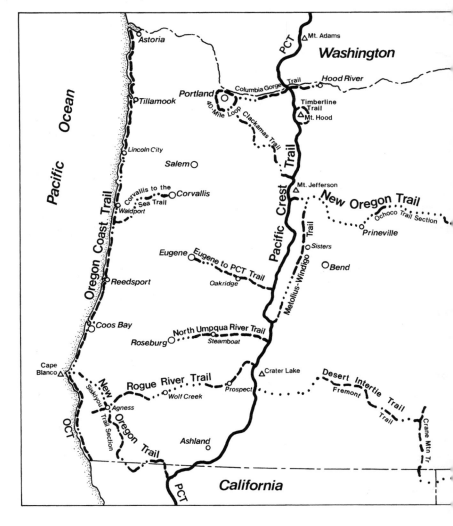

extend the route west to Troutdale, in order to join the 40-Mile Loop around Portland. The proposed Chinook Trail would extend the Columbia Gorge Trail east to The Dalles, cross the Columbia River to Washington, and return to Vancouver along the Gorge rim via Three Corner Rock and Silver Star Mountain. Portions of the Chinook Trail in Washington have already been completed.

The 40-Mile Loop began as a 1910 proposal to link Forest Park trails with a 40-mile route encircling Portland. Growth of the city has lengthened the mapped loop to 140 miles, but the trail's original name remains. Currently hikable throughout, the loop connects existing trails in more than 30 parks (notably the Wildwood Trail in Forest Park and the Marquam Trail at Council Crest) with a variety of sidewalk and roadside routes.

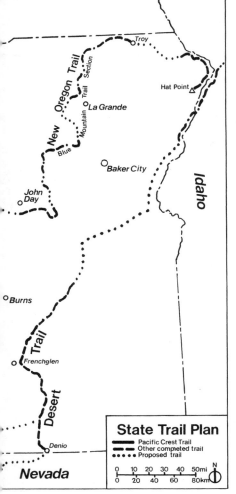

The Clackamas Trail will eventually link the Portland area to the PCT near Mount Jefferson. The plan would use the abandoned Portland Traction Railroad corridor from Gresham to Boring, as well as the existing 7.8-mile Clackamas River Trail, the 4-mile Riverside Trail, the 5-mile Rho Ridge Trail, and the 4.4-mile Red Lake Trail to the PCT at Olallie Lake.

The Corvallis To The Sea Trail currently offers only 15 miles of completed trail, including the Corvallis-Philomath bike path, a trail at Marys Peak, and trails in the Drift Creek Wilderness. The proposed 105-mile route would cross the Coast Range entirely on public land to connect with the Oregon Coast Trail at Cape Perpetua.

The Eugene To PCT Trail, 74 miles long, is about 85 percent complete and is currently hikable from Dexter at Elijah Bristow State Park to the PCT at Bobby Lake, near Waldo Lake. The completed portion follows forested ridges usually free of snow from June to November. Volunteer trail-building efforts proceed on the remaining valley-bottom route that would continue past Mount Pisgah to join the Eugene-Springfield riverside bike path.

The North Umpqua Trail provides 79 miles of completed trail along this forested and often cliff-lined river from its

State Trail Plan
― Pacific Crest Trail
■■■ Other completed trail
●●●● Proposed trail

0 10 20 30 40 50mi
0   20   40   60   80km

headwaters at Maidu Lake in the Mount Thielsen Wilderness. The completed section extends from the PCT west past Steamboat down to Idleyld Park. Volunteers propose continuing construction downriver 23 miles to Roseburg.

The Rogue River Trail consists of three very scenic completed sections. The popular Lower Rogue River Trail extends 40 miles from Grave Creek to Illahe, traversing the rugged Wild Rogue Wilderness. The lesser known Upper Rogue River Trail descends 47.9 miles from the river's headwaters in the northwest corner of Crater Lake National Park down to the town of Prospect. The path then skips 4 miles of private land and continues another 18.3 miles downstream to Casey Park, just below Lost Creek Lake's dam. An ambitious proposal to extend this path 60 miles to join the Lower Rogue River Trail suggests a nonriver route through Wolf Creek.

The Metolius-Windigo Trail features a completed, 45-mile path through central Oregon's pine forests. The route primarily attracts equestrian use and serves as a low-elevation alternative when the nearby, high-elevation PCT is blocked by snow.

The trail crosses Highway 20 at Indian Ford, 5 miles northwest of Sisters. To the north of Highway 20, the path skirts Black Butte and follows Green Ridge, overlooking the Metolius River. To the south, the trail continues as far as Three Creek Lake, near Broken Top. A Forest Service proposal would eventually extend the route south to join the PCT in the Mount Thielsen Wilderness.

The Desert Intertie Trail would link the Desert Trail with the PCT. This east–west route would incorporate the Fremont Trail (147 miles currently complete, in three segments from Yamsay Mountain to the Lakeview area) and the Crane Mountain Trail (34 miles complete, in two segments).

APPENDIX B: MANAGING AGENCIES

UNITED STATES FOREST SERVICE (USFS)

Pacific Northwest Regional Office
333 SW 1st Ave.
Portland, OR 97204
(503) 808-2592
www.fs.fed.us/r6

Columbia Gorge National Scenic Area
902 Wasco Avenue
Hood River, OR 97031
(541) 386-2333

Deschutes National Forest
1645 Highway 20 East
Bend, OR 97701
(541) 383-5300

Fremont National Forest
1301 South G Street
Lakeview, OR 97630
(541) 947-2151

Malheur National Forest
P.O. Box 909
John Day, OR 97845
(541) 575-1731

Mount Hood National Forest
16400 Champion Way
Sandy, OR 97055
(503) 668-1700

Ochoco National Forest
P.O. Box 490
Prineville, OR 97754
(541) 416-6500

Rogue River National Forest
P.O. Box 520
Medford, OR 97501
(541) 858-2200

Siskiyou National Forest
P.O. Box 440
Grants Pass, OR 97528
(541) 471-6500

Siuslaw National Forest
4077 Southwest Research Way
Corvallis, OR 97333
(541) 750-7000

Umatilla National Forest
2517 Southwest Hailey Avenue
Pendleton, OR 97801
(541) 276-3811

Umpqua National Forest
P.O. Box 1008
Roseburg, OR 97470
(541) 672-6601

Wallowa-Whitman National Forest
P.O. Box 907
Baker, OR 97814
(541) 523-6391

Willamette National Forest
P.O. Box 10607
Eugene, OR 97440
(541) 465-6521

Winema National Forest
P.O. Box 1390
Klamath Falls, OR 97601
(541) 883-6714

BUREAU OF LAND MANAGEMENT (BLM)

Oregon State Office
P.O. Box 2965
Portland, OR 97208
(202) 452-5125
www.or.blm.gov

Burns District
HC 74-12533, Highway 20 West
Hines, OR 97738
(541) 573-4400

Coos Bay District
1300 Airport Lane
North Bend, OR 97459
(541) 756-0100

Eugene District
2890 Chad Drive
Eugene, OR 97401
(541) 683-6600

Lakeview District
1300 South G Street
Lakeview, OR 97630
(541) 947-2177

Medford District
3040 Biddle Road
Medford, OR 97501
(541) 618-2200

Prineville District
3050 NE Third Street
Prineville, OR 97754
(541) 416-6700

Salem District
1717 Fabry Road
Salem, OR 97306
(503) 375-5646

Vale District
100 Oregon Street
Vale, OR 97918
(541) 473-3144

OTHER AGENCIES

Confederated Tribes of the Warm Springs Indian Reservation
Natural Resources Department
P.O. Box C
Warm Springs, OR 97761
(541) 553-2001

Crater Lake National Park
P.O. Box 7
Crater Lake, OR 97604
(541) 594-2211

Crooked River National Grassland
813 Southwest Highway 97
Madras, OR 97741
(541) 475-9272

Hart Mountain Refuge / USFWS
P.O. Box 111
Lakeview, OR 97630
(541) 947-3315

Hells Canyon National Recreation Area
88401 Highway 82
Enterprise, OR 97828
(541) 426-4978

Nature Conservancy
1234 Northwest 25th
Portland, OR 97210
(503) 228-9561

Newberry National Volcanic Monument

Fort Rock Ranger District
1230 Northeast 3rd
Bend, OR 97701
(541) 383-4000

Oregon Caves National Monument

National Park Service
Cave Junction, OR 97523
(541) 592-2100

Oregon Department of Fish and Wildlife

2501 Southwest 1st Avenue
Portland, OR 97207
(503) 872-5268

Oregon Dunes National Recreation Area

855 Highway 101
Reedsport, OR 97467
(541) 271-3611

Oregon State Parks and Recreation Division

1115 Commercial Street Northeast
Salem, OR 97301
(503) 378-6305

APPENDIX C: TOPOGRAPHIC MAP PUBLISHERS

Bureau of Land Management (BLM)
P.O. Box 2965
Portland, OR 97208
(503) 952-6001

The Bureau of Land Management publishes several river-recreation-oriented topographic maps for $4 each: the Lower Deschutes River, the Lower John Day River, and the Upper John Day River, all at a scale of 1:100,000. A $4 map of Central Oregon is also available at this scale. If you're traveling by car, the BLM's district maps, at a scale of ½ inch = 1 mile, are extremely useful, especially for negotiating the maze of dusty tracks near roadless areas in eastern Oregon. These maps cost $4 each. Although there are nine BLM districts in Oregon, there are thirteen maps in the series because it takes two or three maps at this scale to cover the larger districts. Among the most popular is the Burns District South Half, which includes Steens Mountain. All BLM maps show public and private land ownership.

Desert Trail Association
P.O. Box 34
Madras, OR 97741
www.madras.net/dta.htm

This nonprofit association publishes topographic maps of the Desert Trail route. The maps include detailed notes for following the trail route, but are broad enough to cover alternative hiking terrain. The six maps available in Oregon so far cover the Pueblo Mountains, the Alvord Desert, Steens Mountain, the Donner und Blitzen River, the Malheur Wildlife Refuge, and Diamond Craters. Price is $7 each, postpaid. The maps are also available in some bookstores, including the Book Parlor at 181 North Broadway in Burns.

Geo-Graphics
970 Muirfield Court
Beaverton, OR 97006
(503) 533-5121

This publisher offers high-quality topographic maps of popular Cascades wilderness and winter sports areas. The Mount Hood Wilderness map ($6) covers the Mount Hood Wilderness at a scale of 1:24,000 on the front, and the Columbia, Badger Creek, and Salmon-Huckleberry Wildernesses at a scale of 1:100,000 on the back. Trails of the Columbia Gorge ($6) covers the Hatfield Wilderness and surrounding areas at a scale of 1:64,267. The Bull of the Woods Wilderness map ($5.95) by David Imus also covers the Opal Creek Wilderness, Table Rock Wilderness, Middle Santiam Wilderness, and Menagerie Wilderness, all at a scale of 1:63,360. The Mount Jefferson Wilderness map ($6) covers the peak itself at 1:30,000 and the rest of the wilderness at 1:62,000. The Three Sisters Wilderness map ($6) covers the entire Three Sisters Wilderness and half of the Mount Washington and Waldo Lake Wildernesses at a scale of 1:70,000. The Mount Washington Wilderness map ($6) covers that area at 1:30,000. The Diamond Peak Wilderness map ($5.95) by David Imus has a scale of 1:42,240. The Wallowa Mountains map ($6) by David Imus covers the Eagle Cap Wilderness at a scale of 1:100,000. Other topographic maps cover the winter sports areas at Santiam Pass ($4.75) and Willamette Pass ($3). Postage is $1 per map. The maps are also available at many bookstores and outdoor stores in northwest Oregon and Bend.

Green Trails
P.O. Box 77734
Seattle, WA 98177
(206) 546-6277
www.greentrails.com
   Green Trails publishes fifteen topographic maps for Oregon, covering the Northern Oregon Cascades at a scale of 1:69,500. These frequently updated maps each cover about 12 by 18 miles, showing trails, cross-country skiing routes, and other recreational data. The maps are available for $3.60 in many outdoor stores in Washington and northwest Oregon. A set of any twelve selected maps can be ordered at a discount directly from the publisher.

Imus Geographics
P.O. Box 161
Eugene, OR 97440
(541) 344-1431
   Imus Geographics has won the nation's highest award for cartography four times. The prize-winning maps are handsome indeed, with shaded relief, topographic contour lines, forest cover in green, and precise mileages. The Oregon Topographic Road Map covers the entire state at a scale of 1:800,000 and includes an Oregon Travel Guide on the back by author William L. Sullivan. It is available in many bookstores and outdoor stores or can be ordered by mail for $9.95 apiece (folded) or $12.95 (rolled), postpaid. Many other Imus maps are now carried by Geo-Graphics, listed above.

United States Forest Service (USFS)
319 SW Pine Street
Portland, OR 97208
(503) 221-2877
www.fs.fed.us/r6
   The U.S. Forest Service publishes convenient topographic maps for a few of the designated wilderness areas under their management, generally at a scale of 1:62,500. The maps often exclude adjacent roadless areas. The USFS also offers special topographic

maps covering the Pacific Crest Trail through Oregon and winter ski trails in certain areas. Finally, nontopographic recreation maps cover each of the thirteen National Forests in Oregon, showing major roads, most trails, and other data at a scale of ½ inch = 1 mile. District offices generally stock all the maps, while ranger stations only keep maps of local interest on hand.

The Forest Service now cooperates with the United States Geological Survey (USGS) to include road numbers and some recreation information on USGS topographic maps.

United States Geological Survey (USGS)

Box 25286 - Denver Federal Center
Denver, CO 80225
1-800-ASK USGS
http://mapping.usgs.gov

The U.S. Geological Survey has completed its effort to produce topographic maps for all of Oregon in its 7.5-minute series, a format that shows great detail but can be unwieldy for large areas (in Oregon 1 minute is approximately 0.8 mile). Unless otherwise noted, the USGS maps recommended in the area descriptions are in this series. USGS maps with a 1:250,000 scale span 100 miles but show insufficient detail for most uses.

USGS topographic maps can be downloaded from the Internet for free at *www.topozone.com*. The maps are available for sale at a few outdoor stores and bookstores. USGS maps can also be ordered direct, either online, by phone, or by mail. The 7.5-minute maps cost $4; the 1:250,000 series maps and a special 25-minute Crater Lake map cost $7 postpaid. There is a $5 handling fee for each order. The USGS will send a free state index map on request.

Many university and large city libraries in Oregon stock all Oregon USGS topographic maps and allow them to be checked out or photocopied.

APPENDIX D: SELECTED BIBLIOGRAPHY

PLANTS AND WILDLIFE

Ferguson, Denzel, and Nancy Ferguson. *Oregon's Great Basin Country*. Bend, Ore.: Maverick Publications, 1978.

Hitchcock, C. Leo, and Arthur Cronquist. *Flora of the Pacific Northwest*. Seattle: University of Washington Press, 1973.

Horn, Elizabeth. *Wildflowers 1: The Cascades*. New York: Touchstone Press, 1972.

Jolley, Russ. *Wildflowers of the Columbia Gorge*. Portland, Ore.: Oregon Historical Society, 1988.

Matthews, Daniel. *Natural History of the Cascades and Olympics*. Portland, Ore.: Portland Audubon, 1988.

Niehaus, Theodore F. *A Field Guide to Pacific States Wildflowers*. New York: Houghton Mifflin, 1976.

Pandell, Karen, and Chris Stall. *Animal Tracks of the Pacific Northwest*. Seattle: The Mountaineers Books, 1981.

Peterson, Roger Tory. *A Field Guide to Western Birds*. New York: Houghton Mifflin, 1961.

Ross, Charles R. *Trees to Know in Oregon*. Corvallis, Ore.: Oregon State University Extension Service, 1975.

Ross, Robert A., and Henrietta L. Chambers. *Wildflowers of the Western Cascades*. Portland, Ore.: Timber Press, 1988.

Taylor, Ronald J., and Rolf W. Valum. *Wildflowers 2: Sagebrush Country*. New York: Touchstone Press, 1974.

Whitaker, John O., Jr. *The Audubon Society Field Guide to North American Mammals*. New York: Knopf, 1980.

Whitney, Stephen R. *A Field Guide to the Cascades & Olympics*. Seattle: The Mountaineers Books, 1983.

GEOLOGY

Alt, David D., and Donald W. Hyndman. *Roadside Geology of Oregon*. Missoula, Mont.: Mountain Press Publishing, 1978.

Bishop, Ellen Morris, and John Allen. *Hiking Oregon's Geology*. Seattle: The Mountaineers Books, 1996.

Harris, Stephen L. *Fire & Ice: The Cascade Volcanoes*. Seattle: The Mountaineers Books, 1980.

Mitchell, James R. *Gem Trails of Oregon*. Baldwing Park, Cal.: Gem Guides, 1998.

Orr, Elizabeth L. *Geology of Oregon*. 4th ed. Dubuque, Iowa: Kendall/Hunt, 1992.

HISTORY

Ashworth, William. *Hells Canyon.* New York: Hawthorn Books, 1977.

Brogan, Phil F. *East of the Cascades.* Portland, Ore.: Binfords & Mort, 1964.

McArthur, Lewis A. *Oregon Geographic Names.* Portland, Ore.: Western Imprints, 1982.

Sullivan, William L. *Hiking Oregon's History.* Eugene, Ore.: Navillus Press, 1999.

Williams, Chuck. *Bridge of the Gods, Mountains of Fire: A Return to the Columbia Gorge.* New York: Friends of the Earth, 1980.

HIKING AND BACKPACKING

Barstad, Fred. *Hiking Oregon's Eagle Cap Wilderness.* Helena, Mont.: Falcon, 1996.

Henderson, Bonnie. *Best Hikes With Children in Western and Central Oregon.* 2d ed. Seattle: The Mountaineers, 1992.

————. *120 Hikes on the Oregon Coast.* Seattle: The Mountaineers, 1998.

Judd, Ron C., and Dan A. Nelson. *Pacific Northwest Hiking.* Emeryville, Calif.: Foghorn Outdoors, 1999.

Kerr, Andy. *Oregon Desert Guide: 70 Hikes.* Seattle: The Mountaineers Books, 2000.

Lorain, Douglas. *Backpacking Oregon.* Berkeley, Calif.: Wilderness Press, 1999.

————. *50 Hikes in Hells Canyon & Oregon's Wallowas.* Seattle: The Mountaineers Books, 1997.

————. *75 Hikes in Oregon's Coast Range & Siskiyous,* 2d ed. Seattle: The Mountaineers Books, 2001.

————. *100 Hikes in Oregon,* 2d ed. Seattle: The Mountaineers Books, 2000.

Plumb, Gregory A. *A Waterfall Lover's Guide to the Pacific Northwest.* Seattle: The Mountaineers Books, 1989.

Prater, Yvonne, and Ruth Mendenhall. *Gorp, Glop & Stew: Favorite Foods From 165 Experts.* Seattle: The Mountaineers Books, 1982.

Schaffer, Jeffrey P., and Andy Selters. *The Pacific Crest Trail, Vol. 2: Oregon and Washington.* Berkeley, Calif.: Wilderness Press, 2000.

Sullivan, William L. *100 Hikes in the Central Oregon Cascades.* Eugene, Ore.: Navillus Press, 1998.

————. *100 Hikes in Northwest Oregon.* Eugene, Ore.: Navillus Press, 2000.

————. *100 Hikes in Southern Oregon.* Eugene, Ore.: Navillus Press, 1997.

————. *100 Hikes/Travel Guide: Eastern Oregon.* Eugene, Ore.: Navillus Press, 2001.

————. *100 Hikes/Travel Guide: Oregon Coast & Coast Range.* Eugene, Ore.: Navillus Press, 2002.

Vantilburg, Christopher. *Emergency Survival.* Seattle: The Mountaineers Books, 2001.

Wood, Wendell. *A Walking Guide to Oregon's Ancient Forests.* Portland, Ore.: Oregon Natural Resources Council, 1991.

CLIMBING

Graydon, Don, and Kurt Hansen, eds. *Mountaineering: The Freedom of the Hills*, 6th ed. Seattle: The Mountaineers Books, 1997.

Thomas, Jeff. *Oregon High: A Climbing Guide*. Portland, Ore.: Keep Climbing Press, 1991.

Watts, Alan. *Climber's Guide to Smith Rock*. Portland, Ore.: Chockstone Press, 1992.

WINTER SPORTS

Gilette, Ned, and John Dostal. *Cross-Country Skiing*. Seattle: The Mountaineers Books, 1988.

Lund, John W. *Southern Oregon Cross-Country Ski Trails*. Klamath Falls, Ore.: Lund, 1987.

Prater, Gene and Dave Felkley, ed. *Snowshoeing, 4th ed*. Seattle: The Mountaineers Books, 1997.

Vielbig, Klindt. *Oregon Cross-Country Ski Routes*. Seattle: The Mountaineers Books, 1998.

BOATING

Boater's Safety Handbook. Seattle: The Mountaineers Books, 1982.

Campbell, Arthur. *John Day River Drift and Historical Guide*. Frank Amato Publications, 1980.

Jones, Phil. *Canoe and Kayak Routes: Northwest Oregon, 2nd ed*. Seattle: The Mountaineers Books, 1997.

Keller, Robb. *Paddling Oregon*. Helena, Mont.: Falcon, 1998.

Quinn, James M. *Handbook to the Illinois River Canyon*. Waldport, Ore.: Education Adventures Inc., 1979.

———. *Handbook to the Rogue River Canyon*. Waldport, Ore.: Educational Adventures Inc., 1978.

Willamette Kayak and Canoe Club. *Soggy Sneakers: A Guide to Oregon Rivers, 3rd ed*. Seattle: The Mountaineers Books, 1994.

INDEX

362   ■   INDEX

ABOUT THE OREGON NATURAL RESOURCES COUNCIL

The Oregon Natural Resources Council (ONRC) is Oregon's largest conservation organization. A nonprofit, tax-exempt corporation, the ONRC has more than 6500 individual members. The Council addresses major conservation and natural-resource-management issues facing Oregon's forests, rivers, coast, and rangelands. Wilderness protection, especially through legislation, has long been an organizational priority and is viewed as vital for preserving the state's resources, both for environmental and economic purposes. The areas described in this book are that resource. With a staff of seventeen, including regional field coordinators who live and work in each corner of Oregon, the ONRC's strength is its strong and active grass-roots citizen network of volunteers. The Council coordinates public involvement in Oregon conservation issues at the agency-planning level, represents its members in court, and lobbies with them directly at the State Legislature and in Congress. Its educational programs provide information and assistance to all members of the public interested in management of Oregon's lands, waters, and natural resources.

The ONRC is a publicly supported educational, scientific, and charitable organization dependent upon private donations and citizen support. Memberships and contributions are tax-deductible.

Oregon Natural Resources Council
5825 North Greeley Street
Portland, OR 97217
(503) 283-6343

Western Field Office
P.O. Box 11648
Eugene, OR 97440-3848
(541) 344-0675

Eastern Field Office
16 Northwest Kansas Street
Bend, OR 97701
(541) 382-2616

Southern Field Representative
HC 63, Box 332
Chiloquin, OR 97623-5757
(541) 783-2206

ABOUT THE AUTHOR

WILLIAM L. SULLIVAN began hiking in Oregon at the age of five and has been in love with adventure ever since. He left high school to study at remote Deep Springs College in the California desert. He went on to earn a B.A. in English from Cornell University and an M.A. in German from the University of Oregon. He and his wife, Janell Sorensen, bicycled 3000 miles through Europe, studied two years at Heidelberg University, and built a log cabin by hand on Oregon's Siletz River. They live in Eugene.

In 1985, Sullivan backpacked 1360 miles across the state—from Oregon's westernmost point at Cape Blanco to the state's easternmost point in Hells Canyon. His journal of that two-month trek, *Listening for Coyote,* was a finalist for the Oregon Book Award.

Sullivan has authored nine books about Oregon's outdoors and writes a column for Eugene's *Register-Guard.* A schedule of his slide shows and more information about hiking, skiing, bicycling, kayaking, and rafting in Oregon is available at his website, *www.oregonhiking.com.*

THE MOUNTAINEERS, founded in 1906, is a nonprofit outdoor activity and conservation club, whose mission is "to explore, study, preserve, and enjoy the natural beauty of the outdoors . . . . " Based in Seattle, Washington, the club is now the third-largest such organization in the United States, with 15,000 members and five branches throughout Washington State.

The Mountaineers sponsors both classes and year-round outdoor activities in the Pacific Northwest, which include hiking, mountain climbing, ski-touring, snowshoeing, bicycling, camping, kayaking and canoeing, nature study, sailing, and adventure travel. The club's conservation division supports environmental causes through educational activities, sponsoring legislation, and presenting informational programs. All club activities are led by skilled, experienced volunteers, who are dedicated to promoting safe and responsible enjoyment and preservation of the outdoors.

If you would like to participate in these organized outdoor activities or the club's programs, consider a membership in The Mountaineers. For information and an application, write or call The Mountaineers, Club Headquarters, 300 Third Avenue West, Seattle, WA 98119; 206-284-6310.

The Mountaineers Books, an active, nonprofit publishing program of the club, produces guidebooks, instructional texts, historical works, natural history guides, and works on environmental conservation. All books produced by The Mountaineers Books fulfill the club's mission.

Send or call for our catalog of more than 500 outdoor titles:

The Mountaineers Books
1001 SW Klickitat Way, Suite 201
Seattle, WA 98134
800-553-4453
mbooks@mountaineersbooks.org
www.mountaineersbooks.org

The Mountaineers Books is proud to be a corporate sponsor of Leave No Trace, whose mission is to promote and inspire responsible outdoor recreation through education, research, and partnerships. The Leave No Trace program is focused specifically on human-powered (nonmotorized) recreation.

Leave No Trace strives to educate visitors about the nature of their recreational impacts, as well as offer techniques to prevent and minimize such impacts. Leave No Trace is best understood as an educational and ethical program, not as a set of rules and regulations.

For more information, visit *www.LNT.org,* or call 800-332-4100.

50 Trail Runs in Washington by Cheri Pompeo Gillis. $16.95 paperback. 0-89886-715-0.

75 Scrambles in Washington: Classic Routes to the Summits by Peggy Goldman. $18.95 paperback. 0-89886-761-4.

Snowshoe Routes: Washington by Dan A. Nelson. $16.95 paperback. 0-89886-585-9.

100 Classic Backcountry Ski and Snowboard Routes in Washington by Rainer Burgdorfer. $17.95 paperback. 0-89886-661-8.

Animal Tracks of the Pacific Northwest by Karen Pandell and Chris Stall. $6.95 paperback. 0-89886-012-1.

A Field Guide to the Cascades & Olympics by Stephen Whitney. $18.95 paperback. 0-89886-077-6.

Northwest Trees by Stephen F. Arno and Ramona P. Hammerly. $14.95 paperback. 0-916890-50-3.